Junian Latinity in the Roman Empire
Volume 1: History, Law, Literature

Edinburgh Studies in Ancient Slavery
Series editor: Ulrike Roth, University of Edinburgh

Original research in ancient slavery studies

The study of slavery is an essential element of the study of the ancient world. This series publishes the latest research on ancient slavery, including Greek, Roman and Near Eastern slavery, as well as Jewish and early Christian slavery, from c. 1000 BC to AD 500.

Written by experts in the field, from the rising star to the well-established scholar, the books offer cutting-edge research on key themes in ancient slavery studies, which will enhance as well as challenge current understanding of ancient slavery. The series presents new insights from a range of disciplines, including history, archaeology and philology.

Advisory board
Dr Bassir Amiri
Professor Jean-Jacques Aubert
Dr Lisa Fentress
Professor Jennifer A. Glancy
Professor Deborah Kamen
Professor Noel E. Lenski
Dr David Lewis
Professor Henrik Mouritsen
Professor Walter Scheidel
Dr Jane Webster
Dr Cornelia Wunsch
Professor Rachel Zelnick-Abramovitz

Books available
Kostas Vlassopoulos, *Historicising Ancient Slavery*
Pedro López Barja, Carla Masi Doria and Ulrike Roth (eds), *Junian Latinity in the Roman Empire Volume 1: History, Law, Literature*

Forthcoming books
Peter Morton, *Slavery and Rebellion in Second Century* BC *Sicily: From Bellum Servile to Sicilia Capta*

Visit the series webpage: edinburghuniversitypress.com/series-edinburgh-studies-in-ancient-slavery

Junian Latinity in the Roman Empire
Volume 1: History, Law, Literature

Edited by Pedro López Barja,
Carla Masi Doria and Ulrike Roth

EDINBURGH
University Press

Edinburgh University Press is one of the leading university presses in the UK. We publish academic books and journals in our selected subject areas across the humanities and social sciences, combining cutting-edge scholarship with high editorial and production values to produce academic works of lasting importance. For more information visit our website: edinburghuniversitypress.com

© editorial matter and organisation Pedro López Barja, Carla Masi Doria and Ulrike Roth, 2023, 2024
© the chapters their several authors, 2023, 2024

Edinburgh University Press Ltd
13 Infirmary Street, Edinburgh, EH1 1LT

First published in hardback by Edinburgh University Press 2023

Typeset in 10 / 12 Bembo by
IDSUK (DataConnection) Ltd, and
printed and bound by CPI Group (UK) Ltd,
Croydon, CR0 4YY

A CIP record for this book is available from the British Library

ISBN 978 1 3995 0746 2 (hardback)
ISBN 978 1 3995 0747 9 (paperback)
ISBN 978 1 3995 0748 6 (webready PDF)
ISBN 978 1 3995 0749 3 (epub)

The right of Pedro López Barja, Carla Masi Doria and Ulrike Roth to be identified as the editors of this work has been asserted in accordance with the Copyright, Designs and Patents Act 1988, and the Copyright and Related Rights Regulations 2003 (SI No. 2498).

Contents

Series Editor's Preface   vii
Acknowledgements   ix
Abbreviations   xi

Introduction: 'There was even mention of Junian Latins'   1
Pedro López Barja, Carla Masi Doria and Ulrike Roth

I. THE HISTORICAL AND LEGAL CONTEXTS FOR JUNIAN LATINITY

First Prologue: A Millennium of Legislation on Junians and Other Latins   15
Ulrike Roth

1. Municipal Latin Rights from the Social War to Hadrian   21
Estela García Fernández

2. The Legal Foundation: The *leges Iunia et Aelia Sentia*   56
Luigi Pellecchi

3. The Republican Background and the Augustan Setting for the Creation of Junian Latinity   80
Pedro López Barja

4. Imperial Legislation Concerning Junian Latins: From Tiberius to the Severan Dynasty   104
Jacobo Rodríguez Garrido

5. Of Mice and Junians: On the Latin Condition   123
Pedro López Barja and Jacobo Rodríguez Garrido

6. Junian Latinity in Late Roman and Early Medieval Texts: A Survey from the Third to the Eleventh Centuries AD   132
Simon Corcoran

II. JUNIAN LATINS IN THE LATIN LITERARY SOURCES

Second Prologue: The Latin Literary Universe of Junian Latinity   155
Ulrike Roth

7. Promoting Junian Latinity: Columella, *De re rustica* 1.8.19   160
Ulrike Roth

8. Reading Pliny's Junian Latins   167
Ulrike Roth

9. The Name, the Garb, the Cap: A Plea for the Renunciation of *civitas*   188
Ulrike Roth

10. 'They live as freeborn, and die as slaves': Junian Latins and *filii religiosi* in Salvian's *Ad ecclesiam* 3   203
Chris L. de Wet

Appendix: List of Legal Enactments (with Key Sources)   216
Pedro López Barja and Jacobo Rodríguez Garrido
Bibliography   220
Index Locorum   242
General Index   250

Series Editor's Preface

Edinburgh Studies in Ancient Slavery provides a forum for the latest research on all aspects of slavery and related forms of unfreedom around the Mediterranean basin and in its hinterland in antiquity. The exploration of slavery has been critical to research on this ancient world from the beginning of concentrated study in the nineteenth century. This is in many ways unsurprising given that there exists plenty of evidence for slavery and other forms of unfree labour and enforced subordination in antiquity, from the British Isles in the northwest, to the Persian Gulf in the southeast, from the Sumerian to the Visigothic kingdoms. Slavery in the ancient Mediterranean and beyond has manifested itself in myriad ways. The surviving evidence stretches the full panorama of our sources, material and textual, documenting cogently the pervasive nature of slavery in ancient society, across uncountable contexts and disparate settings. The diversity of the source material forcefully underpins the need for multi- and interdisciplinary approaches, including collaborative and comparative efforts; the intricate nature of the evidence calls moreover for a preparedness to combine traditional with innovative methods, empiricist work with theoretical perspectives. Notwithstanding these evidential, contextual and methodological challenges that the study of slavery brings with it, in the light of the influence that the history of the region has had on the evolution and development of numerous modern societies and the world at large, the study of ancient Mediterranean slavery is imperative for a full understanding of the contemporary world.

The present series is not the first to give ancient slavery centre stage. The study of especially classical slavery has been an academic battle-ground at prominent modern historical crossroads, framed by its exploration under the abolitionist banner in the nineteenth century at one end – combatting the apologist uses to which the study of the classical past had been put by pro-slavery advocates, and its mobilisation on both sides of the Iron Curtain during the Cold War in the twentieth century at the other. Research agendas on ancient slavery have thus at times been powerfully influenced by modern, socio-political concerns. But even when the large political stage was not a key driver, work on ancient slavery has more often than not been inspired by, and reflective of, contemporary developments. Pioneering work on enslaved women, for example, was carried out in the 1970s, when the feminist movement was at its first peak in Western society; a decade or so later, an interest in the labour roles of enslaved individuals, and the ways in which they mobilised the world of work in creating their own identities, changed the modern appreciation of enslaved life at a time when labour force participation in Europe and the US – the hubs of research on ancient Greek and Roman slavery – was broader than ever before. It is fair to say that each generation of scholars brings its own preoccupations to the drawing-board of slavery studies, thereby ensuring the regular adjustment of our analytical gaze, and enabling the steady discovery of new facets of an institution that is not only as old as our historical records, but that has profoundly shaped social relations at the critical intersections of age, class, gender and race for generations to come. The rapid changes and momentous transformations that characterise contemporary society, often directly related to the many deeply troublesome legacies of slavery across human history, beget an opportune moment, and indeed constitute an urgent call, for a fresh, concentrated effort to reflect on the world we live in through the lens of an institution that was not less peculiar in antiquity than it is, sadly, still today, drawing on as wide a set of questions, approaches and perspectives as possible, thus also to reflect on and challenge the scholarly implication in the maintenance of the noted legacies.

Ulrike Roth

Acknowledgements

Of the many reasons that make people flock to the Galician capital Santiago de Compostela, the search for Junian Latins is located at the eclectic end of the spectrum. Nevertheless, it was in this fine city, in the autumn of 2019, that a gathering of Roman historians, lawyers, epigraphists and papyrologists unfolded, in the beautiful surroundings of the Consello da Cultura Galega, and generously supported by a Spanish government grant awarded to Pedro López Barja of the Universidade Santiago de Compostela (HAR2017-86523-P): 'Beyond the Black Hole: Locating Junian Latins in the Roman Empire' – was the theme tune of the meeting, joining forces across disciplinary niches and academic cultures, in the hope of unleashing renewed interest in a Roman legal status and lived reality that has been of as little scholarly interest as it may have been of actual importance in antiquity. We here present the first results of this effort, followed, in a second volume, by 'the other half' of our activities in Santiago, including in both volumes additional contributions solicited after the event, to close gaps that became evident during our gathering and that we felt important to address in the ensuing publication.

It goes without saying that as editors, and joint conference organisers, we are especially grateful for the enthusiasm of the colleagues who have answered our call to tackle the conundrum of Junian Latinity from the angle of their particular scholarly expertise as well as for the engaged exchange in person, via screen and text, then and since. We are also enormously grateful for the financial support that various institutions and organisations have provided for the project. Apart from the already mentioned Consello da Cultura Galega, and the Spanish government – that is, the Ministerio de Ciencia, Innovación y universidades, under its 'Programa estatal de fomento de la investigación científica y técnica de excelencia', with funding from the European Union's European Regional Development Fund (ERDF) – we owe a debt to the research group 'Synkrisis. Investigación en formas culturales' and to the research network 'Consiliencia', both at the Universidade Santiago de Compostela.

We accrued several personal debts in the course of our activities. First, we must thank Estíbaliz García for her impeccable organisation of the practical aspects of the 2019 conference. We also owe a debt to Michael Crawford for his generous assistance with the English of several chapters; to Chantal Gabrielli for her help with securing photos of the Riccardi fragment of the *lex Aelia*; to Edinburgh University Press's peer reviewers for their passionate engagement with our submission and keen support of the project as a whole; and, last but not least, to Carol Macdonald, Rachel Bridgewater, Isobel Birks, Fiona Conn and Grace Balfour-Harle of Edinburgh University Press, and the Press's production team, as well as our copyeditor Eliza Wright, for their hugely supportive and highly professional handling of, first, our publication proposal and, thereafter, the manuscript submission, all the way to publication.

Pedro López Barja
Carla Masa Doria
Ulrike Roth

ABBREVIATIONS

Abbreviations of classical authors follow the *Oxford Classical Dictionary*. Abbreviations of epigraphic and papyrological sources follow the standard conventions in these two respective fields. Other abbreviations of sources, corpora and repositories, especially legal, employed in this volume, are as follows:

CJ	The Justinian Code (*Codex Iustinianus*).
Coll.	*Collatio Legum Mosaicarum et Romanarum / Lex Dei*.
CPL	Cavenaile, R. 1958. *Corpus Papyrorum Latinarum* (Wiesbaden).
CTh	The Theodosian Code (*Codex Theodosianus*).
Digest	The Digest of Justinian (*Digesta Iustiniani Augusti*).
FIRA	*Fontes iuris Romani anteiustiniani*.
Flammini *Hermeneumata*	Flammini, G. 2004. *Hermeneumata Pseudodositheana Leidensia* (Munich and Leipzig).
Frag. Aug.	*Fragmenta Augustodunensia*.
Frag. Dos.	*Fragmentum Pseudo-Dositheanum*.
Frag. Vat.	*Fragmenta Vaticana*.
Gai. *Inst.*	The Institutes of Gaius (*Gai Institutiones*).
HD	Epigraphische Datenbank Heidelberg (EDH: https://edh.ub.uni-heidelberg.de/).
Inst.	The Institutes of Justinian (*Institutiones Iustiniani*).
Lepor	Lepor. Leges Populi Romani (http://www.cn-telma.fr//lepor/accueil/).
Pauli Sent.	*Pauli Sententiae*.
PG	Migne, J.-P. ed. 1857–86. *Patrologiae cursus completus: Series graeca* (Paris).
PL	Migne, J.-P. ed. 1844–64. *Patrologiae cursus completus: Series ecclesiae latinae* (Paris).
RGDA	*Res Gestae Divi Augusti*.

RRC	Crawford, M. H. 1975. *Roman Republican Coinage*, 2 vols (Cambridge).
RS	Crawford M. H. et al. 1996. *Roman Statutes*, 2 vols (London).
Ulp. *Reg.*	The Rules of Ulpian (*Tituli ex Corpore Ulpiani / Epitome Ulpiani / Regulae Ulpiani*).

Introduction:
'There was even mention of Junian Latins'

Pedro López Barja, Carla Masi Doria and Ulrike Roth

WHY BOTHER ABOUT JUNIAN LATINITY? In the light of the fact that not many do, the question has to be asked. While in the nineteenth century, Junian Latinity attracted the keen attention of several Roman legal scholars whose work laid the foundation for our understanding of the condition, Junian Latinity lost much of its appeal to legal inquiry in the ensuing century. Moreover, it has played virtually no role in Roman historical studies until the last few decades. The scholarly lack of interest that Junian Latinity has suffered for most of the twentieth century is not easy to account for – given the availability of substantial, if complex evidence, and the potential significance of the condition for modern understanding of Roman imperial politics, society, economy and law.

Junian Latinity is the status of formerly enslaved individuals who were manumitted from Roman slavery in the imperial period in ways that, in anglophone scholarship, have become known as informal and imperfect – as a result of which these former slaves gained freedom upon their manumission, but not Roman citizenship.[1] The combination of the award of freedom *and* citizenship was reserved for those manumitted formally and perfectly. Two legal enactments (at least one of which is safely known to have been promulgated in the Augustan age) laid out the criteria that characterised the status: the *lex Aelia Sentia*, from AD 4, and the *lex Iunia* – from which part of the name by which the status was known in antiquity (as today) is

---

The texts of the quoted legal sources are taken from the standard editions; the translations are adapted from those given there.

[1] Expressions and concoctions similar to the English 'formal/informal manumission' (or similar) are also used in other modern languages; some recent examples in the languages in which most of the relevant scholarship is written: 'une *manumissio* informelle', 'les esclaves affranchis de manière informelle', 'une *manumissio* régulière', 'affranchir régulièrement' (Corbier 2008, 315–16); 'feierlichen und offiziellen Formen', 'formlose Freilassungen', 'vollen Freilassung' (Herrmann-Otto 2009, 199–200); 'manomissioni informali', 'manomessi senza formalità' (Masi Doria 2018, 555, 559); 'manumisión informal' (López Barja 2007, 19, 27, 30; 2008, 223); 'manumisión llamada informal', 'la manumisión formal' (López Barja 2008, 220). The English rendering 'perfect/imperfect manumission' (or similar) is regularly expressed through circumlocution in other languages (often following closely the Roman, Latin usage): some examples: 'les conditions liées à l'âge' (Corbier 2008, 315); 'die Voraussetzungen zu einer vollen Freilassung' (Herrmann-Otto 2009, 200); 'i manomessi minori dei trent'anni in violazione della legge Elia Senzia', 'i minori di trent'anni *manomessi testamento*' (Bisio 2020, 17, 103); 'manumisiones [. . .] de *servi minores*' (López Barja 2018b, 575).

derived – of uncertain date.² The texts of these statutes have not survived intact.³ But in his *Institutes* produced in the second half of the second century AD, the Roman jurist Gaius summed up the key criteria detailed in the *lex Aelia Sentia* for the award of both freedom and citizenship upon manumission – and the award of mere Latinity in their absence – thus:

> Nam in cuius personam tria haec concurrunt, ut maior sit annorum triginta et ex iure Quiritium domini et iusta ac legitima manumissione liberetur, id est vindicta aut censu aut testamento, is civis Romanus fit; sin vero aliquid eorum deerit, Latinus erit.

> For any person who fulfils three conditions – that he is above the age of thirty, that he is in the quiritary ownership of his master, and that he is freed by means of a lawful and legally recognised manumission (that is, by the rod, by the census, or by will) – becomes a Roman citizen; but if any of those conditions is lacking he will be a Latin.⁴

Despite his focus on men in the cited passage, Gaius implied a few paragraphs on that these legal provisions also applied to women.⁵ Moreover, Gaius added information that documents a further limitation in the creation of new Roman citizens from Rome's enslaved population through the *lex Aelia Sentia*: he specified that a manumitter *below* the age of twenty was only able to constitute a Roman *civis* if there existed 'just cause' – *iusta causa* – for the manumission; Gaius comments further that 'just cause' was also required of a manumitter below the age of twenty when manumitting informally *inter amicos* (on which more below). For example, manumission for the purpose of marriage was regarded as such a 'just cause', as was the manumission of one's natural children: in such cases, the stipulated age requirement was rescinded. The same rule applied to those manumitted: if 'just cause' was demonstrated, the requirement to be of thirty years of age to gain Roman *civitas* upon manumission became redundant.⁶

The newly prescribed requirements, however, constituted a steep challenge otherwise: besides being at least thirty years of age and manumitted by whoever held legal

---

² See Gai. *Inst.* 1.22 for an explication of the concoction *Latini Iuniani*.
³ For an attempt at reconstructing the content of the *lex Iunia*, see Sirks 1983, 218–29.
⁴ Gai. *Inst.* 1.17.
⁵ Gai. *Inst.* 1.29.
⁶ The key discussion is in Gai. *Inst.* 1.38–40. For the stipulation that an owner under the age of twenty was required to prove *iusta causa* before a *consilium* (*apud consilium*) to manumit *inter amicos*, see Gai. *Inst.* 1.41. Manumission for the purpose of marriage – *manumissio matrimonii causa* – has attracted the bulk of the scholarly debate on manumission for a 'just cause': for example, Huemoeller 2020; Perry 2014, 90–2; Wacke 1989 (and 2001). Incelli 2017 discusses some (possible) epigraphic cases, contending more broadly that the (indirect) epigraphic evidence for *manumissio matrimonii causa* is considerable. The fundamental legal framework of *iusta causa manumissionis* is discussed in Buckland 1908, 538–42; it has at times been seen as giving enslaved women an advantage over their male counterparts in securing manumission, as, for instance, in Weaver 1972, 70: 'Women in general had a decisive advantage over men as slaves in gaining early manumission; manumission "matrimonii causa" worked in their favour'; similarly Wacke 1989 (and 2001); Weiler 2001, 256 (endorsing Wacke's conclusions). See also Chapter 4 (pp. 118–9).

title over them, of twenty years of age or above, to achieve *civitas* required, as Gaius put it, 'a lawful and legally recognised manumission' (*iusta ac legitima manumissio*), i.e. 'by the rod', 'by the census', or 'by will'.[7] Of these three modes of manumission, manumission 'by the census' (*censu*) could only be achieved occasionally, when a local census was conducted, leaving manumission 'by the rod' (*vindicta*) and testamentary manumission (*testamento*) as the potentially more practicable avenues for gaining citizenship with freedom.[8] The 'formality' of these manumission modes, carried in the English rendering 'formal manumission', was constituted by their public dimension, i.e. the involvement of the state. This is self-evident in the case of manumissions 'by the rod' and 'by the census', given their patent engagement of magistrates who acted on behalf of the Roman state: in the first case through the magistrate who presided over the proceeding at which the manumission was effected;[9] in the second case through the magistrate who sanctioned the entry of the formerly enslaved in the list of citizens. Both manumission 'by the rod' and 'by the census' constitute manumissions *inter vivos* – 'among the living' – given that in both cases the manumitter was alive at the point of manumission. In the case of testamentary manumission, the manumitter was, evidently, deceased, with the instruction to manumit appropriately expressed in their will; the will was in turn expected to be signed by witnesses who, in the imperial period, effectively exercised the original public sanction of wills by the *comitia calata*.[10] The scholarly dispute over the order in which these manumission modes developed in the republican period, their precise functioning and original (legal) aims, need not detain us here.[11] Importantly, however, the Romans also expressed their desire to manumit enslaved individuals without having recourse to any of these formal manumission modes, by declaring their wish to manumit without the participation of the public authority. This so-called informal manumission is attested in diverse sources. Within the remit of the juridical discourse of the early imperial period, Gaius speaks, for instance, about manumission 'among friends' (*inter amicos*).[12] Informal manumission was not affected by the age requirements laid down by the *lex Aelia Sentia*: those manumitted informally became Junian Latins even if aged thirty or above.

While formerly enslaved individuals who were freed from slavery in conjunction with the award of *civitas* faced social and civic disadvantages in Roman society vis-à-vis their freeborn peers, such as (in the case of men) the inability to stand for political office, for Junian Latins, the absence of citizenship came with some significantly more

---

[7] The different manumission modes, and especially their legal dimensions, are fully discussed in Buckland 1908, 437–78; see also López Barja 2007, 15–43; Masi Doria 1993b, 233–40.

[8] Gaius' treatment does not uphold the widespread view that *manumissio censu* had all but disappeared by then, even if he is probably referring to a census of a different kind from the republican one: López Barja 2007, 31–4.

[9] Note, however, also Gaius' comment that manumission 'by the rod' of a person aged thirty or more may also be carried out in what are de facto less formal scenarios, such as when the praetor or proconsul was on the way to the theatre or the baths: *Inst.* 1.20; discussion is in López Barja 2007, 20–1.

[10] For the republican provisions, see Daube 1946.

[11] The issues discussed by scholars are clearly laid out in Daube 1946.

[12] Gai. *Inst.* 1.41, 1.44; see also Ulp. *Reg.* 1.10, 1.18. For the debate on the existence of other forms of informal manumission during the Principate, see, for example, Nicosia 2000.

severe limitations, most notably the inability to pass property upon death through a will. The brunt of these disadvantages was carried by male Junian Latins, for the simple reason that the legal capacities of formerly enslaved females were in any case of a lesser kind compared with those of men. On the other hand, Junian Latins enjoyed the same rights and freedoms during their lifetime as their enfranchised counterparts, i.e. formally and perfectly manumitted men and women; the differences between the two groups of freedpersons were focused, as far as the lawgivers were concerned, on the sphere of family lineage. The key text that provides the relevant information comes once more from Gaius' *Institutes*. Discussing the historical context and legal intentions specifically of the *lex Iunia*, Gaius added the following explication of a chief negative characteristic of the Junian Latin status:

> per legem Iuniam eos omnes, quos praetor in libertate tuebatur, liberos esse coepisse et appellatos esse Latinos Iunianos: Latinos ideo, quia lex eos liberos proinde esse voluit, atque si essent cives Romani ingenui, qui ex urbe Roma in Latinas colonias deducti Latini coloniarii esse coeperunt; Iunianos ideo, quia per legem Iuniam liberi facti sunt, etiamsi non essent cives Romani. legis itaque Iuniae lator cum intellegeret futurum, ut ea fictione res Latinorum defunctorum ad patronos pertinere desinerent, quia scilicet neque ut servi decederent, ut possent iure peculii res eorum ad patronos pertinere, neque liberti Latini hominis bona possent manumissionis iure ad patronos pertinere, necessarium existimavit, ne beneficium istis datum in iniuriam patronorum converteretur, cavere [voluit], ut bona eorum proinde ad manumissores pertinerent, ac si lex lata non esset. itaque iure quodam modo peculii bona Latinorum ad manumissores ea lege pertinent.

> as a result of the Junian Act, all those whose liberty the praetor protected came to be free and were called Junian Latins: Latins, because the Act intended them to have their freedom exactly as if they were freeborn Roman citizens who came to be colonial Latins through emigration from the City of Rome to Latin colonies; Junian, because they were made free by the Junian Act, even though they were not to be Roman citizens. That being so, the draftsman of the Junian Act realised that the result of this fiction would be that the property of deceased Latins would cease to go to their patrons. They did not die as slaves and so their property could not go to their patrons as *peculium*; and the goods of a freedman who was a Latin could not go to his patron by virtue of his manumission. So that the benefit given to Latins should not rebound to the prejudice of their patrons, therefore, he considered it necessary to provide that their estates should go to the persons who manumitted them as if the Act had not been passed; and so by this Act the estates of Latins go to those who manumit them, in a certain sense as being a slave's *peculium*.[13]

Free while alive, Junian Latins died as if they were still enslaved, barred from making wills: 'the estates of Latins go to those who manumit them, in a certain sense as

---

[13] Gai. *Inst.* 3.56. For a recent discussion of this text, see Masi Doria 2018, 558–60.

being a slave's *peculium*.[14] The ability of Junian Latins to build a family lineage was thus severely compromised, in the interest of their patrons. Sherwin-White therefore famously labelled Junian Latins 'under-privileged half-citizens'.[15]

The conceptual gymnastics that the juridical creation of the Junian Latin status required have, quite rightly, been central to the modern scholarly debate. In the present study, the legal foundation of the condition, i.e. the *leges Aelia Sentia et Iunia*, is given pride of place in Chapter 2: in this chapter, Pellecchi outlines in great detail the juridical framework of this particular form of *libertinitas*, 'freed status', with special regard to the dates of the two enactments, their scope and relationship, and the context of their technical provisions. As Gaius' summary also implies, in its legal conception Junian Latinity was crafted from an already existing right – i.e. that of the *Latini coloniarii*, giving the Junian Latin status the second part of its name. Latin status had been around for some time, enabling the Roman state already in the mid-republican period to manage colonial foundations under its control, but without awarding Roman civic status to community or individual.[16] Following the success of Rome in the war against its former Italian allies in the early first century BC, known in English as the Social War, the *ius Latii* found new applications, both in (northern) Italy and further afield from the peninsula, creating the actual and conceptual bases to which, according to Gaius, Junian Latinity related. Crudely put, Junian Latinity grew out of a wider net of Latinity known in Roman law and society for several centuries. In the light of this close relationship between existing forms of Latinity and Junian Latinity, the story of the Roman invention and application of a flexible Latin status – i.e. one that is divorced from its original locational and cultural dimensions – is a critical element of a sound understanding of the Junian Latin status. For this reason, Latin status of the non-Junian type is given full attention in this study in a comprehensive overview of its development from the Social War onwards, in Chapter 1, by García Fernández, thus to embed the dedicated discussions of the many diverse aspects of Junian Latinity in the ensuing chapters in the broader historical developments to which they relate. Indeed, it is only on this basis that it is possible to grasp how the new status could be created quickly as and when it was enacted in the Augustan age. But what drove its enactment at the time? By exploring more closely the late republican context, López Barja argues in Chapter 3 that the *lex Iunia* makes best sense if placed within the context of the *frumentationes* of the late Republic and the sudden increases of (informal) manumissions that they provoked. The chapter also demonstrates that the laws pertaining to Junian Latinity were not mere formalities, but had a direct and significant impact on social relations in imperial society, including between the imperial power and private slave-owners – thereby underlining the importance of the study of Junian Latinity for the modern understanding of the wider history of the period. To complicate the matter of Latinity (yet further), in Chapter 5, López Barja, joined by Rodríguez Garrido, revisits

---

[14] In the republican period, the informally manumitted retained the legal status of the slave also while alive: brief discussion is in Masi Doria 2018, 560–1.
[15] Sherwin-White 1973a, 329–30.
[16] A short historical contextualisation of the origins and development of the status of the so-called *prisci Latini* in the early and mid-Republic is in Cornell 1995, 348–52.

one of the broader questions of the topic, namely the relationship, in the imperial age, of the status of 'mere' Latins and Junian Latins, arguing that there was in fact a single and substantial identity of *Latinitas*, with the differences between 'mere' Latins and Junian Latins deriving solely from the rule of the *lex Iunia* pertaining to the succession rights of specifically Junian Latins.

Whatever view one takes on these various questions, there is little doubt that Junian Latinity was anything but short-lived. Indeed, the status was of notable longevity: following its introduction in the Augustan period, Junian Latinity lasted for over half a millennium, until the emperor Justinian abolished it in the sixth century AD.[17] These, and other developments that follow the period that is at the centre of the modern discussion, i.e. the Principate, are part and parcel of the story too, and need to be taken full account of, not least for their potential to throw light on the ancient understanding of the status: Chapter 6, by Corcoran, offers therefore a comprehensive survey of all explicit (and some implicit) textual references to Junian Latinity from the third century AD via late antiquity and through the early medieval period as far as the revival of Justinianic law in the early second millennium AD – highlighting the likely blow that the facilitation of manumission in the Church on the part of Constantine in the early fourth century AD constituted for the Junian Latin status in practice long before its abolition by Justinian. That there is nevertheless reason to think that Junian Latinity was well known and understood as a condition in late antiquity is not least underscored by its deeply intriguing mention, roughly a century after Constantine, in Salvian's *Ad ecclesiam* – which therefore deserves detailed contextualisation, undertaken by de Wet in Chapter 10.

Whatever the modern appreciation of both the creation and the development of Junian Latinity as a status, and its eventual demise, for those holding the status there were, at least over time, several ways out of it, to acquire Roman citizenship. The principal means to shed the Junian status in favour of *civitas* was by way of a second, formal, and perfect manumission, so-called iteration – *iteratio*. The relevant discussion in Gaius' *Institutes* is preserved in a fragmentary passage:

> Praeterea possunt maiores triginta annorum manumissi et Latini facti iteratione ius Quiritium consequi. quo ------- triginta annorum manumittant -------- vv. 1½ -------- | manumissus vindicta aut censu aut testamento et civis Romanus | et eius libertus fit, qui eum iteraverit.

> Moreover, those of over thirty years who have been manumitted and become Latins are able to obtain the right of citizenship by iteration. So . . . of [over] thirty years, they may manumit . . . a person manumitted by rod, by the census, or by will becomes both a Roman citizen and the freedman of the one who repeated the manumission.[18]

The *lex Aelia Sentia* offered, moreover, the possibility for procreative Junian Latins to acquire Roman citizenship through a process termed *anniculi probatio*, i.e. the presentation

---

[17] *CJ* 7.6.
[18] Gai. *Inst.* 1.35.

to the local authorities of a child of one year of age – an option prolifically discussed on the famous epigraphic dossier of L. Venidius Ennychus from Herculaneum by Camodeca in several publications.[19] Roman *civitas* could also be awarded through a special grant from the emperor – an option that features in Roth's contribution to this volume concerned with one of the most heavily cited literary texts on this topic, i.e. the correspondence of Pliny the Younger, in Chapter 8. Alternatively, at intervals, the Roman state established a number of challenges that, if successfully met, presented a Junian Latin with additional mechanisms to shed Latinity in favour of *civitas*, albeit focused on male Junian Latins: with further conditions and qualifications attached to them, contextualised in Rodríguez Garrido's account of imperial legislation in the early Empire in Chapter 4, these challenges included service with the *vigiles* in the capital, the provisioning of Rome with grain, and the building of a house at Rome. While the creation of Junian Latin status and the key criteria that defined it (as well as some of the ways out of it) were laid down by the *leges Aelia Sentia et Iunia*, the addition of new legislation pertaining to the status was not confined to the examples here listed. Indeed, there was regular legal engagement with the condition: we provide a full overview of all relevant enactments mentioned in the surviving sources in the Appendix.

Besides the provisions promulgated through the *leges Aelia Sentia et Iunia*, a statute known as the *lex Fufia Caninia*, enacted in 2 BC, established related new numerical limits specifically for testamentary manumission: 'moreover', Gaius notes in his *Institutes*, 'by the *lex Fufia Caninia* a certain limit is established with reference to the manumission of slaves by a will'.[20] In effect, the law established a scale for testamentary manumission:

> Nam ei, qui plures quam duos neque plures quam decem servos habebit, usque ad partem dimidiam eius numeri manumittere permittitur; ei vero, qui plures quam X neque plures quam XXX servos habebit, usque ad tertiam partem eius numeri manumittere permittitur. At ei, qui plures quam XXX neque plures quam centum habebit, usque ad partem quartam potestas manumittendi datur. Novissime ei, qui plures quam C habebit nec plures quam D, non plures manumittere permittitur quam quintam partem; neque plures quam D habentis ratio habetur, ut ex eo numero pars definiatur, sed praescribit lex, ne cui plures manumittere liceat quam C. Quod si quis unum servum omnino aut duos habet, ad hanc legem non pertinet, et ideo liberam habet potestatem manumittendi.

> Hence, he who has more than two slaves and not more than ten, is permitted to manumit as many as half of that number. He, however, who has more than ten and not more than thirty slaves, is permitted to manumit a third of that number; and he who has more than thirty slaves and not more than a hundred, is granted authority to manumit one fourth of his slaves. Finally, he who has more than one hundred and not more than five hundred, is not permitted to manumit more than a fifth; and, no matter how many slaves a man may have, he is not

---

[19] See esp. Camodeca 2002, 260–6 (with 2006a, 902–4); 2017, 57–84.
[20] Gai. *Inst.* 1.42.

permitted to manumit more than this, as the law prescribes that no one shall have the right to manumit more than a hundred. Still, where anyone has only one or two slaves, his case does not come under this law, and therefore he has free power of manumission.[21]

Quite evidently, the *lex Fufia Caninia* compromised the discretionary powers of masters to make new Roman citizens from Rome's enslaved population. While not technically a part of the 'creation story' of Junian Latinity, the provisions of the *lex Fufia Caninia* are nevertheless important for the debate on the Junian Latin status, both with regard to the law's impact on the power of slave-owners to manumit and because the numerical limitation of testamentary manumission may well have caused a rise of other manumission types, informal manumission included. Indeed, all three laws are commonly subsumed in modern scholarly parlance under the rubric of the Augustan manumission legislation.[22] In its totality, as the passages cited in this Introduction illustrate, the early imperial legislation pertaining to manumission centred on the link between liberation from slavery and civic enfranchisement, and the role played by masters-cum-patrons in the process, raising the broader question of the legislative aim or aims, with a particular focus on the relationship between slavery, freedom and citizenship. As Atkinson put it in her discussion of the purpose of these enactments: 'it is this close connection in Roman law between manumission and citizenship which gives to this whole question its special interest and permanent importance'.[23]

By its very definition, the study of the status of individuals freed by way of manumission from slavery sits at the heart of our understanding of the relationship between slavery and freedom in the Roman world. The conditions for and consequences of manumission for the individuals concerned, just like the roles and lives of the formerly enslaved in Roman society, have therefore long been allocated centre stage in modern historical analyses: studies of freedmen and freedwomen, their contributions to Roman society, economy and politics, the impact of their former servile status on life after manumission, the opportunities for their children – to name but a few of the areas most discussed – constitute a seemingly ever burgeoning field.[24] At the centre of this debate has been the enfranchised portion of Rome's freed population, i.e. those awarded *civitas* upon manumission. By contrast, beyond intense legal exploration of Junian Latinity in the nineteenth century, the status and its holders have featured primarily in specialist studies, typically focused on particular bodies or snippets of

---

[21] Gai. *Inst.* 1.43 (with 1.44–6).
[22] These laws fall in turn into the broader bracket of Augustus' so-called social legislation, including also enactments pertaining to marriage (the *lex Iulia de maritandis ordinibus*, of 18 BC; the *lex Iulia de adulteriis coercendis* and the *lex Papia Poppea*, of AD 9).
[23] Atkinson 1966, 357.
[24] The scholarship on the topic is vast; we list here merely some sizeable recent contributions: MacLean 2018 (cultural role of freedpersons); Perry 2014 (freedwomen); Bell and Ramsby 2012 (meaning of manumission for the freed); Mouritsen 2011 (historical synthesis); López Barja 2007 (history of manumission); Kleijwegt 2006 (manumission in comparative perspective); Weiler 2003 (exit routes from slavery); Masi Doria 1996 (*bona libertorum*); Waldstein 1986 (freedpersons' *operae*); Fabre 1981 and Treggiari 1969 (late republican freedpersons); Weaver 1972 (imperial freedpersons).

evidence. Overall, this work has had little impact on the wider debate on freed life in ancient Rome. Perhaps unsurprisingly therefore, modern scholarship has generally seen a firm link between manumission and citizenship at Rome. Indeed, the Roman practice of giving formerly enslaved individuals *civitas* has even been credited with the status of a norm: Moses Finley spoke of an 'astonishing rule'.[25]

Sherwin-White's negative assessment of the quality of the civic condition of Junian Latins aside, cited above, the Junians were, at base, a constituent part of Rome's freed population. Their marginalisation in modern scholarly thought concerned with that population and its place in Roman society is perhaps less bewildering than problematic. Quite obviously, separating the sheep from the goats – freedpersons with and without the franchise – is an excruciatingly difficult undertaking. Integrating the story of Rome's freed population in the broader, widely accepted narrative of the desirability of Roman citizenship is on the other hand an attractive alternative to the painstaking work that such differentiation requires – a differentiation that, moreover, is easily subject to criticism given the lack of any clear, agreed criteria. At the same time, the widespread disregard for Junian Latinity is seriously problematic given that the status opens up a massive window precisely on the issue of the relationship between freedom and citizenship in ancient, imperial Rome. Put most sharply: what would happen to Finley's 'astonishing rule' if the Junian element of Rome's freed population were deemed a significant part of that population?

The idea that Junian Latins made up a sizeable proportion of Rome's freed population had in fact long been suspected among the few who accepted the challenge that the status brought to the modern appreciation of freed life in ancient Rome, even if without any in-depth analysis of the issue.[26] Most notably, back in 1997, Paul Weaver – one of the most prolific students of the Junian Latin condition – famously coined the notion of a 'black hole' for the status, i.e. a phenomenon both vast in size but for all practical purposes impenetrable in nature.[27] Weaver's characterisation of Junian Latinity as a 'black hole' went hand in hand with his contention that our evidence brims with hitherto unrecognised Junian Latins. In particular, Weaver regarded the inscriptional evidence as a potential treasure trove for the student of Junian Latinity, reiterating in 2001 that the Latin funerary record from the Roman Empire was probably infested with freed individuals who lacked Roman citizenship: 'if Junian Latins lurk untraced in large numbers in the *sepulcrales*, as I think they must [. . .] they represent a large undetected black hole at the heart of the "slave" society that is Rome, at least in urbanised Roman society'.[28] The contention that Junian Latins may have been numerous throws their importance to the modern study of Roman slavery, freedom and citizenship into stark relief. It also throws into relief the potential set-backs for our understanding of Roman society more broadly that arise from the widespread scholarly inattention to the condition – encapsulated above in the brief aside on Finley's 'astonishing rule'. First and foremost, there is the question of the spread of Roman

---

[25] Finley 1980, 97.
[26] Notable examples are Lemmonier 1887, 225–7; Duff 1928, 75.
[27] Weaver 1997, 55.
[28] Weaver 2001, 103.

citizenship: if Junian Latins constituted a significant portion of Rome's freed population, modern understanding of the numbers of Roman citizens is in need of potentially drastic revision. It is also important to ask in this context to what extent Junian Latinity was a phenomenon *across* the Roman Empire, and especially in the diverse provincial settings. Secondly, and directly related to the numerical point, there is the issue of the role of citizenship at Rome: scholars have been quick to identify Roman *civitas* as a highly desired good among Rome's servile population; but what if fuller and more probing study of Junian Latinity casts doubt on the idea of the importance of Roman citizenship, at least for the formerly enslaved? Thirdly, with some notable exceptions, the study of Rome's freed population has been heavily focused on its male members, leaving open a whole range of questions regarding the consequences of the different manumission outcomes in the lives of female freedpersons.[29] Put differently, to what extent did Roman citizenship matter for former *female* slaves, who had turned into *Latinae Iunianae*, in comparison with their male counterparts? Addressing this question has repercussions for our view of (and obsession with) the routes available for Junian Latins to acquire Roman citizenship – summarised above. In the present volume, the topic of the informal manumission of enslaved women takes centre stage in Chapter 7, with Roth offering a close reading of a well-known literary passage that reveals a fairly casual attitude on the part of slave-owners to the issue; the topic concludes furthermore the contribution by Rodríguez Garrido in Chapter 4 with discussion of a particular case and the issues that may arise for the *Latina Iuniana*. Fourthly, the two-step approach to freedom and citizenship that underlies the Junian Latin condition has regularly been interpreted as providing the manumitters with an important means of social control over their former slaves. The assumption is that if those freed from slavery were still in need of a second manumission to gain citizenship in addition to freedom, their relationship to their masters-cum-patrons is likely to have been close, and perhaps even stronger than that widely assumed between patrons and their enfranchised freedpersons – a point of view that stands or falls with our answers to the first three questions. Conversely, and fifthly, the idea that Roman slave masters used their former slaves' aspiration to Roman citizenship as a means of social control is tied to the broader notion of guarding the civic gates. Mouritsen, for instance, has emphasised the concerns that may be raised through manumission by (what he calls) 'the crossing of boundaries and the transition between supposedly essential categories' – i.e. slavery and citizenship.[30] Understandably therefore, scholars have often talked about a 'merit test' before formerly enslaved persons were allowed entry into the civic community. López Barja, for example, noted that 'Latinity was a very valuable tool with which owners could gradually grant to their slaves the *magnum beneficium* of freedom and citizenship, according to their merits'; seen in this way, Latinity constituted 'a test period before definitely granting Roman citizenship'.[31] Once again, one's view

---

[29] See esp. Perry 2014, with Roth 2016b. The epigraphic evidence for *libertae*, and their role in Roman society, is discussed in detail in another volume in this series: Sandon forthcoming.
[30] Mouritsen 2016, 408.
[31] López Barja 1998, 160. Mouritsen 2016, 407 speaks in consequence of 'a hierarchy of civic statuses to which former slaves in principle would be allocated according to individual merit'.

on this matter is firmly tied to one's perspectives on the issues already raised. Seen in the round, it is quite evident that the study of Junian Latinity is not a mere self-serving exercise; rather, Junian Latinity is an ideal test case for putting a check on our current understanding of a whole range of important elements of the relationship between slavery, freedom and citizenship in the Roman Empire and thus on our view of the nature of Roman imperial society more broadly.

Weaver's attempt at encouraging increased scholarly concern with Junian Latinity arose out of his wider interest in what he called 'slave-born Roman society'.[32] In taking a lead from the work of Rawson on family life among the lower strata of Roman society, Weaver sought to come to terms with the seemingly dazzling legal and civic status mixture in what was by all accounts a highly stratified society. When Rawson noted in 1966 that '[o]ne of the striking impressions gained from a reading of the Roman *sepulcrales* is that of the intermingling of slaves, freedmen, and freeborn', Weaver responded by asking 'why in such a status-conscious "slave" society did the vast majority not use any form of status indication, especially those who had their names on tombstones?'[33] Rawson's way of dealing with the issue was to privilege a reading of the evidence that championed citizenship over Junian Latinity. Consequently, when commenting on the occurrence of numerous freed children in the *sepulcrales*, i.e. individuals who were too young to have been awarded citizenship upon manumission under the Augustan legislation, unless manumitted *iusta causa*, Rawson asked the obvious question – adding what with hindsight appears as a predictable answer: 'Are we to assume that all of these were only Junian Latins? This seems unlikely; at least, there is no evidence in the epitaphs for different classes of freedmen (except for imperial and nonimperial).'[34] The seeming lack of evidence for any status differentiation among these young freedpersons was taken as licence by Rawson to regard them all as endowed with citizenship – without proposing a safe identifier for their status. Instead, Rawson drew on a widespread short-hand, namely the use of onomastic signifiers, in her identification of freed citizens. As mentioned in brief above, Weaver emphasised, in contradistinction and on more than one occasion, the problem with assuming that those identifiable as freed were necessarily endowed with Roman citizenship. Weaver's critique was more than justified; it centred on the unreliability of onomastics, and in particular the *tria nomina* in the case of males, as a safe diagnostic in the identification of Roman citizens, especially in the inscriptional sources. By contrast, Weaver underlined the association of the *tria nomina* with freedom, over citizenship: given how much turns on this matter in the identification of civic status, the *tria nomina* (and friends) are revisited in Chapter 9, by Roth. But despite his critical take on Rawson's preference for interpreting the evidence for freedpersons generically in favour of enfranchised status, Weaver was warmly approving of the fact that, as he put it, '[t]there was even mention of Junian Latins.'[35]

There is more than just 'mention' of Junian Latins in the present volume – concerned in its first part with tracing the historical and legal settings of Junian Latinity, across six

---

[32] Weaver 2001, 101.
[33] Rawson 1966, 72; Weaver 2001, 101.
[34] Rawson 1966, 79.
[35] Weaver 2001, 101.

chapters. The four chapters in the second part of this volume are all concerned with explorations of Junian Latinity in the Latin literary universe, from the early imperial period until late antiquity, seeking to comprehend more fully, or to identify for the first time, particular Roman mentions of Junian Latinity. But our hunt for Junian Latins does not stop there: the body of evidence that has been at the centre of the modern scholarly debate, i.e. the epigraphy, is given centre stage in a separate volume, thus to provide the documentary evidence with the space it deserves, as well as to showcase in a focused fashion a range of scholarly 'laboratories' established to gain a firmer grip on the seemingly elusive condition; we also present in this second volume in-depth socio-historical analyses of the place of Junian Latinity in Roman society, based on diverse bodies of evidence and employing diverse analytical methods.[36] Grouping the chapters in the way here done emphasises that there is enough material for analysis across the different source bodies as well as enough questions to ask still of this material across diverse disciplinary fields, most notably legal and historical studies.

But the thematic and analytical choices behind the presented collection of chapters also necessitates an acknowledgement of an obvious lacuna in the present undertaking, namely the lack of exploration of the archaeological remains. This is an area that has only recently entered the debate on Junian Latinity, in relation to the rich funerary evidence that has long been central to the epigraphic exploration of the condition.[37] That said, the new approaches trialled on inscribed evidence in our second volume open up fresh ways of combining epigraphic and archaeological analysis, to take the debate on the materiality of Junian Latinity further in the future.

Back to the present, as noted at the outset of this Introduction, Junian Latinity continues to be kicked more often than not into the interpretative long grass, even by students of Roman slavery. But this was not always so: at the start of what may be termed the modern analysis of Roman history and law in the nineteenth century, Junian Latinity was given serious attention, especially by the lawyers. When this interest waned, the condition became submerged ever deeper in the 'black hole' that has become typical for its socio-historical study. To challenge this development, the work here presented seeks to rekindle the conversation about a status that has been as elusive to the modern scholarly eye as it may have been pervasive in the Roman imperial age, with a view to encouraging others to join the inquisitive bandwagon. Let there be mention of Junian Latins again.

---

[36] López Barja, Masi Doria and Roth forthcoming.
[37] Emmerson 2011.

I.

The Historical and Legal Contexts for Junian Latinity

First Prologue:
A Millennium of Legislation on Junians and Other Latins

Ulrike Roth

The legal exploration of Junian Latinity has been at the forefront of modern scholarly investigation into this seemingly peculiar status. This is hardly surprising given that the status was framed by a series of laws. These laws, and the surrounding legal discourse, have left conspicuous evidence behind in the surviving source materials. Much of the modern juridical debate has centred on a handful of key questions: in the main, Roman lawyers have debated the chronological relationship of the *leges Aelia Sentia et Iunia*; they have sought to establish each of these two laws' precise provisions; and they have asked after these laws' relationship to other, contemporary statutes. Despite the many insights gained into Junian Latinity that have arisen from this work, there is much that is still unknown, or at least uncertain: at the head of this uncertainty stands the question of the rationale behind the legal innovation, besides that of the association of specifically *Junian* Latinity with other forms of Latinity. Both of these questions are, to a large extent, historical in nature, even if these questions cannot be addressed in separation from their inherent legal dimensions – a point that has been stressed before. In her discussion of the rationale behind the legislation, Atkinson, for instance, formulated the cross-over between legal and historical matter thus:

> The question is a historical rather than a legal one, but is none the less deserving on that account of engaging the consideration of scholars primarily concerned in the study of law, since no law operates in a vacuum, but in the context of human society and affairs.[1]

Atkinson's reference to the operation of law in a historical context provides a motto for this first, opening part of the present study. Here, we present six chapters concerned with roughly a millennium of legislation on Junians and other Latins. This wide chronological vista is a deliberate choice for setting the scene. Historically, the creation, by Rome, of the concept (and reality) of Latin status which was divorced from its geographical and cultural roots is a development of the fourth century BC,

---

[1] Atkinson 1966, 358.

enabling Rome to strengthen its grip in Italy in the shape of Latin colonies, outside Latium.[2] Beginning, then, with the story of the reinvention of coloniary Latinity, followed by municipal Latinity, in the late republican context in Chapter 1, and ending with the known relics of Junian Latinity in the late antique and the first half of the medieval period in Chapter 6, this part sets the discussion of Junian Latinity in the context of several interrelated developments over a *longue durée*: while typically studied primarily by students of the early Roman Empire, Junian Latinity is a historical phenomenon that cannot be fully understood in isolation from other forms of Latinity, both those existing before and those surviving the Junian Latin status. Moreover, by setting the discussion into this wide historical view, the volume follows a long-known role model – for Gaius' attempt at explaining the status in the middle of the second century AD drew, after all, precisely on an analogy with the status of coloniary Latins, in an earlier historical period. Admittedly, Gaius' assimilation of the Junian condition to the status of coloniary Latins ranks among the more bewildering elements of his exposition of the newly created status: the apparent mismatch between the communal nature of the status of coloniary Latins vis-à-vis the focus on individual status that characterises Junian Latinity has, unsurprisingly therefore, caused some considerable modern debate that is far from being settled. Thinking Junian Latinity within the web of Latin statuses can thus not be sidestepped. But irrespective of the conundrum that Gaius has created for us, it is evident that, from the start of its explication – and from its *legal* explication at that – the Junian Latin status has been rendered intelligible through historical contextualisation. History and law, then, must go hand in hand in the exploration of the Junian condition.

This is not to deny that many advances in the study of Junian Latinity have been made in historical explorations of especially social and cultural aspects of the condition. The indispensable work of Weaver illustrates this well, especially regarding the study of epigraphic materials.[3] Obviously, Weaver did not shy away from the analysis of the legal sources either, even if he can be found to express a certain amount of apprehension regarding these: in his discussion of the children of Junian Latins, in which Weaver drew heavily on Gaius & Co., he nevertheless sought, as he put it, 'to keep the more complicated legal material to a minimum'.[4] Weaver's apprehension was not misplaced: broadly speaking, outside of dedicated epigraphic study – fraught with its own problems – students of Junian Latinity find themselves easily on quicksand when approaching the treacherous evidential ground that is undermined by legal dimensions. This point can be elucidated by a recent example.

Thus, in his fine study of the urban economy, Hawkins suggested that a part of the productive contribution of formerly enslaved artisans to the urban labour market was

---

[2] A good overview of the developments reported in the literary sources is in Salmon 1969, 55–69. For a historical interpretation, see Cornell 1995, 347–52. The invention of the Latin colony may not have been as late as 338 BC: see Salmon 1969, 40–54 on the so-called *Priscae Latinae Coloniae*, established by Rome and its allies on land of defeated communities; see also Cornell 1995, 301–4.

[3] Notably Weaver 1990. The contribution of epigraphy to the study of Junian Latinity is in focus in the sequel to the present volume.

[4] Weaver 1997, 55.

made under an agreement for *operae*: with due caution, Hawkins included Junian Latins in this assessment.[5] The inclusion of Junian Latins is underpinned in Hawkins' argument by the realisation that informal manumission granted in exchange for a price may stimulate the accumulation of pay for iteration (which the present author has herself argued for), thus encouraging an agreement for labour obligations in-between manumissions (and potentially also after iteration).[6] Hawkins speaks generally of 'labour hoarding', explicating the various means through which patrons could oblige (and even pressurise) their former slaves to undertake work for them post-manumission. It is instructive to look more closely at how Hawkins straddles the treacherous ground, in a footnote:

> No ancient text directly states that Junian Latins promised *operae* in exchange for their manumission like other freedmen. Waldstein 1986: 162 argues that they did not, but this is the minority view. Most historians assume that Junians could obligate themselves to *operae* in exchange for manumission in the same way as other freedmen (Sirks 1983, 259–60; Lopez Barja de Quiroga 1998, 144).[7]

Despite the lack of evidence, Hawkins sides, according to his own assessment, with a view that is primarily embraced by historical specialists, citing in support López Barja's suggestion that '[i]t is likely that Junian Latins had the same obligations of *operae* and *obsequium* as any other freedmen'; López Barja, too, acknowledged simultaneously that '[w]e have no information at all about *operae*' in our sources relating to Junian Latins.[8] More or less the same remark was made by Sirks in the other cited study, focused on legal issues pertaining to the *lex Iunia*, in which Sirks commented on the possibility of a Junian Latin's obligation to *operae*: 'though we do not know whether this happened, there is no reason not to assume the possibility of it'.[9] As also duly noted by Hawkins, Waldstein's views were different, expressed in what the author himself called a work that may be deemed too 'juristisch-dogmatisch' by ancient historians.[10] Notwithstanding Sirks' pointer towards a *possibility* (rather than a probability), it appears that where juridical dimensions are at the core of the analysis, the notion of obliging a Junian Latin to *operae* is challenged, at least within the formal remit of the law. This is also evident in Chapter 2 in this part, which shows, on the basis of deft legal reasoning, *operae* and *libertas Latina* to be incompatible. The legal perspective on the question of *operae* and Junian Latinity that is offered in this chapter necessitates therefore the search for a different explanation for the mechanism(s) through which the patrons of Junian Latins potentially benefited from their labour.[11] Furthermore, this perspective

---

[5] Hawkins 2016, 146–57.
[6] Roth 2010b; see also Sirks 1983, 259–60.
[7] Hawkins 2016, 156, n. 88.
[8] López Barja 1998, 144.
[9] Sirks 1983, 260.
[10] Waldstein 1986, 9.
[11] Note in this context the emphasis on a (financial) safety net that undergirds the argument for a manumission price in Roth 2010b; *operae* are by contrast not a reliable form of revenue, going by the instances in which a patron sues for *operae* that shine through the legal sources. Note also the comments in n. 12 below.

prompts a broader reconsideration of historical arguments in which *operae* are given a role in explorations of the lives of Latins, Junian and other.[12] Like Waldstein's *opus*, Chapter 2, despite (or perhaps rather because of) its legal focus, makes a powerful case for the interrelatedness of legal and historical analyses on the topic of Junian Latinity, demonstrating in passing just how slippery the ground is for wide-reaching historical interpretation in the context of complex legal issues.[13]

But the need to think widely and across disciplinary and subject partitions is also evident in the *historical* explanation of the condition and its multifaceted dimensions. Indeed, it goes almost without saying that despite the chronological location of the creation of Junian Latinity in what we call the Roman imperial period, the republican background, i.e. the social, economic, political and cultural settings especially in the decades before Augustus came to power, which underpin the legal innovation, cannot be omitted in discussions of the purpose of the laws that framed Junian Latinity. Chapter 3 makes the case for the importance specifically of the actual socio-economic and political situation in the outgoing years of the Republic for our appreciation of the need that the newly created status filled, engaging intensely with the late republican power struggles on the one hand, and the role of the corn dole in the feeding of the city of Rome on the other. The chapter thereby underlines just how important it is to think Roman republican and imperial history in tandem.

The importance of a joined-up historical view can be reinforced by recalling the situation specifically of *women* freed from slavery in the republican period, which Perry has rightly foregrounded for our understanding of the limitations put upon female freedpersons even when they enjoyed citizenship:

> In the early Republic, lawmakers inserted patrons into the existing system governing the affairs of women by categorizing them as de facto agnatic relatives. Since freedwomen lacked agnatic relatives under Roman law, patrons were the first in line to administer and inherit freedwomen's estates. What changed over time was not the control that patrons wielded over freedwomen's property, but rather that basis upon which they exercised these rights. By the late Republic, jurists increasingly indicated that former owners should be entitled to a share of their freedpersons' estates as *patrons* rather than as substitute agnates.[14]

Evidently, the situation that Perry outlines is not concerned with Junian Latinity as such. But the described developments nevertheless highlight that the idea of protecting

---

[12] Two examples: Harper 2010, 624–5, on the Latin status arising for the offspring of unions between a free woman and an enslaved man as a result of the *Senatus Consultum Claudianum*, and the assumed potential burden of *operae* for the children born to such unions; Roth 2010b, 105, including *operae* in a list of possible sources of revenue to pay for manumission, potentially including informal manumission and, hence, Junian Latins.

[13] The importance of legal reasoning for social history was also noted in Wiedemann 1988, 332, reviewing Waldstein 1986: 'The conclusions W. feels entitled to draw from his analyses of points of detail will be of considerable interest to the social historian.'

[14] Perry 2014, 87.

patronal powers over the estates of freed individuals is not an imperial invention. These developments place the legal innovation that created Junian Latinity into a wider historical framework that must play a role in its exploration if it is to be fully understood (as must also, quite obviously, the role of gender, which surfaces in some of the contributions in this volume and its sequel). Similarly, the many later modifications and additions that enabled Junian Latins to shed Latinity in favour of Roman citizenship, often studied as a seemingly static bundle, need to be analysed in their own historical settings – as Chapter 4 illustrates with several examples from a period spanning the rule of Tiberius at one end to the Severan dynasty at the other. But whatever the mechanisms open to Junian Latins to discard their Latin status in favour of Roman *civitas*, the very question of the relationship between their specifically *Junian* Latin status and Latinity as such, in the imperial period, must be given due attention: the issue is not easily addressed, and different approaches and views are presented in Chapters 1 and 5 respectively, designed to stimulate further debate. That there is more work to be done also to understand the later Roman developments pertaining to Junian and other forms of Latinity, as well as the post-Roman references to Latinity, is brought home with force in the concluding chapter to this part, which details the longevity of the legal treatment of the Junian Latin status and its transformation and abandonment over the first millennium of our era, taking the discussion to as late as roughly a millennium after its creation.

In one of his important discussions of the legal aspects of Junian Latinity, Sirks described Junian Latinity as foreign matter – a 'Fremdkörper' – in the writings of Roman jurists: 'In the handbooks of Roman law Junian Latinity turns up as a kind of "Fremdkörper"'; the image of extraneous matter, that has somehow infiltrated a body – here of the discourse on Roman law – and that by its very nature requires removal, is striking, and explained by Sirks thus:

> A Junian Latin was neither a slave, nor a coloniary Latin, nor a Latin in the sense of the grants of Latinity in the beginning of the Principate. And where/of (what) was he a citizen? Why did the Romans make this status, and why this instead of conferring generously the coloniary or other Latinity?[15]

Sirks' own approach to these questions and the broader, underlying puzzles was to set out to show, on the basis of legal argumentation, that Junian Latinity was no 'Fremdkörper' at all but in fact 'a part of the whole system of slavery and patronage'.[16] The same perspective emerges from the ensuing chapters, encouraged, we contend, by the diverse disciplinary and subject matters that are dealt with in the various discussions that follow. It is merely putting the matter in another way to say that, in sum, this following part is framed by three convictions: first, the need for both legal and historical study, and the combination of both approaches; second, the need for a historically contextualised analysis of Junian Latinity, in the sea of other forms of Latinity, before

---

[15] Sirks 1981, 247.
[16] Sirks 1981, 247.

and after; and third, the need for explorations of the various dimensions of Junian Latinity – from the rationale behind the laws that framed it to the changing provisions that the status has attracted – in specific historical settings. That there is more to be said on all of these scores than what the subsequent six chapters cover needs little emphasis: these chapters issue an invitation for a much larger, inclusive conversation on the historical and legal contexts that have fostered Junian Latinity.

1

Municipal Latin Rights from the Social War to Hadrian

Estela García Fernández

Introduction

The study of Latin rights is of great importance in analysing the processes of legal integration of the inhabitants of the western part of the Roman Empire. Moreover, to understand fully the importance of Latin rights in the Roman orbit it is important to stress that, with the exception of the oligarchies of the cities and their kin, a large majority of the population of medium and low social status living in the Roman Empire's western part would have been Latins. In the absence of specific data, this circumstance can be deduced from the widespread diffusion of Latin rights, or the *ius Latii*, in the western provinces, judging by the information provided by the literary sources and the epigraphic documentation.[1]

This chapter will focus on the study of *municipal* Latin rights. This expression refers to the condition enjoyed by the provincial cities that received the *ius Latii*. This right, in addition to modifying the administrative structure of the affected communities and attributing Latinity to their inhabitants, had the important peculiarity of providing access to Roman citizenship that was open only to the municipal oligarchies, a point that will be explored in detail below. It goes without saying that the question of municipal Latin rights is in itself a vast subject, the aspects to be dealt with are numerous, and the bibliography is virtually limitless. It is therefore opportune to note at the outset that the aim of the present chapter lies not in providing a complete overview of the topic. Rather, my focus is on those dimensions that are especially relevant to place the study of Junian Latinity – the topic of this volume – into the wider, contemporary context. To this end, attention will be focused on the discussion and analysis of the provincial Latin condition or, in other words, what it could mean for any individual to be a citizen of a provincial Latin city. Consequently, aspects such as the administration of Latin cities and their forms of government (civic titles, magistracies, local senates,

---

[1] The Latin right or *ius Latii* spread extensively throughout the western provinces of the Roman Empire (except Britannia), specifically Gallia Cisalpina, Gallia Narbonensis, Hispania, Gallia Comata, the Alpine districts, Germania, and the African and Danubian provinces. For the relevant evidence, see Kremer 2006, 121 (Gallia Cisalpina), 150–9 (Gallia Narbonensis), 159–64 (Gallia Comata), 180–8 (the provinces of Hispania, the three Alpine provinces, the Germaniae, the African and Danubian provinces), with detailed discussion.

legislation, etc.) will only be dealt with occasionally and indirectly, with a focus on the most pertinent data for present purposes (such as regarding the section that briefly explores the function of municipal legislation). Notwithstanding notable differences in the diverse forms of Latinity, this chapter thus opens a wider perspective for the study of Junian Latinity, by outlining some of the interrelated historical and legal contexts of Latin rights that surround the development and application specifically of Latinity's Junian dimension.

The Origin of Provincial Latin Rights: The Granting of *ius Latii* to Gallia Transpadana in 89 BC

In the long and complex history of the Latin right, which dates back to the fifth century BC,[2] Latin provincial law has a precise date of origin. In 89 BC, the consul Cn. Pompeius Strabo granted the indigenous communities of Gallia Transpadana the *ius Latii*,[3] turning them into Latin colonies. This episode, important because of its impact on the subsequent history of the Latin right, is known only from a report transmitted by Asconius in a commentary on a passage from a speech by Cicero (*in L. Pisonem*, of 55 BC):[4] in referring to a mention of the Latin colony of Placentia, the author compares the traditional procedure of foundation used for that colony with that used in Gallia Transpadana for the *deductio* of Latin colonies in the area.[5] The passage is highly

---

[2] On the origin of Latin rights as a legal condition established by the *Foedus Cassianum* and its development up to 89 BC, see Kremer 2006, 4–107.

[3] On the author of the law and its date, and the geographical scope of application, see Luraschi 1979, 143–57. Although Asconius refers exclusively to the population of Gallia Transpadana, the application of the procedure is generally extended to the territory of Gallia Cispadana, since it would not make any sense to exclude the federated communities of Gallia Cispadana that were not affected by the *lex Iulia*. On the possible settlements in Gallia Cispadana affected by the measure of Pompey, see Luraschi 1979, 147–61, 157; Bandelli 1990, 260–1, n. 64.

[4] Namely Asconius, *In Pis.* 3 Clark: 'Neque illud dici potest, sic eam coloniam esse deductam quemadmodum post plures aetates Cn. Pompeius Strabo, pater Cn. Pompei Magni, Transpadanas colonias deduxerit. Pompeius enim non novis colonis eas constituit, sed veteribus incolis manentibus ius dedit Latii, ut possent habere ius quod ceterae Latinae coloniae, id est ut †petend<o> magistratus† civitatem Romanam adipiscerentur.' On the passage, see Luraschi 1979, 143–73 with detailed analysis; cf. Barbati 2012, offering discussion of some problems in reading the passage (esp. 1–4); also Barbati 2013 (esp. 86–8, 95 on the acquisition of colonial titles by the communities of Gallia Transpadana with a historiographic review and detailed treatment); Sisani 2018a, 347–53.

[5] The Latin colony of Placentia was established in 218 BC and was part of the group of republican Latin colonies. Its foundation procedure was subject to the requirements of any colonial establishment: population transfer (in this case 6,000 colonists among whom were 200 *equites*), the creation of a new *urbs* and a new citizenship, land distribution to the colonists and the presence of a triumviral commission in charge of organising the new colony (Asconius, *In Pis.* 3 Clark; Polyb. 3.40.3–5; Livy 21.25.2–5). For discussion, see Gargola 1990. Similarly, from the end of the third century BC, a process of founding cities of Latin colonial type began in Hispania, including Carteia (Livy 43.3.1–4), as well as Italica, Tarraco and Cordoba, among others. The unlikely presence of a stable Roman population in these colonies, added to their large indigenous population component, means that their foundation was markedly different from the general course of Latin foundations: discussion is in García Fernández 2009; see also Espinosa-Espinosa 2016, 2018.

relevant because the author provides two important pieces of information for the study of municipal Latin rights. First, that the Latin colonies 'founded' by Strabo in Gallia Transpadana had undergone a different process than the usual one. Although at first the expression used by Asconius, *colonias Transpadanas deduxerit*, might suggest the opposite, a precise clarification by the author makes it clear that there was no arrival of colonists ('non novis colonis constituit'), but that instead it was the existing indigenous settlements and the population living in them ('incolis veteribus manentibus') that were to receive the colonial title and the *ius Latii*.[6] Second, Asconius provides the oldest explicit reference to the *ius Latii* and the procedure for its concession to provincial *civitates*. This right was to be of decisive importance in the integration of provincial elites by opening up a means of access to Roman citizenship through the holding of a local magistracy.[7]

As regards the procedure used for the colonies of Gallia Transpadana, the absence of a population relocated for this purpose would in principle make the customary allocation of land unnecessary, and with it the complex Roman organisation of the land which until then had accompanied any colonial foundation. It is therefore to be expected that the communities of Gallia Transpadana would not have been subjected to a profound territorial or urban reorganisation, as was usual in true colonial foundations, at least in the years immediately following their conversion into Latin colonies. Hence the name of *colonie fittizie*, fictional colonies, coined by Luraschi, which these colonies received.[8]

In fact, the assessment of the urban and territorial documentation of the area has changed since the 1970s and 1980s. While previous studies have interpreted large-scale centuriation as an effect of the concession of Pompey, current archaeological thinking seems to reject the idea that the reorganisation of the Transpadane territory can be attributed to such an early date.[9] Thus, the extensive urban and territorial transformation of the Transpadane region is thought to have begun only after 49 BC, when Roman citizenship was granted to all of Gallia Cisalpina. This fact, and the subsequent suppression of the provincial status of Gallia Cisalpina in 42–41 BC, is seen as marking the starting point of

---

[6] The expression *veteres incolae manentes* would refer to the resident and original population of Gaulish cities, but possibly also to foreign individuals who were domiciled there. The underlying idea is that of *domicilium* by analogy with the *lex Plautia Papiria* (Cic. *Arch.* 4.7): see Luraschi 1979, 171, n. 151. On the passage and the concept of *incola*, see Gagliardi 2006, 3, n. 10, 8–11.

[7] The text of Asconius indicates that this right predates 89 BC. On its possible origin after the revolt of the Latin colony of Fregellae in 125 BC, see Tibiletti 1953; Sherwin-White 1972, 95–6; Luraschi 1979, 301–15; Piper 1988; cf. Brunt 1988, 511–12, n. 2; Crawford 1996, I, 111. For a summary review of the different theses on the origin of the *ius Latii*, see Genovese 2010, 1633, n. 87; and more recently, Balbo 2016.

[8] On the colonial process in Gallia Transpadana, see Luraschi 1979 (with 165–6 for discussion of *colonie fittizie*); Luraschi 1983, 265, stating that the Latin colonies ('neocolonie latine') of Gallia Cisalpina are in many aspects assimilable to *municipia*. On the arbitrary character of Luraschi's expression, which has nothing to do with a legal fiction, see Barbati 2013, 65, n. 26.

[9] For a general overview of the relevant archaeology up to 1979, see Luraschi 1979, 210–17 (largely responsible for the reversal of the trend to argue for a genuine reorganisation of the territory after 89 BC); see also Mirabella Roberti 1990, who does not consider that there are significant signs of urban restructuring in the area, except perhaps at Brixia and Mediolanum (although the latter is not certain).

the reorganisation of the area, which took place in the Augustan period. The recent discovery of a bronze fragment, called the B cadaster, at Verona, has confirmed the general lines of this interpretation, although it has also introduced a number of significant nuances.[10] This cadaster, dated sometime after 89 BC and before 49 BC, appears to prove the intervention of Rome, as a consequence of the granting of the *ius Latii*. This intervention is thought to be reflected in the formal recognition and registration of pre-existing properties with all of the census and fiscal repercussions that this entails.[11] Furthermore, the public display of the cadaster would have had a major symbolic value, reflecting Verona's entry into the Roman sphere and its conversion into a Latin colony. Seen this way, the granting of the *ius Latii* did not lead to a great territorial or urban reorganisation of Gallia Transpadana, as Luraschi advocated, but it does seem to have imposed some institutional modifications and interventions on the territory of which the cadaster is, in a way, an expression.[12]

With regard to the granting of the *ius Latii* to the population of Gallia Transpadana and their exclusion as beneficiaries of the *lex Iulia* of 90 BC, it is highly likely that, regardless of the strategic or political reasons that may have recommended their legal integration, the survival and vitality of the indigenous world in the Transpadane area did not make general access to Roman citizenship advisable. For this reason, a new channel was created which made it possible to promote the indigenous communities through the Latin right, conferring on them the colonial title that had been characteristic of the Latin right up until that time, together with some of its rights (*conubium, commercium* and the so-called *ius adipiscendae civitatem Romanam per magistratum*).[13] However, this path of integration was conceived from a municipal, rather than a colonial perspective, since it was not a question of transferring populations, nor of redistributing land, nor was it necessary to appoint commissioners to provide an *ex novo* Roman legal framework, but rather to legally promote communities that had their own population and their own institutions. These communities' direct conversion into municipalities was not possible because in the first century BC this administrative condition was only accessible through the granting of Roman citizenship, which seems to have been precisely

---

[10] The two bronzes (cadaster A and B) were discovered in the excavations of the *capitolium* of Verona directed by Cavalieri Manasse. Both documents are of extraordinary importance for the study of the effect of the Pompeian concession in the area (cadaster B) and of the subsequent reorganisation carried out following the granting of Roman citizenship (cadaster A). For an overall assessment, see Cavalieri Manasse and Cresci Marrone 2015, 2017; Maganzani 2015, 2017. Specifically on the cadaster A of Verona, see Cavalieri Manasse 2000, dating it to 40–20 BC, thus confirming the intervention of Rome after 49 BC, with Cavalieri Manasse 2004, 2008. For a re-evaluation following the discovery of cadaster B, see Cavalieri Manasse and Cresci Marrone 2015.

[11] The drafting of a cadaster would serve as a basis for establishing the census category of each male member of the community and their participation in elections and in the army or their possibility of access to a magistracy; neither should a fiscal function be ruled out: Maganzani 2015, 103–4; note also the onomastic differences pointed out by the author between the two cadasters (A and B).

[12] Maganzani 2015, esp. 98–9.

[13] On the Latin right of Gallia Transpadana, see Luraschi 1979, 221–5, 233–62. On the absence of the *ius migrandi* and *ius suffragii* in the provincial Latin right, see García Fernández 2001, 87–95. On the controversial *ius migrandi*, see recently Gagliardi 2020, 160–70, with earlier bibliography.

what was intended to be avoided, given the indigenous nature of the population. In my view, this is the reason why the Latin right was used,[14] instead of the Roman citizenship that was offered by the *lex Iulia de civitate*.

The key to the process in Gallia Transpadana and the reason for its success as an integrating mechanism was that it was capable of achieving the legal integration of the provincial populations through a two-pronged approach. On the one hand, the *ius Latii* acted as a filter that ensured access to Roman citizenship only for those of the highest social and economic levels. In fact, given the wide family coverage of this right (see below), members of the city oligarchies may have acquired Roman citizenship in a fairly short period of time, not only through access to local office, but also through filiation. On the other hand, Latin law facilitated the integration of the rest of the population by transforming their original status as *peregrini* into freeborn *Latini*. The latter condition, in contrast to Roman citizenship, had the advantage of making legal integration compatible with various levels of Romanisation or, if preferred, with the greater or lesser dynamism of the indigenous world. This was possible because, in reality, the provincial freeborn Latin who belonged to the middle or lower strata was not only estranged from the imperial system and its administrators, but, unlike other groups such as the Junian Latins, lacked their own means of access to Roman citizenship. The local route open to Roman citizenship in the Latin colonies and municipalities was a prerogative of the upper classes.

The episode in Gallia Transpadana was not an isolated event. At the same time that Roman citizenship was granted to Gallia Cisalpina,[15] thereby leading to the disappearance of the Transpadane Latin colonies, which had been transformed into Roman municipalities, a new process of Latinisation began in Gallia Transalpina in which the local communities, through a concession of the *ius Latii*, would also acquire Latin colonial status.[16] The Latin colonisation of Gallia Narbonensis would confirm that the Transpadane episode was not a one-off measure, and opened the door to the regular application of the *ius Latii* to other provincial territories. Later, in all likelihood during the Augustan period, Latin law underwent a further administrative modification that gave rise to the last of the administrative categories created by Rome, the Latin municipality.[17] This modification was probably due, among other possible reasons, to a desire to attribute a title that was adapted to the genuine characteristics of the *ius Latii*, which were not colonial but municipal in nature. Except for the different titles,

---

[14] The newness of the procedure possibly required the collaboration of some legal expert such as Q. Mucius Scaevola, as the possible architect of this innovative formula: see Luraschi 1979, 331.

[15] Caesar granted the inhabitants of Gallia Cisalpina Roman citizenship in 49 BC: Cass. Dio 41.36.3. The granting by Caesar of the *ius Latii* to Gallia Narbonensis is usually also dated around 49–48 BC: see Christol and Goudineau 1987–8, 90; Christol 1999, 15.

[16] On the Latin colonising process in Gallia Narbonensis and its relationship with Gallia Transpadana, see García Fernández 2001, 31–71. On the non-existence of Latin *oppida*, see García Fernández 2001, 104–24; Sisani 2018a, 352–4. For a different perspective, see Christol 1999; Kremer 2006, 137–59, with earlier bibliography. On the republican Latin *oppida* in Hispania, see Espinosa-Espinosa 2014.

[17] On the origin of the Latin municipality in the Augustan period, see García Fernández 2001, 73–104; Letta 2005, 2006; Sisani 2016, 12–14.

the different tribes assigned or the local magistrates' careers, governed by *quattuorviri* in Gallia Narbonensis and by *duumviri* preferably in Hispania,[18] there does not seem to have been any structural difference between the Latin colonies of Gallia Narbonensis and the Latin municipalities of Hispania. The origins of both lay in a concession of *ius Latii* to an indigenous community.[19] For this reason, the expression municipal Latinity is here used in reference not only to the condition enjoyed by the group of Latin municipalities in the west of the Empire and their population, but also to the Latin cities with colonial status.

Latin Rights in the Time of Augustus: Municipal Latinity in the Provinces and Junian Latinity

With Augustus, not only would the Latin municipality and the *municipes* with similar rights appear, but so also would a new type of Latin freedpersons, the so-called *Latini Iuniani* – the heroes of this volume. This meant that several population groups in the Empire would be called *Latini*: *Latini* were the freeborn inhabitants of the Latin cities in the west of the Empire (living in both municipalities and colonies), and *Latini* were their freedpersons, both private and public, as documented by the *lex Irnitana*.[20] Yet, as various other contributions to this volume emphasise, and as is generally well known, the new Junian freedpersons were also *Latini*.[21] The polysemy of the term probably led to confusion amongst the local magistrates of the provincial communities, not necessarily versed in legal subtleties, about the type of Latin status enjoyed by their fellow citizens. As will be seen below, it is possible that the letter of the emperor Domitian that is appended to the *lex Irnitana* could be a response to conflicts that arose in this respect.

The figures of municipal Latin and Junian Latin have some characteristics in common, but also important differences that are relevant enough to argue that they constitute two different types of Latin right. The characteristics they share are, notably, the same general denomination, the use of a trinominal onomastic system (with the exceptions that will be discussed in due course) and a common link, although of a different nature, with the former *Latini coloniarii*.

---

[18] In fact, with the exception of those cases where the praetorship is mentioned (which for Gallia Narbonensis is interpreted as the translation of an indigenous magistracy and which had not been documented since the time of Augustus, except among the Vocontii), the quattuorvirate is generalised (in addition to the positions of aedile and quaestor). The career progression of the magistracy is uniform in Gallia Narbonensis, where the transition from the quattuorvirate to the duovirate seems to be a reliable indicator of the transition from a Latin colony to a Roman colony: see García Fernández 2001, 31–71, with earlier bibliography; Sisani 2018b, 46–50. In Hispania, although the duovirate was widespread in the Flavian period (in addition to the positions of aedile and, to a lesser extent, quaestor), the career structure of the local magistracy was less stable in the older Latin municipalities: discussion is in Melchor 2013; Sisani 2018b, 50–70.

[19] See García Fernández 2001, 31–124 on the process of creating a provincial Latin municipality.

[20] *Irn.* 28, 72.

[21] Junian freedmen are always referred to as *Latini* without qualification by Gaius: *Inst.* 1.29, 1.31, 1.66, 1.68, 1.70, 1.80; see also Ulp. *Reg.* 5.4, 7.4; Plin. *Ep.* 10.104. For brief modern discussion, see López Barja 1998, 146.

This link is established in the case of the municipal Latins (*ingenui* and freedpersons) because their condition derives directly from the procedure applied to Gallia Transpadana in 89 BC as described above, while in the case of the Junian Latins, it is because their *libertas* was assimilated, by means of a fiction, to that possessed by the former colonial Latins – as elaborated in detail in the ensuing chapter by Pellecchi. Apart from these shared characteristics, each of these types of Latinity has a different legal profile, and each followed its own historical course, as indicated, for example, by their respective dates of disappearance – a point fully discussed for the Junian Latin status in this volume by Corcoran, in Chapter 6.[22]

It is of course correct that our key source for the Junian Latin status – the famous passage from Gaius' *Institutes*, at 3.56 – is as such ambiguous as to which group of Latin colonists is being referred to in explaining the Junian Latin status, i.e. either the earlier *Latini coloniarii* that emerged in 338 BC, or the new Latins from the colonies of Gallia Transpadana.[23] But the precision of the passage clears up, in my view, any ambiguity or misunderstanding as to what type of Latin colonials *Latini Iuniani* were assimilated to: Gaius literally refers to the colonies founded with *cives Romani* from Rome ('cives Romani ingenui, qui ex urbe Roma in Latinas colonias deducti'), whose citizenship they would lose when they became *Latini coloniarii* ('Latini coloniarii esse coeperunt'), which made them citizens of another city ('alterius civitatis cives').[24] Admittedly, Gaius' description does not fit the origin of the settlers of the Latin colonies that emerged in Gallia Transpadana or, shortly thereafter, in Gallia Narbonensis. The latter would no longer be Roman citizens from Rome who had lost their citizenship, but the inhabitants of the peregrine cities of Gallia Cisalpina themselves, the *veterae incolae manentes* of Asconius (*In Pis.* 3 Clark), who transformed their original status as *peregrini* into *Latini* through a concession of *ius Latii*. But if this is so, the obvious question to ask is why Augustus' chancellery sought to define the legal profile of the new freed status, i.e. Junian Latinity, within the frame of the old colonial Latin status that had disappeared almost a hundred years earlier with the *lex Iulia* of 90 BC. In this context, it must also be considered that the contemporary provincial Latin right was rapidly expanding, spawning cities with colonial titles as well as private and public freedpersons with Latin status.

The most likely answer to this somewhat paradoxical circumstance is that Junian Latinity was equated to the status of the republican colonial Latinity because they share a common origin: both *Latinorum genera* are internal categories of the *ius Romanorum* since both were created from Roman citizenship, which was not the case with

---

[22] The municipal Latin right disappeared with the *constitutio* of Antoninus Caracalla in AD 212, over three centuries before Justinian abolished Junian Latinity as a legal status.

[23] Gai. *Inst.* 3.56 is given in full in this volume's Introduction, with translation and discussion.

[24] On the final aspect, see Gai. *Inst.* 1.131. The loss of Roman citizenship was due to two factors: the impossibility of enjoying dual citizenship for a Roman citizen (Cic. *Balb.* 28.30) and the legal design of these colonies, which were conceived, from a formal point of view, as sovereign, and therefore possessing their own citizenship, as Gaius states. On the loss of Roman citizenship of origin of the *coloni Latini*, see Cic. *Caecin.* 98; *Dom.* 78. The colonies' actual status of being subordinate to Rome does not in any way detract from the strength of the legal argument.

municipal Latinity. The colonial Latinity that emerged in 338 BC was forged from Roman citizenship, or – to be more precise – from the loss of this citizenship. The Latin colonist was a *civis Romanus* who necessarily lost his citizenship when he became a colonist and therefore a citizen of another city and no longer of Rome, as previously mentioned.[25] In the same way, Junian Latinity must also be considered as an internal category since it originated in the very heart of the *civitas Romana*, given that this condition could only be achieved through a Roman citizen who carried out a manumission without regard to formal procedure or requirements. In fact, every Junian Latin could have become a Roman citizen, since the Junians had their own means of access to Roman citizenship that were not limited to the *anniculi causae probatio*, as enumerated by Gaius (and briefly discussed, once again, in the Introduction to this volume).[26] Indeed, notwithstanding all the difficulties a Junian Latin may have faced in gaining access to citizenship, they probably still found it easier to die as a Roman citizen than a provincial Latin who did not belong to the oligarchy of their city.[27]

In contradistinction, the colonial Latinity of Gallia Transpadana and, by extension, the subsequent municipal Latinity, is a condition that originated from the very exterior of the *civitas*. The Latin colonist of Gallia Transpadana was a foreigner who had been legally integrated through the concession of *ius Latii* to the community of which he was a citizen. This integration procedure is referred to by Gaius when he mentions that *ius Latii* is granted by the people of Rome, the Senate or Caesar, to some peregrine cities.[28] Through this concession, the *peregrini* population of one or other city became *Latini ingenui*; their community received a precise administrative title, colony or municipality, and their oligarchy could obtain Roman citizenship at a local level through this specific channel. Their origin as *peregrini*, however, made them irrelevant as far as Roman jurisprudence was concerned, and this at least partly explains the dearth of information relating to them.[29]

At this juncture, it is important to emphasise anew that the *libertas* of the Latin colonists, to which the *libertas* of the Latin Junians was assimilated, was defined on the basis of the *civitas Romana*, and in fact on the basis of its loss. The notion forms part of the conceptualisations of the idea of *libertas* that took shape in the republican period and which did not include identification with the *civitas*, despite the well-known formula

---

[25] The legal form was devised for settlers with Roman citizenship from Rome; the fact that later Latin colonial status may be acquired by the surrounding peregrine population (for example, Livy 32.2.6–7, 33.24.8) does not challenge the legal design: a distinction must be made between the legal principle and its subsequent updating.

[26] Gai. *Inst.* 1.28, 1.32b–35.

[27] See especially the case of the freed L. Venidius Ennychus and his wife Livia Acte (*TH* 89), with Camodeca 2006a, 2006b. However complex access to Roman citizenship through the *anniculi causae probatio* may have been for Junian Latins, the only individual route to *civitas Romana* for municipal Latins was solely accessible to the oligarchies and their kin.

[28] Gai. *Inst.* 1.95: 'ius (Latii) quibusdam peregrinis civitatibus datum est'.

[29] The institutions or categories which, in the field of law, serve as a reference point are those which developed within the Roman legal system itself, not those originating in external circumstances, as is the case with the free Latinity of the provinces: see Schulz 1990, 53–4.

of Cicero that freedom is citizenship: *libertas id est civitas*.[30] In the case of Junian and municipal Latinity, it can be seen how the different origins of the two directly influenced the unequal attention paid to them by ancient writers, and especially by jurists. In fact, while the legal sources pay special attention to the situation of *Latini Iuniani*, which ultimately was a figure of the Roman *ius civile*, they barely acknowledge the existence of free provincial Latinity, which does not even have a name of its own, and for which little information is provided beyond the specific means of access to Roman citizenship.[31] Naturally, it could be argued that the legislative compilation made by Justinian removed any reference to the provincial Latins as they would have already disappeared with the *constitutio Antoniana*. But the lack of interest in analysing the provincial Latin condition and its idiosyncrasy demonstrated by Gaius, already in the second century AD, cannot be ignored: in this work, the unbalanced attention that the jurist devotes to both groups of Latins is striking, with his references to provincial Latins being reduced to a few passages.[32]

The type of sources that best inform us about provincial Latinities are neither legal nor literary,[33] but instead are epigraphic and therefore more closely focused on local contexts. As noted earlier, the epigraphic documentation referring to the colonies and municipalities under the *ius Latii* is extraordinarily abundant as a result of the spread of Latin throughout the western provinces of the Roman Empire. In fact, the *ius Latii* was the preferred means of legal integration of the inhabitants of the western provinces in the Roman Empire. If we exclude the oligarchies of the cities and their kin, who would have had immediate access to Roman citizenship, the rest of the population of medium and low social status would have only had Latin status, and would not have had any means of access to Roman citizenship, as also previously mentioned. Only

---

[30] Cic. *Balb.* 24. For discussion, see Arena 2012, 27–8. These new legal categorisations affected the cases classified as *capitis deminutio media*, as citizenship was lost and not freedom, as was the case of the Latin colonists or those Roman citizens who went into exile voluntarily to escape a legal penalty. The definition of this circumstance as *capitis deminutio media* is logically made in reference to the full capacity represented by the possession of Roman citizenship, which was in any case the starting point.

[31] The expression *municeps Latinus* from the *lex Irnitana* (28) cannot be taken into account as a means of denomination since it excludes the *coloni Latini* documented, for example, in Gallia Transpadana and Gallia Narbonensis. Of course, they are neither *prisci Latini*, nor *Latini coloniarii*, nor *Latini Iuniani*, despite the various proposals to identify or assimilate the provincial Latins of the imperial period with this new category of freedpersons. They are only given the generic adjective of *Latini*, either as *cives* (*Mal.* 53; *Tab. Siar.* II A ll. 8–9) or as *municipes*, and in any case as a specific *hominum genus* without a denomination of their own, as Luraschi 1979 noted.

[32] Gai. *Inst.* 1.95–6, referring to the *patria potestas* over the children conferred by the *ius Latii* and the two types of Latin right existing in relation to access to the *civitas Romana*. The *Latini* mentioned in Gai. *Inst.* 1.79 do not, in my opinion, refer to provincial Latins, but to colonial Latins before the Social War: see García Fernández 2018, 390–4.

[33] Although the literary sources are somewhat more generous than the legal ones with information on municipal Latinity, the literary sources are usually restricted to the mention of its specific means of access to Roman citizenship. They succinctly explain the content of the *ius Latii* along with Asconius (*In Pis.* 3 Clark), Strabo 4.1.12, App. *B Civ.* 2.98, Gai. *Inst.* 1.95–6 and *Frag. Aug.* 1. 6–7. Other passages only refer to the concession of the *ius Latii* without further details, such as Tac. *Ann.* 15.32, Plin. *HN* 3.30, 3.135; Cic. *Att.* 14.12.1, or (referring to *Latina condicio*) Plin. *NH* 3.91; cf. *CIL* V, 532.

in Hispania, which, as is known, received the general edict of the Latin right from Vespasian, over three quarters of the cities were Latin, including Baetica, the most Romanised of its territories.[34] In addition, an important collection of municipal laws was found in this province, which provides an exceptional level of documentation, because of its size, coherence and state of conservation, of the regulations concerning municipalities under Latin law.[35]

In the light of the availability of this exceptional source material, one would expect that at least the main issues relating to the provincial Latin right, and Latin municipalisation in general, would be reasonably well established. But this is not the case. Proof of this is that within the research that deals with the study of Latin law at provincial level, there is still debate on issues that are not exactly minor in nature, but which instead play a central role in its study, such as the very existence of free provincial Latinity, the municipalising capacity of the *ius Latii*, or the role attributed to municipal legislation.

The debate on these issues has to do not only with the different lines of interpretation through which the study of Latinity is approached, but also with the elusive nature of the documentation. In principle, one would have expected that the discovery of the *lex Irnitana* in 1981 in El Saucejo, in the province of Seville, would have provided decisive information on the Latinity of the imperial period, bearing in mind that it has made it possible to reconstruct a municipal law, intended for the Flavian municipalities of Hispania, consisting of almost one hundred chapters, three quarters of which have been preserved. However, in a document of these characteristics only Roman law of an administrative and procedural nature is found, and the text even refers back to the *ius civile* in those legal matters not expressly regulated by municipal law. This is notably the case in chapter 93 of the *lex Irnitana*, regarding the rights of the *municipes*.

In communities whose specific characteristic was the institutionalised existence of a population with different statuses, Roman and Latin, it is surprising how few references are made to laws and regulations that expressly take into account the idiosyncrasies of the citizens of Latin status who comprised the majority of the population. The explicit

---

[34] See specifically Plin. *HN* 3.30. The calculation is based on the provincial synopses dating from the time of Augustus and presented by the Elder Pliny in Books 3 and 4 of his *Natural History*, which record a very high number of cities of a stipendary status, and, to a much lesser extent, those that are federated or free:

HN 3.7: of the 175 *oppida* of Baetica, 129 are still peregrine, without including the Balearic Islands (for which see *HN* 3.76–7).
HN 3.18: of the 179 *oppida* of Hispania Citerior, 136 are peregrine.
HN 4.117: among the 59 *populi* mentioned in Lusitania, 36 are still peregrine.

All these peregrine towns were potential recipients of the *ius Latii* of Vespasian, to which should be added the Latin municipalities of the Augustan period. For a complete list (as of the date of publication) of the Latin municipalities in each of the three provinces of Hispania, see Andreu Pintado 2004.

[35] To date, according to the data provided in Caballos 2009, with Caballos 2018, forty-one fragments of laws have been found from different cities in Baetica, among which the most important, because of the volume of information, are still the ancient *lex Malacitana* and *lex Salpensana*, and especially the most recent and extensive *lex Irnitana*.

mentions of the Latin population in the Flavian laws are those referring to the vote of the *Incolae qui cives R(omani) Latinive cives erunt* in a curia extracted by lot (*Mal.* 53), the possibility of manumitting before the *duumvir* that is granted to any *municeps qui Latinus erit* (*Salp.*, *Irn.* 28), and the mention of the free and Latin condition (*liber et Latinus esto*) of the public slave manumitted by the authorised magistrate of a Latin municipality (*Irn.* 72). In addition to these explicit references, there is a chapter on the acquisition of Roman citizenship, together with his family, by a *municeps* who has served as a magistrate (*Salp.*, *Irn.* 21). In turn, the chapters referring to the permanence of family and patronal rights, *manus*, *mancipium*, *patria potestas* and *iura libertorum* (*Salp.*, *Irn.* 22, 23; *Irn.* 97 ext.), are problematic because despite their wholly Roman formulation, they imply that these rights could be enjoyed, before the *mutatio civitatis*, by the municipal population with Latin status. Finally, brief mention should be made of the reference to the *lex Lati* in the letter from the emperor Domitian appended, as noted, to the *sanctio* of the *lex Irnitana* (and discussed more fully in due course).

The municipal legislation does not really take into account the Latin context, but rather extends a uniform mantle of *Romanitas* which conditions, in my opinion, the analysis and interpretation of provincial Latinity. In fact, Chastagnol has already observed that municipal laws erased too much of the importance and influence of the indigenous element in social life, encouraging the view that a city under Latin law was barely different from a Roman one: in his opinion, a Latin community could have kept its local *iura* and *mores*, provided that their use did not affect Roman interests.[36] The municipal legislation refers us to a universe of full *Romanitas* which, nonetheless, the epigraphy denies. The differences between the epigraphic documentation of the various Latin colonies and municipalities in the west of the Empire are too pronounced to be able to give a uniform response that integrates in all cases the presence of municipal legislation. It must also be noted that the standard idea of provincial Latinity is not necessarily provided by the *Irnitanus municeps*, however tempting this notion may be, insofar as the fully Roman profile, in tandem with the sophisticated cultural context of the province of Baetica, clashes with the vitality of the indigenous world which nevertheless appears in the documentation of other provincial territories. Thus, the province of Hispania does not constitute so much a paradigm of accomplished Romanisation, to which the different Latin communities aspired, but rather a true exception within the framework of the provincial territories of the Roman Empire.

Given this situation, any attempt to grasp the nature of provincial Latinity involves *questioning* the role of municipal legislation. The question is of obvious methodological interest: if the municipal law has a constituent character, i.e. if its function is to confer the municipal (or Latin colonial) title on a peregrine city, then it must be concluded that every time the term *municipium/municipes* or *colonia/coloni* is recorded in the epigraphic sources, it indicates that a regulatory statute has been granted to the community, and that wholly Roman forms of organisation have been introduced; Latin status in this case would not be very different from Roman status. However, if

---

[36] Chastagnol 1987a, 16–17.

the *lex* lacks a constituent function, as is assumed in the Roman municipalisation of Italy (and as will be argued in what follows), the Latin condition would offer greater versatility. A concession of *ius Latii* would be sufficient for a peregrine community to become a Latin colony or municipality and, subsequently, a *lex municipalis* which could be granted (or not) would reorganise the community on the basis of a fully Roman template. This idea has the advantage of making legal Latinisation compatible with various Romanising developments; it would explain the widespread diffusion of *ius Latii*; and it would account for the onomastic diversity of cities under Latin law based on their area of settlement.

The Role of the Flavian Municipal Legislation and the *ius Latii*

In the field of provincial studies on Latin rights, it is common to attribute a decisive role to municipal legislation in the constitution of the Latin municipality or colony. The concession of *ius Latii* to a community would not grant it a political, colonial or municipal, status, but mainly the possibility of accessing Roman citizenship, an option that in any case was only available to the civic oligarchy, as stressed in the previous section. The rest of the population would retain their initial status as *cives peregrini*, and the *civitas* affected by *ius Latii* would acquire the status of *oppidum Latinum* or simply *civitas Latina*. The administrative title, i.e. *municipium* or *colonia*, would only be acquired through a *lex* granted subsequently as a 'privilège supplémentaire', which is presumed to be similar in nature to the Flavian municipal laws, as it is the only regulatory reference known to date. The reasons that justify the passing of a law in one community and not in another, when these situations occur, have been focused on the notion of the respective community's broader cultural sophistication, which would make it worthy of the recognition that the law represents.[37]

This constituent function, which is attributed to municipal legislation and which, in my opinion, is not supported by the regulatory Flavian text, is contaminated by the truly constituent nature of colonial legislation. Every colonial foundation required a *lex* that founded the new colony. The colonial law, as in the case of the *lex Ursonensis*, is what gave rise to the new city and organised it.[38] However, the same does not apply to the municipality whose origin presupposes the prior existence of a city with its own *ius civitatis* that originates from the peregrine world and that was subsequently integrated into the state through a concession of Roman citizenship – in the case of a municipality of Roman law, or of the *ius Latii* in the case of a Latin municipality. In fact, none of the preserved definitions of *municipium* provided by jurists and lexicographers refer to or establish a causal relationship between municipalisation or the status of *municeps* and municipal legislation.[39] The close link between a *receptio in civitatem* and the acquisition of municipal status expressed in Ulpian's declaration 'Munícipes appellantur . . . recepti in civitatem' would indicate that in the case of Roman municipalities – the only ones

---

[37] Fundamental to this interpretation are Chastagnol 1987a (esp. 6 – also for the quotation, and 8), 1987b, 1990, with n. 109 below; see also Le Roux 1986, 2017, among other works by this author.

[38] On the *lex Ursonensis* and the colonising process, see Caballos 2006.

[39] See Humbert 1978, 3–43; 2006; note also Crawford 1998.

addressed by the legal sources – the connection between the granting of citizenship and municipalisation was too obvious to be mentioned.[40]

With regard to the Flavian legislation, a number of internal aspects of the law itself can be put forward that challenge the constituent character often attributed to it. First, the fact that the law did not reach every *oppidum*, but rather fully functioning municipalities, seems conclusive to me. It is also significant that this law, of which more than three quarters have been preserved and where many matters of an administrative or jurisdictional nature are regulated in detail, makes no reference whatsoever to its function as an element intended to grant or ratify municipal status. In fact, none of the areas of civic organisation regulated by the Flavian legislation allows us to assume that the law confers or ratifies municipal status.[41] This is a characteristic that the Flavian legislation shares with the preserved Italian municipal laws, from whose provisions a constituent function can also not be inferred. The municipalisation of Tarentum or Heraclea, for example, is recognised as being associated with the acceptance of the *lex Iulia de civitate* of 90 BC, but their respective municipal laws are attributed a later date.[42]

As the law arrived in a fully functioning *municipium*, the Flavian regulatory text took the precaution of ensuring the continuity of the municipal government, regardless of the new developments or new regulations it introduced. The *lex Irnitana* therefore expressly establishes that the magistrates appointed in the municipality, before or after the *lex*, with reference to the aediles (*Irn.* 19 ll. 1–5) and quaestors (*Irn.* 20 ll. 24–8), shared a similar *ius* and *potestas* in carrying out the tasks of their office, as specified by the law. Similarly, in the chapter of the *lex Malacitana* referring to the calling of local elections, a distinction is made between duoviri who were in office when the law arrived in the municipality, and duoviri appointed at a later date (*Mal.* 52 ll. 29–30).

---

[40] Digest 50.1.1.1 The same insistence on the possession of Roman citizenship can be found in Gell. *NA* 16.16.6: 'Municipes ergo sunt cives Romani ex municipiis.' Similarly, the idea of *receptio* in relation to the *lex Iulia de civitate*, responsible for the general process of municipalisation in Italy, is also present in Vell. Pat. 2.20.2: 'recepti in beneficium'. The link between citizenship and municipalisation is not usually expressed in the epigraphic or literary sources, but is constantly implicit; the same observation can be made about the concession of *ius Latii*. This fact explains the absence of testimonies in the Empire referring to the concession of municipal status to a community as observed by Millar 1977, 400–1. On the argument, see García Fernández 2001, 108–12.

[41] The structure of the law shows order and coherence: magistrates, senate, the people, administration and jurisdiction. The entire set of legal regulations that govern these matters and that introduce the Flavian laws is of an administrative and procedural nature, not a constituent one: García Fernández 2001, 163–80. Nor does Bispham 2007, 210–25 seem to conclude, after analysing the *lex Flavia*, that these laws have a constitutive function; rather, their purpose was to provide a set of rules to organise the public life of the citizens as a whole and, to a degree that may vary according to the communities, to maintain some identifying elements of local tradition (pp. 223–5).

[42] On the autonomy of the municipalisation process with regard to the arrival of legislation in the municipality, see Laffi 2007, 58–64 including in his analysis the Flavian legislative material. On the text and structure of the *lex Tarentina* and *lex Heracleensis*, see Crawford 1996, I, 191–231 and 301–12 respectively, where he advocates a Caesarian chronology for the latter. On the *lex Tarentina*, see also Cappelletti 2011, 115, 126 (with 90 BC as a probable date of the municipalisation of Tarentum), 115–33 on the dating of the statute of Tarentum to a time prior to the second half of the first century BC, with earlier bibliography; see further 13–21 (esp. 20–1) regarding the complex *lex Heracleensis*, not strictly a *lex municipalis*, but a document written for practical purposes that includes different regulatory provisions of diverse origin and interest for the government of the cities of southern Italy (on which see also Sisani 2016, 29–47, esp. 43).

The *lex Irnitana* also mentions the former existence of a *curia* normally consisting of sixty-three members (31 ll. 42–3): 'Quo anno pauciores in eo municipio decuriones conscriptive quam LXIII, quod ante h(anc) l(egem) rogatam iure more eiius municipi fuerunt <erunt>.' The use of the term *mos* suggests that the text foresees that the municipality, with respect to the *ordo* and presumably in relation to other matters (*Irn*. 81), could have been regulated by its own customs, a situation which the municipal law would bring to an end by introducing new organisational guidelines. In fact, by appointing *senatores* together with *decuriones*, chapter 30 of the law of Irni seems to seek to cover all the different municipal regimes, since it is precisely the *curiales* that predate the law, whose appointment the law respects and confirms, while for those appointed after it, it exclusively refers to *decuriones conscriptive*. Furthermore, prior to the arrival of the law, the municipality did not lack legislative provisions, since it could have made use of all those issued since the time of Augustus that could be applied at a local level, and which are briefly mentioned in the *lex Irnitana*.[43]

The care with which the law differentiates between magistrates appointed *ex edicto* and magistrates appointed *ex lege* seems to indicate that different procedures were followed for their appointment (or at least that such a possibility existed as a feature of municipal autonomy). This fact is corroborated by chapter 50 of the *lex Irnitana*, which establishes that the first *duoviri iure dicundo* in the municipality of Irni, within ninety days of the arrival of the law in the municipality, would have to establish twelve *curiae* ('Ut IIvir(i) iuri dic[un]do curias d(um) t(axat) XI constituant'), proof that previously they did not exist, even if they were indispensable for voting, as the vote was channelled through them. The length and detail of the electoral procedure introduced by the *lex Malacitana* allows us to deduce either that no previous elections had been held in the municipality to appoint local magistrates, or that an election was not necessarily carried out in accordance with Roman customs, as these were introduced by the law.

However, the fact that the magistrates of a municipalised community were not elected according to Roman rules, or that they were elected according to local customs or even that these customs governed the whole internal organisation, as was the case at least in municipalities prior to the Social War, does not necessarily undermine the municipal status they enjoyed, nor does it mean that this status was provisional or transitional. The conversion of a community into a municipality and the possible, but not essential, administrative reorganisation to which Rome could submit a municipality through a *lex* are processes of diverse natures (although they could occur simultaneously), and therefore it is not necessary to establish a causal relationship between the two events, nor to compromise the dating of a municipal statute according to the date of municipalisation of a given *civitas*.[44]

---

[43] Regardless of the specific legislation that may have been introduced in the municipality with the advent of the *lex municipalis*, all of the legislation passed since the time of Augustus with local application could be used (*Irn*. 19, 20, 40, 81). See the comments on the *lex Irnitana* by González and Crawford 1986; Lamberti 1993.

[44] On this argument see García Fernández 2001, 176–7. In the case of Hispania, the dating of some inscriptions to the years immediately after the date of Vespasian's edict on Latinity (AD 73), where some towns are listed as municipalities before the arrival of the *lex municipalis* (AD 91), corroborates the autonomy of the two processes. Similar are also Igabrum (AD 75: *CIL* II, 1610 = *CIL* II^2, 5, 308), Cisimbrium (AD 77: *CIL* II, 2096 = *CIL* II^2, 5, 292) and Monturque (Cordoba) (AD 69–79: *CIL* II, 1631 = *CIL* II^2, 5, 615), all from Baetica.

It is opportune, moreover, to highlight that the functions of municipal legislation are not limited to administrative reorganisation. Chapter 19 of the *lex Irnitana*, which refers to the powers of aediles, introduces an innovation which only concerns future magistrates, appointed by the electoral procedures established by law, and which consists of giving magistrates, duoviri and aediles a jurisdictional capacity which enables them to intervene in cases where the amount of the case does not exceed 1,000 sesterces (*Irn*. 19 ll. 13–16). This pecuniary limit of municipal jurisdiction appears again in chapter 84 of the *lex Irnitana*, where it is established that the *duoviri iure dicundo* are to have jurisdiction over those matters whose pecuniary value does not exceed 1,000 sesterces (*Irn*. 84 ll. 1–5).[45] This fact must be understood in relation to the possibility that was now available to the citizens of Irni to bring private lawsuits within the limits prescribed by the law.

With the arrival of the *lex municipalis*, the nature of the legal autonomy previously enjoyed by the municipality was altered and extended. In turn, the widespread entry of Roman law into the municipality required that the juridical powers of the magistrates now acquired a technical profile and were redefined in relation to the *iurisdictio* of the provincial governor. It is this autonomy, not the municipal status, that has its basis in the *lex municipalis*.[46] It can therefore be deduced that if the community to which the municipal law was addressed previously enjoyed the title of *municipium*, as expressly indicated, and in addition the regulations introduced by the law itself were of an administrative and procedural nature, it is frankly difficult to attribute constitutive capacities to the Flavian legislation, which if they existed should have been mentioned, given their importance, in some part of the law.

In the Flavian municipalisation process, as it occurred in Baetica – the only province with the information required to support the presented argument – a distinction can be made between what the edict of Vespasian grants and what the legislation introduces, as these seem to be matters of diverse natures, without prejudice to the relationship that can be established between the two processes. Thus, following the framework laid out above, the edict on Latinity would grant the prerogative of the *ius Latii* (on which more in due course) and could provide for the replacement of the local magistrates by duoviri or the conversion of their local *senatores* into *decuriones* (although perhaps not even this, as the reform of the local senate is provided for in chapter 30 of the *lex Irnitana*) and some additional regulation in matters of civic organisation. Concerning the rest, the municipalised communities, as previously existing and therefore organised communities, could continue to make use of their *iura* and *instituta* because, as the emperor Hadrian recalls, this was an inherent characteristic of municipal status in a Roman municipality, and even more so in a Latin municipality, where the majority of its population was not allowed to participate in the administration of the Empire.[47] To my mind, only the most Romanised municipalities would be in a position to receive a *lex municipalis* that would enable them to be governed exclusively by Roman law in

---

[45] Even beyond the financial limit of 1,000 sesterces laid down in the legislation (*Irn*. 19, 84), if there was agreement between the parties the case could be settled locally; there was no need to refer it to the provincial governor's court: Lamberti 2016.

[46] Torrent 1970, 145–55.

[47] See above, with n. 40.

all areas of their public life and to extend their jurisdictional autonomy, since the law removes jurisdictional competences from the provincial governor to the advantage of the municipality. The equivalence with a *municipium Italiae* (*Irn.* 72) did not seem to be within the reach of all the communities that received the *ius Latii*.

This lengthy detour to clarify the role played by municipal legislation is critical to a proper understanding of municipalisation processes in general, but even more so in the particular case of Latin municipalisation. If the law lacks a constituent function, as I have sought to demonstrate, this would imply that the profile of the *municeps* (or *colonus*) *Latinus* does not necessarily respond to the Romanised pattern of the municipality of Baetica reflected in the municipal legislation. The municipal or colonial status would then have its origin in the granting of the *ius Latii* and not in a *lex municipalis*, if we adhere to the type of municipal legislation that existed until this time. By not imposing an exclusively Roman pattern on provincial Latinity, this perspective has the methodological advantage to open the way to defining a common Latin condition,[48] capable of integrating the varied circumstances of the different provincial territories.

The *lex Lati* and *epistula* of Domitian (*Tab. Irn.* X, col. C)

Claiming that the *lex municipalis* does not have a constitutive character does not imply that the information transmitted by the law should be disregarded. This is especially so because the regulations referring to the way of accessing Roman citizenship (*Irn.* 21) and to private matters (*Irn.* 22, 23) was already provided for in the edict of Vespasian. For this reason, it would be more a question of trying to differentiate, as far as possible, between what the *ius Latii* could have granted and what would later be introduced by the municipal law, which was responsible for bringing the city more closely in line with a fully Roman model of government and organisation.

In the final tablet of the *lex Irnitana*, which does not form a part of the regulatory text, there is precisely a thread that can lead directly to the matter at stake. I refer to the already mentioned epistle of Domitian, recorded after the *sanctio*, which brings the document to a close, which speaks of a *lex Lati*, or *legge sulla prerogativa Latina*, as Lebek called it. This epistle is a reply to a previous consultation made by the local magistrates that was addressed to the emperor.[49] We do not know anything about its specific content, although, according to the indications in the letter, it can be inferred that the consultation was directly related to a number of doubts or problems that had arisen regarding the legitimacy of certain marriages (*conubia*) that had been formalised in the municipality of

---

[48] See Plin. *HN* 3.91.
[49] [Epistle of Domitian] *Tab. Irn.* X, C (chapter 98): 159–87: 'Conubia conprehensa quaedam Lege Lati scio et postea aliqua, sic u[[i]]t sollicitudo vestra indicat, parum considerate coisse; quibus in praeteritum veniam do, in futurum exigo, memineritis legis, cum iam omnes indulgentiae partes consumptae sint. Litterae datae IIII idus Apriles Cerceis, recitata<e> V idus Domitianas anno M(ani) Acili Glabrionis et M(arci) Ulpi Traiani co(n) s(ulum). Faciendum curaverunt L(ucius) Caecilius Optatus IIvir et Caecilius Montanus legatus.' See Lebek 1993 on the text, reading and meaning of the *lex Lati*. An initial interpretation of the *lex Lati* is already in Fernández Gómez and del Amo y de la Hera 1990, 69. This interpretation has also been accepted in Crawford 2008, correcting also the phrase *lege late* to *lege Lati*.

Irni. From the emperor's words, two pertinent issues can be deduced: that the *lex Lati* authorised some marital unions ('conubia conprehensa quaedam lege Lati scio'), and that some other unions had subsequently taken place without respecting the provisions of the law, as mentioned above. Domitian acknowledges the facts, and accepts the *fait accompli* in the case of the latter ('in praeteritum veniam do'), but demands that in the future, the citizens abide by the law ('in futurum exigo, memineritis legis').

The reading of the *lex Lati* was interpreted by Lebek as the *lex rogata domitiana* (as referred to in chapter 31 of the law) on which the municipal legislative documents depended that would reproduce it at local level. Apart from the unusual fact that a *lex rogata* would exist at this time, it is more significant that this *lex* is not mentioned in any section of the Flavian legislation as a statutory reference,[50] but rather only with regard to unauthorised *conubia* whose precise legal circumstances are unknown. Its mention as a regulatory framework for a conflict of private law may suggest that this law should perhaps be attributed a narrower scope than that suggested by Lebek. In this case I suggest that the *lex Lati* should not be identified with a *lex municipalis* responsible for introducing Roman administrative and procedural law into the community (it would also be surprising if a provision that was conceptually Roman in all of its dimensions was referred to as such), but should rather be interpreted as the law that regulated the capacities that the *ius Latii* conferred on every community and its population. This *lex Lati* could perhaps even be identified with the very *ius Latii* that the Flavian edict granted to the three provinces of Hispania in the early years of Vespasian's reign.[51] This law was responsible for attributing the basic capabilities shared by all Latin cities and their populations, regardless of their location in different parts of the Empire, and therefore regardless of their greater or lesser degree of Romanisation.[52] There is also a chronological argument that prevents identification of the *lex Lati* and the *lex Irnitana* itself. With the arrival of the latter in the municipality in AD 91, the *lex Lati* did not arrive, but rather the emperor's response to a conflict that had arisen in the municipality of Irni, possibly for a certain length of time, over contravening the provisions on marriage of that set of rules. It can therefore be understood that the *lex Lati* was the general law that had regulated authorised *conubia* since the time of Vespasian, i.e. since the initial constitution of Irni as a Latin municipality, and therefore before the arrival of the *lex municipalis* under Domitian.[53]

---

[50] The implicit or explicit legislative references mentioned in the Flavian municipal laws were always Roman non-municipal laws from a significant part of the Augustan period, in addition to Vespasian's own edict, the edict of the provincial governor, or the *ius civile*: see García Fernández 2001, 166–8. For a more systematic discussion, see Sisani 2016, 13–21.

[51] On the universality and scope of the concession made by Vespasian to Hispania, see Andreu Pintado 2004, offering a detailed and comprehensive study of the process (with 14–20 for the date of the edict).

[52] See García Fernández 2001, 167–9; see also Sisani 2016, 12–13, 25–6.

[53] Published in Circei, where Domitian had a villa, on 10 April 91, and read publicly in Irni the following 11 October, meaning it took six months for the transfer of the original and the preparation of the copy: see Fernández Gómez del Amo y de la Hera 1990, 33. I am aware of the objection in Lamberti 1993, 56 that this dating corresponds to the epistle, not the *lex Flavia*. In any case, it is clear from the *lex Irnitana* that by the time the law reached the city, it had been operating as a municipality since the time of Vespasian, whose edict is expressly referred to in the law.

The powers introduced by the *lex Lati* would be more limited in the sphere of civic organisation and local jurisdiction: they probably focused on the introduction of provisions relating to private law, given the scant attention paid to this in municipal legislation.[54] Taking into account the available documentation, the powers that the *ius Latii* was to grant to any community, in addition to conferring an administrative title to the community, could take the following form: the granting of their specific right of access to Roman citizenship by serving as magistrates in local offices under the conditions established by law; the legal nature (*iusta*) of *iure Latino* unions according to the *ius civitatis* of each municipality or Latin colony and therefore the possibility of having children under *patria potestas* (*Irn.* 21, 22) – if they obtained Roman citizenship by its specific route, as Gaius claims;[55] and surely *manus* over wives, the existence of *conubium* with Roman citizens, and consequently the possibility of legally marrying these Roman citizens, whose children would follow the *ius civitatis* of the father (to which we will return below), the general ability to participate in an act of the *ius civile* with a Roman citizen (which was in keeping with the law or the authorisation, not requirement, of the Latin population of the municipality or colony to use the trinominal onomastic system). All of the above can be understood as Latin prerogatives that would be achieved through the granting of the *ius Latii* (or of the *lex Lati* according to Lebek). However, in my view, the *ius Latii* or *lex Lati* did not automatically enable Latins to make use of the *ius civile* as if they were *cives Romani*, or to organise their city as if it were a Roman municipality in Italy. This equivalence was a matter that was probably enabled by much more demanding municipal laws, as already mentioned, in relation to the degree of Romanisation of the target community, rather than by the simple granting of the *ius Latii*.

Provincial Latinity: An Attempt at Reconstructing a Common Condition

The common Latin status possessed by the provincial *Latini ingenui* and their freedpersons, both private and public, was defined earlier by the rights conferred by the *ius Latii* or *lex Lati* than by the Roman administrative and procedural regulations introduced by municipal legislation. However, notwithstanding the solid regulatory framework provided by the Flavian municipal legislation, the nature of Latinity is somewhat blurred. The various indigenous constitutions are not conserved, and we know nothing, for example, of the various marriage rituals that may have survived and been legitimised through the Latin right. From the Roman point of view, the literary and legal sources, as already mentioned, barely provide any information on provincial Latinity, beyond its particular means of access to Roman citizenship. Some fragments of information offer an insight into other characteristics of the Latin condition that only appeared at the moment when the Latin became Roman through their specific route, such as access to

---

[54] Gagliardi 2016, 382 referring to the *lex Tarentina*.
[55] Gai. *Inst.* 1.95.

the *patria potestas* over their children (noted at the end of the previous section) or the granting of the *iura cognationis* and exemption from inheritance tax for relatives with a second degree of kinship, recognised by Trajan;[56] in addition to this is the protection against *coercitio* by magistrates, suggested by a passage from Cicero.[57]

In reality, we know very little about the circumstances of the provincial Latin population that did not belong to the oligarchy of their city. Even the *ius* that best defined their condition was extraneous to them, as they could not access a magistracy due to their lack of the stipulated census and social requirements. Latinity should therefore be understood as the result of interweaving the rights (and conditions) incorporated in the *ius Latii* or *lex Lati*, with the *iura* of the local *civitas*. This implies that specific indigenous or local features were not extraneous to the Latin condition, but that on the contrary, they were implicit, as revealed by the rich and complex epigraphy of the western provinces in the form of local magistratures, but above all in the survival of onomastic customs that were not fully adapted to the Roman naming conventions (to which we will return below).

In this way, when Rome conceded the *ius Latii* to a community, it acknowledged that the local customs that regulated relations within the *civitas* were in keeping with the law. This recognition could refer to the political organisation of the community, as well as to family and social relations in the private sphere under the conditions established by the *ius Latii*, as was the case with *iure Latino* marriages (on which also more below). All of these aspects were independent of any subsequent full adaptation to Roman forms. Logically, the granting of the *ius Latii* to a Transpadane community in 89 BC would not incorporate the same unifying guidelines as the same law granted from the time of Augustus, when Rome already had a great deal of experience following the process of municipalisation in Italy.

Access to Roman Citizenship at Local Level, and the Question of Dual *civitas*

Access to Roman citizenship at the local level known as *ius adipiscendae civitatis Romanae per magistratum* is the only substantive right that seems to be held by provincial Latinity, or at least the only one which, from a Roman perspective, is considered relevant.[58] As mentioned so far only in passing, through this right, members of the local senate who were elected to a magistracy in their municipality or colony, after being elected in regular elections, obtained Roman citizenship for themselves and their families. It is important to note that Roman citizenship could only be obtained

---

[56] See Plin. *Pan.* 39.
[57] Cic. *Att.* 5.11.2: Cicero's criticism of the episode of the whipping of a citizen of the Latin colony of Novo Comum, possibly a former magistrate, ordered by the consul in 51 BC Marcus Claudius Marcelus, is ultimately based on his status as a Transpadanus – '*erat tamen Transpadanus*'; see also Plut. *Vit. Caes.* 29; App. *B Civ.* 2.98. For modern discussion, see Luraschi 1979, 406–11, 457–86; Sisani 2018b, 57–8.
[58] On the origin of this right, see n. 7 above. The first explicit mention is given by Asconius (*In Pis.* 3 Clark) in a passage already commented on; see also the comments and sources in n. 33 above.

after serving as a magistrate during the magisterial year and not by being elected a magistrate. The most complete formulation of this law is found in the Flavian legislation. Chapter 21 of the law of Irni and Salpensa specifies that the citizenship obtained by the former magistrate is extended to his entire family including his ascendants, under the conditions established by law:

> Rubric. How they may acquire Roman citizenship in that municipium. Those among the senators, decuriones or conscripti of the Municipium Flavium Irnitanum who have been or are appointed magistrates, as is laid down in this statute, when they have left that office, are to be Roman citizens, along with their parents and wives and any children who are born in legal marriages and have been in the power of their parents, likewise their grandsons and granddaughters born to a son, who have been in the power of their parents, provided that no more may become Roman citizens than the number of magistrates it is appropriate to appoint under this statute.[59]

If the formulation of this right contained in the Flavian legislation is accepted as universal, access to Roman citizenship would be available not only to the outgoing magistrate, but also to his entire family, including the parents of the magistrate, under the conditions stipulated by law.

Obviously, the possibility could be considered that this extensive formulation was the result of a gradual extension of the coverage of the *ius Latii*, or even that this extension was not universal in nature and was a feature introduced by the Flavian municipal law itself. This would not be exceptional since it is known that the *ius Latii* modified its coverage over time, as suggested by the appearance in Hadrianic times of a new formulation of this law that extended the number of members of the local oligarchy who benefited from Roman citizenship. Notably, according to information transmitted by Gaius, in the second century AD the *ius Latii* was classified as the minor Latin right (*ius Latii minus*) and major Latin right (*ius Latii maius*).[60] The latter, which was more recent, gave access to Roman citizenship not only to outgoing magistrates, but also to those who were granted decurion status, presumably together with their respective families;[61] the minor Latin right, characteristic of Flavian municipalities and

---

[59] *Irn.* 21 ll. 38–45, with the *lex Salpensana*: 'R(ubrica). Quae ad modum ciuitat[em] Romanam in eo municipio consequantur. Qui ex senatoribus decurion[ib]us conscriptisue municipii Flaui Irnitani magistratus, uti h(ac) 1(ege) [co]mprehensum est, creati sunt erunt, ii, cum eo honore abierint, cum parentibus coniungibusque ac liberis, qui legitimis nuptis quaesiti in potestate parentium [fu]er[i]nt, item nepotibus ac neptibus filio [n]atis, qui quaeue in potestat[e par]entium [fu]er[i]nt, ciues Romani sunto, dum ne plures ciues Romani sint, quam quod ex h(ac) l(ege) magis[t]atus creare oportet.' See González and Crawford 1986, 154 and 182, for the text and English translation respectively.

[60] Gai. *Inst.* 1.96. On the difference in Gaius' interpretation between *honos* and *magistratus*, see Russo 2018, 483–5, who, moreover, considers (p. 486) the possibility that the *Latium minus*, as presented in the summary of Gaius, would extend the *ius adipiscendae civitatis Romanae* not only to those who have served in ordinary magistracies from regular elections, but also to those who have served in any position of honour in their community of origin; see also n. 62 below.

[61] The expression used in Gai. *Inst.* 1.96, 'qui decuriones leguntur', seems to lean towards the acquisition of the *civitas* only as a result of having been elected, regardless of the subsequent performance of the office: see Bravo Bosch 2009, 47.

all previous, only granted access to citizenship to ex-magistrates and their families.[62] Nevertheless, it does not seem that the *ius Latii maius* was universal either, as it seems to have been a privilege that was only granted to the African municipalities.[63]

In this context, the evolution of the epigraphic documentation of the Latin colonies and municipalities suggests, in some cases, the possibility that the relationship of the family members who benefited from Roman citizenship obtained by an ex-magistrate may have varied depending on the period and the territory. In fact, according to *Irn.* 21, access to Roman citizenship by the magistrate's father is not in compliance with the edict of Vespasian, but in accordance with the municipal law.[64] The existence of a number of inscriptions from different sources where the parents of the ex-magistrate seem to be excluded from the benefit of Roman citizenship opens this possibility.[65] In principle, it cannot be ruled out that the immediate explanation is the correct one, i.e. that the respective parents of the magistrates may have died prior to their offspring's acquisition of citizenship. The matter remains subject to debate.

The right to obtain Roman citizenship at a local level introduces an additional complexity in the colonies and municipalities under Latin law, insofar as it implies accepting the institutionalised coexistence of two types of citizenship within the same community. This aspect, which is far from being legally irrelevant and which clearly distinguishes Latin colonies and municipalities from the other administrative categories created by the Roman state, raises various questions of interest. The most immediate is undoubtedly that which forces us to ask where this legal singularity lies in relation to the impossibility of enjoying a dual citizenship that would affect any *civis Romanus*. Moreover, the coexistence of two citizenships implies that there inevitably existed diverse interpersonal relationships within the community itself, which made it necessary to establish legal links that allowed cohesion between individuals who had different types of citizenship, but who shared the same *origo* and *domicilium*.

The principle of the incompatibility of Roman citizenship with any other, formulated by Cicero in several passages of his work,[66] would not lose its validity in the Empire, although it was resolved in various ways, in some cases in such a flexible manner that it could be considered non-existent. Although the matter is subject to endless discussion, I would like to point out that the existence of municipalities under

---

[62] It is important to note that, strictly speaking, the Flavian formulation may not be a case of *ius Latii minus* — for it does not fully coincide with Gaius' definition thereof. According to the Flavian law, having served in a magistracy was not sufficient, requiring instead also membership of the *curia*; see also Russo 2018, 485–7.

[63] On the origin of the *ius Latii* in Hadrian's time in Africa, see Sherwin-White 1973a, 255–6; Millar 1977, 405–6.

[64] See Kremer 2006, 147–8.

[65] This can be seen in *CIL* XII, 516 (Aquae Sextiae): Sex(tus) Acutius Volt(inia) / Aquila praetor / Acuto patri / Ingenuae matri / Severae sorori / Rufo fratri. Note also the case of a former magistrate from the Latin municipality of Brigantium, who was a duovir and quaestor, and who made a dedication to his father and mother, both with similar non-Roman names: *CIL* XII, 95 (Alpes Maritimae); and that of M. Fidius Fidi f. Quir. Macer from Capera, in Lusitania, whose father is Fidius Macri f. (*CPIL* 818 and *CIL* II, 834 respectively).

[66] See Cic. *Balb.* 28, 30; *Caecin.* 100. On the loss of the original Roman citizenship of the *Latini coloniarii*, see Cic. *Caecin.* 98; *Dom.* 78. On the validity of the principle of incompatibility, see Sherwin-White 1973a, 291–316; Genovese 2010 (with a critique of the opinions of De Visscher); Marotta 2016.

Roman law is, in my opinion, important proof that the principle of incompatibility operated even in the Empire. The granting of Roman citizenship to a community had always had the effect of reducing peregrine citizenship to *origo*, and consequently its disappearance from the public sphere of action that can only correspond to the *civitas Romana*.[67] In the case of individual concessions of Roman citizenship, the problem is more complex and the casuistics are varied, since the application of the Ciceronian principle results in the legal disconnection of the *novus civis Romanus* from their family and political environment, which remains that of a peregrine community. Without wishing to enter into a detailed discussion of the evidence, which has already been analysed by other scholars, it may be sufficient to recall the unique status acquired by the Syrian Seleukos of Rhosos, who was granted Roman citizenship together with his family, together with fiscal immunity, among many other *beneficia*, as opposed to Roman citizenship without fiscal immunity, which was granted to the two *Zegrenses principes* of the Tabula of Banasa.[68]

The various updates of the principle of incompatibility in the case of individual grants of citizenship are a consequence of the absence of any pre-arranged mechanism, since the grant was made on an ad hoc basis and its updating depended on the circumstances surrounding the grant. However, in the case of the Latin colonies and municipalities, these were communities that in a stable and institutional way produced a precise number of *cives Romani ingenui* each year. It is possible that the legal effects of the introduction of the *ius Latii* could have been established, without denying the possibility of later adjustments, at the time when this right was incorporated into Latinity, at a time prior to the Social War.[69] In fact, in the Flavian corpus of laws, it can be seen that the relationship between the two citizenships, Roman and Latin, is in line with what Cicero prescribed, since the law did not grant any dispensation to Latin citizens who obtained Roman citizenship through their specific route, but instead they had to abide by the rules of the *ius Romanorum* with regard to their family relations and patronal rights (as if they had always been Roman). Therefore, there did not exist a condition that reconciled the two worlds, but instead an almost complete turnaround of the Roman world as far as private law is concerned (*Irn.* 22, 23).[70] However, as far as the political life of the community is concerned, there seems to have been no need for clauses that allowed, as in the case of Seleukos of Rhosos, the holding of offices and priesthoods. As observed above, the law stipulates that Latin and Roman citizens share in the government of the city, limited at most by social and census-related criteria, in terms of access to the magistracies, the local senate, the *decuriae* of judges or the right

---

[67] Humbert 1978, 300–4.
[68] On Seleukos of Rhosos, see Raggi 2006; Genovese 2010, 1619–31, with earlier bibliography. For the Tabula of Banasa, see Euzennat and Marion 1982, no. 94; Sherwin-White 1973b, 86–98; Marotta 2016, 470–5.
[69] Talamanca 1991, 715. Determining the moment when the *ius Latii* was introduced is neither easy nor the goal of the present chapter, but no doubt Asconius' text indicates that this law predates 89 BC (see also n. 7 above). It is highly unlikely, as Galsterer 1976, 100 suggested, that this right was created for the Latin colonies of Hispania, given their peculiar nature with respect to their origin, population profile and means of foundation; see further García Fernández 2009.
[70] Marotta 2016, 477–9.

to vote in local elections (*Irn.* 31, 86; *Mal.* 53, 54), among other subjects. In the Latin municipality of Irni, with the arrival of the legislation, Roman administrative and procedural law was applied in matters affecting civic organisation and jurisdiction, while in the area of private law, the *ius Romanorum* applied to Romans, and for Latins, local law and the capacities and conditions introduced by the *ius Latinum* applied.

Provincial *ius Latinum*

The stable and institutional coexistence of two citizenships in the same community does not mean that both groups of citizens led their lives in parallel, even if just because the system of reproduction of Roman citizenship would not survive by resorting only to endogamic marriage practices. As pointed out in the previous section, it should be noted that in every Latin city, whether a municipality or a colony, there were several levels of legal relationship between its population: the relationship maintained by Latin citizens among themselves, as well as the relationships that may have been established between them and the Roman population generated by the Latin community, and finally, the relationships of Roman citizens among themselves, which would logically be in accordance with the *ius Romanorum* (and are not the subject of the present chapter).

Some sections of the Flavian legislation, probably contained in the edict on Latinity, allow us to refer to the existence of provisions that regulated the relations of the non-Roman population with each other in the private sphere and which could be expressed by recognising previously established family and patronal relationships, under the conditions established by the *ius Latii*. This was the case of the *iure Latino* marriage. Thus, among the conditions established for accessing the *civitas* formulated in chapter 21 of Irni, if we exclude the obligation of the magistrate to serve for one year, the most relevant for our purpose is the requirement of prior legitimacy of the Latin marriage. The law authorises the extension of citizenship obtained by an ex-magistrate to his parents, his wife and children born of a legitimate marriage and grandchildren under the authority of their parents, i.e. *iusti* children born of a Latin marriage (*Irn.* 21 ll. 41–2, 44: 'ac liberis qui legitimis nuptis quae/ siti in potestate parentium fuerint ... cives Romani sunto'). Without the recognition of the *iure Latino* union, whose formalisation procedure would be dictated by the *ius civitatis* of the city concerned, there could be no legitimate offspring, nor could the children inherit, nor benefit from the Roman citizenship their father obtained. The legitimacy of marriage between Latins is confirmed by the supplementary chapter of the *lex Irnitana* (i.e. chapter 97). This chapter, which aims to protect the rights of patrons over freedmen in the face of any change in their citizenship, alludes to the possibility of a *liberta* obtaining Roman citizenship through the access of her son or husband to the magistracy. This fact suggests that the *lex Lati* contemplated the legitimacy of marriage between Latins, whether *ingenui* or freed, since the husband of the *liberta* had to be an *ingenuus* in order to be accepted as a candidate for the magistrature (*Mal.* 54).

In turn, the demand for the legitimacy of the marriage of the magistrate and of his descendants forces us to assume that it was previously necessary to establish which unions were considered *iustae* and the conditions that granted this legitimacy, a particularly delicate matter in such complex communities as the Latin ones. This question, like others referring to the private sphere, were previously regulated by the aforementioned *lex*

Lati, as demonstrated by the fact that it referred to the types of marital unions that were permitted. It should be borne in mind that marriage in a city governed by Latin law was a complex matter, especially concerning the Latin population, given the different groups of Latins who could live together in a Latin colony or municipality: *Latini ingenui*, *Latini liberti*, both private and public, and *Latini Iuniani*. Although the last are rarely taken into account in the analysis of municipalisation processes, it is to be expected that they would have existed in Latin communities where irregular manumission could have been frequent, given the impossibility of formal manumission under Roman law at a local level.[71] These Junian Latins, unlike the municipal *optimo iure* Latins, whether *ingenui* or freed, would lack *conubium* and could not enter into a *iustum matrimonium* with Roman citizens except via the procedure established for their status.[72]

With regard to other private relationships characteristic of the Latin population, the wording of chapter 21 and the use of the past tense *fuerint*[73] would suggest, in principle, that Latins had *patria potestas* over their children, a right which was specific to Roman citizens.[74] In order to reconcile this possible contradiction, Hanard argued that the term *potestas* used by the Roman legislator in the *lex Irnitana* should be understood in the general sense of 'power' and not in the technical sense of *patria potestas*. However, the legislator composes the law from a fully Roman perspective so there is no reason to downplay the technical value of the expression. Nonetheless, the chapter could be indicating, indirectly, that the *lex Lati* with the recognition of the *iure Latino* marriage also confers parental power over legitimate children resulting from that marriage, understanding this power in a general sense as Hanard affirms and as Pliny expresses when he writes that it is *vis* and *lex naturae* that children are always subject to their parents.[75] In this sense, both the character of the *iure Latino* marriage and the type of parental power exercised could be dictated by the *ius civitatis* of the Latin community, which, depending on the area, could even be very similar to the Roman one. It was only when the Latin gained access to Roman citizenship that this parental power would acquire the technical name of *patria potestas* and would be adjusted to its precise legal profile.[76] The granting of this specifically Roman capacity to those who acquired Roman citizenship through the *ius Latii* stemmed then from the prior recognition of the legitimacy of the Latin marriage.

---

[71] On manumission in the municipalities, and the need for Roman citizens to appeal to the provincial governor to carry out a *vindicta* manumission, at least in Latin municipalities, see López Barja 1998, 157–9.

[72] The Junian freedman could celebrate a *iustum matrimonium* through the procedure established for his status (see Gai. *Inst.* 1.29), as was the case with L. Venidius Ennychus and his wife Livia Acte: see n. 27 above.

[73] Although the use of the past tense has been insisted on, it seems necessary to qualify that the past perfect *fuerint* is a form of the subjunctive and as such has no defined temporal value. It seems to be used in this section of the law rather with its perfect meaning that alludes to the possibility that 'something has happened', in this case the existence of a parental power analogous to the *patria potestas*, but not necessarily that this, or rather its analogue, may exist.

[74] See Gai. *Inst.* 1.55.

[75] See Hanard 1987, 173–6. The Plinian comment (*Pan.* 38.7) refers to Trajan's abolition of the requirement of being under *patria potestas* in order to be exempt from inheritance tax.

[76] See Hanard 1987, 177–9; Lamberti 1993, 71–3.

The recognition by Rome of the other family ties and patronal rights that existed among the Latin *municipes*, of whatever kind, can also be inferred from the provisions of chapter 22 of the *lex Irnitana* (ll. 50–3): 'is ea in eius qui civis Romanus ... erit potestate/ manu mancipio cuius esse deberet si civitate mutatus/mutata non esset'. It was only with the acquisition of Roman citizenship that these relationships acquired a technical legal content, thereby receiving the *nomen iuris*, and becoming known as *manus*, *mancipium* and *potestas* (and *optio tutoris*: ll. 53–4) from the point of view of the *ius civile* according to which they should reorganise their characteristics. This explains the need to introduce the clause 'si civitate mutatus/mutata non esset', whose function is to presuppose that they had always been Roman citizens and no change in citizenship had occurred in order to be able to apply the rules of the Roman *ius civile*.[77] This does not mean that these Roman institutions defined or regulated relations within the Latin population, but others which, at most, could be comparable to the Roman ones dictated by their own tradition and which Rome would recognise as being in accordance with the law under certain conditions.

In fact, the imposition of these conditions can be seen in the sphere of family relationships. It does not seem that Rome transferred without further ado the pre-existing, understood as 'indigenous', family structure to the *civitas Romana*. Rather, I hold that the granting of the *ius Latii* introduced the criteria that had to be applied in order to give legal recognition to the *iure Latino* marriage and to make possible its potential conversion into a Roman family, if this occurred. It is clear from the Flavian legal text that the pre-existing family structure was recognised in a restrictive way as it only included children born from lawful marriages, excluding adopted and emancipated children. These legitimate children would be under the *patria potestas* of the father, if he became a Roman citizen, as this was a prerogative of the *ius Latii*, which gave them the advantage that they could benefit from the Roman laws of succession, for example. However, those kinship relationships that previously existed between siblings, between mothers and illegitimate children, grandparents and grandchildren, not only disappeared with the change of citizenship, but were not recognised by the *ius Latii* for legal purposes, as demonstrated by their subsequent recognition in matters of inheritance and payment of the *vicesima hereditatium*. It was the emperors Nerva and Trajan who were responsible for granting *iura cognationis* to those who were granted Roman citizenship *per Latium*.[78]

Similarly, in a Latin colony or municipality there was a second level of legal relationship, which was established in the private sphere by the Latin and Roman

---

[77] On the reservation of *ius tutoris optandi* in the law to male *municipes*, see Lamberti 1993, 69–71, and 74 for the clause.

[78] The *ius Latii* granted the automatic renewal of relationships under *potestas*, therefore of the inheritance and tax exemption only to *sui heredes*, as should have been established in the law approved by Augustus (see Cass. Dio 55.25.5). Subsequently, both Nerva and Trajan extended the legal recognition of inheritance claims between cognates: for the case of maternal inheritance, see Plin. *Pan*. 37.5–6. For the recognition of second-degree relations between siblings and grandparents and grandchildren, and specifically granted also to those who gained Roman citizenship *per Latium*, see Plin. *Pan*. 39.1. Finally, Trajan allowed children to inherit regardless of whether or not they were under *patria potestas*. Cognate inheritance was an instrument of the *ius honorarium* and not of the *ius civile* and was therefore not granted by the Flavian municipal law. For detailed analysis, see Gardner 2001.

population among themselves. It was desirable that, in a mixed community, the necessary mechanisms were in place so that rifts did not arise between two citizenships, whose respective *cives* not only shared *origo* and *domicilium* and jointly received the title of *municipes* or *coloni*, but also jointly exercised the administration of the city. Both the right of *conubium* and the *commercium*, closely linked to the history of Latinity (although not exclusive to it) were *iura* that allowed cohesion within mixed communities, overcoming the isolation to which the principle of exclusive Roman citizenship would lead (already discussed above).

The effect of *conubium* was to make legitimate, in accordance with Roman law, a mixed union that would come under the *ius civitatis* of the husband. This would mean that the union between a Roman citizen and a Latin woman would result in children who were citizens of Rome, while the legitimate children of a union between a Latin citizen and a Roman woman would inherit Latin citizenship (which would materialise in local citizenship).[79] The possibility of legitimate marriages between Latins and Romans was essential for the social cohesion of the city. Without the recognition of this type of union the system of reproducing Roman citizens was not viable, and it resulted in endogamic marriages or the search for spouses outside of the city. By way of contrast, one can cite Marotta's analysis of the serious problems that the absence of *conubium* caused for the children of Roman citizens living with local women in the provinces of the Greek East, where the *ius Latii* was not widespread; or the endogamic marriage practices of the oligarchy, to avoid illegitimate births.[80] Moreover, onomastic transmission through the male side, whether Roman citizens or Latins, which was implicitly recognised by the Flavian legislation (*Irn*. 86), and above all the stable patrilineal transmission of the *nomina*, whether of Italian-Roman or indigenous origin (which reflects, in general terms, the epigraphic evidence of the Latin cities in the west of the Empire, regardless of their location in one or another province), appears to corroborate the existence of the right of *conubium*.[81]

---

[79] Here I endorse the view of Humbert 1981, 216–17, for whom the Latins in the provinces only existed within the framework of their own local citizenship; see also González and Crawford 1986, 148. Unlike the *Romani cives*, there is no general and abstract Latin *civitas* to which they could refer and from which they derived *iura* and *instituta*. The expression *cives Latini* used in the *lex Malacitana* should be understood as a generic formula which refers to residents of Latin condition coming from one or another Latin city. This does not detract from the value of citizenship in Latinity, but simply means that this citizenship, like the different peregrine citizenships, did not exist in the abstract but through concrete citizenships such as the *cives Baesuc(itani)* (*CIL* II, 3251) or the *cives Singilienses* (*CIL* II, 3008). Nor does it prevent, nor contradict, that these local citizenships could compete, within the respective municipality or colony, with Roman citizenship (*Irn*. 22, 23, 97).

[80] See Marotta 2012, 203. On *conubium* as a right of provincial Latins, see Chastagnol 1987a, 16–19. On the necessary presence of *conubium* for the reasons given in the text, see Dardaine 2003, 104; García Fernández 2018.

[81] For the existence of *conubium* in the epigraphic record, see Christol 1989; Raepsaet-Charlier 2001. The epigraphic records from Hispania also corroborate the correct patrilineal transmission, except in the cases of illegitimate descent and transmission of the maternal *nomen* (for which see Armani 2003), or specific problems of legibility and interpretation. I am aware of Rodríguez Garrido's 2018, 604–5 objection concerning the impossibility of demonstrating that an individual with *tria nomina* or *duo nomina* and no tribe has Roman or Latin status; however, the epigraphic records from Baetica generally confirm the correct transmission of *nomina*.

To be sure, it is precisely in the field of studies on Junian Latins that the existence of *conubium* is questioned as an inherent right of freeborn provincial Latins. Based on the idea that there was only one Latin condition in the Empire, combined with the availability of more, and relatively abundant and precise legal information on Junian Latins, as was already mentioned, some scholars have extended the more restrictive legal regime pertaining to Junian Latinity to the whole category.[82] The absence of *conubium* with Romans, unless expressly granted, was one of the shortcomings of Junian Latinity which was also extended to municipal Latinity, by identifying the Latins from the legal sources with the municipal Latins.[83] The discovery of the *lex Irnitana* in 1986 has strengthened this position in recent years. The restrictions imposed on unions without *conubium* established by the *lex Minicia* dated to the imperial period and intended for provincial Latins in Luraschi's interpretation would have been confirmed in Domitian's letter appended to the *lex Irnitana*.[84] According to Mancini, the reference to *conubia* authorised by the *lex Lati* would confirm the exceptional nature of this right and the fact that it was normally absent, as established by the *lex Minicia*. As I illustrated elsewhere, the letter at no time mentions or questions the right to marriage (*conubium*), nor is this consulted or ruled on. The use of the plural *conubia* does not seem to refer to the right of *conubium*, but to the different types of marital unions that the *lex Lati* or *ius Latii* recognised as legitimate, and others that it would appear to exclude.[85]

It may be relatively easy to identify the *conubia* covered by the *lex Lati*. First of all, the legal marriage of a Roman citizen with a Latin citizen was important to maintain social cohesion within the community, as has already been noted;[86] similarly, the *iure Latino* marriage, whose legitimacy was essential in order for the magistrate's family

---

[82] For Mancini 1997, 4–42, for example, the defence of *Latini Iuniani* and *coloniarii* as two conditions of a differentiated legal nature lacks any foundation; similarly López Barja 2008 (arguing in favour of integrating Latin conditions into a single *genus Latinorum*); Rodríguez Garrido 2017.

[83] The existence of *conubium* is denied in López Barja 1998, 143; 2002–3, 69–70. But note Gai. *Inst.* 3.56 and Ulp. *Reg.* 5.4 ('Conubium habent cives Romani cum civibus Romanis; cum Latinis autem et peregrinis ita, si concessum sit') referring to Junian Latin freedmen. On the identification of the Latins mentioned in the *Tituli Ulpiani* with Junian Latins only (except, obviously Ulp. *Reg.* 19.4), see Luraschi 1979, 242–7, who presents a convincing argument.

[84] As reinterpreted by Luraschi, the *Latini* that Gaius (*Inst.* 1.79) speaks of must be from after the Social War. Assuming that before 90 BC the Latins had *conubium*, he rules out the possibility that the restrictive reform introduced by the *lex Minicia* was introduced with the Latin rights of 89 BC, as it would be tantamount to sanctioning those who were to be compensated with integration. This means that the approval of the *lex Minicia* and the revocation of *conubium* from provincial Latins would have to be dated to the imperial period: Luraschi 1976, 437–8.

[85] García Fernández 2018.

[86] It would be strange indeed if the members of the *ordo decurionum*, Romans and Latins, governed the city together and yet could not establish political-family ties through marriage within their own social class. Similarly, as Dardaine has observed, the fact that the wife of an outgoing magistrate was granted Roman citizenship, as provided for in the relevant chapters of the *lex Irnitana* and *lex Salpensana*, cannot be considered an indication of the absence of *conubium*; their obtaining Roman citizenship could be guaranteed by the subsequent access of a child to the magistrature. The difference in treatment between the remaining wives of the auxiliary soldiers of the Roman army and the wives of the members of the local oligarchies was not so much due to legal reasons as to sociological and class-related matters: see Dardaine 2003, 102.

to have access to Roman citizenship (also already noted); and, of course, marriage between Roman citizens. These would be the three types of marital union which, with relative certainty, could be covered by the *lex Lati*. Indeed, it is more difficult to specify what type of unions would have been excluded. These may have been marriages between Roman citizens and *peregrini*, as reflected in the *tabula Clesiana*.[87] However, it would not be necessary to allude to a *lex Lati* to exclude this union, as this is already done by the Roman *ius civile*.

In this context, it must be noted that the lack of familiarity with or knowledge of the complexities of the *ius civile* by the city's magistrates could have led to the recognition of legitimate marriages in the heart of the municipality of Irni, which were not. I am thinking of the marriages between Junian Latins and Roman citizens, but perhaps the problem could lie in the fact that the marriages between *Latini* (*Iuniani*) and municipal *Latini* were verified as legitimate, whether they were *ingenui* or *liberti*, given the similar designation they shared.

It could be suggested that the question addressed to Domitian may have been connected to a matter concerning freedmen, due to the fact that the additional chapter inserted between the *sanctio* and Domitian's letter alludes to a specific circumstance of this condition.[88] But two other factors seem to me to be more relevant. One of them, already mentioned, is that the common name given to the different groups of Latins would make it difficult to distinguish them locally, especially among magistrates who were not particularly well versed in legal technicalities. Moreover, it is also relevant that Domitian, in his reply to the Irnitani, does not appeal to the *ius civile* in the letter, which is mentioned in chapter 93, but to the *lex Lati*. This fact would suggest that in one way or another the unauthorised *conubia* were to be related to the specificity of the Latin condition, and not to the matrimonial peculiarities of the *ius Romanorum*.

The second right that would be inherent to the provincial Latin right in its relationship with the Romans would be the *commercium*, through which Latins were granted the power to participate in an act of the *ius civile* with a Roman citizen (but not the general and global power to use the institutions of the *ius Quiritium*, access to which was provided by municipal laws, not the concession of *ius Latii*). Both the *conubium* and the *commercium* acted functionally as judicial channels that permitted legal, social and economic cohesion within mixed communities, and which allowed a *civis Latinus* to interact in a Roman environment.[89]

Thus, the provincial Latin condition was the result of interweaving the rights and conditions that the *ius Latii* incorporated into every community, with the *iura* and *mores* of local citizenship. Subsequently, a *lex municipalis*, whose existence was not necessarily compulsory, could standardise, from a Roman perspective, the internal organisation of the municipality or Latin colony and extend its jurisdiction. At the same time, if the characteristics of the provincial Latin condition made it possible to incorporate and maintain, under the conditions established by the *ius Latii*, the indigenous element in

---

[87] *CIL* V, 5050.
[88] Mourgues 1987, 85–7.
[89] On *commercium* in relation to the Latins, see Kremer 2006, 9–15, 113–18.

the Latin legal community (and consequently its effectiveness as an instrument of integration), then the presence of elements belonging to the local tradition in its material register (ceramics, architecture, iconography, etc.) should not come as a surprise, nor should the variety of its forms of denomination.

Municipal Latins: Some Methodological Problems of Identification

While municipal Latins and Junian Latins have different origins, different legal systems and historical backgrounds, and would ultimately constitute two different types of Latin right, they shared the same name in the sources, *Latini*, a common link, although of a different nature, with former colonial Latins, besides some shared difficulties in terms of their identification in the sources, an aspect that now requires discussion.

In the context of the present work, there is no need to explain here the difficulties of identifying Junian Latins in the epigraphic or literary evidence, and of differentiating them, for example, from a freedperson with Roman citizenship, not least because both make use of the Roman *tria nomina* as a denomination system – as emphasised in Chapter 9; moreover, multiple attempts at identifying individual Junian Latins especially in the epigraphic sources are trialled in the partner volume to the present undertaking.[90] The same, of course, is true for provincial Latins. The use of Roman forms of denomination means that in the epigraphic material of many Latin colonies and municipalities, it is also impossible to discern the Roman or Latin condition of the population in the absence of the mention of tribes or magistracies, or to distinguish between a Latin freedperson and another freedperson with Roman citizenship.[91] However, in the case of provincial Latins, the question of onomastic identification is not restricted to the use of *tria nomina* but has added complexities for different reasons, one of a documentary nature and another of historiographic origin.

If we first consider the documentary issue, we can see that, as a consequence of the widespread diffusion of the *ius Latii* throughout various provinces of the Empire, the nature of provincial Latin onomastics is much less homogeneous than that of Junian Latins. This situation poses problems of statutory interpretation which are very difficult to resolve. It has been documented that there are a significant number of cities under Latin law whose populations generally used Roman forms of denomination, but depending on the greater or lesser vitality of the indigenous tradition in a province, the onomastic practices recorded in the epigraphic sources can be much more flexible.

It is precisely this greater onomastic flexibility that characterises the provincial Latin condition in contradistinction to Junian Latins, which is due to the different origins of both in relation to the *civitas Romana*. In the case of a Junian Latin, this could only come about as a result of being manumitted by a Roman citizen, which is

---

[90] López Barja, Masi Doria and Roth forthcoming. Among earlier studies, see esp. Weaver 1990; Hirt 2018; López Barja 2018b; see also the relevant comments and cited bibliography in this volume's Introduction.

[91] With the exception of public freedmen whose Latin status is certain: see Dardaine 1999 (and further below).

why their system of denomination is the same as that of their manumitter (except for the tribe) and therefore more uniform. On the contrary, provincial Latins come from peregrine cities with different cultural traditions that Latinity integrated, assimilated and expressed, which explains the greater onomastic *variatio* and the complexity of its analysis and statutory interpretation. In fact, it can be easily observed how in cities with the same administrative title, *municipium* or *colonia*, the onomastic characteristics of their population can be diverse, even in the case of their non-Roman oligarchy.[92]

This does not mean that the Latins did not have their own onomastics. The onomastic characteristics of the population of the province of Baetica, which had a much higher number of Latins than Roman municipalities and colonies, and where the onomastics of *peregrini* was irrelevant, would reveal that the Latins used a Roman personal denomination system (*duo nomina* or *tria nomina*). Proof of this is that in the absence of tribes and magistrates it is not possible to differentiate in Baetica between a Roman citizen and an individual who was not. It is also quite unlikely that in a Latin municipality it was only the traditionally minority group of Roman citizens who left behind a record of their existence through epigraphy. It is therefore to be expected that a sizeable number of individuals attested in the epigraphic register of Baetica had Latin legal status.[93] Whether or not they can be identified is another matter.

In any case, an additional conclusion can be drawn from this situation. If the population of a predominantly Latin province made widespread use of the Roman form of denomination, it is reasonable to assume that they did not use it illegally. It is precisely the zeal shown by the emperor Claudius to prevent the fraudulent use of Roman names by persons with peregrine status (*peregrina condicio*) that suggests that it was impossible for provincials not legally authorised to do so to make regular use of the Roman onomastic structure and the *nomina* associated with it.[94] The onomastic practices of the population of Baetica would then suggest that the granting of the *ius Latii* may have

---

[92] Here, for example, I refer to the aediles of Andelos (Navarra) Carus Silvini f(ilius) and Lucretius Martialis Lucreti f(ilius) Andelo (*HEp*. 1, 1989, 491 = *AE* 1989, 456). On their Latin status, see García Fernández 2012, 430–5. This group could include the aediles from the territory of the Latin colony of Nemausus, Sex(tus) Vetto C(aius) Pedo aed(iles) (*CIL* XII, 4190); cf. Christol 1989, 91 (modified in Dondin-Payre 2001, 269, n. 209). Their onomastics contrast with those of other aediles who served in the Flavian municipality of Malaca, L(ucius) Octavius Rusticus and L(ucius) Granius Balbus (*CIL* II, 1967); it is true that in this case the absence of tribe does not prevent these incumbent aediles from being Roman citizens in the Flavian municipality of Malaca through kinship. Furthermore, the onomastic record of the Latin municipalities of Aurgi (González Román and Mangas Manjarrés 1991) or Lucentum (Abascal Palazón and Rabanal Alonso 1985) contrasts, for example, with that of the Latin municipality of Caesarobriga in Lusitania (consultable online in Adopia, *Atlas Digital Onomastique de la Péninsule Ibérique Antique*, at http://adopia.huma-num.fr/en/atlas), or the Latin colony of Nemausus in Gallia Narbonensis (Christol 1989).

[93] In the same sense, see the comments of Dardaine 1999, 213–14.

[94] This was the case with the Anauni attributed to Tridentum who, believing they were in possession of Roman citizenship, incorporated Roman names into their names, a fact that the emperor Claudius had to accept because it was an ancient practice, so as not to harm the Roman municipality: 'nomina ea/quae habuerunt antea tanquam cives Romani, ita habere is permittam' (*CIL* V, 5050). In general, we know from Suetonius that Claudius forbade the use of Roman *nomina gentilicia* by people of peregrine status: 'peregrinae condicionis homines vetuit usurpare Romana nomina dumtaxat gentilicia' (Suet. *Vit. Claud*. 25.7). In the republican period, the *lex Papia de peregrinis* instituted an extraordinary *quaestio* to expel *peregrini* from Rome: Cic. *Leg. Agr*. 1.13; *Arch*. 10; *Balb*. 52; *Off*. 3.11.47; Schol. Bob. 175 Stangl;

been accompanied by a general authorisation for the population of Latin status to construct and use the Roman trinominal structure, with the possibility of making use of *nomina* of Roman or even indigenous origin; otherwise the widespread use of Roman onomastic structures by the population of the many Latin municipalities in the province of Baetica is difficult to explain. Dardaine arrives at the same conclusion, and has demonstrated the use of the *tria nomina* structure by persons of Latin origin, analysing the onomastics of the public *liberti* that were manumitted by magistrates of Latin communities.[95] The Latin status of these freedpersons is expressly confirmed in chapter 72 of the *lex Irnitana* on the manumission of public slaves, which states that once they are manumitted, they will be Latin and *municipes* of the Flavian municipality.[96] This possibility is further supported by the obligation on the part of *municipes* elected to the list of judges to register their full names, as established by chapter 86 of the *lex Irnitana*.[97]

Nevertheless, an authorisation does not mean an imposition; ultimately, except for magistrates, Latinity did not immerse the individual into the world of the administrators of the system and its direct benefits. In areas where local onomastic traditions were still alive and Romanisation was less pronounced, tensions and adjustments could occur between the entrenched indigenous and Roman modes of denomination, which were resolved onomastically in a variety of ways, as Alföldy duly noted.[98] This may explain the different onomastic practices in cities with a Latin legal status, whether they were

---

Cass. Dio 37.9.5; Val. Max. 3.4.5; Cicero's comment on the subject – 'Nam esse pro cive, qui civis nos sit rectum est non licere' (*Off.* 3.11.47) – likely covers the (mis)use of Roman names. On the difficulties of the idea of onomastic *imitatio* to explain the use of Roman onomastic structures, see García Fernández 2015; the relevance of onomastic misappropriation is denied by Dondin-Payre 2011b, 14–15.

[95] Dardaine 1999, 225–7 provides a list of epigraphic sources from various communities in the west reflecting the use of *tria nomina* by the public freedmen of different Latin cities: Sex(tus) Publicius Antenor (at Aquae Sextiae: *CIL* XII, 523), Ti(berius) Claudius Favor (at Celeia: *CIL* III, 5227) and C. Publicius Asiaticus (at Virunum: *CIL* III, 4870) – the latter two both from Latin municipalities in Noricum. Note also T. Publicius Tertius, from the Latin colony of Augusta Treverorum; however, he is included in the list of Roman citizens of the colony by Raepsaet-Charlier 2001, 384.

[96] *Irn.* 72 ll. 16–19: 'Qui ita manumissus liberve esse iussus erit, liber et Latinus esto, quaeve ita manumissa liberave esse iussa erit, libera et Latina esto, eique municipes municipi Flavi Irnitani sunto.' I am mindful of the objections of Fear 1990, who interpreted chapter 72 of the *lex Irnitana* in the same sense as Millar regarding the public manumission of slaves. The most important objection is the chronological argument, since it was not until the SC Neratianum, in the Hadrianic period, that provincial communities were authorised to manumit public slaves, and therefore after the *lex Irnitana* (i.e. AD 91). This would suggest that before this emperor, the provincial communities could only manumit informally, i.e. they could only confer the legal status of *Latini Iuniani*. However, this reasoning has to be applied to *optimo iure* communities, which were the only ones that could confer Roman citizenship on their public slaves, while the citizenship that a Latin municipality could confer was in any case not Roman but Latin. This circumstance explains why the consent of the provincial governor was not necessary for the community to be able to grant a citizenship that was actually second-rate. For the discussion, see further López Barja 1991b, 55–60, refuting Fear's argument; note further Dardaine 1999, 217, arguing that the freedmen in the Latin communities are full Latins and not Junians (with 214–15 for his objections to Fear).

[97] Local judges and *recuperatores*, as the latter were selected *ex iis qui in iudicum numero erunt* (*Irn.* 88 l. 4): see Lamberti 1993, 168–9. On the (tralatician) requirement for the judges to have tribes, see González and Crawford 1986, 232. However, it can also be deduced that the law took into account that some judges were Roman citizens and therefore had tribes; those other judges who were Latin and therefore did not have tribes were simply not specified.

[98] Alföldy 1966, 39.

colonial or municipal, located in different provincial territories. This is not to advocate an uncritical flexibility, but rather to highlight the capacity of Latinity to adapt to the different indigenous traditions with which it came into contact. This adaptive process is documented in the Gallic provinces and in the Germanies, where it has been analysed in detail. For example, it is detected in the process of creating 'patronymic *nomina*', which is interpreted as a subtle adaptation of two onomastic traditions, the local and the Roman.[99]

While the onomastic *variatio* contained in the documentation of Latin municipalities and colonies in the provinces of the western part of the Empire introduces great complexity into the onomastic analysis of the municipal Latin right, there is a second issue of a historiographic nature which introduces new difficulties, by erasing all reference to provincial Latins. Thus, in the field of onomastic studies, especially those that focus on the study of Gallic or Germanic documentation, there is a line of research that denies the existence of a Latin population, whether *ingenui* or freed. From this standpoint, it is argued that the citizens of any community under Latin law, whether a municipality or a colony, could only be Roman citizens or *peregrini*.

This interpretation is not directly derived from the analysis of the sources, but, as noted, from a historiographic standpoint. The idea of the absence of free individuals of Latin status is based on a suggestion made by Millar back in 1977 in his *Emperor in the Roman World*, which denied the existence of freeborn Latins following the Social War.[100] The result of this thesis was that the legal status enjoyed by the population of communities with Latin law after 90 BC could only be Roman or peregrine. The express mentions of Latins (even freeborn Latins) which were recorded in municipal legislation and legal sources such as the *Pauli Sententiae* were to be understood as references to Junian Latins, the only existing Latins in Millar's opinion following the proclamation of the *lex Iulia de civitate*, which extinguished all freeborn Latins in Italy and in Gallia Cisalpina by making the *Latini coloniarii* Roman citizens.[101] Consequently, for Millar, the citizens of a Latin colony or municipality would be *peregrini* if they were not Romans.[102] It should be noted that Millar devotes a mere six pages to this thesis in a fairly lengthy book, adding that he

---

[99] See Dondin-Payre 2001, 243–52, who analyses in detail the suggestive phenomenon of 'patronimia' ('patronymie'), the name given to the formation of an element of the onomastic nomenclature of a son (in principle the *nomen*), from an element of his father's nomenclature. This practice differs from the Roman practice of transmitting *nomina* without modification and from the indigenous practice of changing names from generation to generation; see 246–8 for a list of patronymic *nomina* in Central Gaul. See furthermore Chastagnol 1995, 167–80 for discussion of the change of name from one generation to another as a characteristic of the Three Gauls, the Germanies and Noricum; and inter alia Raepsaet-Charlier 2001, 2011, and Dondin-Payre 2011b on the onomastic process of adaptation.

[100] Millar 1977, 630–5.

[101] López Barja 1991b offers a solidly argued criticism of Millar's proposal and accepts on good grounds the value of the relevant text of the *Pauli Sententiae* in which freeborn Latin status is mentioned (2.21a.1, 4.9.8, 4.10.3), which Millar dismisses because of the text's late origin. Similar to López Barja is also Dardaine 1999, 214–16 (accepting the existence of freeborn status); García Fernández 2010. Note also that Millar 1977, 634 accepts that the expression *Latina ingenua*, documented in the *Pauli Sententiae*, may refer to a daughter of a Junian Latin woman, constituting in the view of López Barja 1991b, 54 an 'abuse of vocabulary' because if no other personal *Latinitas* apart from the Junian is accepted, it would be difficult for the son of a Junian to take refuge in a non-existent *civitas*.

[102] The scarcity of references to freeborn Latins in the legal documentation emphasised by Millar 1977, 632–3 with special reference to the *Institutes* of Gaius has already been commented on above.

did not intend to deal with the subject in depth, that it occupies a peripheral place in his work, and above all that he is not convinced that some references to *Latini* do not in fact refer to freeborn provincial Latins.[103]

Notwithstanding Millar's disclaimers, his thesis was accepted by such influential scholars as Chastagnol and Christol because it resolved the question of the presence of onomastics of the peregrine type or onomastics that were not fully adapted to Roman usage, that are documented in the complex epigraphic record of the different Gallic provinces.[104] From this new vantage point, all references to the *ingenua* or *liberta* Latin population of the imperial period disappeared from onomastic analysis, as they were considered to be non-existent. In a city under Latin law, there would therefore only be Roman citizens and *peregrini*, thereby simplifying Millar's standpoint, which did recognise the existence of Latins of Junian condition. Roman citizens would be identified among those individuals who bore *tria nomina* or *duo nomina* (*nomen* and *cognomen*), while the group of *peregrini* would have comprised the population that used the single name plus the filiation (or at the most the patronymic idionym).[105] This statutory classification is in open contradiction with the epigraphic record of cities that combine Latin municipal status with a high degree of Romanisation, as is the case with *Latinorum Lucentum*, for example, or the numerous Latin municipalities from Baetica where the entire population, as has been observed before, used the Roman denomination.[106] Moreover, rejecting the existence of a population of Latin origin in communities where the *ius Latii* had been granted in order to defend the existence of only a Roman or a peregrine population does not appear to enable the elaboration of more precise criteria for the classification of the population. In fact, the identification of individuals with a two-part onomastic structure with Roman citizens is not always reliable, nor do the onomastics of *peregrini* respond, as would be expected, to a structure consisting of a unique name (idionym) plus their filiation (patronymic), as this group also includes individuals whose names have a two-part structure.[107] To deal with

---

[103] For example, in reference to the formula *cives Latini* (*Mal.* 53), Millar 1977, 633 notes merely the rarity of this expression, recognising that it may be referring to Latin citizens from other municipalities who resided in Malaca, while not ruling out that the expression could refer to slaves who were incompletely manumitted, i.e. to *Latini Iuniani*, and concluding that '[t]he alternative hypothesis, that no such class existed (i.e. *Latini*, free-born), is put forward purely tentatively' (p. 635).

[104] See Chastagnol 1990, 575–6 for discussion of the source for his perspective in Millar's work; see also Christol 1989, 90; Christol and Deneux 2001, 39, n. 3.

[105] Chastagnol 1990, 576 = Chastagnol 1995, 54. The identification of Roman citizens in all individuals with *duo nomina* or *tria nomina* is beyond question for Dondin-Payre and Raepsaet-Charlier 2001, iii–iv, iv–viii, describing their analytical criteria; see also Dondin-Payre 2001; 2011b, 14–16.

[106] See Plin. *HN* 3.20. For the epigraphy, see the volumes of *CILA* 1991.

[107] Dondin-Payre 2001, 259–83 explains the criteria for identifying the peregrine population. Examples of binomial structures whose bearers are classified among the *peregrini* include Iulianus Crescens (*CIL* XIII, 2726), Apronianus Saserus (*CIL* XIII, 2912) or the Aeduan Cosuobnus Priscus Tatiri f. (*AE* 1922, 14 = *ILAfr* 645 = *IAM* 2, 508), an *eques* of the *ala Taurina* among others: Dondin-Payre 2001, 273–83. A similar approach is taken to two-part structures formed by a Roman *praenomen* plus an individual name that by reference to Roman onomastics would be a *cognomen*, or two-part structures formed by two unique names juxtaposed. Examples include Q. Caletedo (*AE* 1995, 1067) and Q. Caranto Endami f. (*AE* 1995, 1066) from the Latin colony of Nemausus, who are both classified among the peregrine population of the colony, while the aediles Sex(tus) Vetto and C(aius) Pedo (*CIL* XII, 4190), magistrates still in office and from the territory of the same city in Gallia Narbonensis, and with a similar onomastic structure to the previously listed men, in which the *nomen* also seems to be absent, are classified among Roman citizens.

this obvious hurdle, individuals with two-part naming structures are regularly identified as *peregrini* on the assumption that their onomastic elements do not have the strict meaning that they would have in a Roman citizen's nomenclature: they are seen as 'loans' that lack both function and significance, enabling the individuals' supposed identification as peregrine. Thus, despite the staunch defence of the idea that onomastics express a precise status and that onomastic usurpations are irrelevant,[108] in some circumstances of difficult classification – such as the group of persons with two-part naming structures – the concept of 'cultural Romanisation' is then drawn on to account for the onomastic practices in which the population, despite being peregrine, expressed their desire to be integrated into the system from which they were temporarily excluded. Put the other way round, this desire for integration is supposedly manifested in the use of types of denomination which in principle are not those proper to an individual with peregrine status. In these cases, the noted onomastic practice is understood not as a desire to feign a condition that one does not possess, among other things because the citizen oligarchies would closely monitor any attempt at usurpation, but rather as a desire for emulation while awaiting legal ratification.[109]

In contrast to this interpretative approach, the introduction of Latin status, whose existence is unequivocally documented by municipal legislation in Hispania, would, in my view, allow for a more precise analysis of the population, encompassing a variety of onomastic circumstances, and more coherently integrate the legal, literary and epigraphic information available in the study of Romanisation processes. The municipal Latin was authorised to make use of the Roman *tria nomina* (but not tribes) for the reasons given above. However, the more or less deeply rooted nature of the onomastic usages of local tradition could affect and condition the onomastic structure to be used. It was only through access to citizenship that the Latin would necessarily adopt fully Roman forms of denomination, irrespective of whether they lived in one part of the Roman Empire or another.

Conclusion

After this comprehensive survey into municipal Latinity, it is high time to conclude that Junians were not the only Latins in the Roman Empire. In fact, Latinity reveals itself as a crafty instrument used by Rome to provide different solutions to different problems: from integrating provincial communities with various levels of Romanisation on the one hand, to giving legal sanction to informal manumissions in the case of Junians

---

[108] Dondin-Payre 2011b, 14–15.
[109] Dondin-Payre 2001, 217: 'la romanisation est là encore culturelle, avant d'être entérinée par la loi'. The arrival of the law, a piece of municipal legislation similar to those known for Baetica, should be understood, according to Chastagnol 1987a, 6, as a 'privilège supplémentaire' (as noted above, on p. 32) which gives the city a colonial or municipal administrative title. One of the problems with this interpretation, and an important one, is that it is indifferent to whether the city is an *oppidum Latinum*, a *civitas*, a colony or a municipality, since the arrival of the law and the important impact it has on the community do not seem to modify the status of the population. In any event, the entire analysis is reduced to the identification of the Roman population or peregrines, whether in the Latin colony of Nemausus or the Latin municipality of Ercavica: further discussion is in García Fernández 2020, 67–9.

on the other. Indeed, the pervasiveness of Latin status, combined with its intricacies, causes precisely the kinds of scholarly disagreements that are evident also in the present volume – such as the quite different view on imperial Latinity expressed in Chapter 5 by López Barja and Rodríguez Garrido. Moreover, once the internal complexities underlying the term *Latini* are openly faced, serious epigraphical difficulties arise. Excluding the public freedmen of a Latin colony or *municipium*, who can be identified more or less easily, in most cases, no criteria, to this date, allow us to decide, for instance, whether Q(uintus) Cornelius Secundinus (*CIL* II², 5, 832) from the Latin *municipium* of Singlia Barba (Baetica) was a Roman citizen or a Latin; likewise, Sex(tus) Vetto and C(aius) Pedo (*CIL* XII, 4190), incumbent aediles in Nemausos (Gallia Narbonensis) could be either peregrini or Roman citizens or Latins; also, in the case of T(itus) Minucius T(iti) lib(ertus)/Meleager (*CIL* II², 5, 324) from Igabrum (Baetica), and in that of M(arcus) Rutilius M(arci) l(ibertus) Diomedes (*CIL* II², 5, 976) from Ostippo (Baetica), it is not possible to know if these freedmen were Roman citizens, municipal Latins or Junian Latins. The fact that we cannot tell is annoying: but this is not a good reason for closing one's eyes to the historical and legal developments pertaining to Latinity, and its diverse forms, that this chapter has sought to highlight by focusing on municipal Latinity. Instead, acknowledging and understanding the complexity of Latinity in the Roman Empire is the natural starting point for a better appreciation of any one form of Latinity, Junian Latinity included, and the interrelatedness of these diverse statuses and their historical development.

2

THE LEGAL FOUNDATION: THE *LEGES IUNIA ET AELIA SENTIA*

Luigi Pellecchi

Introduction

THIS CHAPTER SETS OUT the legal framework that shaped the status we call Junian Latinity – *libertas Latina*. Describing this legal framework involves discussing two statutes, the *leges Iunia* (*Norbana*) and *Aelia Sentia*, that created this particular form of *libertinitas*, 'freed status'. Such a discussion cannot avoid the fact that what has to be dealt with are essentially problems: of the dates of the two enactments, of their scope and relationship, of the context of their technical provisions. The difficulties are evidently determined by the state of the sources: the *ipsissima verba*, the 'actual wording' of the two measures, do not survive (as is usually the case with Roman assembly legislation). Nor are the literary sources much help: as far as the *lex Iunia* is concerned, they are simply non-existent; and if the *lex Aelia Sentia* does appear, it appears only rarely and in a way that does not help us to understand its relationship with the *lex Iunia*. But the most serious problem is the result of the policy of Justinian: the reform of AD 531, which abolished *libertas Latina* and which Theophilus describes as one of his finest measures, has rendered almost useless the two main collections of juridical texts of late antiquity.[1]

Without being able to turn to either the *Codex* or the Digest of Justinian, the sources for the original nature of Junian Latinity are three introductory treatments, not even all preserved entire. The legal dimension of the history of the Junian Latins is thus marked by sources that are summary and incomplete, creating the 'black hole', so to speak, in which almost every aspect of the position of these particular individuals is hidden. Given a source problem of this kind, any discussion of the legislative basis of the status has no choice but to follow a largely traditional path: first to organise the source material in such a way as to be able to formulate, if not to answer, the fundamental questions that we wish to pose, i.e. what kind of measure introduced Junian Latinity (§1), in relation to whom (§2), at what date (§§3–4), and with what end in view (§5); I shall then collect and contextualise (§6) such little information as there is on the original legislative position of Junian Latins; at this point, one seriously enters the 'black hole', with an attempt to characterise particular features of the status, in relation both to Latinity (§7) and to the position of the patron and of the freedperson (§§8–9).

---

[1] See *CJ* 7.6.1; Theophilus, *Paraphrasis Institutionum* 1.5.3.

Nine Steps into (and out of) the 'Black Hole'

§1 *The* lex Iunia *and Latin status: the central provision of the statute*

The measure that underpinned freed Latin status is the *lex Iunia*. This measure affected those who were in freedom, 'in libertate erant' (according to some sources[2]), or who lived in a state of freedom, 'in libertate morabantur' (according to other versions[3]), following prior subjection to slavery: to be precise, to those people to whom their owner had granted 'de facto freedom', the statute assigned the status of *Latini coloniarii*, 'colonial Latins'.

This provision may be regarded as the central feature of the *lex Iunia* for two reasons. On the one hand, all the sources make it clear that the acquisition of a more complete '*de iure* freedom' depended on this provision.[4] Before the statute, without a formal or perfect process of manumission, those who lived in freedom merely by the wish of their master – the *morantes in libertate voluntate domini* – had to be satisfied with the protection of the praetor, which was limited, as far as we know, to preventing masters from revoking their grant and using *uindicatio in seruitutem*, a 'claim for enslavement', to bring such people back under their control.[5] On the other hand, we shall see (further below and in §5) that the other, better-known, provision of the *lex Iunia*, according to which on the death of a Junian Latin their property passed to their former owner, is seen by the sources as an adjusting mechanism, to avoid what would otherwise have been an inevitable consequence of assimilating those living in freedom (the above mentioned *morantes in libertate*) to colonial Latins (the also already mentioned *Latini coloniarii*).

This assimilation is thus the central element of the statute, in both a positive sense and a negative sense: the former, because the equation with colonial Latins was the technical manoeuvre which allowed its beneficiaries to acquire legally protected freedom, not available up till then; the latter, since to avoid the equation having consequences not desired by the legislator, it was necessary to include in the statute certain supplementary provisions.

On a technical level, the assimilation prompts two further observations. The first is that it was achieved by means of a fiction: the statute provided that its beneficiaries

---

[2] *Frag. Dos.* 5, 7; Ulp. *Reg.* 1.12; [Quint.] *Decl. Min.* 340pr., 342pr. On the latter texts, as indirect evidence for the statute, see the full account in Bettinazzi 2014, 45–62.

[3] Digest 40.12.24.3 (Paul); *CJ* 7.4.4 (Severus Alexander).

[4] *Frag. Dos.* 6: 'sed nunc habent propriam libertatem inter amicos manumissi et fiunt Latini Iuniani' ('but now those who are manumitted in the presence of friends possess their freedom and become Junian Latins'; Ulp. *Reg.* 1.10: 'hodie autem ipso iure liberi sunt ex lege Iunia, qua lege Latini Iuniani nominati sunt inter amicos manumissi' ('but today they are free by the law itself under the *lex Iunia*, by which the name of Junian Latins is given to those who are manumitted in the presence of friends'); Gai. *Inst.* 1.22: 'homines, Latini Iuniani appellantur; Latini ideo, quia adsimulati sunt Latinis coloniariis, Iuniani ideo, quia per legem Iuniam libertatem acceperunt, cum olim servi viderentur esse' ('men, they are called Junian Latins, Latins because they are assimilated to colonial Latins, Junian, because they acquired freedom through the *lex Iunia*, although previously they seemed to be slaves').

[5] See *Frag. Dos.* 5, which seems to show that the protection of the magistrate did not extend to the property of those *in libertate esse voluntate domini*, i.e. those who enjoyed freedom solely through their master's wish.

should be regarded as if they were freeborn Roman citizens who had decided to take part in the foundation of a colony of Latin status;[6] such a manoeuvre, it is argued, brought the reform within the framework of Roman private law.[7]

The second observation is that the relevant provision of the *lex Iunia* worked on the assumption that, for an individual slave, living in freedom solely by the wish of their master fitted into the norms established in the praetorian edict to allow them to benefit from the protection of that magistrate.[8] This link with the praetorian edict remains obscure,[9] not least because we do not know how many actual cases the magistrate refused to offer his protection to (but clearly several, *plures causae*: see the *Fragmentum Pseudo-Dositheanum*), despite the fact that it was with the agreement of the master that the slave was free. In granting even only de facto liberty, an owner could infringe various legitimate expectations, either their own[10] or above all those of third parties, as in the case of a co-owner of the slave, or a praetorian owner, or the usufructuary, or someone who had him or her as a pledge, or even a creditor, if the estate of the owner became inadequate to meet their debts as a result.[11] It is possible that already in such cases the praetor refused to protect the de facto freedom of the slave, and that the *lex Iunia* borrowed the whole procedure, in order to exclude in such cases the acquisition of (legally protected) Latin liberty.

§2 The complex of beneficiaries of libertas Latina

Leaving aside any exceptions provided for in the praetorian edict, the *lex Iunia* laid down that the status of a Roman citizen who moved to a Latin colony, i.e. of a 'colonial Latin', should be attributed to all those who lived in freedom with the authorisation of their master; but exactly who made up the category in question? To answer this question from a juridical point of view, it is necessary to operate a preliminary distinction between people on whom their owner, even though they

---

[6] See Gai. *Inst.* 3.56: 'lex eos liberos proinde esse voluit, atque si essent cives Romani ingenui, qui ex urbe Roma in Latinas colonias deducti Latini coloniarii esse coeperunt' ('the statute wished them so to be free, as if they were freeborn Roman citizens who, having been led out from the city of Rome to join Latin colonies, became colonial Latins'). It is perhaps as a result of a back-translation of a Greek version of the original Latin that *Frag. Dos.* 6 talks of *liberti*: see the bibliography cited in Wilinski 1963, 379, with n. 6; see also n. 8 below.

[7] See Bianchi 2012, §3, according to whom the fiction in question, on the one hand, kept intact the equation of (full) liberty with Roman citizenship, but, on the other hand, deprived it at the same time of meaning by regarding Roman citizenship as lost by enrolling for a Latin colony, with *capitis deminutio* as a result.

[8] See *Frag. Dos.* 8: 'similiter, ut possit habere servus libertatem, talis esse debet, ut praetor sive proconsul libertatem eius tueatur; nam et hoc lege Iunia tutatum (?) est' ('likewise, in order that the slave may have their freedom, they must be such that a praetor or proconsul may protect their freedom; for this is what is ensured (?) by the *lex Iunia*'); the word *tutatum* probably reflects a mistaken back-translation from the Greek (ἠσφάλισται) of the probable Latin original *cautum est*, 'it is provided'.

[9] For further details, see Impallomeni 1963, 39–58, at 46–8; and more recently, Pellecchi 2015, §2.2.

[10] As in the case in which the person who granted the possibility of living in freedom was an under-age master, who had not consulted and obtained the approval of their guardian: see *Frag. Dos.* 15.

[11] The various possibilities are considered in *Frag. Dos.* 9–11, 16.

could, had *not wished to confer* full freedom, *iusta libertas* (**a** below), and those whom they had wished to benefit with full manumission, but *without having the legal power to do so* (**b** below).

(**a**) The decision to attribute something different from and less than *iusta libertas* might depend on two factors: (**a.i**) practical difficulties linked to the technicality and formality of full manumission,[12] or (**a.ii**) economic reasoning, i.e. the choice of the manumitter not to renounce rights which would have been weakened if the freed slave had attained Roman citizenship.[13] The resulting act is that which the sources describe as manumission in the presence of friends (*manumissio inter amicos*), even though this could take place in forms different from a declaration made in the presence of witnesses.[14]

(**b**) One can also subdivide the second group of those living in freedom by the wish of the master, i.e. those on whom the master would have wished to confer full freedom, but without having the legal power to do so. On the one hand (**b.i**), there is the case in which the manumitter did not have formal *dominium ex iure Quiritium*, but only what modern scholars call bonitary rights, or praetorian rights, given that it was the praetor who agreed to protect possession of an asset, until usucapion was completed.[15] On the other hand (**b.ii**), there might be the case of a *dominus ex iure Quiritium*, who had manumitted a slave not yet thirty years of age, without observing the statutory provisions relevant to this particular case; the statute in question was the *lex Aelia Sentia*, of AD 4, which prescribed that slaves under thirty years of age should only be freed by the rod (*vindicta*) and after a suitable *consilium* had approved the reason for the manumission.[16]

Even leaving aside this last possibility, given that it is not certain whether the *lex Iunia* followed the *lex Aelia Sentia* or not (see §4 below), the subdivision that I have suggested illustrates that from the outset there were various ways in which de facto freedom might be converted into *libertas Latina*. Indeed, the *lex Iunia* furnished for all such ways the same essential regime, without operating any distinction based on the different presuppositions of living in freedom by the wish of the master. This uniformity is to be explained by the fact that the obstacles, not only practical (**a.i**), but also legal, which circumscribed the position of the bonitary owner (**b.i**), as also

---

[12] For which, see López Barja 1986/7, 129–31.
[13] For a fuller account, see Pellecchi 2015, §2.1.2, on the basis of Gai. *Inst.* 3.56 (on which, see further §5 below); Tac. *Ann.* 13.27.2; *CJ* 7.6.1.6.
[14] One could, for instance, make one's wishes known by means of a letter (for example, *Pauli Sent.* 4.12.2), or record them in other documents (suggested on the basis of *CJ* 7.6.1.6), or let them be inferred from having authorised behaviour of the slave incompatible with slave status (suggested on the basis of *CJ* 7.6.1.5, 7.6.1.9; also [Quint.] *Decl. Min.* 340 and 342). On the way in which this freedom of choice of form of manumission coincides with the likely letter of the *lex Iunia*, see Eisele 1912, 70–1, 95–9.
[15] On manumission by the so-called bonitary or praetorian owner as likely to generate *libertas Latina* (and therefore, before the *lex Iunia*, only de facto liberty authorised by the owner), see Gai. *Inst.* 1.17. On bonitary ownership, see in general Johnston 1999, 58–60.
[16] See Gai. *Inst.* 1.18; Ulp. *Reg.* 1.12; see further §4 below.

of the master who intended to manumit a slave not yet thirty years of age (**b.ii**), were not absolute. In the case of the bonitary owner, the problem would solve itself at the latest at the end of the period of a year of usucapion.[17] In the case of the slave below the legal age, the period required could obviously be much longer, though it must be remembered that *iusta libertas* was not totally excluded; it was only excluded for someone unable to certify that there was a satisfactory justification, of which legion were legally recognised.[18]

All these observations suggest that the author of the *lex Iunia* saw as underpinning *libertas Latina* a certain uniformity, even in relation to someone who manumitted (only) in the presence of friends (*inter amicos*), for economic reasons (**a.ii**). This underpinning is invoked in the *choice* of an owner *not to be circumscribed* by the forms, procedures and timetable prescribed by the law, for the freed slave to achieve full Roman *libertas*. I shall come back to this point when I come to the aims and purpose of the *lex Iunia* below.

§3 Date of the lex Iunia: problems of its authorship

When was it decided that slaves who lived in freedom by the wish of their master – i.e. those *qui in libertate morabant voluntate domini* – should be equated to colonial Latins? It is well known that the question of the date of the *lex Iunia* is complicated: various attempts at addressing the question by numerous Roman legal scholars are reviewed in this volume's Introduction, while López Barja attempts a socio-historical contextualisation in the chapter that follows the present inquiry. In my view, the question is complicated, not to say made unanswerable by two factors: one linked to the identity of the proposer, i.e. the *rogator* (or the *rogatores*) of the *lex*, the other to its juridical content.

The identity of the proposer, and hence the authorship of the measure, has two aspects, one associated with the name given to the statute by the sources, the other with its nature, consular or tribunician. The question of the name is so well known that I do not need to go into detail; in fact, either one accepts Justinian's *Institutes*, the only text that calls the measure the *lex Iunia Norbana*,[19] or one does not, given that all the other sources always call it only the *lex Iunia*.[20] If the statute was consular (see below), the first alternative directs us to the Principate of Tiberius, under whom there was a Iunius and Norbanus consular pair in AD 19; the second, tribunician alternative allows us to point to plausible proposers early in the Principate of Augustus, notably 25 and 17 BC.[21]

---

[17] For the year of usucapion for moveable property, including slaves, see Johnston 1999, 57–8.
[18] See Digest 40.2.15.1 (Paul): 'et longum est, si exequi voluerimus, quia multa merita incidere possunt, quibus honestum sit libertatem cum decreto praestare' ('and it would take a long time, if we wished to go through the matter, since many services may be relevant which make it honourable to offer liberty with justification').
[19] *Inst.* 1.5.3; the testimony of Theophilus (*Paraphrasis Institutionum* 1.5.3) is less clear, but appears to follow the Justinianic handbook.
[20] Gai. *Inst.* 1.22–3, 1.80, 1.167, 2.110, 2.275, 3.56–7, 3.70; Ulp. *Reg.* 1.10, 3.3, 11.16, 11.19, 20.14, 22.3; *Frag. Dos.* 6–8, 12; *CJ* 7.6.1.1a, 7.6.1.12a; *Inst.* 3.7.4; *P. Vindob.* L 26.
[21] See López Barja 1998, 138.

Despite the support which it has,[22] the high date has no decisive arguments in its favour, leaving aside the problem, to which I come in the next section, of the relationship between the *leges Iunia* (*Norbana*) and *Aelia Sentia*, in terms of their juridical content. In fact, there is no reason to reject the testimony of Justinian's *Institutes*. Despite the authority of Mommsen,[23] the hypothesis that the compilers of the imperial handbook might have added the name *Norbana*, so that the statute could be presented as with two names, like the *lex Aelia Sentia*, is in the last resort unconvincing, if only because this would be a concern that the compilers do not seem in general to have felt.[24] Nor should we be particularly surprised that in juridical texts the statute should normally be listed simply as *Iunia*. As has been demonstrated,[25] this is a practice that indeed appears consistent with the economy with which the jurists dealt with other *leges Iuniae*, such as the *lex Iunia Petronia* or the *lex Iunia Vellaea*, both regularly cited by the name of the second consul only, probably indeed to avoid confusion with the *lex Iunia Norbana de manumissionibus*.

If then we accept the information provided by Justinian's *Institutes*, the only way to date the *lex Iunia Norbana* to the reign of Augustus is to abandon the consular *fasti* and suppose that the statute was proposed by an unattested pair of tribunes; but even this idea, propounded in the ensuing chapter by López Barja, is not without its difficulties: in fact, on the one hand, the only text cited in support of the idea, Dionysius of Halicarnassus 4.24.8, offers only indirect confirmation; on the other hand, the idea that a reform of such importance to society should have been entrusted to a plebiscite is contrary to what seems to be the pattern of Augustan legislation.[26] The problem remains.

§4 Date of the lex Iunia; relationship with the lex Aelia Sentia

The second factor that militates against the possibility of offering a precise date for the *lex Iunia* is the irremediable confusion in our sources between its provisions and those of the *lex Aelia Sentia*. I have already mentioned (in §2 above) one overlap between the latter and *libertas Latina*, in the context of the rule that introduced a minimum age for someone to be manumitted; but there must also have been an overlap in the case of two other rules of the *lex Aelia Sentia* that limited access to Roman citizenship, those

---

[22] To the bibliography in Pellecchi 2015, §3.1, add, for an Augustan date, Evans Grubbs 2013, 46; Ligios 2018, 284, n. 10, 298–9; Masi Doria 2018, 557, n. 12; Rodríguez Garrido 2018, 599; for a Tiberian date, Koops 2014, 114; neutral, Ando 2015, 316; Roth 2016a, 622, n. 43; Schipp 2017, 23, n. 65.

[23] Mommsen 1889, 248, n. 1.

[24] See Justinian, *Inst.* 1.20pr., 2.6.2. Equally unprovable, though more plausible, is the suggestion that the compilers might have added the name *Norbana*, misunderstanding either the consular lists for the two-year period 25–24 BC or those of AD 15. For these hypotheses, see López Barja 1998, 138 and Sherwin-White 1973a, 332, n. 2 respectively, the latter now followed by Bisio 2020, 107–8.

[25] See Ferrary 2012a, 583–4.

[26] Given, in particular, the fact that with the attribution of tribunician power to Augustus the tribunes seem to have renounced, at least de facto, their right to legislate: see Ferrary 2012a, 577–8. Note also that from 7 BC begins the period in which legislative reforms were presented as consular proposals, to which alone Augustus lent his authority: see Ferrary 2012a, 582–5.

dealing with the age of the person manumitting and with the behaviour of the person manumitted; the nature of the three cases is as follows:

(a) A slave guilty of one of the kinds of behaviour pilloried by the *lex Aelia Sentia* could indeed be manumitted, but was assigned to the category of *peregrini dediticii*.[27] As in the case of Latinity, the status was assigned by a legislative fiction, equipped with a series of specific norms;[28] in this case, the fiction equated the person manumitted with a foreigner, who had surrendered unconditionally to the Roman people and as a result had no citizenship of any kind.[29]

(b) The law denied any master younger than twenty any right of manumission, except by the rod and where an appropriate *consilium* had approved the *iusta causa manumissionis*, 'proper grounds for manumission'; otherwise, the manumission was void.[30]

(c) The procedure in the previous case was the same as the one discussed already,[31] regarding slaves freed under the age of thirty; the only difference is that in this case the *lex Aelia Sentia*, instead of ruling that manumissions that infringed the rule were void, provided that slaves younger than thirty freed by will were to be equated with those who were in freedom solely through and by the wish of the master, i.e. those *in libertate erant voluntate domini*.[32] In the absence of explicit testimony, it is furthermore probable that most jurists attributed the same status to under-age slaves manumitted by the rod, but without the prior approval of the *causa manumissionis* by a *consilium*.[33]

The problem of the chronological relationship between the two statutes arises principally in relation to the problems posed by the first and third cases just described. As for the first case (**a** above), it is certain that, in the period of Gaius, a delinquent slave manumitted in the presence of friends became a *peregrinus dediticius*.[34] So one wonders if this consequence was or was not already regulated by the *lex Aelia Sentia*, and hence also

---

[27] See Gai. *Inst.* 1.13, 1.15.

[28] Listed in Gai. *Inst.* 1.27, 3.75; also in *Fragmentum Berolinense de iudiciis* 1.2.

[29] Gai. *Inst.* 1.14. Some legal consequences of the equation are discussed in Gai. *Inst.* 1.25, 1.67–8; Ulp. *Reg.* 20.14, 22.2.

[30] See Gai. *Inst.* 1.38, 1.40; Ulp. *Reg.* 1.13; *Frag. Dos.* 13.

[31] See above, §2, with n. 16.

[32] Ulp. *Reg.* 1.12 (second part): 'testamento vero manumissum perinde haberi iubet (lex Aelia Sentia) atque si domini voluntate in libertate esset; ideoque Latinus fit' ('it [the statute] orders someone manumitted by will to be regarded as if they were free by the wish of their master; and so they become a Latin'). On the significance of the end of the passage, see n. 35 below.

[33] This is inferred from the contrast between the consequence described in Gai. *Inst.* 1.17, on the one hand (namely Latinity as the result of enjoying de facto freedom in accordance with the master's wishes), and the isolated view stated in the first part of Ulp. *Reg.* 1.12, on the other hand (namely the persistence of slave status as a consequence of the nullity of the manumission): see Pellecchi forthcoming, §II.4.1.d.

[34] Gai. *Inst.* 1.15: 'huius ergo turpitudinis servos quocumque modo et cuiuscumque aetatis manumissos, nisi pleno iure dominorum fuerint, numquam aut cives Romanos aut Latinos fieri dicemus, sed omni modo dediticiorum numero constitui intellegemus' ('we shall say that slaves (guilty) of such delinquency, in whatever way or at whatever age they have been manumitted, unless they were in the full legal control of their owners, never become Roman or Latin citizens, but we shall understand them to be settled in every respect in the category of *dediticii*').

whether or not this statute already took into consideration the civil freedom of people manumitted among friends. As far as the third case is concerned (**c** above), we have just seen that the *lex Aelia Sentia* prescribed that under-age slaves manumitted by will (and, implicitly, those manumitted by the rod, but without the decision of a *consilium*) were assimilated to those living in freedom by the wish of their master. One wonders also in this case whether the statute related to these persons as already enjoying the status of *libertas Latina*, or as persons who were only under the protection of the praetor.

In relation to both cases, the first option implies that the *lex Iunia* is to be dated before AD 4 and that the *lex Aelia Sentia* affected Junian Latinity, in two ways; the second option implies the exact opposite, and hence that the *lex Iunia* is to be dated after AD 4 and that it was this statute that, in introducing *libertas Latina*, affected the positions regulated by the *lex Aelia Sentia*.[35] While aware that no decisive answer is possible, I have the impression that the second option is preferable and in consequence that the *lex Iunia* is the later of the two statutes. This option depends on what the sources have to say about two further provisions of the *lex Aelia Sentia*, whose function was to complete the complex of rules relating to the two cases just described, and to which we must now turn.

(**a**) As far as delinquent slaves are concerned who have been manumitted, the further provision in question related to the succession to them: we know that the *lex Aelia Sentia* provided that on the death of a *libertus dediticius* their property descended to the person who had manumitted them or to their successors; we know also that in order to bring this about the statute made use of a second fiction, which meant in practice that their property was disposed of according to the rules relating either to Roman freedpersons (i.e. to freedpersons endowed with Roman *civitas*) or to *liberti Latini*, depending on the status which the slave would have had if not delinquent. At the end of a passage designed to explain this mechanism, Gaius comments that in the case of the succession of a *dediticius* who would have become a Latin if they had not suffered from some defect ('si in aliquo vitio non esset') the intentions of the legislator were nonetheless not clear.[36]

Without going into detail, it seems to me that the most economical way to explain this judgement is to suppose that the *lex Aelia Sentia* preceded the *lex Iunia*, rather

---

[35] In this case also, there are two consequences: on the one hand, we must suppose that the norms relating to *liberti dediticii* were extended also to those manumitted *inter amicos*, either by a specific rule of the *lex Iunia* or just by the jurists – if the *lex Aelia Sentia* related to delinquent slaves simply as manumitted persons as such; see further Pellecchi forthcoming, §2.2.3b. On the other hand, we may suppose that the recognition of *libertas Latina* was beneficial not only to those manumitted *inter amicos*, but also to those manumitted according to the legal formalities, which was entrusted to praetorian protection according to the *lex Aelia Sentia* and the majority view of the jurists pertaining to it (see n. 33 above), i.e. slaves under thirty manumitted by will or by the rod (without the endorsement of a *consilium*). Seen this way, the phrase which Ulp. *Reg.* 11.2 adds to the paraphrase of the clause of the *lex Aelia Sentia*, namely *ideoque Latinus fit* (see n. 32 above), must be taken as relating to a consequence of the passage of the *lex Iunia*; see further Pellecchi 2015, §3.1.2.

[36] Gai. *Inst.* 3.74–6; the relevant lines are in 3.76: 'eorum vero bona, qui si non in aliquo vitio essent, manumissi futuri Latini essent, perinde tribuuntur patronis, ac si Latini decessissent; nec me praeterit non satis in ea re legis latorem voluntatem suam verbis expressise' ('but the property of those who when manumitted would have been Latins, if they had not been (guilty) of some delinquency, falls to their patrons, as if they had died as Latins; and I am not unaware that the legislator has not expressed his intention clearly enough in that matter').

than the other way round.[37] The clause of the statute expounded by Gaius, the *caput legis*, seems in fact to have been conceived and drafted with reference above all to the succession of delinquent slaves freed by means of one of the proper and legal forms of manumission – *iustae ac legitimae manumissiones*; this would explain how in relation to manumission in this form one managed to interpret it straightforwardly. On the other hand, the clause of the statute posed problems if one wished to apply it to the succession to delinquent slaves manumitted in the presence of friends, i.e. *inter amicos*. Given this state of play, the easiest thing to do is to suppose that a clause of this type was the work of a legislator who did not yet have to face the legal effects (i.e. *libertas Latina*) of manumission *inter amicos*.[38]

(**c**) As far as slaves under thirty are concerned, who might have been manumitted without observing the conditions imposed by the *lex Aelia Sentia*, the additional rule laid down a procedure that might make it possible for them to regularise their position. It was laid down in fact that if they married a Roman or a Latin or someone of their own status and had a child who survived to the age of one, such people would transfer from Latin status (*libertas Latina*) to full freedom (*iusta libertas*) and hence to Roman citizenship. This procedure, known as *anniculi causae probatio* (the 'documentation of the position of a one-year-old child'), is attributed by numerous sources to the *lex Aelia Sentia*.[39] Nonetheless, it must be admitted that other passages of the same juridical sources either attribute the whole procedure to the *lex Iunia*,[40] or cite the two statutes together on the legitimacy to be attributed to marriage between Junian Latins and Romans.[41] Here also, without going into detail, one can say that the only way of reconciling the two groups of texts is to suppose that the procedure of *anniculi causae probatio* was indeed introduced by the *lex Aelia Sentia*, but only for slaves formally manumitted, and that the *lex Iunia* took the whole matter up again, extending the procedure to under-age slaves informally manumitted.[42]

---

[37] For fuller details, see Pellecchi forthcoming, §II.2.3e.

[38] For a different view, see Ligios 2018, 295–8, who leaves open the possibility that the *lex Aelia Sentia* dealt with the succession to a *libertus dediticius* with two provisions, one expressly related to someone formally manumitted and the other related to someone manumitted *inter amicos* (and further inferring that the *lex Aelia Sentia* was later than the *lex Iunia*). This reconstruction, however, fails to explain how the (assumed) provision reserved specifically for those manumitted *inter amicos* relates to the view expressed by Gaius at the end of *Inst.* 3.76, namely that the legislator had not expressed his intention clearly enough. On the other hand, the hesitation of Gaius is easily explained if one supposes that the *lex Aelia Sentia* contained only a single clause, which referred to *liberti dediticii* simply as freed slaves as such (which in abstract terms allowed to include those manumitted *inter amicos*), but in addition dealt with their succession, using terms such as *hereditas* and *bonorum possessio* strictly applicable to those formally manumitted. For further discussion, see Pellecchi forthcoming, §II.3.2c (2–3).

[39] See Gai. *Inst.* 1.29: 'ex lege Aelia Sentia cautum est' ('it is provided by the *lex Aelia Sentia*'); Ulp. *Reg.* 7.4: 'ex lege Aelia Sentia nupta' ('[a woman] married according to the *lex Aelia Sentia*'); *TH*² 89: 'e lege Aelia Sentia causam probare' ('to document the position (of a child) according to the *lex Aelia Sentia*').

[40] See Ulp. *Reg.* 3.3: 'liberis ius Quiritium consequitur Latinus, qui minor triginta annorum manumissionis tempore fuit; nam lege Iunia cautum est, ut [. . .]' ('a Latin, who was under thirty at the time of manumission, acquires the right of citizenship by means of children; for it is provided by the *lex Iunia* that [. . .]').

[41] See Gai. *Inst.* 1.80: 'per legem Aeliam Sentiam et Iuniam conubium inter eos dari' ('for the right of intermarriage to be granted between them by means of the *lex Aelia Sentia* and the *lex Iunia*').

[42] For further discussion, see Pellecchi 2015, §3.1.3, with the bibliography there listed.

§5 Aim(s) of the lex Iunia

The uncertainty over the exact date of the *lex Iunia* carries with it further uncertainties regarding the legal contents of this statute and the *lex Aelia Sentia*.[43] These uncertainties have in any case relative importance with regard to another fundamental question about the original form of *libertas Latina*, i.e. the aim or aims of the *lex Iunia*.

As noted on numerous occasions also in other chapters in this study, on this issue, scholars are divided: the majority hold that the aim was to provide for the *morantes in libertate voluntate domini*, i.e. for those who enjoyed freedom on the basis of the wish of their master, to escape from the limbo of not civil (*iure civili*) but de facto freedom, where they depended on praetorian protection.[44] In this perspective, something that the magistrate could not guarantee, in particular being able to start a family and create a legitimate descent, was now guaranteed by the statute. Other scholars hold that the statute, rather than being concerned with the problems and aspirations of people who benefited from praetorian protection, was concerned to offer their former owners new and more effective means of exploiting those who were subject to them.[45]

This second view is based on the rule that has contributed most to interest in Junian Latinity, already in antiquity,[46] and to which we must now return. Thus, and as noted earlier (see §1 above), the *lex Iunia* provided that at the death of a Latin freedperson their property did not pass to their descendants (or to someone else chosen by them), but to their former owner. This meant that the freedperson continued to work for the person who had freed him or her. As a result, it has been held that Latin liberty was a screen, from a juridical point of view, introduced above all to benefit those who manumitted; these could in fact continue to exploit the labour of their freedpersons, as if they were still slaves, or in any case without certain juridical constraints that slavery involved, to the disadvantage of the owner: it has been held in particular that the reform allowed the owner to trade through an intermediary in sectors debarred on social grounds to the elite and on legal grounds if the manumitter was a senator.[47]

Although attractive, the hypothesis does not convince. There is no doubt that one of the consequences of the *lex Iunia* was to simplify a legal framework that in relation to property could only be managed with considerable difficulty by means of praetorian protection. As a result of the availability of *libertas Latina*, owners were relieved of the burden of providing for representation in court of the *morantes* in relation to third parties.[48] But that this simplification should have been sought in order to strengthen the position of

---

[43] It is hard to decide how, whether by statute or by interpretation, and in the case of the former, by what linking mechanism the later statute related to the preceding statute, where the two sets of provisions overlapped: on this problem, partly dealt with here, see for a fuller exposition Pellecchi forthcoming, §§2.2.3, 2.3.3, 2.4.2, 2.6.3, 3.3e, 3.4e, 3.5d.

[44] See above all López Barja 2008, 219–22; Mouritsen 2011, 85–7.

[45] See esp. Sirks 1981, 257–74; see also Roth 2010b, 110–11, who sees the economic advantage on the part of the masters-cum-patrons as a welcome side-effect of the statute.

[46] See Salv. *Eccl.* 3.7.33: 'quos scilicet iubent [the owners rather than the Junian Latins] quidem sub libertorum titulo agere viventes, sed nolunt quidquam habere morientes' ('those whom their owners order to live under the name of freedpersons, but whom they wish to have nothing when they die'), with the discussion by de Wet in Chapter 10.

[47] Brief discussion is in Sirks 1981, 269; Roth 2010b, 110.

[48] See Pellecchi 2015, §2.1.1b.

patrons goes against the only ancient evidence for the aims of the person(s) who drafted the *lex Iunia* and presented it to the assembly. Such evidence is provided by Gaius in his *Institutes*, at 3.56, the full text of which, together with an English translation, is given in the Introduction to this volume;[49] here, it is necessary to requote the relevant lines of interest to the present inquiry:

> legis itaque Iuniae lator cum intellegeret futurum, ut ea fictione res Latinorum defunctorum ad patronos pertinere desinerent, quia scilicet neque ut servi decederent, ut possent iure peculii res eorum ad patronos pertinere, neque liberti Latini hominis bona possent manumissionis iure ad patronos pertinere, necessarium existimavit, ne beneficium istis datum in iniuriam patronorum converteretur, cavere [voluit], ut bona eorum proinde ad manumissores pertinerent, ac si lex lata non esset. itaque iure quodam modo peculii bona Latinorum ad manumissores ea lege pertinent.

The starting point of the reasoning of Gaius is that the decision to attribute the status of colonial Latins to those whom their owners had authorised to live in freedom would effectively throw a spanner in the patronal works, concerning the economic expectations of their owners. On the one hand, given their legally free status, one could not claim that the *morantes* died as slaves (with an estate that in such a case would have belonged to whoever had conceded the de facto enjoyment of freedom to them). On the other hand, insofar as they had been declared Latins, one could not claim in any way to apply to them the rules of succession pertaining to *Roman* freedpersons, which attributed to the patrons financial expectations that varied according to the gender of the deceased freedperson, to the nature of their estate, to the existence of a will, or to the existence of children, or their number.[50] As a result, an ad hoc measure was necessary to prevent the benefit of *libertas Latina* resulting in the loss by the manumitter of such property as would have fallen to them if the statute had not changed the status of those whom they had authorised to live in freedom:[51] as Gaius explains, 'so that a benefit conferred on them [i.e. the freedpersons] should not cause damage to the patron' ('ne beneficium istis datum in iniuriam patronorum converteretur').

From this complex account there emerge two clear facts. The first is that the perspective of the legislator was not that suggested by some modern scholars. In the account given by Gaius, the concern of the statute for the financial interest of the manumitter is summed up in the phrase 'damage to the patron': Gaius, in talking

---

[49] See above, p. 4.

[50] For a comprehensive account, dealing with the complicated relationship between praetorian provisions, for estates worth less than 100,000 sesterces, or those of the *lex Papia Poppaea*, for estates worth more, see Voci 1963, 27–8, 31–2, 742–3.

[51] As Gaius puts it, the author of the *lex Iunia* would have framed his measure in such a way that the estate of the manumitted person belonged to their patron as if the statute had not been passed. The normal interpretation is that the statute involved a second fiction, that cancelled out the fiction involved in the primary provision, in effect pretending not to have pretended that those who enjoyed liberty solely on the basis of the wish of their master were colonial Latins. On this matter, see most recently Ando 2015, 316–17; more cautiously, Bianchi 2012, §4, suggesting that it was only Gaius who summed up the actual effect as being 'as if the statute had not been passed'.

of *iniuria*, 'damage', to someone who had authorised their slave to live in de facto freedom, does so precisely for the reason indicated above (in §2), in asking why the *lex Iunia*, although there were various circumstances that could create *libertas Latina*, created a single regime. Leaving aside the question of the time necessary for usucapion and the procedures called for to enfranchise someone under thirty, the reason is that when a slave found themselves authorised *only* to live in de facto freedom, instead of being formally manumitted by the rod, through the census, or by testament, they could see their position as objectively the result of a decision by their owner to grant *only* partial freedom, without compromising the financial expectations that would have been lost with the grant of formal freedom. The damage to the owners-cum-patrons, i.e. the *iniuria patronorum*, thus consisted in the fact that, by transforming the *morantes* from persons who enjoyed de facto freedom to persons who enjoyed freedom *de iure* (i.e. as Latins), the manumitters would have deprived themselves of estates which they had not at all expected to renounce. Precisely the fact that Gaius presents the matter as damage, *iniuria*, that would have been the result of assimilating the persons in question to colonial Latins shows that what the legislator had in mind was the *beneficium* of freedom, a gift that the state had granted to the *morantes*, and in their interest. It is true that the state protected also the interest of the manumitter, but it did so by way of a provision that was additional to the satisfaction of the aspiration of the manumitted slave to be able to finally enjoy freedom, even if limited, as of right.

It is obvious that the interpretation here proposed of *Inst.* 3.56 does not exclude the possibility that the solution devised by the *lex Iunia* may have given the owner further ways of using those subject to them to greater advantage, in business or otherwise. But it is hard to believe that this was the original aim of the reform; furthermore, the existence of a procedure such as the *anniculi causae probatio*, allowing the Junian Latin to escape from the limitations on their freedom, supports my argument. For we have already seen in the previous section that this procedure allowed the transfer from *libertas Latina* to the status of *Roman* freedpersons (i.e. those who enjoyed *civitas*) by means of a provision that was probably introduced by the *lex Aelia Sentia* to the advantage of slaves under thirty manumitted by will, then picked up by the *lex Iunia* and extended to slaves under thirty who had been manumitted informally. It is to be emphasised that by becoming a *Roman* freedperson by the rule relating to a one-year-old son, the person freed *inter amicos* transferred under the law of succession as applicable to (enfranchised) Roman freedpersons, which was obviously much more disadvantageous to the former owner. Given that there was this right for a Latin to acquire Roman citizenship by means of their children, i.e. this *ius adipiscendae civitatis per liberos*, it is hard to suppose that the *lex Iunia* saw the (private) interest of the patron as the centrepiece of the reform that it introduced; rather, it did not hesitate to prefer to the protection of the latter the (public) interest of the state in population growth.[52]

Against this interpretation, resulting from the *anniculi causae probatio*, the uncertainty over the chronological relationship between the *leges Iunia et Aelia Sentia* is of little significance. It is true that the *lex Iunia* might be datable earlier, in theory to 25 or 17 BC (see §3 above); it is also true that it could be the *lex Aelia Sentia* that

---

[52] See on this Koops 2014, 123–4.

included those freed *inter amicos* among the beneficiaries of the *anniculi causae probatio*, thus reducing the rights of their manumitters. There would remain the problem of explaining such a radical change in the socio-political significance of *libertas Latina* in the course of the twenty or thirty years between the two statutes.

§6 The legal status of Junian Latins: the origins of a (partial) 'black hole'

Having discussed the reasons for the *lex Iunia*, the problem of its date, its principal provisions and other matters that it has been necessary to recall, it is now time to lay out the remaining materials in order to complete the analysis of the rules that the statute made for the new category of freed individuals.

Thus, we know that Junian Latins had *commercium*,[53] but that not all jurists agreed that they had rights to intermarry with Roman citizens (see §7 below). This relationship was further constrained by the rigid complex of rules concerning inheritance rights: Junian Latins could not accept legacies or inheritances left them by Roman citizens (which thus fell to the imperial treasury) if within 100 days from the opening of the will (or the *dies cretionis*) they had not themselves acquired the citizenship of the deceased person(s).[54] As a consequence of the general lack of succession rights, they also could not be made guardians under the terms of a will;[55] our sources discuss, moreover, whether a Junian Latin could be assigned to an under-age Roman as a *tutor Atilianus*.[56] Completely excluded, finally, was any right to make a will.[57] This rule was the corollary of the fact that at the death of a Junian Latin their estate went to the person who had manumitted them, discussed in the previous section; their descendants were therefore also excluded from intestate succession to them.

A summary such as I have just offered, in more or less detail, forms a traditional and useful part of any account of Junian Latinity. At the same time, a fundamental question is still unanswered: how can we really understand the nature and the composition of the problems with which the *lex Iunia* grappled? As I have mentioned in my introduction, the sources that allow us to draw up our account of the original content of *libertas Latina* consist essentially of three pieces of juristic writing of the imperial period: the *Commentarii institutionum* of Gaius, the *Liber singularis regularum* of Ulpian (or attributed to him), and the so-called *Fragmentum Dositheanum de manumissionibus*. The last two are not even preserved complete.[58] A further problem concerning the *Fragmentum Dositheanum* is that it is not the original text but a Greek version, undertaken as a school exercise in translation, with a back-translation into Latin, full of grammatical errors and even misunderstandings.[59] Whether complete or not, and in the original

---

[53] See Ulp. *Reg.* 19.4.
[54] Gai. *Inst.* 1.23, 2.275; Ulp. *Reg.* 17.1, 22.3, 25.7; *Gnomon* of the *Idios Logos* 19.
[55] See Gai. *Inst.* 1.23; Ulp. *Reg.* 11.16.
[56] See Pellecchi 2015, §2.1.2a.
[57] See Ulp. *Reg.* 20.14.
[58] On the two works, see the important discussions of Daalder forthcoming; Mitchell forthcoming.
[59] For a couple of examples, see nn. 6 and 8 above.

version or not, the essential feature of all three works is that they are introductory pieces, intended to offer only a brief and general account of the law of the Roman people. The effect of all this on our understanding of *libertas Latina* is directly intertwined with the work of Gaius: it is the only one of the three to have been transmitted more or less complete, and is thus the fullest account of the matter, even though a substantial lacuna falls precisely in the course of one of the discussions of Junian Latins.

That said, Gaius' *Institutes* do not offer an organic treatment of *libertas Latina*; rather, the material is distributed in the three parts into which the work is famously divided – persons (*personae*), things (*res*) and actions (*actiones*). In the first part (*personae*), the subject is directly addressed at the outset, with the division into the three categories of freedpersons (*tria genera libertinorum*), i.e. Romans, Latins and *dediticii* (§12). Inverting, however, what seems the natural order,[60] Gaius begins by explaining how a freedperson becomes a member of the third category (§§14–15), rather than the first (§§16–21) or the second (§22). At the point at which the discussion moves from Roman to Latin freedom, there is the lacuna that I have mentioned. Nonetheless, from what survives at the end of the lacuna and later (§§23–35), it appears that Gaius privileged the factors that made it possible to compare the status of Junian Latins with that of *dediticii*, in particular in relation to the right to make a will and to the possibility of acquiring Roman citizenship.[61]

When the matter reappears, still in the first part, the focus is no longer on *libertas Latina*. Thus, in relation to *patria potestas*, Gaius recalls in fact the *anniculi causae probatio* (§§65–6) and then links this with a further procedure that regularises the family, known as *erroris causae probatio*, 'documentation of the position of error' (§§67–86). Both procedures allowed the persons concerned to acquire Roman citizenship, either a whole family or individuals begotten by a Roman father. This involved the remarkable consequence that someone might find themselves under the (Roman) power of their biological father, not at the moment of their birth, but only later.[62] Seen this way, it is obvious that Gaius returns to the topic in the context of (one of) the distinctive rights of the Roman people. Similarly, when the treatise has moved on to dealing with things (*res*), Gaius returns to the position of a Junian Latin, in relation first to the various rules for Roman wills (in Book 2),[63] and

---

[60] For a possible explanation, see Battaglia 2020, 209–10.

[61] The right to make a will or to inherit in relation to the two categories of freedpersons are compared in §§24–5; the greater restrictions on *dediticii* form the bridge to the greater limitations in relation to personal status (§§26–7), above all the impossibility of acquiring Roman citizenship; this then leads by way of contrast (*per differentiam*) to the existence of this possibility in the case of Junian Latins (§§28–35).

[62] Gai. *Inst.* 1.65–6: 'aliquando autem evenit, ut liberi, qui statim ut nati sunt, parentum in potestate non fiant, ii postea tamen redigantur in potestatem, velut si Latinus ex lege Aelia Sentia uxore ducta filium procreaverit etc.' ('but sometimes happens that children do not enter the power of their parents at the moment of their birth, but are later brought under power; as in the case of a Latin according to the *lex Aelia Sentia*, who after marrying begot a child etc.').

[63] This normally occurs in the context of a freed Latin person as the beneficiary of the dispositions made in the will of a Roman citizen, in connection either with the problem of the missing right to inherit (§§110, 275) or with the rule that the birth of a son invalidates the will (§§142–3, where the birth is seen metaphorically as the acquisition by the son of Roman citizenship, thanks to *anniculi causae probatio*). On the problem passage §195, which seems to refer to a Junian Latin, not as the subject of a disposition of a Roman will, but as its object, in fact by means of a legacy *per vindicationem*, see Sirks 1983, 274–7.

then to the expectations of Roman manumitters as to the estates of their deceased freedpersons (in Book 3).[64]

The (piece of) information offered by Gaius on Junian Latins is then of two kinds: the first devoted precisely to *libertas Latina*, but with material chosen to highlight specificities and presented through the topic of *differentia*, involving the lacuna at §§21–2 of Book 1;[65] the second, less specific, because presented in the context of different institutions (*patria potestas* and the law of succession), treating *libertas Latina* as something that might have an impact on the rights of the Roman people. It is as a result of this strategy that the image of Weaver's famous 'black hole' comes to relate not only to the family relationships and social position of Junian Latins, but also to their juridical definition. The fact that the handbook of Gaius is our principal source for the juridical position of this particular category of freedpersons means that the category can only be understood insofar as it can be fitted into the analytical structure adopted by Gaius. In other words, if *libertas Latina*, and in particular the *lex Iunia*, had an impact only on one of the many topics not treated by Gaius, his work would not have helped us to understand the institution.

In sum, fundamental questions on the legal status of Junian Latins cannot be resolved, given the poverty and the nature of the other available legal sources,[66] and similarly of the occasional fragment of a new document which raises issues that cannot at the moment be answered.[67] But this means that Gaius' *Institutes* and the other introductory handbooks constitute a limit beyond which one proceeds as if walking on quicksand.

§7 The 'black hole' and questions of Latinity

The fragmentary nature of their textual transmission and the elementary content of the available legal sources are not the only factors that limit our capacity to reach an understanding of the original legal status of Junian Latins; two other factors deepen the 'black hole'. One concerns the technicalities that the *lex Iunia* uses to create *libertas Latina*; the other (to which I come in the next section) involves the relationship with the *lex Aelia Sentia*, but from a point of view that is different from that of earlier scholarship, including my own treatment in §4 above.

---

[64] The account of intestate succession to the estate of Latin freedpersons occupies §§55–73, split between the regime of the *lex Iunia* (§§55–62, contrasting it with intestate succession to *Roman* freedpersons) and the changes made by the *Senatus Consultum Largianum* (§§63–73) as well as by later imperial legislation (§§72–3).

[65] The *differentia*-pattern is the one most frequently adopted by Gaius, along with *diaeresis*, 'definition', textual commentary, or example: see Battaglia 2020, *passim* and the conclusion at 275–6.

[66] One should consider the question of the ability of Junian Latins to marry and have legitimate offspring (on which, see in general Weaver 1997, 57, 60–4). From the point of view of the legal sources, the question can be addressed only indirectly, on the basis of scattered and indirect pieces of evidence concerning dowries: see *CJ* 7.6.1.9, for a dowry created by a patron for a *Latina Iuniana*, as well as the *Gnomon* of the *Idios Logos* 26, for a dowry created by a *Iuniana* herself. Nothing appears in Gaius on this, since he excludes dowry from the subjects to be discussed (see esp. Stagl 2014).

[67] The reference is to *P.Vindob.* L 26; a draft of a new edition by S. Ammirati, D. Mantovani and P. Mitchell (from the Pavia REDHIS project) is available at http://papyri.info/dclp/64818. A fragment of what was certainly the work of a classical jurist (the editors think of Callistratus) attributes to the *lex Iunia* (recto, col. II, ll. 2–3) a 'dare eos inter Latinos', which for syntactical and lexical reasons cannot relate to any of the known rights under the law (*libertas, testamenti factio, tutela,* and so on). Furthermore, the mystery is deepened by the fact that the text seems to include a reference to aediles (in line 1, integrated), a magistracy that the sources had so far in no way related to the *lex Iunia*.

To contextualise the first set of problems, we must return to the fundamental provision of the *lex Iunia*, discussed in §1 above, namely the fact that in order to confer freedom as of right on the *morantes in libertate voluntate domini*, the statute uses the trick of pretending that they were freeborn Roman citizens who had enrolled in a Latin colony. For the new category of freedpersons, it was thus the juridical status of colonial Latins that the legislator took as his model, with the limitations that we have already in part considered and to which I return shortly.

There were, however, two types of colonial Latins: the original category consisted of freeborn Roman citizens who renounced their citizenship to enrol in a newly founded Latin colony; the category ceased to be used after about 180 BC (or perhaps about forty years later in Spain),[68] but was joined after the Social War by the category of so-called fictitious colonial Latins, not of Roman origin but members of foreign communities, advanced in their relationship with Rome by the grant of the Latin right.[69] The question is then to which category Junian Latins were assimilated – the original category or the category created after the Social War (see Chapter 1 in this volume, where García Fernández argues for the former of these options).

The question arises above all with regard to *conubium*, the 'right of intermarriage' with Roman citizens: by reason of their Roman origin, the original Latin colonists certainly had it.[70] In the case of Junian Latins, I have already noted that juristic opinion was divided, with some, albeit a minority, holding that if the statute conceded the right to Latin freedpersons, it did so by virtue of the *anniculi causae probatio* and the marriage in question.[71] It is therefore easy to suppose that the *lex Iunia*, apart from the measures relating to a one-year-old child, did not have a chapter specifically relating to *conubium*. One has then to suppose that this fact enabled the majority of juristic opinion to deny that the statute made any change to the status that was its model, namely that of Latins who must at the latest with the *lex Minicia*[72] have lost *conubium* (with Romans).[73]

---

[68] See Sisani 2018a, 335–47.

[69] On the limited and ambivalent nature of the concept of 'fictitious' Latin colonies, see Maganzani 2017 *passim*, with the conclusions at 79–81.

[70] See Kremer 2006, 27–30, 116–17; Roselaar 2013, 109.

[71] See Pellecchi 2015, §§2.1.2a, 3.1.3b, arguing from Gaius, *Inst.* 1.80. For the text of the passage, see also Briguglio 2020, 396–402, especially regarding doubts of a palaeographical nature about the reading adopted following the edition by Studemund.

[72] See Gai. *Inst.* 1.78–9: 'quod autem diximus, inter civem Romanam peregrinumque nisi conubium sit (?), qui nascitur peregrinum esse, lege Minicia cautum est, ut is quidem deterioris parentis condicionem sequatur; eadem lege ex diverso cavetur ut si peregrinam, cum qua ei conubium non sit, uxorem duxerit civis Romanus, peregrinus ex eo coitu nascatur; [. . .] adeo autem hoc ita est ut ex [lacuna of 2½ lines] non solum exterae nationes et gentes, sed etiam qui Latini nominantur; sed ad alios Latinos pertinet, qui proprios populos propriasque civitates habebant et erant peregrinorum numero' ('but in relation to what I have said, that unless there is right of intermarriage between a Roman citizen woman and a foreigner, any offspring is a foreigner, it was provided by the *lex Minicia* that such offspring should have the status of the lesser partner; the same statute, on the other hand, provides that if a Roman citizen marries a foreign woman, with whom he does not have the right of intermarriage, offspring of such a union is a foreigner; this is so to such an extent that [lacuna of 2½ lines] not only external [to Italy] peoples, but also those who are called Latins; but this relates to other Latins').

[73] The date of the statute may belong anywhere between 121 BC and the Augustan or Tiberian period: see most recently García Fernández 2018, 387, with nn. 31 and 34. It is also true that the innovation attributed by Gaius to the *lex Minicia*, namely that in the absence of the right of intermarriage offspring

The relationship between Latinity and freedom according to the *lex Iunia* is complicated by a further factor, linked to the difficulty of pinpointing the criteria according to which the statute, on the one hand, adopted assimilation to colonial Latins, but then, on the other hand, derogated from this status in order to create Junian Latinity by means of supplementary measures. To these chapters belonged above all the chapter that reserved for the manumitters the estates of deceased Junian Latins. As we have seen, Gaius is explicit that this measure formed a derogation to the rest of the statute, in the sense that it was included in the *lex Iunia* to prevent the assimilation to colonial Latins having as an unwanted consequence the loss by the manumitters of the estates of those manumitted in the presence of friends. The need for such supplementary measures is the result of the fact that any issue on which the statute lacked a specific provision was determined as for colonial Latins, as we have seen in the case of the right of intermarriage. Seen in this complementary fashion, one may wonder whether one may extend the argument and deduce that every specific chapter of the *lex Iunia* was the consequence of the need to apply to Junian Latins rules different from those that applied to the status on which theirs was modelled. Put in such rigid and schematic terms, the question is perhaps false, since any reply would homogenise a richer and more complex historical reality.

A good example of the need for caution is the group of measures of the *lex Iunia* which together relate to what the Roman jurists described as passive *testamenti factio*, i.e. the right to receive under a will and to appear in a will (of a Roman citizen) as heir, or legatee, or guardian. For the Junian Latin, as we know (and discussed in §6), to be named as a guardian was wholly excluded, to be an heir or legatee only slightly less absolutely – either of these was possible with the acquisition of Roman citizenship within 100 days of the opening of the will. That these prohibitions formed part of the *lex Iunia* is certain. What is less certain is that they applied to colonial Latins, whether original or fictitious; one might infer from Cicero that the rights in question belonged only to the citizens of some Latin colonies,[74] therefore as a privilege, whose date, recent or not, we do not know.[75]

With such limited information, it is obvious that anyone who tried to contextualise the logic behind the drafting of the *lex Iunia* could not in fact rule out *any* solution. In theory, it is clearly possible that, apart from a few exceptional cases, colonial Latins laboured under a general ban on being heirs or legatees of Roman citizens, a ban to

---

acquired the status of the lesser parent, not necessarily that of the mother, as under the *ius gentium*, does not necessarily mean that the statute had also removed the right of intermarriage from Latins. The measure that infringed, at any rate in the sphere of marriage, the original Latin right, could thus be earlier than the *lex Minicia*, whatever its date. Some scholars in fact attribute the removal of the right of intermarriage between Romans and Latins to the creation of fictitious Latinity, with the *lex Pompeia* of 89 BC on Cisalpine Gaul: see Barbati 2013, 104.

[74] Cic. *Caecin*. 102: 'iubet enim [i.e. the *lex Cornelia* on removing citizenship from the Volaterrani] eodem iure esse quo fuerint Ariminenses; quos quis ignorat duodecim coloniarum fuisse et a civibus Romanis hereditates capere potuisse?' ('for it [the *lex Cornelia*] orders them [the Volaterrani] to have the same rights as the Ariminenses; and everyone knows that they were one of the twelve colonies and could be heirs to Roman citizens').

[75] See Roselaar 2013, 114, with n. 61 for the bibliography.

which the *lex Iunia* had no choice but to have recourse. It is also possible that the statute indeed took up the ban, but added some supplementary element, for instance the period of 100 days granted to Junian Latins to regularise their position. From this would follow that the general ban and that of the *lex Iunia* did not coincide in every particular. There is, however, a third possibility, namely that the statute took up the ban simply to avoid a lack of clarity, given that Latin colonies did not enjoy a single, uniform status.

Faced with such a slippery state of affairs, one can only maintain an open mind: for situations not explicitly ordered by the statute, it is likely that the rules applicable to colonial Latins were effective; where these rules had undesirable consequences, it was necessary to adopt specific measures, to order the matter differently. It does not, however, follow that every such specific measure responded to the need to remove those who had been assimilated to it from the complex of rules for colonial Latins.

§8 The 'black hole' and patronal dimensions (honor, operae, bona)

As we have seen (in §1 above), as a result of the *lex Iunia* and the use of the juridical status of colonial Latins, informal manumissions finally came within the purview of Roman private law, transforming those enjoying de facto freedom based solely on the wish of their master from being slaves into being freedpersons. Leaving aside the derogations from that status imposed by the same statute, there is thus no doubt that the Junian Latin status depended directly on their assimilation to (colonial) Latins. But there is a further question: did the content of this statute depend also in part on norms relating to freed status in general, in particular on those laid down by the *lex Aelia Sentia*?

This further question needs to be asked, because the *lex Aelia Sentia* was not confined to regulating what may be described as the *modus manumittendi*, the mode of manumission, dealing with the conditions and procedures relating to full and legal manumission. To the norms concerned that we have already discussed (in §4 above), the statute linked various other measures relating to patronage, above all in order to avoid manumission imposing overly burdensome obligations, incompatible with the freed status being conferred. At the same time, precisely with regard to the rules relevant to the *modus manumittendi*, we have already seen (also in §4 above) that neither the statute nor the jurists were unaware of the problem of extending the existing rules to informal manumission. Hence my further question: apart from the rules pertaining to the modes of manumission, might the *lex Aelia Sentia* have had an impact on *libertas Latina* by means of the rules relating to patronage?

Before beginning a detailed discussion of the legislative rules involved, it is necessary to offer some general introductory remarks on how patronage of *Roman* freedpersons was related to that of Junian Latins: since the one was not the same as the other, one cannot avoid considering whether and how far norms for patrons and Roman freedpersons applied also to patrons and Latin freedpersons. To begin with, the main prerogatives of the manumitter in patronage of Roman freedpersons were three: the *honor*, i.e. the respect due to the patron, which prevented the freedperson from suing the patron or their close relatives, without first being authorised by the praetor; a series of expectations in relation to the property of a deceased freedperson, i.e. their *bona*, differently affected by the praetorian edict and by the *lex Papia Poppaea*; and finally, the right to demand and impose *operae*.[76] With regard to Junian Latins, there are no issues pertaining to the first two topics. As regards the *bona*, I have mentioned several times that the *lex Iunia* ruled on this subject in a completely different way than with regard to Roman freedmen. The law destined the whole of a patrimony, not a part, to the manumitter and regardless of whether the freedman left a will or a legitimate offspring or not.[77] As far as respect is concerned, the situation is different, namely that the Latin freedperson was also constrained by the so-called *venia edicti*: it is true that the text on which such a conclusion is based relates to a particular case, in a period that is later than the *lex Iunia*; but there is no reason to doubt that the privilege belonged to the patron of a Latin freedperson as such.[78]

Quite different, partly because of the outcome, but also because of the complexity of the scholarly discussion, is the question of *operae*: the sources never present them as an additional feature of *libertas Latina*.[79] This 'black hole' within the 'black hole', so to speak, has been variously interpreted: by some as an indication that *operae* were juridically incompatible with *libertas Latina*, by others as an area where the absence of evidence made it impossible to draw any conclusions.[80] An attempt has recently been made to prove the first view on the basis of the fiction involved in the *lex Iunia*. As we have seen (in §1 above), our *morantes in libertate voluntate domini* were granted legally protected freedom by means of the fiction that one was dealing with freeborn Roman citizens, who had left the city of Rome to join a Latin colony and become colonial Latins – thus referred to by Gaius: 'cives Romani ingenui, qui ex urbe Roma in Latinas colonias deducti Latini coloniarii esse coeperunt'.[81] Given that they were being equated with freeborn persons, one may suppose that precisely the *lex Iunia* would have prevented them being saddled with a burden that was typical of freedpersons.[82]

This position, which certainly has the merit of having addressed the problem from a technical point of view not hitherto adopted, is, however, not wholly convincing. The Junian Latin, as we have seen, owed respect to their manumitter in the same way as a *Roman* freedperson, and on their death their whole estate passed to their

---

[76] See in general Albanese 1979, 72–95, also for discussion of other minor provisions, not known in detail and not considered here.

[77] See §5 above, with n. 50.

[78] The text in question is Digest 2.4.10.1 (Ulpian), discussing whether the protection of *venia edicti* extends to the owner who, having sold a female slave and then reacquired her, invoking the resolutory clause relating to the situation in which a seller prostituted a slave that they had acquired, continued to prostitute her themselves. That such a case involved *libertas Latina* follows from *CJ* 7.6.1.4, leaving aside the breach of the rule against the prostitution of a slave, if the contract of sale had not included an appropriate clause. We remain ignorant of how imperial legislation managed to subsume such a case under the *lex Iunia*: see Pellecchi 2015, §4.1b.

[79] See Masi Doria 2018, 556, with bibliography.

[80] For different views, see Sirks 1983, 259–60; Waldstein 1986, 162; López Barja 1998, 144.

[81] I.e. in the key passage again: Gai. *Inst.* 3.56.

[82] Masi Doria 2018, 568.

manumitter. This means that the fiction of free birth did not *ex hypothesi* prevent the subordination of the freedperson to their manumitter, but involved the adoption of particular supplementary provisions.[83]

If *operae* and *libertas Latina* were indeed incompatible, this must have been a decision made on the basis of already held values, not one made for technical reasons. Seen this way, it may be better to hypothesise that for Roman freedpersons *operae* and *bona* (i.e. days of labour service and forfeiture of their estate at their decease) were alternative burdens. Despite doubts that have been raised, it seems certain that the praetor, and through him the *lex Papia Poppaea*, prevented the estate of a former slave – the *bonorum possessio liberti* – from passing to a patron who had already exacted days of labour service, i.e. *operae*.[84] If this is right, it looks as if it was precisely the *lex Iunia*, in providing that the estate of a Latin freedperson should fall to their patron, that denied the patron the possibility of demanding days of labour service from them during their lifetime.

§9 The 'black hole' and the lex Aelia Sentia

Having described the legal framework of patronage over Junian Latins, we can return to the question left in suspense, namely whether the *lex Aelia Sentia* contributed to the definition of *libertas Latina* precisely in the field of the rights of patrons.

As we know, there were several rules that the statute devoted to the relationship between a Roman freedperson and their former proprietor. Duties and restrictions affected above all the manumitter, with loss of rights of patronage as the punishment for infringement of the rules. On the one hand, they were obliged to look after an impoverished freedperson, by providing for their upkeep (*alimenta*).[85] On the other

---

[83] As shown by the measure relating to their estate (*bona*), which based the rights of the manumitter on a counter-fiction, or at least on an explicit legislative enactment (see n. 51 above).

[84] The edict denied acquisition of the estate to a patron who had either exacted *operae* or taken money in lieu: see Lenel 1927, 351, basing the first alternative on *Pauli Sent.* 3.2.5 and *CTh* 6.13.2, and the second on Digest 38.1.41 (Papinian) and 50.16.53pr. (Paul). Following Lenel, also Voci 1963, 745; Albanese 1979, 85–6, with n. 304. A different view has been advanced in Masi Doria 1996, 462–77, namely that the edict only dealt with the case in which a patron had forced a freedperson to pay money instead of providing days of labour service ('*operas vendere*'), to be distinguished from the (voluntary) exchange of *operae* with a money payment ('*operas emere*'), where the exchange of money in place of *operae* occurred on the free initiative of the freedperson, not of the patron; for precisely this reason, the praetor did not deprive the patron of the possession. In the present state of our knowledge, this explanation of the edict seems to me both over-complicated and unsatisfactory. On the one hand, it presupposes a radical difference of structure between the two procedures – between *vendere* and *emere operas* – which are rather the two sides of the same coin. The exchange of *operae* is in fact a bilateral agreement. Indeed, it is not apparent why the sources should have spoken of sale (*vendere*) when the patron had enforced the other party to accept the proposal (how?), and of purchase (*emere*) when the initiative was that of the freedperson (without accounting for the fact that for this to work the agreement of the patron would still have been essential). On the other hand, the hypothesis leaves unresolved a textual problem: the edict contains the words 'si donum munus operas redemerit', attested in Digest 50.16.53pr. (Paul). This means that, on the one hand, one has to allow (as Masi Doria in effect does: 1996, 467) that the presumed edictal clause on '*operas vendere*' is not directly attested; on the other hand, one would need to explain why the praetor, alongside the figure of sale (*vendere*), should have also considered that of purchase (*redimere*), something that Masi Doria does not do.

[85] Digest 25.3.6 and 38.2.33 (both Modestinus), 37.14.5.1 (Marcian).

hand, they were denied certain exploitative forms of behaviour, such as demanding money instead of days of labour service, or seeking to impose an oath not to marry.[86] In contrast, the statute threatened with punishment (whose precise nature is not known) a freedperson who turned out to be disrespectful towards the person who had manumitted them.[87] A further provision, that touches on both the *iura patronatus* and the *modus manumittendi*, prevented a freedperson from themselves freeing slaves, if the value of the slaves compromised the expectations of the patron from the inheritance of the freedperson.[88] Of this complex of provisions only the last attracts some attention from Gaius (and from the *Regulae* and the *Fragmentum Dositheanum*) – precisely because it involves the mode of manumission. For all the others, however, it is to the Code and the Digest to which one must turn, not forgetting that the compilers started from the presupposition of the abolition of *libertas Latina* (as mentioned in the introduction to this chapter). The nature of the sources thus produces two complementary consequences. The first is that one cannot expect to find in the Justinianic material any evidence that there may once have been for any extension of this aspect of the *lex Aelia Sentia* to Junian Latins. The second is that the investigation allows only an indirect approach, or rather that one must proceed on a theoretical basis, with all the uncertainties that this implies; in effect, one has to consider the rationale and content of and sanctions for each chapter, and try to assess how far it is reasonable to suppose that any one of them might have been made to cover Latin freedpersons.

In this context, the chapter easiest to deal with is certainly that concerned with *operae*, and the related provision known as *mercedem capere*, i.e. the ban on the patron converting into money the days owed to them. If it is the case that patronage over Latin freedpersons did not involve a right to days of labour service (as proposed in §8 above), it follows that there is no reason to wonder about an extension of the ban; this rule of the *lex Aelia Sentia* therefore remained relevant only to the patrons of *Roman* freedpersons. The position is different for the other two rules by which the *lex Aelia Sentia* allowed for the loss of patronal rights. The first – the obligation to provide for the upkeep of a destitute freedperson – goes back to very ancient norms, entrusting to the *fides* of the patron the assurance to the freedperson of help and protection.[89] The justification of the norms lay obviously in the state of partial dependence of the freedperson, a state which in the case of those manumitted *inter amicos* was even more loaded in favour of the manumitter. So it is possible that the need was here felt to prevent the owner from profiting from the manumission to relieve themselves of the cost of upkeep, the more so in that general morality saw the expense as owed to the actual person of the slave.[90]

---

[86] *Operae*: Digest 38.1.25 (Julian), 40.9.32.1–2 (Terentius Clemens); *CJ* 6.3.7 (Severus Alexander); oath: Digest 38.2.24 and 38.16.3.5 (both Julian), 2.4.8.2 (Ulpian), 37.14.15 (Paul).

[87] See Digest 40.9.30 (Ulpian), 50.16.70 (Paul), who both, however, only discuss who was entitled to present the *accusatio ingrati*. For the content of the sanction involved, see n. 93 below.

[88] See Gai. *Inst.* 1.37; Ulp. *Reg.* 1.15; *Frag. Dos.* 16; Digest 40.12.9.2 (Gaius), 38.5.11 (Paul).

[89] See Pellecchi forthcoming, §3.2c.

[90] See Sen. *Ben.* 3.21.2, along with the rescript of Antoninus Pius, reproduced in *Coll.* 3.3.4. On both texts, see now Liebs 2017, 22–3, 26. In this context, it must be remembered that the position of Latin freedpersons was even more unfavourable because of their exclusion from corn distributions, in contrast, it seems, to the position of *Roman* freedpersons: the matter receives detailed discussion by López Barja in Chapter 3.

A similar approach may be valid for the ban on seeking to impose on the freedperson an oath not to marry, or, alternatively, not to have children. It is plausible, even if not directly attested, that such an oath was motivated by economic factors, to prevent (Roman) freedpersons from having legitimate offspring and thus compromising, or even destroying, the expectation of the patron to inherit.[91] As far as succession is concerned, it is clear that the patrons of Latin freedpersons had nothing to fear. But, if it is the case that the *lex Iunia* guaranteed the manumitters rules of succession that were unequivocally in their favour, it is also the case (at least as argued in §4 above) that it also included the possibility of promotion linked to the presence of a one-year-old child. Given that *anniculi causae probatio* provided for transfer from Latin to Roman status, with all that that implied for questions of succession, it is clear that someone who manumitted *inter amicos* (whether or not the slave was under thirty) had an interest in trying to bind the freedperson with an oath not to marry (and not to have offspring). In this case, as in the previous one, it is thus plausible that the provision of the *lex Aelia Sentia* was extended to patrons of Latin freedpersons, threatening those who infringed it with the loss of property and of immunity from court proceedings – the *bona* and *honor* discussed above (in §8).[92] The hypothesis, that harassment by patrons was forbidden in the same way in the case of both categories of freedpersons, makes it plausible that the same was true in the opposite sense, namely in relation to the rules that protected patrons. Such perfect symmetry, however, can only be hypothesised in relation to the so-called *accusatio ingrati* and its (unknown) sanction.[93] As far as the rule is concerned that protected patrons from fraudulent manumissions by freedpersons, the essential basis of freed Roman and Latin persons was so different that the discussion has to follow a different course.

The ban imposed by the *lex Aelia Sentia* on manumission in order to defraud a patron (*in fraudem patronorum*) complemented two measures of the praetorian edict that allowed a patron to demand the cancellation of gifts by which the freedpersons had reduced their patrimony below what the jurists called the *portio debita*, 'the portion due', namely the amount to which the patron was entitled on the basis of the praetorian edict or the *lex Papia Poppaea*.[94] It is then natural to hold that these rules would not have been applicable as such to manumissions by and gifts from Latin freedpersons during their lifetimes. On the one hand, in a set of rules which assured to the patron the entire patrimony of the freedperson, the very concept of *portio debita* does not fit, given that any manumission or gift by a freedperson would amount to defrauding the patron. On the other hand, the very fact that a Latin freedperson could not dispose at death of any of their property was in itself an even greater temptation to attempt to defraud the patron.

---

[91] See Moreau 2017, §4.6, on the analogous ban, even if the sanction was differently formulated, in the *lex Iulia de maritandis ordinibus*.

[92] There need be no consequences as far as *operae* are concerned, if it is true that such a right was excluded *ab initio* in the case of manumissions *inter amicos*: see §8 above.

[93] Both the possibilities, for which Tac. *Ann.* 13.26.2 provides the evidence, either exile or reduction to the status of *libertus dediticius* (see Pellecchi forthcoming, §3.5c–d), are compatible with the view that the *accusatio ingrati* could be brought against both Roman and Latin freedpersons.

[94] See in detail Masi Doria 1996, 180–224.

In the light of all these considerations, it is unimaginable that the *lex Iunia*, even more than the *lex Aelia Sentia*, should not have dealt with the problem. But how? One may offer a guess, following the logic of the statute in regulating the succession to a Latin freedperson. In discussing the solution which I have mentioned several times (in particular in §5 above, with full quotation), Gaius observes that the statute provided that at the death of a Junian Latin their estate passed to their manumitter, as it were, like a *peculium* – *iure quodammodo peculii* – in other words, as if the deceased should have regarded themselves simply as holders of a *peculium*, ceasing to exist with their death and therefore falling automatically into the hands of their patron. The regime of the *peculium* was not, however, limited to this question of succession: it restricted the holder also during their lives, whether slaves or sons-in-power, because they could not dispose of it freely, by either gift or manumission.[95] It may therefore be that the *lex Iunia* reactivated, as it were, the regime of the *peculium*, not only in matters of succession, but also to cancel liberalities, for which the freedperson had been responsible without the authorisation of the patron.

Conclusion

The above exposition has provided an extensive overview of the chief dimensions of the *leges Iunia et Aelia Sentia*, from a legal point of view, including discussion of some of the main issues that have vexed modern scholarship – such as the question over the chronological order of the two statutes, their relationship in terms of contents, as well as their respective aims. Tying together the strands from the end of the discussion in the previous section (§9), it is now possible to foreground, by way of a more general conclusion, some critical features that have a wider bearing on our appreciation of the statutes and their operation.

Through the *leges Iunia et Aelia Sentia*, slaves informally manumitted finally obtained full legal recognition. The regulation was complex. On the one hand, these people were assimilated to *freeborn* colonial Latins. On the other hand, this assimilation did not give them all the legal rights originally granted to the Latins, and it did not mean that Junian Latins were not above all *freedpersons*, over whom their patrons exercised rights that were sometimes identical with those exercised by patrons over *Roman* freedpersons, sometimes reformulated. If the position with regard to *honor*, i.e. actions in court, was identical, the rights over the estate of the deceased freedperson were substantially greater, indeed complete; so complete that the alternative obligation of *operae* could not be imposed on Junian Latins.

It is on this basis that one must approach the relationship between *libertas Latina* and the norms that form the second part of the *lex Aelia Sentia*: to suppose that they were norms that applied only between patrons and *Roman* freedpersons would make little sense, any more than to suppose that the norms were extended *en bloc* to Junian Latins, rather than there being differences. It is plausible to hold that there were rules

---

[95] Digest 39.5.7pr. (Ulpian), 37.14.13 (Modestinus).

that applied in both contexts, such as the obligation to provide for the upkeep of a destitute freedperson, the ban on imposing an oath not to have children, and the *accusatio ingrati* (see §9 above). Other rules, such as the ban on taking payment, it is plausible to hold applied only in the case of *Roman* freedpersons. Finally, still other rules, such as the ban on defrauding a patron, had to be specifically redrafted in the *lex Iunia*.

As has been seen throughout this chapter, the main obstacle that must be overcome in the study of the complex topic that we are dealing with is the state of the available legal evidence: these are sources that Justinian reduced to a few elementary texts, where the subject matter is dealt with in a concise and selective way, which aim, above all, to establish a harmony with the *iura populi Romani*. Moreover, since *Latinitas Iuniana* is primarily a legal creation, the formation of the 'black hole' in which it has been engulfed is mainly to be ascribed to the aforementioned state of the legal sources. With the subject thus defined therefore, the interdisciplinary approach chosen in the present undertaking by the editors is not only useful, but absolutely essential.

3

The Republican Background and the Augustan Setting for the Creation of Junian Latinity

Pedro López Barja

Introduction

It is part of the historian's craft not only to tell what happened in the past, but also to explain why it happened. When it comes to a legal enactment or statute, historians therefore usually try to reconstruct the objectives of those who drafted it, to identify their motives. This approach has regularly been applied to the laws that created and expanded Junian Latinity (i.e. the *leges Iunia et Aelia Sentia*), with inconclusive results. Part of the reason for this is that we must rely on sources, such as Suetonius or Cassius Dio, that are chronologically far removed from the point in time when these laws were passed. We do not have any statement on the topic by Augustus himself, not even an indirect mention in the *Res Gestae Divi Augusti*; consequently, the door is open to speculation. The method adopted in the present chapter is somewhat different. Without entirely discarding the information given by our sources, we will focus on the content of the laws and their implications, within a very specific historical context, namely a late period of the Augustan Principate, from c. 7 BC to AD 4, but also taking note of a kind of prologue, the late Republic.

Thus, besides taking account of the contributions of the (later) source material, there are two chief axes to this chapter: the contents of these laws and the historical context. As regards the former, the following discussion will rely heavily on what has been said by Pellecchi in the preceding chapter, as well as on the more general comments made in the Introduction to this volume. It is thus assumed here that the reader is familiar with the main features of the statutes and the legal sources for them. As regards the latter, the argument presented here is, perhaps surprisingly, different from that offered by Pellecchi, who champions a late(r) date for the *lex Iunia*, after the *lex Aelia Sentia*. I say 'perhaps surprisingly' because both our contributions appear in one and the same volume. But as just summarised, the following discussion explores the *historical* context that drove the enactments here discussed, in order to understand in this way the legal changes – and the dates of the statutes – in their contemporary socio-political settings. As will be seen, this socio-political setting supports, in my view, an early date for the *lex Iunia*, before the *lex Aelia Sentia*.

A Short Review of the Historiography

The development of the historiography on the 'Junian' question is a complex issue that cannot be summed up in a few pages: it receives full discussion in the sequel to the present volume to reflect on past and present approaches and future openings. Here, I will concern myself with the different explanations scholars have propounded for the laws themselves, including also the *lex Fufia Caninia*. Both issues are obviously related to each other, but the problems pertaining to the manumission laws of Augustus call for a more precise focus on the social policy of the first Princeps.

First and foremost, for much of the twentieth century, the dominant explanation for the Augustan laws was that their aim was to limit manumissions, i.e. to reduce their frequency in absolute terms. The intention, it was thought, was to preserve the racial purity of the Roman people from the intrusion of people of Eastern origin who would eventually corrupt it. This was Duff's opinion, based on conclusions reached earlier by Frank. Duff even rejected the idea that the institution of *anniculi probatio* was intended to increase the number of citizens, claiming that this would have required not just one child, but more than one. In fact, in his opinion, the aim of this measure was strictly to limit the number of manumissions, suggesting that, by making it seemingly easy for Junian Latins to become Roman citizens, Augustus tried in effect to alert slave-owners to what was assumed to be an undesirable possibility, so that they would liberate fewer slaves.[1] This hypothesis, which sees the Augustan laws as restrictive in aim regarding manumissions, acquired considerable traction when it was adopted by Last in the corresponding chapter of the *Cambridge Ancient History*.[2] Subsequently, the idea has continued to be defended, both in its original form, i.e. with an emphasis on racial purity, as well as in a diluted form, avoiding the term 'race', but insisting on the protection of the Roman people as a declared aim of the legal innovation.[3]

In an article published in 1966, Atkinson paved the way for a different approach. In her opinion, the sources that inform us about Augustus' motives, i.e. Suetonius and Cassius Dio, and which focus on the idea of preserving the purity of the Roman citizen body, are both tainted by the prejudices of their own days. Atkinson argued that Augustus was, in contrast, pursuing a totally different goal, shown by the fact that he rewarded with Roman citizenship those Junian Latins who had at least one child, through *anniculi probatio*. Augustus' intention, according to Atkinson, was not to limit the number of manumissions, but instead to ensure the necessary manpower for army recruitment, through child-bearing incentives tied to the acquisition of Roman citizenship.[4]

---

[1] Duff 1928, 82, with Frank 1916. See the fuller discussion of the historiographical developments in López Barja, Masi Doria and Roth forthcoming.

[2] See esp. Last 1934, 434: 'Together these laws [i.e. the *leges Fufia Caninia* and *Aelia Sentia*] cannot have failed to secure a drastic reduction in the number of persons alien both by culture and by blood.'

[3] For the former, see, for instance, Rodríguez Álvarez 1978, 169–70: 'Esta idea de preservación de la raza [. . .] es a nuestro juicio la que preside de una forma constante toda la política de Augusto en materia de manumisiones.' For the latter, see, for instance, Richardson 2012, 160–1 (on the reasons for the passing of the *lex Fufia Caninia*): 'fears that excessive use of manumission might pollute the purity of the Roman people'; see also Eck 2007, 108–9.

[4] Atkinson 1966, 365: 'The *Lex Iunia* was looking forward to the establishment of a new source of recruits for the city troops (in the first instance) and, in the second generation, for the legions'; cf. Robleda 1976, 156.

Although it cannot be said that Atkinson's proposal has met with unanimous agreement, the truth is that the idea of seeing the Augustan laws as purely limiting manumissions has gradually lost its force.[5] Indeed, it cannot have been their aim, for not even the manumission of 'dangerous' slaves was forbidden; if freed, they simply became *dediticii*. In recent years, historians have preferred demographic explanations or, in any event, have stressed that Augustus intended not to limit access to the citizen body but, rather, to regulate it.[6] In some cases, the intention has been to maintain both perspectives simultaneously. For example, for de Dominicis, the *lex Iunia* was both generous and restrictive: generous, because by granting full rights to the manumitters over the Junians' inheritance, it encouraged manumission, but at the same time restrictive, because the manumission was no longer revocable, and the former slave-owners would therefore grant it with greater caution.[7]

In a way that is, shall we say, secondary to this series of interpretations that have dominated the twentieth century, other scholars have recently focused on the economic dimensions of the statutes. One argument suggests that the aim of these laws was to allow patrons to make better use of their freedmen in profit-making activities: slave-owners could use informal manumission to put out capital and secure its safe return, together with the profits made.[8] A related argument has foregrounded the economic benefit for the masters-cum-patrons in potentially being able to charge twice for manumission, if the freed slaves, now Junian Latins, sought citizenship through iteration, i.e. a second manumission at the hands of their (now) patron.[9] A third variant of this line of thought (the one I myself prefer) emphasises the patrons' rights to their freedpersons' inheritance, which were considerably enhanced by the combined action of the *leges Iunia et Aelia Sentia*.

Thus the historians' chief approaches to these crucial laws. There are, moreover, two very important methodological points that need emphasis before proceeding to the analysis of the republican background for the Augustan reform. First, in my view, it is a mistake to propose a single explanation as common to all three laws, which, in fact, obey a logic of two different kinds. Thus, the *lex Iunia* seeks to solve a serious problem that had caused unrest in the past among the plebs of Rome, i.e. a problem caused by informal manumissions, and affecting those cases in which the will of the master to free the slave is clearly expressed, but without following any of the three established procedures (*vindicta, censu, testamento*).[10] The law regulates the slave-owner's

---

[5] López Barja 1998, 140: 'there was no attempt to limit manumission in absolute numbers'.
[6] Demographic: for example, Mouritsen 2011, 87: 'A central motivation behind many of the new provisions appears to have been population growth.' Regulatory: for example, Treggiari 1996, 896: 'Though the Fufio-Caninian law may have reduced the number of manumissions, the rest of his legislation blocked only criminal ex-slaves and made access to citizenship easier for others. He [i.e. Augustus] wanted to regulate, not to stop the talented and energetic.'
[7] De Dominicis 1973.
[8] See Sirks 1981. I consider as overly contemporary the opinion of some scholars who believe that the aim of these statutes was to reduce the competition between freedmen and free commoners in small-scale trades and crafts. For this view, see, for instance, Schumacher 2001, 295; Schipp 2017, 16. Indeed, it is not at all clear why Junian Latins should have been less successful competitors than enfranchised freedpersons.
[9] See Roth 2010b, with earlier bibliography.
[10] Discussion of the issues caused by informal manumission in the period is in López Barja 2007, 37–40.

expressed volition. In the case of the *lex Iunia*, then, the law does not interfere with the will of the *dominus*, but, rather, the statute gives it a certain official sanction. By contrast, the *leges Fufia Caninia* and *Aelia Sentia* constitute the first cases in Roman history of the intervention of the public power in the private sphere of relations between slave-owners and their slaves. From now on, the former can no longer grant freedom to as many slaves as possibly desired in their will, nor reward a potentially unlimited number with Roman citizenship if they do not meet the new legal requirements, especially if they are not of the required age. As with the new statutes pertaining to marriage (i.e. the *leges Iuliae*), the emperor interferes through the *leges Fufia Caninia* and *Aelia Sentia* in the previously private business of Roman citizens, depriving them of the almost absolute power they had hitherto enjoyed vis-à-vis slave manumission. Seen in this way, the *beneficium* of Roman citizenship upon manumission became the shared gift of private citizen *and* Roman emperor, to the former's slaves. It follows that in contrast to the *lex Iunia*, the *leges Fufia Caninia* and *Aelia Sentia* do not simply support the volition of the slave-owner; rather, those two laws *interfere* with the slave-owner's volition. This has to be borne in mind in any contextualisation of the three laws here discussed.

My second point arises in fact from the first one. In essence, it is of course entirely reasonable to assume that the laws under scrutiny here expressed the point of view of the slave-owners, and that these laws responded therefore to what we moderns think were the reasons why they manumitted their slaves. But the distinction stressed in the previous paragraph between the different operating logics of these laws complicates matters. In my view, Augustus had his own axe to grind, irrespective of – and in fact in contradistinction to – the motivations of private slave-owners: he did not try to satisfy only the ambitions and expectations of his subjects, but sought to advance an imperial policy. With these two sets of preliminary yet critical considerations regarding the statutes' fundamental logic clarified, this chapter can progress to outlining its argument on the motives behind the legal innovation, seen against the republican background.

The Republican Background

In Book 3 of the *Institutes*, Gaius explains the origin of Junian Latinity; he does so only in brief, noting that he has already dealt with the matter before, in another passage, which we cannot read because it corresponds to an unhappy gap of twenty-four illegible lines in the Verona manuscript, in paragraph 1.21. We must therefore make do with this later brief summary, in which Gaius reminds the reader that the driver for the law is to be found in the situation of freed slaves whose freedom had hitherto been protected by the praetor,[11] which enabled them to live in a kind of freedom; the *lex Iunia*, then, turned these individuals into Latins, by assimilating them to the Latins of the Latin colonies: I refer of course to our famous passage *Inst.* 3.56 – the text of which is given in full in this volume's Introduction.

Even less full is the information that we find in the *liber singularis regularum* of pseudo-Ulpian, also with a gap in the most inopportune place, since it only tells us that

---

[11] We are not told the reason for this praetorian protection.

'today' these freed slaves are free by virtue of the *lex Iunia*, and that those who have been freed *inter amicos* are called Latins:

> hodie autem ipso iure liberi sunt ex lege Iunia. Qua lege Latini sunt nominati inter amicos manumissi.
>
> but today they are legally free, according to the *lex Iunia*; by this law those freed in the presence of friends are called Latins.[12]

We are luckier with the *Fragmentum Pseudo-Dositheanum*, which faithfully follows the text of Gaius, because this part has been better preserved. Here we can read that in the past some slaves lived in a state of freedom in accordance with the will of their master, but that if the latter tried to reduce them again to slavery, the praetor intervened and did not allow it. To these, that is, to those who were manumitted *inter amicos*, the *lex Iunia* gave a freedom of their own, equating them with the Latins of the Latin colonies.[13]

From these three fragmentary texts it can be inferred that the *lex Iunia* addressed a problem of a certain gravity, posed by those slaves who had not been 'correctly' manumitted – i.e. who had been informally manumitted, the term used hereafter – but who lived in a state of de facto freedom, with the consent of the owner and under the protection of the praetor. The problem must have been particularly serious in Rome itself, since we are only told about the praetor, but not about what was happening in the provinces or even in the rest of Italy. Clearly, the number of slaves in this precarious situation must have been high enough to attract the attention of the legislator when the time came. Thus, although there is little evidence, we should never lose sight of this essential fact: the main objective of the *lex Iunia* was to solve a serious problem pertaining to or arising from those manumitted slaves who lived as free men, even if they were still slaves in the eyes of the law; any other motive we wish to attribute to the drafter of this measure can only be secondary – a crucial point, also made by Pellecchi in Chapter 2. Unfortunately, the texts mentioned above do not give any precise chronological indication: they only provide a summary description of the situation that existed prior to the *lex Iunia*, but they do not specify when the praetor had begun to protect these informally manumitted slaves. Nevertheless, we have enough information to suspect the origin of the problem and to be able to place it in a broader context.

To begin with, in 58 BC Clodius passed into law the free distribution of grain to the plebs to help with ongoing food scarcities, giving to his lieutenant Sextus Cloelius full

---

[12] Ulp. *Reg.* 1.10; the translation is my own.

[13] The reference is to *Fragmentum Pseudo-Dositheanum* 5–6: 'Antea enim una libertas erat et manumissio fiebat vindicta vel testamento vel censu et civitas Romana competebat manumissis: quae appellatur iusta manumissio. Hi autem, qui domini voluntate in libertate erant, manebant servi; sed si manumissores ausi erant in servitutem denuo eos per vim ducere, interveniebat praetor et non patiebatur manumissum servire. Omnia tamen quasi servus adquirebat manumissori, velut si quid stipulabatur vel mancipio accipiebat vel ex quacumque causa alia adquisierat, domini hoc faciebat, id est manumissi omnia bona ad patronum pertinebant. Sed nunc habent propriam libertatem qui inter amicos manumittuntur, et fiunt Latini Iuniani, quoniam lex Iunia, quae libertatem eis dedit, exaequavit eos Latinis colonariis, qui cum essent cives Romani liberi, nomen suum in coloniam dedissent.'

control of the *annona*.[14] The situation, however, very quickly worsened, because of the grain shortage suffered during that summer (but also very probably because the law did not set a limit to the number of recipients, or clearly specify the personal circumstances of those who were to receive the handout).[15] In September of the following year, 57 BC, when the situation was threatening to get out of control, Sextus Cloelius was replaced by Pompey (under the *lex Cornelia Caecilia*).[16] The consequences of Clodius' grain distribution law had been immediate, given that it improved on earlier schemes by offering the grain entirely for free to the recipients. In consequence, Pompey had to deal with a sudden increase in the number of manumissions, made with the sole aim of benefiting from the distribution, as Cassius Dio reports:

> While these men kept up their conflict, Pompey, too, encountered some delay in the distribution of the grain. For since many slaves had been freed in anticipation of the event, he wished to take a census of them in order that the grain might be supplied to them with some order and system. (tr. Cary, LCL)[17]

It is likely that many of the cited manumissions were carried out without abiding by the established legal procedure; consequently, once the 'freedman' had received his ration of grain, his owner could, whenever desired, rightfully reclaim him as a slave, an abuse so flagrant that it caused the praetor to intervene: these were probably the bulk of the slaves described by Gaius and the *Dositheanum* as 'qui domini voluntate in libertate erant auxilio praetoris'.[18] We do not know exactly what the situation was immediately before the *lex Clodia*, but it is likely that the recipients had been only 40,000 under the *lex Terentia Cassia* of 73 BC.[19] This number increased to an unknown extent with the *lex Porcia*, in 62 BC;[20] the distributed grain was still not free, which means that the incentive for informal manumission was greater now under the *lex Clodia*.[21] Clodius may have cast the net as widely as possible because he wanted the handout to cost so much money that the public treasury would be exhausted, thereby leaving Caesar's agrarian policy without the necessary funding.[22]

---

[14] Cic. *Dom.* 10.25, with Ruffing 1993.
[15] The key source is Cic. *Dom.* 10.26.
[16] Brief discussion is in Vervaet 2020, 155.
[17] Cass. Dio 39.24.1: 'Οὗτοί τε οὖν ἐμάχοντο, καὶ ὁ Πομπήιος ἔσχε μὲν καὶ ἐν τῇ τοῦ σίτου διαδόσει τριβήν τινα. Πολλῶν γὰρ πρὸς τὰς ἀπ' αὐτοῦ ἐλπίδας ἐλευθερωθέντων, ἀπογραφήν σφων, ὅπως ἔν τε κόσμῳ καὶ ἐν τάξει τινὶ σιτοδοτηθῶσιν, ἠθέλησε ποιήσασθαι.'
[18] Gai. *Inst.* 3.56; *Frag. Dos.* 5.
[19] On this point, see Garnsey 1988, 212.
[20] The precise nature of the *lex Porcia* (possibly in fact a *senatus consultum*) is not clear.
[21] Unconvincingly, Rising 2019, 192–3 argues for a drastic increase resulting from Cato's measures in 62 BC. In his view, the number of recipients would have increased to 300,000 during the next thirteen years, and Clodius' law would have had very little impact. Regardless of whether the law was indeed a law or a *senatus consultum*, it is likely that the measure was temporary: see Pina Polo 2021a.
[22] For the idea that the objective of Clodius was to hinder the development of Caesar's *lex agraria* of the previous year, see Manni 1940; Fezzi 2001b, both of whom point out that in April 56 BC the Roman Senate had to provide *in re frumentaria* 40 million sesterces to Pompey (see Cic. *QFr* 2.6.1). Fezzi 2001a makes a good case for an opposition between Clodius' objectives (to maintain the plebeians living in the city through his *lex frumentaria*) and those of Caesar (to settle many of them in the countryside with his *lex agraria*).

Faced with these difficulties, Pompey then proceeded to make a detailed investigation. He prepared a census (*apographe*) that was in all likelihood limited to the population living in Rome, in order to eliminate the names of those who did not rightfully qualify for the handout; among these were presumably the above mentioned informally manumitted slaves. But the lists that had been prepared and deposited in the temple of the Nymphs on the Campus Martius, where the *memoria publicae recensionis* was kept, were destroyed by a fire. Clodius and his followers are to be held responsible for the arson, if we are to believe Cicero's repeated claim:[23] they sought to destroy these lists (we may assume) so that every freedman, whatever his personal status, even those who were still slaves according to the law, gained access to the *frumentum publicum*.

A few years later, in January of 52 BC, as a candidate for the praetorship, Clodius made several proposals prepared specifically to benefit freedmen. At least, this is what Cicero states in his speech in defence of Milo for murdering Clodius, in which he tries very hard to present the victim as an evil man who was a threat to the Republic. Cicero of course sought to render Clodius' assassination at Bovillae on 18 January in 52 BC acceptable, in order to achieve the acquittal of his client. There are two very vague references, in which Cicero is clearly not interested in going into detail regarding Clodius' plans, but merely aims at presenting him to the judges in the most unfavourable light possible. In the first case, Cicero states that 'laws' (*leges*) were prepared in the house of Clodius that would have placed all Romans under the control of their own slaves, a phrase that is difficult to understand and which Asconius interprets as follows: if approved, Clodius' bill would have distributed the freedmen's votes in all of the tribes, including the rural ones, which until then had been reserved for the freeborn.[24] The change in tribal affiliation would have had dramatic and very negative consequences for the voting of the *comitia*, altering the distribution of power. It is not the first time that Cicero resorts to this kind of exaggeration, since in 55 BC he had already described with great drama the attempts to distribute the freedmen among all the tribes, which he considered a threat to the *res publica*.[25] The second case is equally mysterious, but with the added difficulty that we do not have the help of Asconius, who does not comment on it. This is a new Clodian law, which would have made 'our slaves his [i.e. Clodius'] freedmen'.[26] It is tempting to think that this law sought to favour precisely those slaves whose precarious freedom the praetor had been protecting, i.e. those we know of from Gaius and the *Dositheanum*, thus forming a sort of precedent for the *lex Iunia* (even if we may presume that Clodius would in fact have

---

[23] Cic. *Mil.* 73; *Har. resp.* 27.57; *Cael.* 78 (where the accused is Sextus Cloelius). For discussion, see Nicolet 1976.

[24] Cic. *Mil.* 87: 'incidebantur iam domi leges quae nos servis nostris addicerent', with Asconius (52C): 'Significasse iam puto nos fuisse inter leges P. Clodi quas ferre proposuerat eam quoque qua libertini, qui non plus quam in IIII tribubus suffragium ferebant, possent in rusticis quoque tribubus, quae propriae ingenuorum sunt, ferre.' Schol. Bob. *De aere alieno Milonis* fragm. XVII (ed. Hildebrandt 156, 15) says more or less the same.

[25] Cic. *De or.* 1.38; cf. López Barja 2022.

[26] Cic. *Mil.* 89: 'lege nova, quae est inventa apud eum cum reliquis legibus Clodianis, servos nostros libertos suos effecisset'; cf. Favory 1978/9; Loposzko 1978/9.

conferred on them full Roman citizenship). It is easy to see how, in the highly charged rhetoric of the orator, these informally manumitted slaves would become 'Clodius' freedmen', not because they actually were, but because they owed their new status as freedmen to him, given that until that moment, according to the law, they were still slaves. If we are to believe Cicero, Clodius had already promised freedom to some slaves on a previous occasion, a mention that could also refer to informally manumitted slaves (almost in anticipation of the proposals in 52 BC); or it may be nothing other than a simple invention of our orator.[27]

With all the restraint required by the scarcity of our sources and by the intense prejudice against Clodius that motivated Cicero, we can conclude that the problem of these slaves *in libertate*, which probably already existed before, was considerably aggravated following the *lex frumentaria* of Clodius in 58 BC, because the free grain distribution encouraged many Romans to informally free some of their slaves, so that they could be fed at the expense of the treasury. In the ensuing years, Clodius continued to favour this policy, perhaps because the large number of informally freed slaves made them a useful instrument for keeping a significant part of the urban plebs under his control.

Other *popularis* politicians, however, refused to go along with this strategy. Notably, in around 47 BC, Sallust advised Caesar to deprive the urban plebs of these handouts and to distribute the monthly rations of grain throughout the colonies and municipalities, among those veterans who had returned to their homeland after long years of service.[28] Caesar himself was not in favour of following the 'open door' policy for one and all that Clodius followed. We do not know if the grain distributions continued during the Civil War, although it is likely that there were many difficulties in maintaining these and that they were often interrupted, from the beginning of the conflict in 49 BC. Maritime traffic must have been severely affected (at least while Africa was in Pompeian hands, between August 49 and April 46 BC, it is very unlikely that any number of ships could sail from African ports to provide food for Rome), affecting in turn the grain supply, and the money available was primarily used to pay troops. When a certain stability was finally achieved, once control of Egypt and Africa was recovered, and Caesar decided to resume distributing grain to the urban plebs, he did so not in a disorderly manner, but following the example of Pompey and his census of 56 BC. Consequently, after the crushing victory at Thapsus, in a moment of exaltation and, hence, in the context of the fourfold triumph over his enemies, Caesar undertook a specific census, limited to residents of Rome – a *recensus*, which did not follow the usual procedures. Thus, Suetonius reports that it was done by neighbourhoods and taking as reference points the owners of the *insulae*:

> Recensum populi nec more nec loco solito, sed vicatim per dominos insularum egit atque ex viginti trecentisque milibus accipientium frumentum e publico ad

---

[27] Cic. *Att.* 4.3.2 (SB 75, November 57 BC) accused Clodius of 'vicatim ambire, servis aperte spem libertatis ostendere'.

[28] [Sall.] *Ep. Caes. Sen.* 1.7.2. Much of the discussion has centred on the authenticity of these letters to Caesar: see Pina Polo 2021b.

centum quinquaginta retraxit; ac ne qui novi coetus recensionis causa moveri quandoque possent, instituit, quotannis in demortuorum locum ex iis, qui recensi non essent, subsortitio a praetore fieret.

The *recensus* of the people he conducted in neither the usual manner nor the usual place, but street by street, through the owners of the apartment blocks; and he reduced the number of those who received grain at the public expense, from three hundred and twenty thousand to a hundred and fifty thousand. To prevent anyone ever causing tumults on account of the *recensus*, he ordered that the praetor should every year fill up by lot the vacancies occasioned by death, from those who were not enrolled in the *recensus*.[29]

As the text makes sufficiently clear, the result of this *recensus* was a drastic reduction in the number of beneficiaries, from 320,000 to only 150,000. We do not know where the first figure comes from, although it is tempting to attribute it to the census taken by Pompey in 56 BC. Perhaps the fire at the temple of the Nymphs did not have as devastating an effect as Cicero would have us believe or, at least, despite the damage, the final figure for those entitled to participate in the distributions was recorded. Yet, Caesar did not want the number to grow, but for it to remain fixed from then on; we will see that this did not happen and that Augustus had to face the same problem again. As we will also see, he succeeded by following a procedure like the one deployed by Caesar: first, a local census, in Rome, which greatly reduced the numbers, and after that, the *numerus clausus*.

Our sources agree in attributing the bulk of the reduction in the number of the recipients to casualties in the Civil War, which only makes sense if we accept that the military implication of the urban plebs was higher than usually believed.[30] Nevertheless, modern interpretations of this evidence have preferred a different explanation. Thus, while van Berchem accepted the implications of the ancient sources at face value, he considered that half of the total reduction of 170,000 corresponded to people who had been illegally inscribed in the list.[31] With Brunt the approach developed significantly: 'war casualties were not severe' in the city of Rome; therefore the presumed increase in the number of recipients before the Civil War, noted above, was assigned to widespread fraud; in particular, Brunt pointed to those who had been informally manumitted.[32] Given that according to Roman law, these informally manumitted slaves were still slaves, Caesar would have been in a position to erase their names from the list. This explanation, which underestimates war casualties in favour of

---

[29] Suet. *Iul*. 41.3. Special thanks to Michael Crawford for the English translation.
[30] Liv. *Per*. 115; Plut. *Vit. Caes*. 55.5–6; App. *B Civ*. 2.102; Cass. Dio 43.21.4. Even if he was convinced that the bulk of the legionaries belonged to the *plebs rustica*, Brunt 1971, 381 duly registered three references to recruitments in the city of Rome or its vicinity (Caes. *BC* 1.14.4; Cic. *Phil*. 10.21; Cic. *Fam*. 11.8.2). To these should be added [Caes.] *B. Hisp*. 31.9. Brunt's view relied on the assumption that most of the urban plebs were freedmen, who were ineligible for the legions; cf. now López Barja 2022.
[31] Van Berchem 1939, 22.
[32] Brunt 1971, 381. This idea had already appeared in his seminal paper of 1962, and is still in the edition of 1988: Brunt 1988, 243, 245, 250.

a gigantic fraud, has become the standard view on this issue.[33] Even when scholars do not speak of fraud, they assume that Caesar excluded all freedmen from the handout.[34] But this view is untenable, because it depends on a grossly exaggerated estimation of the number of freedmen in Rome: few scholars would accept today that almost half of the *plebs frumentaria* were freedmen.[35]

In my opinion, we should return to van Berchem's view and accept that war casualties were responsible for the biggest part of the reduction, while acknowledging that some fraud occurred. Several groups can be mentioned as included in the rounded-up figure, such as the 80,000 Roman citizens who were sent to colonies abroad,[36] as many of them were surely inhabitants of the capital city. It is very likely that both the very rich (the property owners or *domini insularum*) and the very poor were also excluded from the *recensus* – the latter simply because lacking a domicile they could not be counted (this had also happened in the census conducted by Pompey in 56 BC).[37] Consequently, soldiers killed or missing in action, house owners, and those sent to new colonies, were probably the groups that made up the vast majority of those eliminated by the *recensus* of 46 BC. Even so, informally manumitted slaves should probably also be mentioned: notwithstanding our inability to ascertain their numbers, and even if we do not accept that they can have made up the bulk of the numbers eliminated from the grain handout, they were certainly a sizeable group in 46 BC. Thus, at least in the city of Rome, and over time, they could not simply be ignored, not least because politicians could use them as an instrument to achieve their own objectives. Whatever the precise figures, given the circumstances that our sources portray, we must start from the assumption that the risk of social unrest was very real.

The *lex Iunia*: The Date of the *lex*

The situation outlined above provides a new context for understanding the Augustan measures that are the subject of this chapter. In short, it seems evident to me that Augustus found the solution to the problem. He could not leave the danger of social unrest to grow out of control, precisely when its connection with the corn dole was apparent and the emperor was committed to solving this issue once and for all. In other words, the historical context provides both the rationale and the (most likely) date for the *lex Iunia*.

As we have seen, the social group that legal sources place at the origin of the *lex Iunia* (i.e. the slaves who *domini voluntate in libertate manebant*) grew exorbitantly and began to cause serious problems as a result of Clodius' *lex frumentaria* of 58 BC.

---

[33] Virlouvet 1995, 168–9, 184; Giovannini 2004, 199; see also Scheidel 2004, 14 ('Caesar's sharp cut suggests the possibility of widespread fraud and corruption in previous years'); Courrier 2014, 355.

[34] See, for instance, Mouritsen 2011, 121.

[35] Mouritsen 2011, 121–2 allows for the possibility that, out of the 170,000 excluded, 90,000 were freedmen and that an indeterminate number of the 80,000 Roman citizens sent to colonies were also *liberti*. Further discussion is in López Barja 2022.

[36] See Suet. *Iul.* 42.1.

[37] See Lo Cascio 1997; Tarpin 2002, 117–18.

Pompey was then faced with a drastic increase in informal manumissions, and it seems that Clodius sought the support of these slaves who lived in de facto freedom, protected by the praetor, promising them, in 52 BC, to resolve their precarious condition by giving them protection by law. Then, in 46 BC, Caesar adopted a policy contrary to that of Clodius, expelling them from the *recensus* and therefore also from the distribution of grain. Augustus soon had to face the same problem: the *frumentatio* encouraged large-scale manumission. This was commented on by Dionysius of Halicarnassus, who singles out, among several 'immoral' motives for granting freedom to slaves, specifically that many owners did it only with the intention of having their slaves included in the corn dole:

> Some are freed in order that, when they have received the monthly allowance of wheat given by the public or some other largesse distributed by the men in power to the poor among the citizens, they may bring it to those who granted them their freedom. (tr. Cary, LCL)[38]

Suetonius agreed with Dionysius on this point but added an important detail: he says that the manumitted slaves had become Roman citizens, the implication being that they were not informally manumitted, a detail left unclear in Dionysius' account; but Suetonius also commented that Augustus refused to accept these new citizens for the corn distribution.[39] As is often the case with Suetonius, the lack of a precise date obscures the issue. All the same, everything seems to indicate that already at that time Augustus had announced that the distribution would benefit Roman citizens exclusively, causing an increase in formal manumission, i.e. manumissions carried out by the consul or the praetor.

We have no proof that anyone would want, as Clodius had done, to now seek the support of the *morantes in libertate*, but we do know that the urban plebs could show their discontent in a forceful and violent way. In the year 22 BC, M. Egnatius Rufus, as aedile, used his own slaves to put out a fire in Rome, a gesture that made him very popular. He became praetor two years later, and tried, in 19 BC, to present himself for the consulate, but was prevented from doing so, because the two statutory years between magistracies had not yet passed. This caused serious disturbances in Rome, and eventually brought about his execution.[40] Importantly for present purposes, the episode shows that even in Augustus' time some believed that they could base their political career on the support of the urban plebs. Indeed, the case makes it difficult to believe that the issue of those who had been informally manumitted could remain unresolved for long, especially when the problem of *frumentationes* – i.e. the uncontrolled increase in the number of those who received the grain for free every month – had not yet found a definitive solution, which would happen in 2 BC, as we will see later on.

---

[38] Dion. Hal. *Ant. Rom.* 4.24.5–6: 'οἱ δ' ἵνα τὸν δημοσίᾳ διδόμενον σῖτον λαμβάνοντες κατὰ μῆνα καὶ εἴ τις ἄλλη παρὰ τῶν ἡγουμένων γίγνοιτο τοῖς ἀπόροις τῶν πολιτῶν φιλανθρωπία φέρωσι τοῖς δεδωκόσι τὴν ἐλευθερίαν'.

[39] Suet. *Aug.* 42.2: 'cum proposito congiario multos manumissos insertosque civium numero comperisset, negavit accepturos quibus promissum non esse'.

[40] The chronology of the events is not entirely clear. Discussion is in Richardson 2012, 109; see also Vell. Pat. 2.91.3, 92.4 (*florentem favore publico*), with Cass. Dio 53.24.4–6, 54.10.1–2; Suet. *Aug.* 19.1.

The historical context is one reason why we should date the *lex Iunia* in the Augustan Principate, but it is not the most important one. In my opinion, a careful reading of the texts involved leads us to the conclusion that the *lex Iunia* is earlier than the *lex Aelia Sentia* of AD 4, even if it does not definitively prove it.[41] The alternative hypothesis (as presented by Pellecchi in Chapter 2) holds that the *lex Aelia Sentia* conceded the status of *morantes in libertate* to those slaves under thirty years of age manumitted without *iusta causa*. Yet it is very difficult to understand how the *lex Aelia Sentia* could have envisaged a certain kind of matrimony – which was assumed by the *anniculi probatio* provision – for people who were then simply slaves living in de facto freedom.[42] The main argument in favour of this alternative view is the name of the law as given by Justinian – the *lex Iunia Norbana*. But Justinian's officials did not always get it right. In fact, we know of some cases in which they were mistaken, and the same could also have happened this time. Perhaps the law had only one name, as was the case with the *lex Quinctia de aquaeductibus* from 9 BC, which was named solely after the consul T. Quinctius Crispinus (who had Drusus as his colleague). In sum, Justinian's officials may have wrongly added a second name – i.e. Norbana.[43]

But there is in fact a third option, which allows to accept both the name Norbana *and* a date before the *lex Aelia Sentia*, namely that it was a tribunician law, presented by two tribunes of the plebs, hence *Iunia Norbana*. Attributing this law to tribunes of the plebs makes sense, for its aim was to solve a nagging problem, that of the *morantes in libertate*, which affected the plebs greatly. It is true that most tribunician laws bore just one name, but there are exceptions, such as the *lex Acilia Rubria de cultu Iovis Capitolini*, which was a plebiscite with two proponents (M. Acilius Balbus and C. Rubrius Publilius).[44] Tribunician is also the mysterious *lex Mamilia Roscia Peducaea Alliena Fabia*, or the well-known *lex* of the ten tribunes from 52 BC which allowed Caesar to file his candidature for the consulship while still in Gaul. Another example is the *lex Plautia Papiria* of 89 BC, on the granting of Roman citizenship to honorary members of Italian communities.

Unfortunately, we cannot test this hypothesis, for only very few tribunes are known for this period. We have only six names between 32 and 2 BC,[45] when the total

---

[41] For a detailed discussion of the argument, see Balestri Fumagalli 1985, claiming that the *lex Iunia* was passed earlier than the *lex Aelia Sentia*. For the opposite view (*lex Iunia Norbana*, under Tiberius), see Venturini 1995/6; Pellecchi 2015, in addition to Chapter 2 in this volume.

[42] Cf. Venturini 1995/6, 232, who holds (with Ulp. *Reg.* 3.3) that the *lex Aelia Sentia* transformed these *servi minores*, when manumitted *vindicta*, into *servi populi Romani* (assuming that the anonymous epitomator subsumed these under the term *servus Caesaris*). Venturini, however, refuses to accept the very same source in the part where it claims that according to the *lex Aelia Sentia*, a *servus minor*, when manumitted by will, became a Latin (*ideoque Latinus fit*). This contradiction means that we would need to accept that in the same paragraph the drafter has mixed up two different chronological horizons: in the first case, he was supposedly referring to the moment the *lex Aelia Sentia* was passed (without noticing later developments), while in the second, he is describing the juridical facts of his own time.

[43] Recently, Bisio 2020, 107–8 has also argued that the Justinian commissioners were wrong about this law, even though he dates it to AD 15 (when C. Norbanus Flaccus was consul and M. Iunius Silanus *consul suffectus*), since in his opinion it must, in any case, be later than the *lex Aelia Sentia*.

[44] See Rotondi 1912, 315.

[45] See Kondratieff 2003.

of those who held this magistracy was perhaps 300, that is, assuming that a majority of the ten posts were filled every year (although this could not be achieved in some years, such as between 16 and 14 BC and in 12 BC).[46] It is true, as Pellecchi observes in Chapter 2, that after Augustus assumed the *tribunicia potestas*, as a logical consequence, tribunes of the plebs might have stopped using their right to present new laws to the plebs; but there is no firm evidence on this.[47]

An indirect argument in favour of my hypothesis can be found in the very famous passage of Dionysius of Halicarnassus commenting on the practice of manumission in contemporary, i.e. Augustan, Rome. Here, Dionysius defends his view that the link between manumission and citizenship (established, according to him, by Servius Tullius) should be maintained, but with some modifications. The solution, in his opinion, would be simple — i.e. to expel from the citizenship those who are deemed unfit, under the pretext of sending them to a colony:

> After which, they [i.e. the censors] should enrol in the tribes such of them as they find worthy to be citizens and allow them to remain in the city, but should expel from the city the foul and corrupt herd under the specious pretence of sending them out as a colony. (tr. Cary, LCL)[48]

This is certainly similar to the content of the *lex Iunia*, for this law converted some of the manumitted (i.e. those who have been informally liberated) effectively into *Latini coloniarii*: they were assimilated to those Roman citizens who were sent out to found new (Latin) colonies. There is a difference, though: the *lex Iunia* made use of this legal fiction with regard to those slaves who had been informally manumitted; Dionysius suggested this measure, on the other hand, for those slaves whose conduct was below expectations, 'the foul and corrupt herd'. When this measure was eventually approved, in AD 4 by the *lex Aelia Sentia*, they were not sent to a fictional colony; rather, their status was transformed into that of *dediticii*.[49] It is plausible that when Dionysius was writing (in the years before 7 BC) these ideas were common knowledge in senatorial circles and therefore subject to discussion, but eventually modified. The recently published *lex municipii Troesmensium* teaches us that senators wrote *commentarii* with ideas that four years later could find their way into a law.[50] The same procedure was perhaps followed in our case. In the discussions among senators about slavery and manumission, the idea of a fictional *colonia* could have filtered into some of these *commentarii*, and later, somewhat transformed, into the law. Therefore, this testimony can allow us to conclude, albeit tentatively, that the *lex Iunia* was a tribunician law passed later than 7 BC (i.e. the year Dionysius' *Roman Antiquities* was published), but probably not many years after that date.

---

[46] For 16 BC, see Cass. Dio 54.16.7; for 12 BC, see Cass. Dio 54.30.2.

[47] See Pellecchi in Chapter 2: p. 61, n. 26.

[48] Dion. Hal. *Ant. Rom.* 4.24.8: 'ἔπειθ' οὓς μὲν ἂν εὕρωσιν ἀξίους τῆς πόλεως ὄντας, εἰς φυλὰς καταγράψουσι καὶ μένειν ἐφήσουσιν ἐν τῇ πόλει· τὸ δὲ μιαρὸν καὶ ἀκάθαρτον φῦλον ἐκβαλοῦσιν ἐκ τῆς πόλεως εὐπρεπὲς ὄνομα τῷ πράγματι τιθέντες, ἀποικίαν'.

[49] Detailed discussion of the status is in Bisio 2020, 142–66. For an exploration of the status in the literary universe of the early imperial period, see Roth 2011.

[50] AD 5–9: 'commentarius ex quo lex Papia Poppaea lata est', with Dion. Hal. *Ant. Rom.* 55.4.1; Eck 2016.

The *lex Iunia* and the Corn Dole

In the year 5 BC, the emperor gave 60 denarii apiece to 320,000 people as a celebration for his adopted grandchild Gaius' coming of age.[51] This amount would provide for one year of corn on a 5 modii per month basis (estimating a cost of 1 denarius per modius, 5 x 12 months = 60). Three years later, Augustus repeated the gift. The occasion was his adopted grandchild Lucius' coming of age.[52] Again, he gave 60 denarii per person, but the crowd this time was not 320,000 people, but 'a little more' than 200,000. The name of the group receiving the corn also changed: in 5 BC, it was the *plebs urbana*, but now, in 2 BC, the group is referred to as the *plebs quae tum frumentum publicum accipiebat*. Augustus had taken the radical measure of fixing a limit to the number of people receiving the corn dole. As Cassius Dio said, from that moment onwards, the number was no longer 'indeterminate'; this 'closure' was probably preceded by the *recensus* Augustus conducted using the *vicus* as the unit, as we know from Suetonius, but, as is so frequent in his case, without a date.[53] This *recensus* was instrumental in the huge reduction in numbers: around 100,000 people disappeared from the lists between 5 and 2 BC: not as many as those eliminated by Caesar, but still a substantial figure. Augustus surely knew of the problem Pompey had faced in 56 BC and that he himself had also experienced, associated with the increase in manumissions.[54] Viewed against this backdrop, it is now possible to see that, in order to avoid riots and disturbances, he took three interconnected measures in a very short time span: first, the *lex Iunia*, which gave a juridical status to all those *manentes in libertate*, while simultaneously excluding them from the Roman citizenship; second, the *recensus*, where these Junian Latins (as well as many other people) were not included in those eligible for distributions of corn (which allowed for a dramatical reduction in the figures, as we have just seen); and third, the limitation of the *plebs frumentaria* to a number that was meant to be stable for the future. This seems a logical course to follow, but unfortunately, we have no sources to confirm this chain of events. We only have an annoyingly vague reference in Cassius Dio corresponding to the year 2 BC:

> on one occasion, when the people [. . .] gathered together and were asking that certain reforms be instituted and had sent the *tribunes* to Augustus for this purpose, the emperor came and consulted with them about their demands; and at this all were pleased. (tr. Cary, LCL, my emphasis)[55]

Annoyingly, Dio does not say what problems the tribunes wanted to address, but we may guess that the *frumentationes* were at the top of the list.

As we have seen, in the three cases (Pompey in 57, Caesar in 46 and Augustus in 2 BC) the chain of events was similar: the free distributions of corn caused a huge surge in the number of manumissions, which forced some sort of *recensus* to lower the

---

[51] See *RGDA* 15.2.
[52] See *RGDA* 15.4.
[53] Suet. *Aug.* 40.1: 'Populi recensum vicatim egit.'
[54] See Suet. *Aug.* 42.2.
[55] Cass. Dio 55.9.10.

alarming figures of recipients (which were considerably reduced as a result), followed, finally, by the 'closure' of the list. (The 'closure' was not attempted by Pompey, as far as we know.) The decision over who was to be included in the list must have been a very delicate matter; it was made not by throwing lots, but by excluding those who seemed unfit for the dole. The *lex Iunia* implemented a very cautious solution, namely that of excluding informally manumitted slaves from the list of recipients while giving them a legally defined status in exchange. It is difficult to estimate how many of the 100,000 excluded were Junian Latins, but it was probably less than half, if we bear in mind the likely number of freedmen who lived in Rome (not more than 100,000, according to the highest estimates).[56]

The evidence so far reviewed suggests that, from the outset, Junian Latins were excluded from the free distribution of corn because they were not Roman citizens. It is necessary now to comment on the view that the beneficiaries of the corn dole were of *freeborn* status only. In particular, Virlouvet has claimed that freedpeople who were Roman citizens were excluded from the *frumentationes*, because, in her view, being freeborn was a requisite for those who participated in the corn dole.[57] But the evidence seems to support the opposite conclusion, namely that any (male) Roman citizen, either freed or freeborn, could participate. The evidence can be summed up as follows, under three headings.[58]

1. The testimony of Persius. Persius (5.73–6) states the following: 'What we want is true liberty; not by that kind is it that any Publius enrolled in the Veline tribe becomes the possessor of a ticket for a ration of mangy spelt. O souls barren of truth, you who think that one whirling can make a Roman citizen!' (tr. Ramsey, LCL).[59] The scholiast explains this passage by saying that it was customary in Rome that all those who became Roman citizens upon manumission participated in the corn dole among other citizens.[60] Virlouvet thinks that the scholiast was ill-informed and that Persius was not necessarily talking about a freedman.[61] However, the explanation given by the scholiast to the verses seems the most likely: 'whirling' (*vertigo*) is a direct reference to the turning around of the slave in the ceremony of manumission *vindicta*, which made slaves into Roman citizens (*Quirites*), something that is rarely attested.[62] In short, according to Persius, freedmen were not excluded from the public handouts.

---

[56] Morley 2013, 42.
[57] Virlouvet 2009, 2–3. Following the interpretation of Virlouvet, Bisio 2020, 66 argues that the *lex Aelia Sentia* imposed on the patron the duty to feed his freedmen, and that failure to do so was punishable by the loss of *operae* and in particular of inheritance rights – citing Digest 38.2.33 (Modestinus) – precisely because Augustus had forbidden freedmen to participate in the *frumentationes*.
[58] In the same vein, see Lo Cascio 1997, 18, n. 49: freedmen were included in the distribution.
[59] 'Libertate opus est. non hac, ut quisque Velina/ Publius emeruit, scabiosum tesserula far/ possidet. heu steriles veri, quibus una Quiritem/ vertigo facit!'
[60] *Schol Pers.* (ad loc.): 'Romae autem erat consuetudo ut omnes qui ex manumissione cives Romani fiebant in numero civium Romanorum frumentum publicum acceperent.'
[61] Virlouvet 1995, 224–6.
[62] See my earlier comments in López Barja 2007, 22.

2. The Digest evidence. In several passages from the Digest, a freedman is given a *tessera* for the corn dole as a testamentary gift, which makes little sense if freedmen were categorically excluded from the handout.[63] Virlouvet argues that the gift was not the *tessera* but money, the estimated value of the *tessera*, but this is clearly not what the texts say.

3. Epigraphic evidence. On some tombstones from the city of Rome the fact of having received *frumentum publicum* is mentioned. This is a small corpus of only fourteen inscriptions (not including the inscriptions related to the *vigiles*), where twenty-nine people are mentioned: six *ingenui*, one freedman and twenty-two *incerti*. Despite their small number, we find one freedman in this select group, Ti. Claudius Aug. lib. Ianuarius, which means that they were not automatically excluded, although Virlouvet sees this as an exceptional grant.[64] For the rest, we have three *ingenui* (*tria nomina* with filiation)[65] and three others who say they are *ingenui* or members of a *tribus ingenua*. According to Virlouvet, in these latter cases, they proclaim their freeborn condition precisely because this was a *conditio sine qua non*.[66] However, it cannot be ruled out that they mentioned their *ingenuitas* for an entirely different reason. For example, fifteen of these twenty-nine people carry a Greek *cognomen*, which may be taken as evidence of a freedman social milieu: perhaps the men who proclaimed their freeborn status insisted on displaying it to differentiate themselves from these freedmen. We may also take recourse to a hypothesis put forward by Panciera: in analogy to what happened in Oxyrhynchus (Egypt), Panciera suggested that people entitled to the corn dole were distributed into several different lists – one for the *ingenui*, another for *liberti*, and so on.[67]

---

[63] Digest 5.1.52.1 (Ulpian): 'Si libertis suis tesseras frumentarias emi voluerit, quamvis maior pars hereditatis in provincia sit, tamen Romae debere fideicommissum solvi dicendum est, cum apparet id testatorem sensisse ex genere comparationis.' But see also Digest 32.35pr. (Scaevola): 'patronus liberto statim tribum emi petierat'; further Digest 31.87pr. (Paul).

[64] Virlouvet 2009, 56, with no. 13 = *CIL* VI, 10223: Ti(berius) Claudius Aug(usti) lib(ertus)/ Ianuarius, curator/ de Minucia die XIIII ostio XLII, et/ Avonia Tyche uxor eius/ Pituaniani solaria de sua/ impensa/ fecerunt. Virlouvet concludes that 'il prouve que l'accès au privilège frumentaire était loin d'aller de soi pour un affranchi, même pour un affranchi impérial'. But we can read nothing of this sort into the inscription, only that Ianuarius was an imperial freedman and had access to the corn dole.

[65] Virlouvet 2009, no. 14 = *CIL* VI, 10224b; no. 15 = *CIL* VI, 10225 = 33991; no. 19 = *CIL* VI, 2584. There is also a fourth case, likely to be an *ingenuus*, for the child, with *tria nomina*, but without filiation, belonged to a *tribus rustica*, Oufentina: Virlouvet 2009, no. 11 = *CIL* VI, 10221.

[66] Virlouvet 2009, 56. The three inscriptions are:
[1] Virlouvet 2009, no. 10 = *CIL* VI, 10220: D(is) M(anibus)./ L(ucio) Aurelio Tycheniano,/ L(ucius) Aurelius Stephanus pater,/ filio dulcissimo et pientissi/mo bene merenti, feci(t) titulu(m)./ [T]ychenianus dicit: 'fatis ab/[r]eptus hic iaceo; reliqui tri/[bu]m ingenuam, frumentum/ [publi]cum et aenatorum/ [---; quicun]que leget, nolo/ [experiatur luc]tum sic/ [ut pater expertus est]'.
[2] Virlouvet 2009, no. 18 = *CIL* VI, 10228: D(is) M(anibus)./ Eutycheti filio,/ qui vixit annis VI,/ diebus VI, incisus/ ingenu(u)s qui accepit/ congiarium (denariorum) C; fecit pater be/ne merenti.
[3] Virlouvet 2009, no. 23 = *AE* 1998, 285: D(is) M(anibus)./ L. Ploti[o] Liberali,/ ingenuo frumento publico,/ collactaneo L(ucii) Ploti(i) Sabini,/ pr(aetorici) candidati, sodalis Titialis/ Flavialis,/ posuit Florentia/ Domitilla.

[67] Panciera 1998.

In short, Persius, the texts of the jurists, and the inscriptions all point in the same direction, in accordance with what has been argued here. To this we can add that two other passages explicitly state that freedmen could participate in the public distribution of grain. The first is a very obscure and difficult text, belonging to the so-called *Sententiae Hadriani*, in which the emperor Hadrian is furious with the complainant, because he considers his request immoral. Apparently, the complainant had obtained the condemnation of his freedman to the quarries, under the *lex Aelia Sentia* (supposedly for ingratitude, but the text does not say so), but now he intends to collect the *congiarium* that pertains to the unfortunate man. It is not clear why the sentence was handed down by the *praefectus aerarii*, and this is possibly an error, as it was the *praefectus urbi* who dealt with complaints against ungrateful freedmen. Nor do we understand the brutality of the punishment, although it is difficult to judge, since we do not know what the offence was. In any case, the emperor rejected the request, leaving us, however, with evidence that is indicative of the right of a freedman (a Roman citizen, evidently) to take part in the *congiarium*.[68] That said, we must of course also bear in mind that these *Sententiae Hadriani*, if they really incorporated actual decisions by the emperor, have been substantially altered by textual corruption and rhetorical invention.[69]

Fortunately, we have another text that adds clarity. Referring to the Jewish community living in Rome on the other side of the Tiber, Philo notes that 'most of them were Roman citizens emancipated. For having been brought as captives to Italy they were liberated by their owners and were not forced to violate any of their native institutions'; Philo adds a comment regarding Caligula's tolerance vis-à-vis the Jews in Rome, noting that 'he neither ejected them from Rome nor deprived them of their Roman citizenship'; finally, Philo notes that 'in the monthly doles in his own city when all the people each in turn receive money or corn, he never put the Jews at disadvantage in sharing this bounty' (tr. Colson, LCL).[70] In short, although he certainly had a 'political agenda', Philo testifies that, in Caligula's time, the freedmen who were Roman citizens (even those of Jewish origin) were part of the *plebs frumentaria*.[71]

As we have already seen, in 2 BC, Augustus created the *plebs frumentaria* with a *numerus clausus*, but this does not mean that the creation of Junian Latinity was rendered useless. A larger number of citizens through manumission would have implied lower chances when casting lots to get a *tessera* for the grain handouts; this, in turn,

---

[68] *Sent. Hadr.* §2: 'Per libellum petente quodam, ut suum libertum perderet, quem ante tempus iussu praefecti aerarii secundum legem Aeliam Sentiam in lautumias miserat, et modo <cum> congiarium eius peteret, Adrianus dixit: "Quid quaeris perdere hominem et congiarium auferre, ex quo iam vindicatus es? Improbus es".' I have reproduced the text as in Flammini *Hermeneumata*, which has minor differences with Goetz 1892, 31–2. See Lewis 1991, 275, who suggests that *praefectus aerarii* can be a corruption for *praefectus Aegypti*. In *Sent. Hadr.* §10 (Goetz 1892, 35) a woman appears before the emperor whose son is entitled to the *congiarium*: in the Latin version, she is described as 'Latin' (but without indicating if she is a freedwoman or not), while in the Greek version she is termed a Roman ('ἀπεκρίθη ἡ γυνὴ Ῥωμαϊκὴν αὐτὴν γεγονέναι').

[69] See Lewis 1991, 280.

[70] Philo *Leg.* 23.155–8: 'Ῥωμαῖοι δὲ ἦσαν οἱ πλείους ἀπελευθερωθέντες· αἰχμάλωτοι γὰρ ἀχθέντες εἰς Ἰταλίαν ὑπὸ τῶν κτησαμένων ἠλευθερώθησαν, οὐδὲν τῶν πατρίων παραχαράξαι βιασθέντες ἀλλ᾽ ὅμως οὔτε ἐξῴκισε τῆς Ῥώμης ἐκείνους οὔτε τὴν Ῥωμαϊκὴν αὐτῶν ἀφείλετο πολιτείαν . . . οὐ μὴν ἀλλὰ κἀν ταῖς μηνιαίοις τῆς πατρίδος διανομαῖς, ἀργύριον ἢ σῖτον ἐν μέρει παντὸς τοῦ δήμου λαμβάνοντος, οὐδέποτε τοὺς Ἰουδαίους ἠλάττωσε τῆς χάριτος [. . .]'.

[71] For a careful analysis of Philo's testimony, see Ben Zeev 2016.

would have increased the level of social unrest in the city of Rome. Moreover, famines were not uncommon when some sort of food rationing was introduced, which very likely benefited only Roman citizens.[72] Seen in this light, the *lex Iunia* can be understood as seeking a solution for the *morantes in libertate* without unduly increasing the size of the *plebs frumentaria*, which Augustus was absolutely committed to keeping within manageable limits. In sum, by a simple stroke of the pen, Augustus was able to exclude a certain number of freedmen from the corn dole, while giving them at the same time something in return: a legally defined status.

The Laws Limiting *patria potestas*: *Fufia Caninia* and *Aelia Sentia*

Apart from the legal sources, we have no direct mention of the *lex Iunia* in our evidence; for the other two laws of interest in this chapter, we have some famous passages that try to explain the objectives they sought. In the first place, Suetonius, referring to Augustus, makes the following well-known statement:

> Not content with making it difficult for slaves to acquire freedom, and still more so for them to attain full rights, by making careful provision as to the number, condition, and status of those who were manumitted, he added the proviso that no one who had ever been put in irons or tortured should acquire citizenship by any grade of freedom. (tr. Rolfe, LCL)[73]

Suetonius here refers to two types or degrees of freedom, one that is complete (*iusta*) and the other that is not, in what is an indirect reference to the *lex Iunia* or perhaps the *lex Aelia Sentia* itself, given that those who are *in dediticiorum numero* live in some kind of freedom, however minimal it may be. Taken literally, the passage is very sparse in information; it only dwells on the case of these so-called *dediticii Aeliani*, referring in a generic way to the 'number and condition' of those who have been manumitted, but does not tell us the reason why Augustus took the relevant steps. However, the passage is embedded in a paragraph in which Suetonius explains that Augustus' policy on citizenship had been very restrictive, because he wanted to prevent the people from being corrupted by servile or foreign blood: 'Considering it also of great importance to keep the people pure and unsullied by any taint of foreign or servile blood, he was most chary of conferring Roman citizenship and set a limit to manumission' (tr. Rolfe, LCL).[74] The testimony of Cassius Dio coincides with this in general terms:

> Since also many were freeing their slaves indiscriminately, he fixed the age which the manumitter and also the slave to be freed by him must have reached and

---

[72] See, for example, Cass. Dio 55.26.2, 55.31.4, for the years AD 5 and 6.
[73] Suet. *Aug.* 40.2: 'Servos non contentus multis difficultatibus a libertate et multo pluribus a libertate iusta removisse, cum et de numero et de condicione ac differentia eorum, qui manumitterentur, curiose cavisset, hoc quoque adiecit, ne vinctus umquam tortusve quis ullo libertatis genere civitatem adipisceretur.'
[74] Suet. *Aug.* 40.2: 'Magni praeterea existimans sincerum atque ab omni colluvione peregrini ac servilis sanguinis incorruptum servare populum, et civitates Romanas parcissime dedit et manumittendi modum terminavit.'

likewise the legal principles which should govern the relations of both citizens in general and the former master towards slaves who were set free. (tr. Cary, LCL)[75]

We have seen already in the Introduction to this volume how these and similar passages have been interpreted by earlier scholarship in a racial fashion. For present purposes, it is by contrast important to highlight that unlike Suetonius, Cassius Dio does not focus on slaves who have behaved badly, but rather on other aspects of the *lex Aelia Sentia*, such as the respective ages of master and slave, even if he also emphasises Augustus' concern for preserving the citizen body unharmed. In the last of the four 'books' (*biblia*) that Augustus left to serve as a guide for Tiberius and the general public after his death, there was, according to Cassius Dio, a recommendation that 'they should not free many slaves, lest they should fill the city with a promiscuous rabble' (tr. Cary, LCL).[76] Paradoxically, however, our author also mentions a speech by the emperor in AD 9 in which, defending the measures taken to increase the birth rate, he proclaims as follows: 'Do we not free our slaves chiefly for the express purpose of making out of them as many citizens as possible?' (tr. Cary, LCL).[77] Since these are two apparently contradictory statements and messages, it is tempting to attribute one of them (or both) to the rhetoric of Cassius Dio, but it cannot be precluded that both coexisted peacefully in the mind of the emperor: manumission is good for Rome, as long as it is done with due caution and restraint; it involves the creation of new citizens and therefore new soldiers, both for the navy, the *vigiles* or the *auxilia* (in the case of freedmen) and for the legions (in the case of their descendants).

Importantly, Augustus was not the first to establish rewards for freedmen who had children. In the census of 169 BC, freedmen with a son over five years of age were enrolled in all the thirty-five tribes, instead of being confined to the four urban ones, a form of reward which in some way equated them with *ingenui*, but which coexisted with deep prejudices against them because of their past enslavement.[78] Against this backdrop, the discourse surrounding the Augustan laws emerges as yet another example, albeit a particularly significant one, of the ambiguity with which the Roman elite perceived the challenge posed by the integration of manumitted persons into the citizenry.

To our dismay, neither Suetonius nor Cassius Dio makes any direct reference to the *lex Fufia Caninia*, and the limits this law established for testamentary manumission. The law was passed in 2 BC, coinciding therefore with the creation of the *plebs frumentaria*. It is difficult to know if we can establish any kind of relationship between these two events, because we do not know what the transitory provisions of the law were; in other words, we do not know what measures were applied to wills drawn up before this date, but which were opened later, that is, whether or not the restrictions imposed by the *lex Fufia Caninia* applied to them. On the other hand, Dionysius of Halicarnassus

---

[75] Cass. Dio 55.13.7: 'πολλῶν τε πολλοὺς ἀκρίτως ἐλευθερούντων, διέταξε τήν τε ἡλικίαν ἣν τόν τε ἐλευθερώσοντά τινα καὶ τὸν ἀφεθησόμενον ὑπ' αὐτοῦ ἔχειν δεήσοι, καὶ τὰ δικαιώματα οἷς οἵ τε ἄλλοι πρὸς τοὺς ἐλευθερουμένους καὶ αὐτοὶ οἱ δεσπόται σφῶν γενόμενοι χρήσοιντο'.
[76] Cass. Dio 56.33.3.
[77] Cass. Dio 56.7.6.
[78] See Livy 45.15.1–2.

reveals the concern that there was at that time, in some circles, over what was seen as a hypocritical display of false generosity at funerals enabled through sizeable testamentary manumissions.[79] Clearly, a moral stance that challenged the 'luxury' that characterised some funerals was one of the main reasons for the law, but perhaps not the only one.[80] Gardner and Sirks have proposed an explanation for the law that seems a little too complicated to my mind. They focus on the consequences for patronal rights that testamentary manumission had in cases when the testator had no children or else the heir was an *heres extraneus*.[81] A far simpler explanation is that the law attempted to avoid a substantial reduction in the number of slaves transmitted in the will of their owner, because this would negatively affect the interests of the legal heir(s): not patronal rights, but instead the squandering of the inheritance; that was the real danger. The most likely background then is to be seen in the deceased's desire to have a splendid funeral, with many manumitted slaves attending, facilitated by the fact that the required manumissions through the will would not cost the deceased anything. It is notable in this context that the emperor Justinian mentioned the case of slaves who were deceived into thinking that they had been liberated in their owner's will; they attended the funeral with the *pilleus*, only to find out later that they were still slaves.[82]

As for the *lex Aelia Sentia*, although it regulated various aspects of the relationship between the freed slave and the former owner, as far as manumission was concerned, it enacted two critical provisions: these are worth reiterating here. First, it provided that a person under twenty years of age could not manumit any of their slaves except for *iusta causa*. Second, it provided that a slave who was freed before the age of thirty (and without *iusta causa*) became not a Roman citizen but a Junian Latin (this is assuming the anteriority of the *lex Iunia*). To understand the reasons for the law, approved in AD 4, the first thing we must do is place it in the context of the reforms that were introduced in AD 4–9. Overall, the aim of these reforms was to provide stability to the Augustan regime when the succession to the throne could already be anticipated, as Dalla Rosa has outlined.[83] As is well known, in February AD 4, Gaius Caesar died and Tiberius was adopted by Augustus. A *lectio senatus* followed, but this time it was carried out not by Augustus himself (as on the other three occasions that preceded this one) but by a senatorial commission.[84] Furthermore, Augustus completed a peculiar census, limited only to Italy and to people with assets valued at least at 200,000 sesterces.[85] The following year, control over the elections was handed over to the senatorial and equestrian *ordines* through the quite complex system known as *destinatio* (via the *lex Valeria Cornelia*).

---

[79] Dion. Hal. *Ant. Rom.* 4.24.6.

[80] There is therefore a clear connection between this Augustan law and the so-called Falcidian Fourth, established by a *lex Falcidia* in 41 or 40 BC. On the dating of the Falcidian law to 41 BC, which depends on Cass. Dio 48.33.5 and Hieron. *Chron. ad ann.* 42 (p. 152 Helm), see Broughton 1952, II, 372; cf. Rotondi 1912, 438, who situates the law in 40 BC.

[81] See Gardner 1991; Sirks 2012.

[82] *CJ* 7.6.1.5 (AD 531); on this issue, see Chapter 9 below, pp.195–6.

[83] See Dalla Rosa 2018.

[84] Cass. Dio 55.13.3, with Suet. *Aug.* 37.1. The role of the senatorial commission explains why the *lectio* is passed over in silence in *RGDA* 8; cf. Cooley 2009, 139.

[85] So reported in Cass. Dio 55.13.4.

Seen against this backdrop, the *lex Aelia Sentia* emerges as being situated in the context in which Augustus sought to bring stability to the regime and prepare for the succession. Since the issue of the *plebs frumentaria* had been settled and the vote of the freedmen no longer posed a threat (because the people had stopped participating in the elections), it was now necessary to address the venerable identity between freedom and Roman citizenship that had surprised Greek observers so much. To this end, the law was adopted, in my view, with a threefold objective: to protect citizens; to improve the inheritance rights of patrons; and to restrict *patria potestas*, i.e. the power of owners over their slaves, which included the right to grant the *beneficium libertatis*. As for the protection of the citizens as a whole, the testimony of Suetonius and Cassius Dio, noted above, should be sufficient, if interpreted not in racial or moral terms, but as an ideological measure with the aim of putting Roman citizenship at the top of a long scale of statuses.[86] However, it is not easy to understand why it was decided to use age as a criterion in the *lex Aelia Sentia*. It is easy to understand that 'dangerous' slaves were taken away from the city of Rome and excluded forever from Roman citizenship. But the age requirement for slaves is not a moral criterion, but a purely objective one, with no automatic relation to the merits that the slave may demonstrate or the slave's general conduct. The various allusions that we find in the sources to the age of thirty do not help much either. We know, for example, that Augustus reduced to thirty the minimum age required for judges of the *decuriae*, which was previously thirty-five.[87] In addition, the *tabula Heracleensis* set the minimum age for a magistrate in a colony, *municipium* or prefecture at thirty.[88] It could be thought, in view of these two examples, that a certain level of maturity was required on both sides when it came to manumitting, in order to achieve the desired citizenship. However, slavery is not a novitiate, but on the contrary, a factor of corruption that does more harm the longer it lasts.[89] This renders the 'maturity' thesis difficult. It seems then rather that the aim was essentially to cover a lot of ground. The legislator chose precisely a relatively mature age with the intention of excluding a large number of slaves from Roman citizenship, knowing that early manumission was a very common practice. In the case of the slaves, moreover, this meant for them that many of their children would be born Latins, and hence without the franchise (thereby boosting the number of those who could be encouraged to accomplish one or other state-desired activity). In practice and effect, the aim was to exclude a large number of slaves from (formal) manumission, without pausing to analyse the circumstances of each case. Conversely, the objective was clearly not to check or reduce the number of manumissions (only the regulation concerning owners below twenty years of age could have had an impact on the figures, which surely was not great), but to control the access of the former slaves into the citizen body.

As for inheritance rights, the prohibition for the informally freed of making a will was certainly the work of the *lex Iunia*, to prevent that the recognition given to the

---

[86] Mouritsen 2011, 91–2; and very much in the same vein, recently Veldman 2020, 47–8.
[87] Suet. *Aug.* 32.3.
[88] *RS* I, no. 24, ll. 89–93.
[89] On the idea of 'early manumission', see Wiedemann 1985.

manentes in libertate led to financial harm for their (former) owners. However, it should be remembered that in the case of the *lex Iunia* the slaves that fell under its provision were those who would otherwise have died as such, i.e. as slaves. Now, with the *lex Aelia Sentia*, the affected individuals became freedpersons who, by becoming Junians, saw their capacity to bequeath their patrimony to their descendants annulled.[90] The strategy culminated in another law, the *lex Papia Poppaea*, in AD 9, which improved patronal rights over the inheritance of *enfranchised* freedmen whose assets exceeded 100,000 sesterces: it would no longer be enough for them, as it had been until then, to have one child *in potestate* to exclude the patron from the inheritance; from now on, they had to have at least three.[91] If we view these three laws together (*Iunia*, *Aelia Sentia* and *Papia Poppea*), we can see that, in the presence of a situation in which some moderately wealthy freedmen begin to appear, the response of the legislator was to increase the patron's rights over the inheritance: this was clearly the concern, rather than the creation of a legal mechanism that enabled business associations between freedmen and their manumitters, favoured by some scholars.[92]

The third objective of the Augustan laws was to put limits on *patria potestas*. When the military aristocracy of the Republic had given way to a service aristocracy, its authority in the private realm was seriously compromised.[93] The new legal regulations deprived the owner under the age of twenty of the full capacity to free their slaves, something that surprised even Gaius, because the provision assumes that a man over fourteen can make a will, appoint an heir and institute legacies, but not manumit slaves until he is twenty.[94] If he were of the required age, he could not freely manumit either, because the law establishes limits as to the number of slaves who could benefit from his generosity. Similarly, it is no longer in his power to grant Roman citizenship to slaves under thirty years of age. In short, through these laws, we can observe a dense network of prohibitions and rules that seriously limit *patria potestas*. From now on, the power to convert a slave into a Roman citizen would no longer be exclusively in the hands of the master – who would henceforth 'share' this power with the emperor. Consequently, the *beneficium libertatis* was integrated into the *beneficium Principis*. If nothing else, this shift entailed a significant symbolic message regarding the role (and power) of the emperor in Roman society, with particular regard to the power relations between the emperor and his peers, i.e. the members of the Roman elite.

Conclusion: From Law to Everyday Life

The impact of the infringement on slave-owners' powers over their slaves that the Augustan laws at the core of this chapter represented must have been acutely felt in terms of the elite's understanding of the citizen's rights, powers and, in short, freedoms.

---

[90] Masi Doria 2018.
[91] Gai. *Inst.* 3.42, with Masi Doria 1996.
[92] See López Barja 2010, 329. Note also the comments by Pellecchi on the relationship between a Junian Latin's *bona* vis-à-vis *operae* in Chapter 2: pp. 74–5.
[93] I have written elsewhere on this topic: López Barja 2020.
[94] Gai. *Inst.* 1.40.

The kind of discourse pertaining to Junian Latinity that is included in Pliny's correspondence and discussed by Roth in Chapter 8 is a relic of the resulting socio-cultural transformation. But not only did the Augustan innovation send a powerful symbolic message that mainly affected the Roman upper crust, it had much further reaching consequences, as the laws were applied across the Roman Empire, of course with the effectiveness that can be expected from a society with a limited bureaucracy such as Rome. This is an important dimension of the matter, which underscores the need to give the topic centre stage to enhance our understanding of Roman imperial society and history more broadly. The noted far-reaching consequences can be seen in several instances in our source material that demonstrate the impact of the Augustan legal programme on everyday life. Indeed, the evidence we have in this regard is abundant and varied. For example, an Egyptian form for drawing up wills specifies that the testator is aware that the limits set by the *lex Fufia Caninia* cannot be exceeded and that fugitive slaves must also be included in the calculations.[95] Several *senatus consulta* were also approved in order to prevent fraud against this law;[96] although we cannot specify either their content or their date, it is clear that the government did not intend to let the statute become a dead letter. As for the *lex Aelia Sentia*, we know of several declarations of birth made, it is said, in accordance with the provisions of this law as well as the *lex Papia*.[97]

It is in fact possible to tentatively propose the inclusion of another source in this list, i.e. the so-called Riccardi fragment. Its origin is unknown; the fragment received its name as a result of being built into a wall at the Palazzo Medici Riccardi, in Florence (as shown on this volume's cover), although it was bought in Rome in 1600. The second column, of interest to the present inquiry, reads as follows:

> s[it, c]uius de ea re cogni[tio erit---]/ eius c(oloniae), ita uti lege Aeli[a --- cautum]/ est, d(ecreto) d(ecurionum) ad pr(aetorem) de ea re refer[to isque pr(aetor) proponere)]/ edicere debeto eam r[em---]

> [may be,] whoever [shall have] *cognitio* concerning that matter [---] of that colony, as is [prescribed ---] in the *Lex Aelia* [---], by decree of the decurions [is to] raise that matter with the praetor [and the praetor] is to be obliged [to publish] and to announce that [matter---].[98]

According to Crawford, this is the fragment of a colonial charter, possibly (judging from the letter forms) of the Augustan period. In his edition, Crawford rejected seeing here

---

[95] *P.Hamb.* 1, 72 = *CPL* 174 = *ChLA* XI 496: 'cum autem' sciam mihi non licere per testamentum [plus -ca.?-] / quam quob(*) in lege Fufia{m} Caninia · conprehensum [-ca.?-] / sit · manu[mittere], rogo, heres · karissime(*) ·, manum[ittas -ca.?-] / ei n(on) obstet fugitivorum · servorum · <m>eorum numer[us -ca.?-]'.

[96] See Gai. *Inst.* 1.46.

[97] *CPL* 148: 'nomina eorum qui e lege Pap(ia) [P]opp(aea) et Aelia Sentia liberos apud [s]e natos [scil. the praefectus Aegypti] sibi professi sunt)'. See also *P.Mich.* 3.169: 'lex Aelia Sentia et Papia Poppaea spurios spuriasve in albo profiteri vetat'; *P.Mich.* 7.436: 'atque se testari ex lege Aelia Sentia et Papia Poppaeae quae de filis procreandis latae sunt nec potuisse se profiteri propter distinctionem militiae'.

[98] *RS* I, no. 34: col. II (text and translation), with *RS* II, plate X.

a reference to the *lex Aelia Sentia* because the relevant supplement appears too short to fill the gap, and because the role of the praetor in a colonial manumission procedure is not clear. The first problem, that is, the space to be filled by the supplement, can be solved, as suggested by Moreau, by reading (in line 2) *ita uti lege Aeli[a Sentia s(enatus) ve c(onsultis) cautum]*.[99] As to the second, I think that Crawford's objection provides a key to the solution, which is the role of the praetor in this context. My hypothesis is to see here a reference not to manumission, but to *anniculi probatio*.[100] In Gaius' text, the married couple themselves must appear before the praetor or provincial governor;[101] yet the law may have envisaged a different procedure. This is what we gather from the case of Venidius Ennychus, where we have, first, the decurions' decision, which was communicated to the praetor, and then the latter's edict (according to the cryptic TH2 89).[102] The same procedure appears also behind the Riccardi fragment: first the decurions' decree, of which the praetor was subsequently notified, who was then to issue the corresponding edict. The *cognitio* briefly mentioned in the preceding line in the Riccardi fragment can equally be explained in the same fashion. Maybe the law required the local council to conduct some investigation into the circumstances of marriage before reporting to the praetor in Rome.

The above considerations suggest that we may have here a hint at least that the provisions of the *lex Aelia Sentia* concerning *anniculi probatio* were written into some colonial charters to communicate the procedures to the local magistrates. In fact, we already know that some other regulations of the *lex Aelia Sentia* were introduced in the municipal charters of Spain: chapter 28 of the charters known from Salpensa and Irni, dated to the age of Domitian, states that manumission by a slave-owner below the age of twenty is permitted only if the decurions approved of the *iusta causa*. The Spanish charters do not mention provisions regarding slaves below the age of thirty: the fact that the slave's age is irrelevant proves that a municipal Latin could not 'create' a *Junian* Latin. It is reasonable therefore to think that colonial or municipal charters of Roman towns from Augustus onwards, on a regular basis, incorporated some of the contents of the *lex Aelia Sentia*, in a similar way as the *Gnomon* of the *Idios Logos* in Egypt did – the details of which are discussed in a dedicated chapter in the present volume's sequel. If this is correct, we may no longer consider these Augustan laws as primarily imbued with symbolic value rather than practical effect, for these provisions were transposed to local charters: these charters and similar evidence thus offer a tiny glimpse of the real-life application of the legal innovation that created a status, and that promoted associated practices, which were as significant in antiquity as they are marginalised in modern scholarship. This mismatch is the motivation behind this chapter and the volume as a whole.

---

[99] Moreau 2014.
[100] In the same sense, see Troiano 2019. I was not aware of this article when I elaborated my hypothesis, and I would like to thank Professors Camodeca and Urbanik for having brought this article to my attention. Moreau 2014 believes that the fragment dealt with the manumission of public slaves, but as far as we know the *lex Aelia Sentia* did not include any regulations on that topic.
[101] Gai. *Inst.* 1.29.
[102] Discussion is in Camodeca 2006b.

4

Imperial Legislation Concerning Junian Latins: From Tiberius to the Severan Dynasty

Jacobo Rodríguez Garrido

Introduction

THE ENACTMENT OF LEGISLATION related to Junian Latins – i.e. imperial constitutions, *senatus consulta* and laws – covers practically the entire Roman imperial period from the very creation of the status in the time of Augustus to its elimination during the reign of Justinian. Thanks to the legal sources, examples of rules concerning or dealing with this seemingly peculiar freed status are preserved for almost all the emperors of the Principate, with some insignificant exceptions (Caligula, Titus and Domitian). That said, discussing legislation pertaining to Junian Latins does not always mean the same thing, because both content and effects differ greatly from one measure to another. In this chapter, the focus is put on the different imperial decisions promulgated during the early Roman Empire that modified or affected in some way the new freed status created by Augustus. Besides providing an overview of these enactments, the chapter offers a thematic categorisation of the surveyed measures promulgated between Tiberius and Severus Alexander that can roughly be grouped under five interrelated headings. First, we have a group of measures which regulated access to the *libertas Latina*. These measures dealt not only with the informal manumission process, but also with specific situations in which a slave could achieve freedom as a Latin when manumitted or freed by other means. The second group of enactments has to do with the next step in the Latin freedperson's path to enfranchisement: access to Roman citizenship. Through their rules, emperors would develop new ways in which Junian Latins could attain Roman citizenship, acting both as reward and as a remedy to specific problems in the city of Rome. The third group of enactments has a direct relation with the general law on marriage, with the specific case of the *anniculi probatio* process, also known as *matrimonium ex lege Aelia Sentia*. This mechanism was, in fact, one of the main ways of access to Roman citizenship, but it was also discussed by the Roman jurists because of its implications for matrimonial law, intermarriage and the situations that fall under the *erroris causae probatio*. Given the source of the freed status carried by Junian Latins, i.e. manumission, the fourth set of rules consists of regulations of the rights of the manumitter towards the Junian freedman or freedwoman (essentially based on the reception of their inheritance at the time of death). Finally, a last group encompasses the rules on *iusta causa manumissionis*, dealing with those exceptions which, in the eyes of emperors and jurists, allowed the age limitations imposed by the *lex Aelia Sentia* to be ignored. The relation of these measures to Junian Latins is incidental because, effectively, their application allowed a *iusta manumissio* of the enslaved, but they can help us to understand better the functioning of the Latin status. In conclusion, this chapter presents a specific case that falls under the provisions of the *lex Aelia Sentia*, dating from the time of Alexander Severus, to enhance our understanding of how the Junian status interacted with Roman law as a whole.

From *servus* to *Latinus*: On the Creation of Junian Latins

In this first section, I will deal with imperial decrees and *senatus consulta* that created – so to speak – new ways of becoming a Junian Latin, leaving aside the case of the *leges Iunia et Aelia Sentia*, already discussed in depth in Chapters 2 and 3. The first on our list is an edict of Claudius (AD 46) which conferred Junian Latinity on an abandoned sick slave, reported in the Digest: 'Under an edict of the deified Claudius, freedom is due to the slave whom the owner treated as abandoned because of grave bodily weakness.'[1] This imperial decision has often been interpreted as a humanitarian measure. Even Bradley, otherwise sceptical about humanitarian explanations, accepts this hypothesis.[2] But there are other motivations to be taken into account. A first possible hint can be found in a passage of Suetonius. Thus, from a brief mention of the matter in Suetonius' *Life of Claudius*, we can assume that this measure was conceived to solve a specific problem in the *urbs*, i.e. the city of Rome:

> As certain people were abandoning their sick and debilitated slaves on the island of Aesculapius, to avoid the expense of having them cured, he passed a law that all who were thus abandoned were to have their freedom and would not be subject to their masters' power, if they recovered. (tr. Edwards 2008)[3]

Given the location of the *insula Aesculapii*, in Rome, it is here that the rationale behind the measure may best be found. Following this text, some authors such as Schmitt and Rödel, or Bellen, have proposed an explanation based on the maintenance of public order in the city.[4] It is doubtful, however, that a simple change of status would have

---

Unless otherwise stated, texts and translations of the cited legal texts have been taken from the following editions: *CJ* = Blume 1952; Digest = Watson 1985 [1998]; Gai. *Inst.* = de Zulueta 1946.

[1] Digest 40.8.2 (Mod. l. 6 *reg.*): 'Servo, quem pro derelicto dominus ob gravem infirmitatem habuit, ex edicto divi Claudii competit libertas.' For further discussion of the edict, see López Barja 2007, 49.
[2] Bradley 1987 [1984], 127.
[3] Suet. *Claud.* 25.2: 'Cum quidam aegra et adfecta mancipia in insulam Aesculapii taedio medendi exponerent, omnes qui exponerentur liberos esse sanxit, nec redire in dicionem domini, si convaluissent.' Notably, Cassius Dio gives this provision general effect (61.29.7 = Xiph. 142, 26–9; Zonar. 11.9). This also appears in later sources, such as the Suda: 'Klaudios', Suda On Line (tr. Abram Ring, 25 November 2003), http://www.stoa.org/sol-entries/kappa/1708.
[4] See Schmitt and Rödel 1974; Bellen 1982.

much effect in this regard, as it would hardly prevent the proliferation of sick people and beggars in the streets of Rome. More likely, we should think about a multicausal explanation, as Major pointed out.[5] In such a multifaceted explanation, humanitarian motivations may well play a role, but this role has more to do with the complex idea of Roman *humanitas* than with the modern concept of humanitarianism. Indeed, we can begin to grasp more fully the thrust of the Claudian edict if we view it against other expressions of Roman *humanitas* – such as a famous passage in one of Pliny's letters:

> Illnesses and also deaths among my servants, some of them young, have affected me deeply. I have two consolations, which though in no way commensurate with the overwhelming grief, are none the less consolations. The first is my readiness to grant them their freedom. [. . .] And the second is my permitting those who remain slaves to make a sort of will; such documents I guard as if they are legal. [. . .] But though these consolations ease my mind, I am badly affected and heartbroken, owing to the same human feelings (*humanitas*) which led me to grant that concession. [. . .] I am well aware that others regard happenings of this kind as nothing more than financial loss, and that they regard themselves on that account as men of importance and wisdom. Whether they are important and wise I do not know; they are certainly not men. (tr. Walsh 2006)[6]

From the Roman (or in any case Pliny's) point of view, the idea of *humanitas* frames the way a Roman individual should behave as a citizen and, in this case, more specifically in their handling of those over whom they exercise the powers of ownership.[7] In Pliny's opinion, he who treats his slaves according to economic criteria only is not *humanus*. In other words, such an individual is not a good Roman, or a good master. Following the same criterion, the edict of Claudius can be seen in a different light, i.e. it can be understood as a punishment for neglectful masters, a logic that perhaps explains the criticism launched against some *domini* that comes through Justinian's description of the enactment in the *Codex*:

> And we also know that this too was introduced by the edict of the divine Claudius, in connection with the ancient Latin right, namely that if a man should publicly eject his slave, stricken with dangerous sickness, from his house, neither caring for him nor commending him to another, although, if he did not have sufficient

---

[5] See Major 1994, 89.
[6] Plin. *Ep.* 8.16: 'Confecerunt me infirmitates meorum, mortes etiam, et quidem iuvenum. Solacia duo nequaquam paria tanto dolori, solacia tamen: unum facilitas manumittendi. [. . .] Alterum quod permitto servis quoque quasi testamenta facere, eaque ut legitima custodio. [. . .] Sed quamquam his solaciis acquiescam, debilitor et frangor eadem illa humanitate, quae me ut hoc ipsum permitterem induxit. [. . .] Nec ignoro alios eius modi casus nihil amplius vocare quam damnum, eoque sibi magnos homines et sapientes videri. Qui an magni sapientesque sint, nescio; homines non sunt.'
[7] On this specific meaning of Roman *humanitas*, see Schulz 1990, 211–13; and 235 for discussion of *humanitas* and slavery; on which, see now more fully also Knoch 2005. The search for humanity in Roman slavery is firmly tied to the work of Joseph Vogt (esp. Vogt 1965). For a critique of Vogt's work, see Finley 1975; 1980, 55–65, 107–22.

property to provide for him, he had the opportunity to send him to a hospital or aid him as far as he could, such slave enjoyed Latin liberty, and when he died, the master received his property, though he abandoned him while dying (*quem ille moriendum dereliquit*).[8]

As we know from Gaius (*Inst.* 3.56), the manumitter of a Junian Latin has the right over the freedperson's entire inheritance. This is a fact that Justinian clearly despises when he describes the master as *quem ille moriendum dereliquit*. A master who abandons their slaves due to illness is not, from the perspective of these emperors, a good master. Leaving aside Justinian's acute awareness of this issue, I suggest that behind Claudius' edict lies, moreover, the same principle that inspired the *lex Iunia* as a solution for those slaves released by their masters without a specific and regulated status – *qui domini voluntate in libertate erant* (*Frag. Dos.* 5, discussed in Chapter 2). This was always extraordinarily unpleasant for the Roman state, which, incarnated in the figure of the emperor, intervenes partially limiting the master's rights for the greater good (*utilitas publica*), an intrusion that can only be understood from the position of authority that the figure of the *princeps* had already acquired in the first century.

A second enactment, probably a senatorial decree from the times of Vespasian, deals with some of the consequences of the well-known *Senatus Consultum Claudianum* (AD 52). The identification of the enactment as a *senatus consultum* of the Flavian emperor was made by Buckland, following a text of Suetonius in which legislation on this subject is mentioned.[9] The original senatorial decree stated that if a woman who had sexual relations with an enslaved man did not cease such relations after three warnings from the *dominus*, she would herself become the slave of the *dominus* (Gai. *Inst.* 1.91; *Pauli Sent.* 2.21a.1). As Masi Doria has emphasised, however, there are multiple parameters contained within the general framework of the SC Claudianum, varying its application according to the status of the free woman, the property of the slave or the psychological position of the master (*ignarus*, *invitus*, *sciens*, etc.).[10] If we follow Buckland's identification, this particular decree of Vespasian regulated the case of the freedwoman who committed *contubernium* with a *servus alienus* without the consent of either the slave's master or her patron. In this situation, the *liberta* was re-enslaved under the dominion of her former master, which, moreover, ruled out her acquisition of Roman citizenship through a future manumission by the *dominus* – a specification not provided in the *Senatus Consultum Claudianum*: 'If a freedwoman, without her

---

[8] *CJ* 7.6.3: 'Sed scimus etiam hoc esse in antiqua Latinitate ex edicto divi Claudii introductum, quod, si quis servum suum aegritudine periclitantem sua domo publice eiecerit neque ipse eum procurans neque alii eum commendans, cum erat ei libera facultas, si non ipse ad eius curam sufficeret, in xenonem eum mittere vel quo poterat modo eum adiuvare, huiusmodi servus in libertate Latina antea morabatur et, quem ille moriendum dereliquit, eius bona iterum, cum moreretur, accipiebat.'

[9] Buckland 1908, 412–18, with Suet. *Vesp.* 11.1: 'Libido atque luxuria coercente nullo invaluerat; auctor senatui fuit decernendi, ut quae se alieno servo iunxisset, ancilla haberetur' ('With no measures to curtail them, lust and luxury had flourished. At his instigation, the senate decreed that if any woman should have a relationship with someone else's slave, she was to be considered a slavewoman'; tr. Edwards 2008).

[10] Masi Doria 2013, 167. On the difficult task of tracing the *Senatus Consultum Claudianum* in the Justinianic sources, made more complex by the fact that Justinian eliminated its use, see generally Masi Doria 2016.

patron's knowledge, lived together with someone else's slave, she would become the slave of her patron, with the consequence that she cannot ever acquire Roman citizenship from him.'[11] It is clear that the change in the procedure here responds to an interest in protecting the rights of the patron, who was, after all, unaware of the affair. The woman is punished with re-enslavement, and the patron is compensated with the recovery of ownership over his former *liberta*. Nevertheless, Buckland infers from the text that the *senatus consultum* only bans a second formal manumission executed by the *same* master.[12] Seen this way, it follows that the re-enslaved woman could be manumitted by the *dominus* as a *Latina* or, alternatively, as a *liberta* endowed with Roman citizenship by a *different* master. More recently, Sirks has argued differently, i.e. that in this kind of situation the state of slavery was necessarily permanent, regardless of who owned the individual in question or the type of manumission.[13] A third possible interpretation can be centred on the only aspect that appears as permanent in the enslaved woman's condition, i.e. her seeming inability to achieve not freed status, but the Roman citizenship. This, then, would make her practically (or literally) a *dediticia*. From my point of view, the key is in the text, and in the expression *ab eo ad civitatem Romanam perducatur* – referring to *the master* (*ab eo*), instead of manumission. Thus, the text seems to be specifically banning a second *iusta manumissio* by the *same* master, as Buckland suggested. If, then, Buckland's hypothesis is correct, the enslaved woman would have been allowed to achieve Roman citizenship even if manumitted as a Latin in the first instance, if she later fulfilled the conditions to obtain the *ius Quiritium* by other means than *iteratio*.

The third rule in our list is closely related with another striking provision, namely the so-called *ne serva prostituatur* covenant on the sale of a slave, i.e. the prohibition to prostitute an enslaved woman after purchase (Digest 18.7.6; Pap. l. 27, *quaestiones*). Justinian tells us in the *Codex* (7.6.4) that slaves used to achieve *Latinitas* if they were sold with this clause and later prostituted by the new owner, a second buyer or even the former owner (if they had recovered the slave through *manus iniectio*, one of the possibilities this covenant envisaged). The legal development of this restrictive covenant is as complex as it is fascinating, with a first reference to a specific imperial decree known from the times of Vespasian.[14] Indeed, in a section from the Digest (37.14.7; Mod. *l. sing. de manumissionibus*) a *lex* prior to Vespasian is mentioned, which was probably the origin of the covenant's institutionalisation. Despite all this, we should not take it for granted that the slave was freed as a Latin already at the point of the rule's enactment. To be sure, the picture in the Justinianic age is clear: the slave sold *ne prostituatur* who was nevertheless prostituted should be freed as a Junian Latin. But the use of the Junian status could have been a later addition not included in the

---

[11] *Pauli Sent.* 2.21a.7: 'Liberta si ignorante patrono servo se alieno coniunxerit, ancilla patroni efficitur ea condicione, ne aliquando ab eo ad civitatem Romanam perducatur' (own translation). For discussion, see Masi Doria 2013, 168.

[12] See Buckland 1908, 416.

[13] See Sirks 2005, 142, 146.

[14] For detailed analysis of the *ne serva prostituatur* covenant, see Sicari 1991; McGinn 1998, 288–319; Rodríguez Garrido 2020.

original clause. Thus, McGinn has argued precisely for such a later addition, placing it, however, in the classical period for Roman law; McGinn argues on the basis of the linkage between the Justinianic text and the Claudian edict on sick slaves.[15] But as noted in the above discussion of the edict concerned with sick slaves, Justinian's own refusal to reward the neglectful master with the substantial profits of the *bona Latinorum* provides a moral bridge between his own stance and that evidenced in the case of the abandoned sick slave freed as a Latin *ex edicto divi Claudii*; therefore, we need not necessarily look for a common basis in the law of the classical period or rule out a post-classical origin for this innovation, perhaps motivated by moral issues that only started to appear, timidly, in the third century, but manifested themselves more firmly under the Christian emperors.

Two additional references in the legal sources put us on the trail of another couple of measures regarding manumissions that created Junian Latins. The first one is a constitution of unknown date but necessarily enacted later than Neratius Priscus' works (at the beginning of the second century),[16] perhaps contemporary to him, which dealt with the capacity of female slave-owners to free *inter amicos* with the permission of their guardian (*Frag. Dos.* 15; also discussed in Chapter 2). The reference is not particularly meaningful except for opening a window on the possibility of a *manumissio per epistula* during the classical period.[17] The second one, mentioned by Justinian in the *Codex* (7.6.8), deals with an old tradition concerned with a slave who had lost a *causa liberalis* against their master. By this rule, if the slave was bought by a third person in order to manumit them, the slave could only attain freedom as a Junian Latin. Buckland considers this rule too precise not to depend on a specific provision.[18] Due to the fact that the freedom of the slave seems to have been automatic, we can assume that the old rule was established after two other enactments that simplified the relevant procedure, i.e. Marcus Aurelius' legislation on the *ut manumittatur* sales and the *redemptiones suis nummis* provision.[19]

From *Latini* to Roman Citizens: The Acquisition of the *ius Quiritium*

The second block of measures to be discussed directly relates to the ways open to Junian Latins to obtain the *ius Quiritium* and thus Roman citizenship through their own efforts, outlined in brief in the Introduction to this volume. Whatever the theoretical chances to gain *civitas* through one or other state-driven remedy, the complexity of the procedures covered by the *lex Aelia Sentia* and subsequent decrees leads us to assume that many Junian Latins died before attaining full citizenship; this is also implied by the

---

[15] See McGinn 1998, 307.
[16] Despite the difficulties in dating this rule, the classical nature of the content of the *Fragmenta Dositheana* suggests its location in the period between the reign of Hadrian and the start of the third century: Nicosia 2000, 223, n. 9.
[17] This possibility has been denied by Nicosia 2000.
[18] See Buckland 1908, 549.
[19] For discussion, see Buckland 1908, 628–40.

length of time taken to undergo *anniculi probatio* by Venidius Ennychus.[20] However, the emperors found in the theoretically provisional nature of the Latin status (as opposed to the permanent one of the *dediticii*) a useful tool for solving specific situations without overburdening the imperial fisc.[21] Generally speaking, much like with the already mentioned Claudian edict, these eventualities typically concerned issues arising in the city of Rome in the first century of imperial rule: problems to do with the grain supply, and the maintenance of infrastructures and of public order. This is the context of the *lex Visellia* of AD 24, which granted Roman citizenship to those Junian Latins who served six years with the *vigiles* of Rome.[22] Later, a *senatus consultum* reduced this six-year term to one of three years only, reported by Gaius in his *Institutes*:

> Moreover, by the *lex Visellia*, persons become Roman citizens, where by manumission they have become Latins, when either under or over thirty years of age, if they have served for six years in the guards at Rome. A decree of the Senate is said to have been subsequently enacted by which Roman citizenship was bestowed on Latins if they had served for three years.[23]

The service in the *militia* of the *vigiles* of Rome has often been interpreted as a heavy task that required incentives to encourage recruitment.[24] It is difficult to identify which percentage of the *vigiles* was constituted by Junian Latins since, despite the abundant epigraphic documentation for its members, listing these by name, scholars are once more faced with the difficulty in distinguishing a free Roman citizen from a Junian Latin using purely onomastic criteria.[25] Another issue that has vexed modern scholarship in analysing this decree is the question of the date of the reduction in the required number of years. For example, Rainbird has suggested that this senatorial decree dates from Trajan's reign, and that it falls into Trajan's introduction of wider reforms in the *vigiles* such as the *subpraefectus vigilum* or the *castra vigilum*.[26] On the other hand, Sablayrolles has stressed that since Gaius does not mention that the three-year service had to be performed in *Rome*, the decree could have been enacted after the establishment of the *militia* in Ostia in the age of Domitian.[27] Back in 1883, Cantarelli had argued very differently: he held that the *senatus consultum* preceded Claudius, arguing for a chronological logic in the text of

---

[20] Since Venidius Ennychus lived before the SC Pegasianum of AD 75 we must assume that he was freed as a Junian Latin when he was younger than thirty years old, sometime before AD 40–1 (Camodeca 2017, 207), and obtained Roman citizenship through *anniculi probatio* in AD 62. The more than twenty years that have elapsed between his manumission and the obtainment of Roman citizenship casts doubt on the provisional nature of the Latin status.

[21] On the permanency of the status of *dediticii*, see Gai. *Inst.* 1.15.

[22] The law was passed during the consulship of L. Visellius Varro: Tac. *Ann.* 4.17.

[23] Gai. *Inst.* 1.32b: 'Praeterea ex lege Visellia tam maiores quam minores triginta annorum manumissi et Latini facti ius Quiritium adipiscuntur, id est fiunt cives Romani, si Romae inter vigiles sex annis militaverint. Postea dicitur factum esse senatusconsultum quo data est illis civitas Romana, si triennium militiae expleverint.'

[24] For example, Duff 1928, 140; de Dominicis 1973, 319; Sablayrolles 1996, 40; *contra* Rainbird 1976, 229.

[25] On this problem, see López Barja 2018b, 585–9.

[26] Rainbird 1976, 252.

[27] Sablayrolles 1996, 290–1.

Gaius.[28] The standard view, here also assumed, is that the senatorial decree is mentioned after the *lex Visellia* not because of their chronological relationship, but because of their related content.

Another provision, this time an edict issued by Claudius,[29] granted Roman citizenship to the Junian Latin who chartered a ship with a carrying capacity of at least 10,000 modii of wheat to supply Rome for, once again, six years (Gai. *Inst.* 1.32c). A passage in Suetonius' *Life of Claudius* is a good example of the contemporary contextualisation of the supply problem and its remedies; thus Suetonius describes in vivid language the causes for the grain shortage in Rome, as well as Claudius' efforts to find solutions to the problem, including the promotion of Junian Latins to Roman citizenship:

> On one occasion, after repeated poor harvests had led to a shortage of corn, he was held up in the Forum by a mob who, hurling insults as well as crusts of bread, attacked him so fiercely that he was scarcely able to escape into the Palace. He then left no means untried of importing supplies even in the winter season. For he offered traders guaranteed profits by undertaking to cover any losses himself, if there should be an accident as a result of bad weather, and to those constructing merchant ships he offered large incentives, corresponding to each person's status: citizens were to be given immunity from the requirements of the Augustan marriage law; those of Latin status were to be given the privileges of citizenship; women were to be given the privileges of those with four children. These prescriptions are still in force today. (tr. Edwards 2008)[30]

Obviously, the group of Junian Latins who were targeted by this decree was of a different socio-economic calibre to that targeted by the *lex Visellia*. But this was not the only time that such wealthy Junian Latins attracted the emperor's attention. Thus, in the aftermath of the great fire of the summer of AD 64, Nero carried through a series of measures for the reconstruction of the city. With these measures, the emperor intended to 'encourage' – if not compel – public and private entities and individuals to contribute to the reconstruction of Rome, as Suetonius details: 'Conlationibusque non receptis modo verum et efflagitatis provincias privatorumque census prope exhausit' (*Ner.* 38.3). In this case, Suetonius does not specify the methods used to

---

[28] Cantarelli 1883, 99, n. 36.
[29] The decree is dated to AD 51 by Sirks 1980, 290.
[30] Suet. *Claud.* 18.2–19.1: 'Artiore autem annona ob assiduas sterilitates detentus quondam medio foro a turba conviciisque et simul fragminibus panis ita infestatus, ut aegre nec nisi postico evadere in Palatium valuerit, nihil non ex eo cogitavit ad invehendos etiam tempore hiberno commeatus. nam et negotiatoribus certa lucra proposuit suscepto in se damno, si cui quid per tempestates accidisset, et naves mercaturae causa fabricantibus magna commoda constituit pro condicione cuiusque: civis vacationem legis Papiae Poppaeae, Latino ius Quiritium, feminis ius IIII liberorum; quae constituta hodieque servantur.' Suetonius narrates a similarly tense episode in *Claud.* 15, which has been employed by Tuori 2016, 164 to suggest that these incidents were highlighted to underline Claudius' weakness, something which is also stressed by Tacitus (for example, *Ann.* 12.43). Even if this view is accepted, it does not invalidate Suetonius' description of the episode as proof of the seriousness of the supply issues in Rome.

involve individuals in the rebuilding of the city, unlike in the case of the grain shortage under Claudius. A passage in Gaius' *Institutes* may come to the rescue, however:

> It was established in an Edict published by Nero that if a Latin who had property worth two hundred thousand sesterces, or more, should build a house in the City of Rome on which he expended not less than half his estate, he should obtain the right of Roman citizenship.[31]

Whether or not Gaius' comment coincides with Suetonius', if we compare this measure with the earlier Claudian edict, a striking difference is immediately apparent that deserves emphasis: thus, under Nero, the requirement to obtain Roman citizenship is not a minimum investment, but a percentage of the Junian Latin patrimony, namely half of it, which is tremendously burdensome – if their patrimony exceeded 200,000 sesterces. Given Suetonius' testimony, this extraordinary high investment may therefore rather be seen as opening up a different interpretation – i.e. the possibility that this procedure was not an option, but mandatory. Put differently, the Neronian measure may in fact constitute a kind of tax on the fortunes of extremely wealthy Junian Latins in Rome, which was off-set by the concession of the *ius Quiritium*.

Less complex was a Trajanic measure that granted Roman citizenship to the Latin who established and ran a bakery in Rome (Gai. *Inst.* 1.34). The voluntary nature of this measure is beyond doubt. Yet, it is interesting how the timeframe for the Junian Latin's accrual of the benefit is not six years, but three – evoking the *senatus consultum* which reduced the term of service in the *vigiles* down to three years, noted above: this may be seen as further evidence that the latter is to be placed in Trajan's reign.

The last path to Roman citizenship to be discussed here was created by a senatorial decree mentioned by Ulpian: this *senatus consultum* granted the *ius Quiritium* to female Junian Latins who had three or more children (*Reg.* 3.1); the SC thus fell within the broader remit of the so-called *ius liberorum*, concerned with rights deriving from having children. As in some of the other cases already discussed, we do not know the date of this decree.[32] Yet, as with all the privileges derived from the *ius liberorum*, there can be little doubt that the measure was an incentive for an increase in the birth rate, something that likely also happened with the procedure of *anniculi probatio* – to which we must now turn.

The *anniculi probatio* Procedure and the Roman Law of Marriage

Regardless of the date on which the last discussed decree was issued, the intention of boosting the birth rate connects directly with the topic of the present section, i.e. the imperial regulations relating to the *anniculi probatio* (also known as *matrimonium ex*

---

[31] Gai. *Inst.* 1.33: 'Praeterea a Nerone constitutum est, ut si Latinus qui patrimonium sestertium CC milium plurisve habebit, in urbe Roma domum aedificaverit, in quam non minus quam partem dimidiam patrimonii sui inpedierit, ius Quiritium consequatur.'

[32] Cantarelli 1883, 108–9 proposed the reign of Hadrian for its enactment because of its similarities with the *Senatus Consultum Tertullianum*.

lege Aelia Sentia), the rules of Junian Latin intermarriage, and the *erroris causae probatio* procedure.

The fundamental provision and the relevant requirements to acquire citizenship through *anniculi probatio*, i.e. the presentation of a child of one year of age, has already been mentioned in the Introduction to this volume. As also stated there, the *anniculi probatio* procedure was established in AD 4 by the *lex Aelia Sentia* for Junian Latins who had acquired this condition because of the age requirement of thirty years for the enslaved upon manumission to gain *civitas*; it was subsequently extended to all Junian Latins in AD 75 via the *senatus consultum* of Pegasus and Pusio – known as the Pegasianum.[33] The more than seven decades that passed between the creation of the *anniculi probatio* and its extension to all Junian Latins are remarkable; but we must at the same time not forget that both elements (the slave freed under the age of thirty as a Latin and the *anniculi probatio*) emanate from the same law (the *lex Aelia Sentia*) and followed a different logic to that of the *lex Iunia*: the latter never limited manumissions, given that slaves freed without *legitima et iusta manumissio* would not achieve Roman citizenship (Gai. *Inst.* 1.17). Apart from cases that claimed what is called *iusta causa* (to be discussed below), this was not the case with the *lex Aelia*, which in effect vetoed the *iusta manumissio* for slaves under the indicated age. The differences in this respect regarding these two laws are discussed in detail by López Barja in Chapter 3. Seen from this angle, the *anniculi probatio* may have acted as some kind of compensation or mitigation of the effects of the law. Later, Vespasian, in some way moved by the *inelegantia* (or incongruence) of the differentiation,[34] decided to equalise the two 'groups' of Junian Latins through a *senatus consultum*, the above mentioned Pegasianum.

Beyond the provisions summarised under the *anniculi probatio* procedure, we know of another senatorial decree of immediate relevance to the present topic – the so-called *erroris causae probatio*. The decree is of unknown date, but was certainly issued prior to Hadrian, as this emperor will again legislate on the subject, as Gaius notes in his *Institutes*.[35] The text is heavily fragmentary, but what survives makes clear that the decree was concerned with marriages regulated by the *lex Aelia Sentia*: its primary target was situations in which there had been some mistake of status identification in the middle of a procedure of *matrimonium ex lege Aelia Sentia* and, subsequently, in the concession of Roman citizenship and *patria potestas* over the offspring of the marital union.[36] We do not have information about the specific processes established to prove these errors. Perhaps this was the function of Hadrian's rescript mentioned by Gaius in the just cited passage in the *Institutes*, and whose content is unknown because of a gap in the *Codex Veronensis*. In any case, it is striking how the senatorial decree was remarkably generous in most of the cases, with the exception of the *dediticii* (whose status was, as said, permanent).

---

[33] Gai. *Inst.* 1.31; Ulp. *Reg.* 3.4.
[34] An example of Vespasian following this criterion is in Gai. *Inst.* 1.85; *inelegantia* as a juridical concept features in Gai. *Inst.* 1.84, 3.100; Digest 28.5.43, 31.66.1, 34.2.2, 36.1.69; *CJ* 7.54.3.1, 6.51.19, 11.48.22.3.
[35] Gai. *Inst.* 1.73. Volterra 1969, 1073, n. 154 and Gardner 1996, 95 consider these two enactments as contemporary, but Castello 1951, 214 and Kaser 1971, 1280 place the general rule during a moment previous to Hadrian (cf. Terreni 1999, 353, n. 35).
[36] It should be noted that this *senatus consultum* only plays a role if there has been *anniculi probatio*, as a possible concession of Roman citizenship comes into play: for discussion, see Terreni 1999.

Regulating marriage between individuals of different legal statuses was undoubtedly one of the obsessions of the imperial chancellery, and Junian Latins were not excluded from this. Much of what is known as the Minician law – the *lex Minicia* – frames our understanding of the rules that governed marriage between Roman citizens and non-Romans.[37] Enacted most likely sometime before the Social War, in the Roman republican period, the *lex Minicia*, by definition, did not address the marriages of Junian Latins.[38] But we have evidence from the imperial period that their marriages were of concern to the emperors. Thus, a *senatus consultuum* enacted by Hadrian established inter alia that the children of a male Latin and a female Roman citizen would always follow the maternal status (Gai. *Inst*. 1.30, 1.80; Ulp. *Reg*. 3.3–4). Overall, this senatorial decree ruled in favour of maternal status in intermarriage, be it those between a Latin woman and a *peregrinus*, a Roman citizen or a *Latinus coloniarius*. As such, the decree does not appear to differ from the regular procedure for intermarriage *sine conubio* and *ex iure gentium*. What was its objective then? The key may be found in another passage in Gaius' *Institutes*:

> There were some authorities, however, who held that where a marriage was contracted under the *lex Aelia Sentia* the child was born a Latin; for the reason that in this instance the right of legal marriage was conferred upon the parties by the *lex Aelia Sentia et Iunia*, and legal marriage always has the effect of giving the child the same condition as its father; for, if the marriage were otherwise contracted, the child, by the law of nations, would follow the condition of its mother, and for this reason would be a Roman citizen. We, however, make use of the rule established by the Decree of the Senate at the instance of the Divine Hadrian, by which it is declared that, in all circumstances, the child of a Latin man and a woman who is a Roman citizen is born a Roman citizen.[39]

From Gaius' text, we can infer that there was a time when some Roman lawyers were not sure if the *leges Iunia et Aelia Sentia* were granting the *ius conubii* to all Junian Latins. If such a debate existed, we must assume that the existing legal provision was not definitive on the subject. Viewed from this angle, the decree of Hadrian appears to seek to clarify the situation: there is no *conubium*, as a general rule, although there can

---

[37] The *lex Minicia* established that in unions between a Roman citizen and an individual of peregrine status, the children emerging from the union took the lesser status of the peregrine parent. For an English-language survey of the law's provisions, see Cherry 1990, esp. 254–60 for discussion of the Roman law of marriage in relation to Junian Latins.

[38] Gaius himself clarified in *Inst*. 1.79 that this law did not affect Latin Junians, since the Latins mentioned in the measure were those 'qui proprios populos propriasque civitates habebant'. On this subject, see García Fernández 2018.

[39] Gai. *Inst*. 1.80: 'Fuerunt tamen qui putaverunt ex lege Aelia Sentia contracto matrimonio Latinum nasci, quia videtur eo casu per legem Aeliam Sentiam et Iuniam conubium inter eos dari, et semper conubium efficit ut, qui nascitur patris condicioni accedat; aliter vero contracto matrimonio eum qui nascitur iure gentium matris condicionem sequi et ob id esse civem Romanum. Sed hoc iure utimur ex senatusconsulto, quo auctore divo Hadriano significatur, ut quoquo modo ex Latino et cive Romana natus civis Romanus nascatur.'

be some exceptions (see Ulp. *Reg.* 5.6, probably hinting at auxiliary troops marrying *Latinae post missionem*).

Hadrian's reluctance in this regard contrasts with the generosity shown by this emperor in another enactment in which the children of a *peregrinus* and a female Roman citizen were considered legitimate (Gai. *Inst.* 1.77). This may at first sight appear to document a distinct privilege, over and above the situation of Junian Latins. But we must not forget that, being affected by the *lex Minicia*, children born of a union between a *peregrinus* and a female Roman citizen would be *peregrini*. From my point of view, this is the key to Hadrian's seeming change of attitude: accepting the foreign children of a foreign father as legitimate is not problematic; on the contrary, subjecting Roman children to the authority of a Latin father would have been aberrant for Roman legal logic.

Junian Latins and the *iura patronatus*

A Junian Latin is first and foremost a *libertinus*. Gaius makes this clear in his *summa divissio personarum* (*Inst.* 1.12). But a Junian Latin is also a freedperson, a *libertus* or *liberta*, because of the fact that he or she is subjected to patronal powers.[40] It is not surprising then that legislation concerning *Latini Iuniani* dealt also with patronal rights, the so-called *iura patronatus*. The *bona Latinorum*, i.e. the *bona libertorum* derived from the freedperson's inheritance, were established already by the *lex Iunia*.[41] Later, the imperial power refocused attention to make implementation more flexible. This is clearly the intention behind the constitution of Trajan that limited the effects of the granting of Roman citizenship via *beneficium principis*:

> For the Divine Trajan decided in a case of this kind that if a Latin obtained the right of Roman citizenship from the Emperor without the knowledge or consent of his patron, the said freedman resembles other Roman citizens, and can beget lawful children; but he will die a Latin, and his children cannot become his heirs.[42]

With this rescript, Trajan sought to counteract the damage that unilateral concession of Roman citizenship could entail for the former master's rights concerning the freedperson's *bona*, a concern that can also be seen in his correspondence with Pliny ('quod a te petente patrona peto', *Ep.* 10.5; 'quod a te volentibus patronis peto', *Ep.* 10.11): the emperor showed himself to be always prudent in granting privileges to formerly enslaved individuals that could negatively affect the freedperson's patron.

---

[40] There is an explicit reference to *liberti Latini hominis* in Gai. *Inst.* 3.56 (quoted fully in this volume's Introduction). Although there is some debate about authenticity and impact (see Nicosia 2007, 1834, n. 16), the constant references in Gaius to *Latini patroni* are, in my view, sufficient to identify Junian Latins as *liberti*. For an analysis of the polysemic nature of these terms, see Cels-Saint-Hilaire 2002.

[41] For discussion, see Masi Doria 2018.

[42] Gai. *Inst.* 3.72: 'Nam, ut divus Traianus constituit, si Latinus invito vel ignorante patrono ius Quiritium ab imperatore consecutus sit, [quibus casibus,] dum vivit iste libertus, ceteris civibus Romanis libertis similis est et iustos liberos procreat, moritur autem Latini iure, nec ei liberi eius heredes esse possunt.'

Trajan's decision was partially reformed by his immediate successor, Hadrian. Moved by the *iniquitas* of the rule, Hadrian established in a senatorial decree that the effects of the Trajanic rescript were not irreversible; thus, if the Junian Latin acquired the right to Roman citizenship through other means, they would indeed die endowed with Roman *civitas*:

> and for the reason that the effect of this Constitution seems to be that men of this kind never die as Roman citizens, even though they may subsequently have acquired the right of Roman citizenship under the *lex Aelia Sentia* or decree of the Senate. The Divine Hadrian, induced by the injustice of this law, caused a decree of the Senate to be enacted providing that freedmen, who had obtained the right of Roman citizenship from the Emperor without the knowledge, or against the will, of their patrons, and afterwards availed themselves of the right by which, under the *lex Aelia Sentia* or decree of the Senate, they would have obtained Roman citizenship if they had remained Latins, should be considered to occupy the same position as if they had acquired Roman citizenship under the provisions of the *lex Aelia Sentia*, or under the decree of the Senate.[43]

It is perhaps surprising that Gaius does not mention here other ways to achieve Roman citizenship, apart from *anniculi probatio* (referring to the *lex Aelia Sentia* and the senate decree of AD 75),[44] thereby ignoring several of the means that he himself describes elsewhere in the *Institutes* (see notably 1.32b–34): most likely, Gaius was not trying to be exhaustive when commenting on Hadrian's intervention, but merely sought to explain the effects of the Hadrianic decree.

But already before the days of Trajan and Hadrian, the *bona libertorum* were the subject of imperial legislation: in AD 42, the *Senatus Consultum Largianum* ruled on the subject, strengthening the claims of a manumitter's children, if these were not specifically disinherited, to the *bona libertorum*. Conversely, thanks to this decree, we know that the *bona Latinorum* could be inherited by an *extraneus heres*, i.e. precisely in the situation where the master's children were specifically disinherited. A window onto this latter scenario is opened in Pliny's letters, concerned with a request for citizenship on the part of three individuals over whom Pliny had received the *iura Latinorum* (i.e. the *bona Latinorum*) from his friend Valerius Paulinus in the latter's will: in the passage in question – discussed more fully by Roth in Chapters 8 and 9 – Pliny states explicitly

---

[43] Gai. *Inst.* 3.73: 'Et quia hac constitutione videbatur effectum, ut ne umquam isti homines tamquam cives Romani morerentur, quamvis eo iure postea usi essent, quo vel ex lege Aelia Sentia vel ex senatusconsulto cives Romani essent divus Hadrianus iniquitate rei motus auctor fuit senatusconsulti faciendi, ut qui ignorante vel recusante patrono ab imperatore ius Quiritium consecuti essent, si eo iure postea usi essent, quo ex lege Aelia Sentia vel ex senatusconsulto, si Latini mansissent, civitatem Romanam consequerentur, proinde ipsi haberentur ac si lege Aelia Sentia vel senatusconsulto ad civitatem Romanam pervenissent.'

[44] We should not rule out the possibility that this was referred to in the *senatus consultum* regulating the *erroris causae probationes* mentioned by Gaius in *Inst.* 1.67–73. It should also be remembered that much of the scholarship places this decree in the time of Hadrian (see also above, with n. 35).

that Paulinus had disinherited his son (*Ep.* 10.104). In practice, this meant that it was possible to bequeath a master's inheritance rights to any private individual, or indeed to a corporate body (which was not the case with regular *bona*). The latter is illustrated in a rescript of Antoninus Pius that is mentioned by Gaius in his *Institutes* (2.195), in which the emperor clarifies that the *bona Latinorum* can also be transferred to a colony as if it were an individual.

Legal sources are not of much help regarding other issues derived from the *iura patronatus*, such as matters to do with the freedperson's duties towards their patron – *obsequium* or *operae*.[45] We cannot count on the Digest or the *Codex* here to provide a reliable account, as any relevant discussion pertaining to Junian Latins may have been erased by the compilers. But a reference can be found in the *Fragmenta Vaticana*, in a difficult text related to the duties of guardianship of the Latin freedman over his master's children:

> When someone creates a Latin, and another person executes *iteratio* on him, it shall be discussed whether this person owes the right of *tutela* to the two of them or not, considering that he has received merits from both. However, following the example of the *munera*, on which the divine Marcus established that they should be fulfilled in the *origo* of the one who made him into a Latin, we can say that only this person's children are owed guardianship rights.[46]

The key question behind the matter is straightforward: if a freedperson has two manumitters, i.e. one whose manumission led to the freedperson's Latin status, and one who subsequently iterates the manumission,[47] which of the two has the right to demand guardianship over their descendants? The answer is equally clear: since a rescript of Marcus Aurelius states that freedpersons manumitted twice should only fulfil *munera* in the place of origin (*apud originem*) of those to whom they own their Latinity, the author of the *Fragmenta* infers that the advantage in the case regarding the tutelage of the manumitter's children should also fall to the person to whom the freedperson owed their Latinity, i.e. the first manumitter. From this it can be concluded that the freedperson owed the same duty also in the absence of *iteratio*, i.e. if they retained their Junian Latinity. More generally, with respect to *operae* and *obsequium*, we can only assume that their functioning did not differ from what we know about their operation pertaining to enfranchised freedpersons.[48] Thus, given its personal and non-transferable nature,

---

[45] For focused discussion of *obsequium* and *operae* in general, see Waldstein 1986; Masi Doria 1993a. For socio-historical contextualisations, see Mouritsen 2011, 224–6; MacLean 2018, 37–40.

[46] *Frag. Vat.* 221: 'Si alius eum Latinum fecerit, alius iteraverit, an utriusque liberorum tutelam suscipiat, videndum, quasi utriusque meritum habeat; nisi forte exemplo munerum, quibus divus Marcus rescripsit apud originem eius qui Latinum fecit debere eum fungi, solius eius liberorum tutelam suscepturum dicemus' (own translation).

[47] This scenario is discussed in Gai. *Inst.* 1.35, detailing that manumission by the bonitary owner of the slave leads to Latinity, while Roman citizenship can be awarded through *iteratio* of the manumission by the quiritary owner; see also the brief discussion of the matter in this volume's Introduction.

[48] For discussion, see López Barja 1998, 144; *contra* Sirks 1983, 259–60.

obsequium was probably only due to the manumitter and their direct descendants. The same is likely true for *operae*, derived from the oath of the former slave to the master (Digest 40.12.44pr.). The fact that the Junian Latin was without citizenship did not affect this oath negatively: when taken before the manumission, the oath only had a religious significance (*religione adstrictus*); but once taken after the manumission, it acquired full legal validity also in the case of a Junian Latin, because Junian Latins enjoyed *commercium*.

Shortcuts Around the *lex Aelia Sentia*: *manumissio iusta causa*

The last section of this journey through imperial legislation on Junian Latins deals with the topic of the *iusta causa manumissionis*, i.e. the procedure mentioned by Gaius in *Inst.* 1.18–20 which allowed slaves under the age of thirty to be freed as Roman citizens *vindicta* and in front of a council of Roman citizens (senators and *equites* in Rome, *recuperatores* in the provinces), claiming a just cause. Unlike other aspects related to the legal dimensions of Junian Latinity, *manumissio iusta causa* partially resisted the Justinianic censorship, thanks to the fact that it shared the procedure with another element of the *lex Aelia Sentia*: the prohibition that prevented masters below the age of twenty manumitting their slaves into Roman citizenship.

It is widely agreed that the reasons considered *iusta causa* had a jurisprudential origin: they are not the result of specific legislation. Thanks to Gaius, we know that, as a general rule, the reasons accepted for manumitters under the age of twenty were also valid for the *servi minores*, and vice versa (*Inst.* 1.39). The roster of admissible reasons must have been large, as Paul states that listing all of them would take a long time (Digest 40.2.15.1; Paul. l. 1 *ad leg. Ael. Sent.*). But imperial legislation had an impact on the subject in reinforcing the irrevocable character of cases already approved. This happens, for instance, with a rescript of Antoninus Pius which established that *iustae causae* already accepted were irrevocable unless a *servus alienus* had been freed by mistake (Digest 40.2.9.1; Marcian. l. 13 *inst.*). Similarly, in AD 215, Caracalla once again declared irreversible the status of someone manumitted *apud consilium*, even if it was alleged that the arguments presented were false (*CJ* 7.1.1). In both cases, the old principle of Roman law – by which manumission was at base a one-way journey – was respected. The same criterion is probably followed in a senatorial decree of an unknown date mentioned by Ulpian which dealt with manumission *matrimonii causa*: 'A virgin or woman may also be manumitted for marriage, provided that the master must first swear an oath to take her as his wife within six months; this was resolved by the senate.'[49] This *senatus consultum* did not create the provision of manumission for the purpose of marriage, nor did it define such manumission as resulting from a just cause. Rather, it established the six-month term to fulfil the stipulated condition. Interestingly, non-compliance did not entail the re-enslavement of the *liberta*, but instead

---

[49] Digest 40.2.13 (Ulp. l. 6 *de off. proc.*): 'Item si matrimonii causa virgo vel mulier manumittatur, exacto prius iureiurando, ut intra sex menses uxorem eam duci oporteat: ita enim senatus censuit.'

led to the termination of the obligation of marrying her master. Gaius (*Inst.* 1.19) mentions *matrimonii causa* as a just cause, but not the six-month term, which may mean that the senatorial decree was passed subsequent to his work (and perhaps during the reign of Antoninus Pius).

A *Latina Iuniana* in the *Codex*: Junian Latins and the Roman Law on Slavery

I will end this tour of the imperial legislation on Latin freedmen and freedwomen with an actual case that I consider to be particularly interesting because of its possible implications for our understanding of the relation between Junian Latinity and Roman law as a whole. I am referring to a rescript of Severus Alexander enacted in AD 224 and compiled by Justinian in the *Codex*:

> If Iusta shall have sold to Saturninus a girl by the name of Firma, then in her seventh year, upon condition that the latter should be free when she should be twenty-five years old, then, although the fact that the purchaser should give her freedom was not inserted in the written pact, but it was (merely) stated that she should be free, then the law of the divine Marcus and Commodus applies. Therefore, upon completion of the twenty-fifth year, Firma became free, nor is she prejudiced because she was manumitted in the twenty-seventh year, when she was already free under the law; and her son, conceived by her after her twenty-fifth year, is free.[50]

The passage talks about an enslaved woman called Firma, who was sold at the age of seven with one condition, i.e. that she should be freed at the age of twenty-five. Her master, Saturninus, does indeed free her, but not on the stipulated date: Firma is manumitted at the age of twenty-seven. From a legal point of view, the purpose of the rescript is to clarify the point in time at which this woman became free, since the status of her son, born sometime between the two dates, depends on it. Technically speaking, the underlying controversy seems to derive from the interpretation of the formula *libera esset*, and whether Firma's case falls under Marcus Aurelius' legislation on sales conducted *ut manumittatur*. Under this legislation, whose functioning we know well because of multiple references to it in the Digest,[51] freedom was secured for a slave

---

[50] *CJ* 4.57.3: 'Si Iusta Saturnino puellam nomine Firmam agentem tunc annos septem hac lege vendiderit, ut, cum haberet annos viginti quinque, libera esset, quamvis factum ab emptore praestandae libertatis pacto non sit insertum, sed ut libera esset expressum, tamen constitutioni divorum Marci et Commodi locus est. Ideoque impleto vicensimo quinto anno Firma libera facta est nec obest ei, quod vicensimo septimo anno manumissa est, quae iam ex constitutione libera erat: et is, quem post vicensimum quintum annum ex te conceptum enixa est, ingenuus est.'

[51] Digest 1.5.22 (Mod. l. 12 *resp.*), 2.4.10 (Ulp. l. 5 *ad ed.*), 24.1.7.8 (Ulp. l. 31 *ad Sab.*), 26.4.3.2 (Ulp. l. 38 *ad Sab.*), 28.5.85.1 (Paul. l. 23 *quaest.*), 38.1.13pr.–1 (Ulp. l. 38 *ed.*), 40.1.10 (Paul. l. 2 *imp. sent.*), 40.1.20.2 (Pap. l. 10 *resp.*), 40.2.20.1 (Ulp. l. 2 *de off. proc.*), 40.8.1 (Paul. l. 5 *Plaut.*), 40.8.6 (Marcian. *ad form. hyp.*), 40.8.9 (Paul. l. 5 *quaest.*), 40.12.38pr.–1 (Paul. l. 15 *resp.*).

who was sold (or gifted)[52] on the proviso of being freed once a term or condition was fulfilled, even if the buyer in charge of manumitting did not, in fact, manumit the slave. If this legislation applied to Firma's case – as Severus Alexander suggests in the rescript – she would be considered free already on her twenty-fifth birthday, and as a consequence also her son.

All ages mentioned in the passage – twenty-seven as the age of manumission and twenty-five as the age fixed in the sale agreement – are below the age requirement of thirty established by the *lex Aelia Sentia*. For this reason, we can presume that what is being discussed in Alexander's rescript is the manumission of a Junian Latin. This possibility was already briefly outlined by Wiedemann, who uses the case to illustrate that manumission before the age of thirty (even if only as a Junian Latin) was embedded in the mindset of Roman *domini*, yet simultaneously challenging the theory of regular early manumission, by age thirty, that had been championed by Alföldy – positing instead a distinction between ideal and reality.[53]

While, as will be seen, there is no reason to doubt Wiedemann's assessment of Firma's status, it is worthwhile briefly considering a number of legal provisos that have a bearing on our appreciation of Firma's case and of the relationship between Junian Latinity and Roman law more broadly. To begin with, and as already noted, the definition of reasons that could be considered *iusta causa* was a favoured subject in legal discourse. But although, as Paul stated, the list was vast, all of the *causae* seem to have to do with kinship, affective bonds or merits of the enslaved. Several extracts from Ulpian's works underline this idea:

> If a man under twenty manumits, grounds of this kind for manumission are usually accepted: that the slave is his son or daughter, brother or sister by birth.
>
> [. . .] or that there is a connection by blood (for account is taken of kinship).
>
> [. . .] that the slave is his foster brother or foster father or schoolmaster or nurse or son or daughter to any of these or his foster child or *capsarius*, that is, one who carries books, or that he is manumitted for the purpose of being his procurator provided that such a person is not under eighteen. It is a further requirement that the manumitter should not have just one slave.[54]

---

[52] See Digest 40.8.8. Buckland 1908, 629 considers the inclusion of the case of a slave who was gifted a later jurisprudential innovation.
[53] See Wiedemann 1985, 170, with Alföldy 1972.
[54] The cited passages are:

> Digest 40.2.11 (Ulp. l. 6 *de off. proc.*): 'Si minor annis viginti manumittit, huiusmodi solent causae manumissionis recipi: si filius filiave frater sororve naturalis sit.'
> Digest 40.2.12 (Ulp. l. 2 *ad leg. Ael. Sent.*): 'Vel si sanguine eum contingit, habetur enim ratio cognationis [. . .].'
> Digest 40.2.13 (Ulp. l. 6 *de off. proc.*): 'Si collactaneus, si educator, si paedagogus ipsius, si nutrix, vel filius filiave cuius eorum, vel alumnus, vel capsarius (id est qui portat libros), vel si in hoc manumittatur, ut procurator sit, dummodo non minor annis decem et octo sit, praeterea et illud exigitur, ut non utique unum servum habeat, qui manumittit.'

As Ulpian also pointed out more generally, *affectio*, in direct opposition to *luxuria*, was a key element in the council's deliberation on manumission motivation:

> It is to be borne in mind by judges when approving grounds for manumission that they are to approve grounds that arise not from *luxuria* but from *affectio*; for it must be supposed that the *lex Aelia Sentia* granted freedom not for self-indulgence, but for affections recognized by law.[55]

As a general rule, 'just cause' derived from a previous, personal relationship of the enslaved individual with their master. This was hardly the case for Firma, however, given she was a newly acquired slave.

On the other hand, it could happen that a sale *ut manumittatur* (or a donation or legacy) could be considered among the *iustae causae* by themselves. This could be the case even when the master in charge of the manumission was younger than twenty years, thus falling short of one of the other provisions established by the *lex Aelia Sentia*. This situation was dealt with by Marcus Aurelius himself, in a letter to Aufidius Victorinus, that commented on a bequest of a slave to a young man under the age of twenty that was made *ut manumittatur*; the rescript ruled that the manumission of the slave at the hands of the 'under-age' master was to be considered fully valid on the grounds that it was undertaken on the basis of a 'just cause':

> A man under twenty who has received the gift of a slave for the purpose of manumission has the most ample justification for manumission since the letter of the deified Marcus to Aufidius Victorinus; in fact, the slave will attain freedom, even if he is not manumitted.[56]

As the passage states unambiguously, if the young master does not execute the manumission, the slave would nevertheless be free under Marcus' legislation on *ut manumittatur* covenants. In this situation, the master's inability (or unwillingness) to manumit is compensated by the mandatory nature of the clause itself. Logically, the 'manumitting impulse', so to speak, does not belong to the master under the age of twenty, but to the seller and former master. In this way, the spirit of the *lex Aelia* was not contravened, i.e. its provision to prevent manumissions executed by immature owners or *ex luxuria*.

In theory, the legal reasoning displayed by Marcus Aurelius concerning the proviso *ut manumittatur* may help explain Firma's case, too. But there is a critical difference: in the case of Firma, it is not the master but the *ancilla* who does not meet the requirements for a full manumission as a Roman citizen. In my view, it is unlikely that the council

---

[55] Digest 40.2.16pr. (Ulp. l. 2 *ad leg. Ael. Sent.*): 'Illud in causis probandis meminisse iudices oportet, ut non ex luxuria, sed ex affectu descendentes causas probent: neque enim deliciis, sed iustis affectionibus dedisse iustam libertatem legem Aeliam Sentiam credendum.'

[56] Digest 40.1.20 (Pap. l. 10 *resp.*): 'Causam minor viginti annis, qui servum donatum manumittendi gratia accepit, ex abundanti probat post divi Marci litteras ad Aufidium Victorinum: etenim, si non manumiserit, ad libertatem servus perveniet.'

could have considered the manumission as *iusta* – given that neither the seller and former master, nor the new owner had the capacity to free Firma as a Roman citizen; nor is *iusta causa* invoked in the evidence at hand. It therefore seems reasonable to think that the freedom of Firma discussed by the emperor is *Latina libertas*: Firma was, as Wiedemann presumed, a Junian Latin.

Even if we end up with a negative conclusion regarding the civic status of Firma, her case highlights a very important matter (besides adding another name to the growing list of Junian Latins!). Thus, although Firma's manumission was not a *legitima manumissio*, her master was quite evidently compelled to execute the manumission as specified, as Firma was protected by Marcus Aurelius' legislation on this kind of agreement; logically, the failure to effect the manumission on time did not lead to a legal disadvantage for Firma (or her son). But this means that we can assume that many of the known regulations applicable to so-called formal and complete manumissions also applied to manumissions that created Junian Latins: the two were conceptually treated in tandem. This is yet another compelling reason to integrate the study of Junian Latinity into the broader remit of research on Roman slavery at large and the legislation pertaining to it.

5

OF MICE AND JUNIANS: ON THE LATIN CONDITION

Pedro López Barja and Jacobo Rodríguez Garrido

Introduction

LET US BEGIN by formulating the hypothesis that we aim to argue on the following pages: from the approval of the *lex Iunia* until the *constitutio Antoniniana* of AD 212 there was a single status of Latin citizenship in the Roman Empire, with different paths to Roman citizenship. Although the prevailing opinion seeks to establish a clear distinction between Junians and provincial Latins, our intention here is to defend the opposite idea, that is, a single and substantial identity, with the logical differences deriving from the rule of the Junian law on the succession rights of Junians.[1] In so doing, this chapter provides also critical reflection on the various contributions offered in the preceding four chapters and the diverse arguments presented in these regarding the location of Latinity in Roman imperial society.

Latins and Junian Latins

To begin with, those Latins who were also freedmen and whose patrons were Roman citizens were known in the technical language of the jurists as Junian Latins. It should be noted, first of all, that the latter were, in fact, *liberti*, not only *libertini*, because as manumitted slaves (*libertini*) who had a patron, they must have been freedmen. This is unequivocally indicated by some texts.[2] These are few in number because the jurisconsults preferred to reserve the term *liberti* for those who were Roman citizens, probably to avoid confusion and for the sake of brevity. A good instance of this practice is found in the third book of Gaius' *Institutes* (Gai. *Inst.* 3.39–53), where the simple term *libertus*

---

[1] For the mainstream opinion, see Chapter 1 by García Fernández, with the relevant bibliography. The exception is Mancini 1997, 42, who argues for an essential unity between Junian Latins and the *Latini coloniarii*.

[2] Plin. *Ep.* 10.6: '*Libertae*' (see also the brief discussion by Roth in Chapter 8: p. 180, with n. 44); Gai. *Inst.* 3.56: 'neque liberti Latini hominis bona possent manumissionis iure ad patronos pertinere' (on this debated passage in Gaius, see for present purposes López Barja 2018a, 263; although the expression *libertus homo* is redundant, we do have some parallels, such as Cic. *Cat.* 8.16, which mentions *libertini homines*); Ulp. *Reg.* 1.5: 'Libertorum genera sunt tria, cives Romani, Latini Iuniani, dediticiorum numero'; Salv. *Eccl.* 3.7.34: 'Ita ergo et tu religiosos filios tuos quasi Latinos iubes esse libertos' (with n. 18 below); *CJ* 7.6.1.8: 'et mortis liberti tempore denuo eum in servitutem deducere'.

is used to mean freedmen who were Roman citizens; in contradistinction, a few lines on (Gai. *Inst.* 3.56–66), Gaius balances between *bona Latinorum* on the one side and *civis Romani liberti hereditas* on the other.

As for the name *Latinus Aelianus*, this is a modern expression, used by some supporters of a Tiberian dating for the Junian law, to refer to the status of the Latins created first by the *lex Aelia Sentia*, at least during the time that elapsed between the promulgation of this law and the Junian law, because later, for purely practical reasons, it no longer made sense to manumit a *servus minor vindicta* without just cause and it was preferred to undertake the manumission *inter amicos*.[3] Such an expression does not appear, nevertheless, in the documentation we have, nor is it necessary for those who (as in our case) maintain the chronological anteriority of the *lex Iunia* over the *lex Aelia Sentia*. On the other hand, the name *Latinus Iunianus* is relatively frequent in the legal sources. While in Gaius we find it only twice (*Inst.* 1.22, 3.56), there are eight mentions in the *liber singularis Regularum* attributed to Ulpian, and one in the *Fragmentum Pseudo-Dositheanum*, the *Pauli Sententiae* and the *Institutiones Iustiniani* respectively.[4] Everything indicates that this is a jurisprudential denomination, proper to technical language, but not strictly legal. The Junian law certainly did not give them such a designation, because when we have the literal text of some of the rules that affected them, the name that appears is simply *Latinus*, without any further precision. This is clearly seen in the rules issued by Constantine and contained in the *Codex Theodosianus*, which are as follows:[5]

- Concerning a freedman who, as a result of being punished, has lost his Roman citizenship and has been reduced to the status of a Latin: his patron, as well as the children and grandchildren of the latter, may claim all the property he leaves behind when he dies.[6]
- As for the senators, if they had children with a freedwoman or her daughter, whether Roman or Latin: whatever they donated to them is annulled for the benefit of the legitimate kinship.[7]
- In a modification of the *Senatus Consultum Claudianum*, the son of a *servus fiscalis* and a mother *ingenua* will be Latin, 'who, while escaping the obligation of slavery, is subject to the privilege granted to the patron'.[8]

---

[3] Wilinski 1963, relying on the phrase 'Latini ex lege Aelia Sentia' in Gai. *Inst.* 1.29, 1.68; see also the recent contribution in Reiner 2021, defending more radically, but without new arguments, the coexistence of both Latinities over the centuries.

[4] Gai. *Inst.* 1.22, 3.56; Ulp. *Reg.* 1.5, 11.16, 17.1, 19.4, 20.14, 20.8, 22.3, 25.7; *Frag. Dos.* 6 (both Latin and Greek: 'Λατῖνοι Ἰουνιανοί'); *Pauli Sent.* 2.27.6 = *Frag. Vat.* 172 (corrupted text, on the excuses for not being a guardian); *Inst.* 1.5.3.

[5] Fuller discussion is in Chapter 6 by Corcoran.

[6] *CTh* 2.22.1: 'Si is, qui dignitate Romanae civitatis amissa Latinus fuerit effectus . . . Interpretatio: Si quis civis Romanus libertus intercedente culpa Latinus libertus fuerit effectus, si in eadem Latinitate sine reparatione prioris status ab hac luce discesserit.'

[7] *CTh* 4.6.3: 'Senatores seu perfectissimos [. . .] si ex ancilla vel ancillae filia vel liberta vel libertae (filia), sive Romana facta seu Latina [. . .], (suscep)tos filios in numero legitimorum habere voluerint.'

[8] *CTh* 4.12.3: 'subolem vero, quae patre servo fiscali, matre nascetur ingenua, mediam tenere fortunam, ut servorum liberi et liberarum spurii Latini sint, qui, licet servitutis necessitate solvantur, patroni tamen privilegio tenebuntur'.

- A slave who denounces the kidnapping of a virgin will be granted Latinity or, if he is a Latin, Roman citizenship.[9]

The same is found in Justinian's detailed regulation that suppressed this Latinity, where again and again only the term *Latinus* is mentioned without any reference to the epithet *Iunianus* (*CJ* 7.6). In these passages of the *Codex*, Justinian gives a brief review, probably in chronological order, of the history of Latinity, showing how, after the passing of the Junian law, new cases were added in which the slave did not obtain Roman citizenship along with freedom.[10] Thus, he mentions Claudius' edict on the sick slave abandoned by his owner (*CJ* 7.6.1.3), on the slave defeated by his owner in a *causa liberalis*, if his price is paid by a third party who manumits him (*CJ* 7.6.1.8), along with other cases in which the owner's willingness to free the slave can be inferred. Justinian notes that the Latin condition was introduced in a variety of ways, 'almost innumerable' (*CJ* 7.6.1.1a); in fact, he does not enumerate them all, but only those which he considers worthy of being transformed into ways of access to Roman citizenship.

The term *Latinus* is the most frequent in legal sources, but it is also the only term used in non-legal texts. Among the former, it is quite frequent in Gaius. In the fragmentary texts of classical and post-classical jurisprudence, this name is also the most common, even in passages that do not refer to these Latins' wealth, but to other aspects of their lives. Hence, for example, we are told that the husband can kill his adulterous wife with impunity if the lover, among other categories, is one of his or his father's freedmen and a Roman or Latin citizen.[11] We also know that the Latin had to fulfil the *munera* in the city where his manumitter had his *origo* and that he could not be an Attilian tutor.[12] We even have two mysterious references in the Egyptian documentation: on the one hand, a reference to *lex Iunia dedit eos/i(nter) Latinos*, in a fifth-century parchment scroll; on the other, the mention of the intriguing *cives* [sic] *Latinus* in a papyrus of AD 165.[13] To these must be added the cryptic *Cives L[a]t(ini) negot(iatores) Brig[a]ntiens(es)*, mentioned in an inscription from *Brigantium*, in Raetia.[14] As for literary sources, the evidence is scarce, but unanimous, in our view:

- Claudius granted the Roman citizenship to Latins who chartered a grain ship for Rome.[15]

---

[9] *CTh* 9.24.1.4: 'Si quis vero servus raptus facinus dissimulatione praeteritum aut pactione transmissum detulerit in publicum, Latinitate donetur aut, si Latinus sit, civis fiat Romanus.'

[10] That the order is chronological is inferred from the fact that the passage begins with the *lex Iunia* and ends with 'ille novissimus antiquae Latinitatis modus' (*CJ* 7.6.1.11).

[11] *Coll.* 4.3.3: 'Sed et . . . licet interficere in adulterio deprehensum, vel libertinum vel suum vel paternum, et tam civem Romanum quam Latinum.' On mentions of *Latini* in post-classical jurisprudence, see more extensively Corcoran's discussion in Chapter 6.

[12] *Frag. Vat.* 221: 'exemplo munerum, quibus divus Marcus rescripsit apud originem eius qui Latinum fecit debere eum fungi'; *Scholia Sinaitica* 17: 'Nam Latinus et lege Atilia tutor dari non potest.'

[13] I.e. the puzzling *P. Vindob.* L 26 (discussed by Pellecchi in Chapter 2: p. 70, n. 67); and *P. Wiscon.* 2.50.

[14] *CIL* III, 13542, with *AE* 1986, 530; HD007878. Alföldy 1986, 204, suggested, quite rightly, that under the denomination *cives Latini*, both freeborn and (Junian) Latins can be included. In addition, we should also mention the *Cohors II Tungrorum miliaria equitata c(ivium) L(atinorum)*, although there is no agreement on whether to accept the interpretation of the abbreviation *C.L.* as *cives Latini*; see Saddington 2004.

[15] Suet. *Claud.* 19: 'civi vacationem legis Papiae Poppaeae, Latino ius Quiritium, feminis ius IIII liberorum; quae constituta hodieque servantur'.

- Flavia Domitilla had been a Latin freedwoman before regaining free birth and Roman citizenship to marry the future emperor Vespasian.[16]
- C. Valerius Paulinus bequeathed to Pliny the Younger the rights to the goods of all his Latins. To do so, he had to disinherit his own son according to the provisions of the *Senatus Consultum Largianum*.[17]
- Salvian of Marseilles explains that those who consider their slaves unworthy of Roman citizenship bind them to the yoke of Latin freedom. These Latin freedmen, he adds, live as if they were freeborn and die as slaves.[18]

From the texts analysed we can infer that where we find a freedman of Latin status and a Roman patron, we are dealing with a Junian Latin. Once we have ruled out the *Latini Aeliani* as inexistent, there is no other alternative. This is perfectly clear. While the jurisprudential texts speak of Junians, as a technical term, both in law and in common usage they are known simply as *Latini*. It is conceivable that, at some point in time, the manner, or the rule by which one had attained Latinity or, as the case may be, Roman citizenship, was important, because these details often had relevant implications, which, however, at no time affected their status, which was Latin. Thus, for example, in the case of a Latin who obtained Roman citizenship by concession of the emperor, it was necessary to distinguish whether or not the consent of his patron had been given, but this was relevant only at the time of his death, not during his lifetime. The same was true of the *anniculi probatio*, an alternative which, since the *lex Aelia Sentia* and until the approval of the SC Pegasianum (i.e. between AD 4 and 75), could only be used by those Latins who had been manumitted before they reached the age of thirty, but not by those who had already exceeded it at the time of being set free. In other words, although it might be affected by different regulations, prerogatives or limitations, there was only one Latin condition or citizenship, just as there was only one Roman citizenship. In some texts we see how the two are placed in parallel, as equivalents: *Latinus/civis Romanus*.[19]

Things become trickier when we are dealing with Latins who are of free birth, a category that is mentioned in the jurisprudential texts, albeit very rarely. Specifically, we have only three passages from the *Pauli Sententiae*. We know, thanks to them, that if a freeborn woman, whether a Roman or a Latin citizen, has a relationship with a slave against the clearly stated will of the slave's owner, she is severely punished by being made a slave.[20] This means that the SC Claudianum was also applied to freeborn

---

[16] Suet. *Vesp.* 3: 'olim Latinaeque condicionis, sed mox ingenuam et civem Rom. reciperatorio iudicio pronuntiatam'.

[17] Plin. *Ep.* 10.104: 'Valerius, domine, Paulinus excepto Paulino ius Latinorum suorum mihi reliquit' (with Gai. *Inst.* 3.63). The text is discussed in Chapter 8, by Roth.

[18] Salv. *Eccl.* 3.7.31, 3.7.34: 'More ergo illorum uteris qui servos suos non bene de se meritos, quia civitate Romana indignos iudicant, iugo Latinae libertatis addicunt ... Ita ergo et tu religiosos filios tuos quasi Latinos iubes esse libertos, ut vivant scilicet quasi ingenui et moriantur ut servi', with the discussion by de Wet in Chapter 10.

[19] See, for instance, *Pauli Sent.* 4.12.1; *Coll.* 4.3.3.

[20] *Pauli Sent.* 2.21a.1: 'Si mulier ingenua civisque Romana vel Latina alieno se servo coniunxerit, si quidem invito et denuntiante domino in eodem contubernio perseveraverit, efficitur ancilla.'

Latinae. In contrast, it seems that they could not benefit from the SC Tertullianum (of the Hadrianic age), by which a mother with *ius liberorum* was granted the right to the legitimate inheritance of her children who had died without descendants or siblings by blood. Only when they obtained the *ius Quiritium* did these *Latinae ingenuae* enjoy this right.[21] Nor does it seem that the SC Orfitianum affected them either: the Latins have no right to the legitimate inheritance of their mother, who died intestate;[22] although the text does not specify whether they are *Latini ingenui* or not, we must assume that they are the former, since freedmen are automatically excluded.

From among the various *Sententiae Hadriani* we find a case in which a Latin woman complains that her son's *congiarium* has been taken away by the man who claims to be the latter's father. It is not specified whether she is of free birth or, on the contrary, a *liberta*. However, the reference to the marriage not yet formally contracted suggests that she is a (Junian) Latin and he is a Roman citizen, so that, in the absence of *conubium*, the father has no *patria potestas* over the son and therefore no right to appropriate the *congiarium*.[23] However, the alternative works equally well if we assume that she was a freeborn Latin, who had had a child with a Roman citizen, with whom there was no *ius conubii*. Ultimately therefore, the reference is ambiguous.

The distance that separated the Latins – the freeborn and the freedmen – from the full enjoyment of the *ius conubii* is another element that points to a unitary consideration of the Latin condition in imperial times. As a general rule, there was *conubium* only between Roman citizens, although exceptionally there could also be *conubium* with Latins and with *peregrini*.[24] These Latins, according to what we have seen so far, have a generic meaning, which implies that, in some specific cases, but not as a general measure, *some* Latins, whether freedmen or not, enjoyed *ius conubii* with Roman citizens.[25]

The Junian Latins were merely Latins who had been manumitted by Roman citizens. In other words, just as both *ingenui* and freedmen were (that is: could be) Roman citizens, among the Latins were both *ingenui* and those formerly enslaved. It is striking that when someone belonging to either of these two categories obtained Roman citizenship, they also automatically obtained the *patria potestas* over their children, unlike

---

[21] *Pauli Sent*. 4.9.8: 'Latina ingenua ius Quiritium consecuta si ter peperit, ad legitimam filii hereditatem admittitur: non est enim manumissa.' Some authors (such as recently Ruggiero 2017, with earlier bibliography) consider that by *Latina ingenua* the text refers to the daughter of a Junian, but there is nothing that forces us to introduce substantial differences between her and a freeborn *Latina* in a municipality.

[22] *Pauli Sent*. 4.10.3: 'Ad legitimam intestatae matris hereditatem filii cives Romani, non etiam Latini admittuntur.'

[23] Flammini *Hermeneumata* 3.10. This is, essentially, Sirks' 1995 reconstruction of the case, but without assuming, as he does, that the woman feigned her status, for which there is no evidence in the text as preserved. In the Latin text, the woman is a *Latina*, but in the Greek one she is a Roman, which is not surprising as there are many translation errors in these *Hadriani Sententiae* (see Lewis 1991).

[24] Ulp. *Reg*. 5.4: 'Conubium habent cives Romani cum civibus Romanis; cum Latinis autem et peregrinis ita, si concessum sit.'

[25] García Fernández 2018 offers a fierce defence of the implicit recognition of the right of *conubium* to all Latins in the communities that were beneficiaries of the *ius Latii*. The main argument lies in the integrative nature of the Latin status, incompatible with the hypothetical situation of internal endogamy (or proliferation of illegitimate children) to which the absence of this right would have led.

what happened to the *peregrini*.[26] Moreover, both the *ius adipiscendi civitatem Romanam per honorem* and the *anniculi probatio* coincide in enabling a concession of citizenship that extends to the wife and offspring of the promoted Latin. In both cases we can speak of a recognition of the previous marital union, understood as a *iustum matrimonium*, which clearly identifies the spouses and their descendants, even though it was not a union between Roman citizens.[27]

Although they had a common condition, this does not mean that all access to Roman citizenship was equally open to all. Clearly, the *anniculi probatio* established by the *lex Aelia Sentia* was only accessible to Junians. The same was true, for obvious reasons, for the *iteratio*.[28] However, the other ways seem to be open to all. We see this in the passage in the *Regulae Ulpiani* in which the various ways by which a Latin obtains citizenship are listed: 'beneficio principali; liberis, iteratione, militia, nave, aedificio, pistrino'. On two occasions, the author specifies that they refer to manumitted slaves (*liberis*, 3.2; *iteratione*, 3.3), but in the other cases, there is no such restriction. It is also specified that, by virtue of a *senatus consultum*, a woman who has had three children obtains *ius Quiritium*: 'praeterea ex senatus consulto mulier quae sit ter enixa' (3.1). The same way of access to Roman citizenship (i.e. three children) is found in the *Pauli Sententiae*, but in this case, as we have seen above, explicitly referring to the freeborn *Latina*: 'Latina ingenua ius Quiritium consecuta si ter peperit'.[29] This coincidence supports the idea of a single, common condition that encompassed all Latins. Moreover, the information we obtain from Gaius regarding these procedures coincides with that of the *Regulae Ulpiani*: the *anniculi probatio* and the *iteratio* are restricted to freedmen, while in the other cases, our author speaks of *Latini* in general.[30] In short, certain ways of access to Roman citizenship were open to all Latins, freedmen or freeborn, while others were more restrictive in nature, depending on the provisions of each of the rules. We should think that the *ius Latii*, i.e. the *ius adipiscendae civitatis Romanae per magistratum*, does not appear in this list because it is not a personal right, but (as Gaius points out) a right granted to certain cities. However, the inhabitants of these communities, as Latins, could also avail themselves of these other ways of obtaining Roman citizenship, namely, in Ulpian's enumeration, *militia, nave, aedificio, pistrino*. Of these, only *nave* is mentioned elsewhere, in a passage in the biography of Claudius written by Suetonius: the text is generic, from which we can infer that all Latins (freed or not) were eligible for the imperial benefit.[31] The same was true, then, for Nero's and Trajan's offerings.

Analysed as a whole, the ways of access to Roman citizenship listed by Ulpian – especially those opened by Claudius, Nero and Trajan – speak clearly of a patent desire

---

[26] Gai. *Inst.* 1.66, 1.95.
[27] The recognition of the legitimacy of marriage as if it had been ruled *conubium* is, for Mancini 1997, 32, one of the most characteristic elements of the Latin condition.
[28] Gai. *Inst.* 1.35.
[29] *Pauli Sent.* 2.21a.1. On the relation between both texts, see Corcoran's comment in Chapter 6: p. 133, with n. 8.
[30] Gai. *Inst.* 1.28–34. Huschke's editorial reconstruction of the passage referring to the *vigiles* explicitly restricts this possibility to the manumitted (at 1.32b), but this lacks any foundation.
[31] Suet. *Claud.* 19. Sirks 1980, 285, n. 7 suggests that *Latinos* here refers only to Junians.

on the part of these emperors to engage individuals from outside the citizen body, but with considerable wealth, in the urban and frumentary support of the city. Within this logic, the contributions of wealthy Junian Latins, wishing to avoid the burdensome testamentary regime that weighed on their status, would be equally welcome, as would those of wealthy Latins from the communities with *ius Latii*. In the same way, it is conceivable that access to Roman citizenship through the magistracies was also available to the sons of Junian Latins living in the Latin communities of the imperial west, since, as *ingenui*, they were completely freed from the limitations imposed by the *lex Visellia*. The situation in which these *Latini ingenui* – children of Junian Latins – found themselves is in many ways obscure to us, but it seems that their prospects for promotion would be quite limited, especially if we place them in a context different from that of the Latin communities in the provinces. As freeborn individuals, they could not have recourse to *anniculi probatio*, nor to *iteratio*, and they would find it difficult to gain access to magistracies in order to avail themselves of the *ius Latii* (perhaps, hypothetically, by moving to one of the communities that enjoyed this privilege). Apparently, the only escape routes for these freeborn Latins seeking the *ius Quiritium* would be those guaranteed directly by the emperors (*beneficium principis*) or for their services to the common Roman interest (*militia, nave, aedificio, pistrino* and, for the *Latinae*, a particular *ius trium liberorum*).

Latins in the *municipia*

There should be no doubt that the *municipes* of a *municipium Flavium* were Latins, for this is indicated by the Flavian laws, which refer to these 'Latins' in three different chapters: 53, 28 and 72. First of all, when dealing with elections, the *lex Malacitana* provides, in chapter 53, that a *curia* must be drawn in which the *incolae, qui cives R(omani) Latinive cives erunt*, cast their votes. The category of 'Latin citizens' is thus recognised, in this case referring to persons who do not have their *origo* in the *municipium Flavium Irnitanum*.[32] Second, in chapter 28, preserved in both the *Salpensana* and the *Irnitana*, which reads as follows:

> R(ubrica). De ser{v}vis aput IIviros manumittendis. Si quis munic[eps] municipi Flavi Irnitani, qui Latinus erit, aput IIvirum iure dicundo eiius municipi, ser[v]um suum servamve suam ex ser[vi]tute{m} in libertatem manumiserit, l[i]b[er]um liberamve e[s]se iusserit dum ne quis pupillus neve quae virgo mulierve sine tutoris auctoritate quem quamve manumitt[a]t, liberum liberamve esse iubeat, qui ita manumissus liber{um}ve esse iussus erit, liber esto, quaeque ita manumissa

---

[32] This expression is 'incorrect' according to Mommsen 1887, 611, n. 2, a rejection later seconded by others (see recently Spichenko 2018, 616, n. 27), However, Alföldy 1986 has provided sound arguments for accepting the validity of this *civis Latinus*, to which should now be added, first, its reappearance in *Tab. Siar.* II A ll. 8–9 and, second, the reference to a *mutatio civitatis* in *Salp., Irn.* 22, 23. The legislator considers that there are two citizenships in the municipality and therefore discusses what happens when one (Latin) passes to the other (Roman).

> liberave esse ius[s]a erit, libera esto, uti qui optumo iure Latini libertini liberi sunt erunt, dum {i}is qui minor XX annorum erit ita manumittat, si causam manumittendi iustam esse is numerus decurionum, per quem decreta h(ac) l(ege) facta rata sunt, censuerit.

> Rubric. Concerning the manumission of slaves before the duumviri. If any *municeps* of the Municipium Flavium Irnitanum, who is a Latin, in the presence of a duumvir of that municipium in charge of the administration of justice manumits his male or female slave from slavery into freedom or orders him or her to be free, provided, that no ward or unmarried or married woman may manumit or order to be free anyone, male or female, without the authority of a guardian, any male slave who has been manumitted or ordered to be free in this way is to be free, any female slave who has been manumitted or ordered to be free in this way is to be free, in the same way as Latin freedmen with the fullest rights are or shall be free; provided that someone who is under 20 may only manumit if the number of decurions necessary for decrees passed under this statute to be valid decide that the grounds for manumission are proper.[33]

There are two persons involved in this chapter. On the one hand, we have the manumitter, who is a Latin; there is no reason to think that he is Junian, as long as it is not specified that he is a freedman. The only thing that matters to the legislator is that he is Latin, since this is the nuance that prevents the Roman citizens of Irni and Salpensa from manumitting their slaves before the duoviri.[34] On the other hand, as a result of the manumission the slave turns into a *Latinus libertinus*. The addition *optimo iure* is not intended to distinguish this *Latinus* from the Junians, but only to specify that they have been freed with full rights and that the correct procedure has been followed.[35] At the end of the chapter, we find the rule of the *lex Aelia Sentia* that forbade the manumission of slaves when the owner was under twenty years of age except for *iusta causa*, a precaution that was intended for Roman citizens, but which here is extended to the Latins, although modifying the composition of the *consilium*, since here it is not made up of twenty Roman citizens.[36] There is no mention of the thirty-year limit, because in the case contemplated by the law it is not possible for the freedmen to become Roman citizens.

The third mention of *Latini* is found in chapter 72 of the *lex Irnitana*, which regulates the manumission of the municipal slave. It is specified that, after the manumission, the slave will be *liber et Latinus*, as well as *municeps municipi Flavi Irnitani*. There are some

---

[33] Text and translation as in González and Crawford 1986.

[34] In *Irn.* 72 the consent of the provincial governor is not required as in *CJ* 7.9.1, 7.9.2. The reason, probably, is that in Irni the slave did not obtain Roman citizenship, contrary, we must presume, to the other cases.

[35] See the texts cited in López Barja 1998, 149, n. 37. Other examples can be added in which it is not possible to differentiate between two categories or classes, such as Cic. *Phil.* 11.29 or Livy 9.34; *contra* González and Crawford 1986, 206, who are of the opinion that 'll.11–12 *uti qui . . . liberi sunt erunt* no doubt serves to make it clear that slaves manumitted or freed under the terms of this chapter are not Junian Latins'. It should be noted that in chapter 72 this expression – *optimo iure* – does not appear.

[36] Gai. *Inst.* 1.20.

differences with respect to what we have seen in chapter 28, because now it is not indicated that they are freedmen, but it is specified, instead, that they acquire the status of *municipes*, something that in chapter 28 was probably implied. Once again, we are dealing with a Latin freedman, but not necessarily a Junian.[37] The law determines that the municipality will have rights over the *hereditas* of the freedman, which is a perplexing fact, given that *hereditas* is never mentioned, but rather a generic *bona* to refer to the patrimony that the Junians leave at death. It is likely, however, that the law takes into account the possibility that this freedman might subsequently obtain Roman citizenship and thus wants to ensure that the municipality retains its inheritance rights in any case.

These Latins of the *municipia* were freedmen, although it may be doubted whether they bore the distinctive mark of the Junians, namely the fact that, on their death, their patrons (whether private individuals or the municipality itself) could claim all their property. The reason for such a drastic measure, as Gaius famously tells us, lies in the different statuses of the two, because the owner, being a Roman citizen, would have been deprived of any right over the property of his Latin freedman, hence the Junian law resorted to a fiction. This discordance does not occur with the municipal Latins, because here patrons and freedmen are both Latins and it is reasonable to think that the rights of patrons are safeguarded *Latini iure*,[38] although we know nothing about this point, other than that they did indeed have certain rights as inferred from *Irn.* 23 and 97.

Conclusion

There is no need for a long conclusion here. As noted at the outset of this chapter, it is widely held that that there existed a clear distinction between Junians and provincial Latins. But as the foregoing pages have shown, this distinction is more apparent than real: the difference between Junian Latins and provincial Latins limited itself mainly to the regulation of the succession rights of the Junians instituted in the *lex Iunia*. It follows that the story of Junian Latinity is at once simpler than often thought, and yet at the same time more complicated. Either way, there should no longer be any doubt that Junian Latinity must be studied in combination with, not in isolation from, the diverse social and legal statuses that characterised Roman imperial society.

---

[37] Fear 1990 considers this to be a Junianus, arguing that the manumission of municipal slaves was forbidden in the provinces until the SC Neratianum under Hadrian (*CJ* 7.9.3). However, the text of the *Codex* explicitly refers to obtaining Roman citizenship, which is not the case here. On this passage see specifically Giménez Candela 1984, 45–6, with the remarks of Lamberti 1993, 111.

[38] This expression appears in Gai. *Inst.* 3.72.

6

JUNIAN LATINITY IN LATE ROMAN AND EARLY MEDIEVAL TEXTS: A SURVEY FROM THE THIRD TO THE ELEVENTH CENTURIES AD

Simon Corcoran

Introduction

THIS CHAPTER IS INTENDED to provide a comprehensive and contextualised survey of all explicit (and some implicit) textual references to Junian Latins and the works in which these occur from the third century AD through the early medieval period as far as the dawn of the revival of Justinianic law.[1] The sources are mostly, but not entirely, normative legal texts. This fact always raises the issue of how far these can illuminate social realities of any period, especially where so much material is being recopied and recycled over a long time in significantly varying places and circumstances. Nonetheless, it is still important to understand the full range of our sources and evidence base to place any one mention in its due context. Additionally, since *dediticii* of freed status are so often mentioned in related contexts and share a cognate origin in the Augustan legislation, I note in passing associated references to these also.

AD 212 and All That

The starting point is the period following the *Constitutio Antoniniana* (AD 212), which, by extending citizenship to almost the entire free population of the empire, greatly increased the number of persons theoretically living under Roman law and so capable of generating Latins in their grants of manumission. Although relevant documentary sources for 'real' Latins in the later empire are few, I start with a rare and clear example of a manumission creating a Latin, since it is explicitly described as being *inter amicos* (= in Greek μεταξὺ φίλων). In a bilingual Latin and Greek text, enacted at Hermopolis in AD 221, M. Aurelius Ammonion, presumably a recent beneficiary of Caracalla's generosity, frees for a price (2,200 dr.) his *verna* Helena, about thirty-four years of age.[2] Two other third-century manumissions of 'house-born' women over thirty and for a

---

[1] This chapter significantly repeats, but revises, expands and updates the information in my earlier study on this topic: Corcoran 2011.
[2] *P.Amherst Lat.* = *M.Chr.* 362 = *FIRA* III, no. 11 = *CPL* 172.

price μεταξὺ φίλων are known.[3] By contrast with these clear examples, the sacred manumissions attested in the Leukopetra corpus in the aftermath of AD 212, although clearly being regarded as valid under some precedential ruling by the governor of Macedonia, remain essentially unchanged in form.[4] Thus, the texts do not make it clear whether, in Roman law terms, this process is creating Latins.

Of normative texts, one pseudonymous work gives significant coverage of the formal legal rules of the third century. The *Tituli ex Corpore Ulpiani*, known also as the *Epitome Ulpiani* or *Regulae Ulpiani*, cited for obvious reasons in several other chapters in this volume, survives in a single ninth-century manuscript, in which the deceptively tidied text masks a beginning both disordered and incomplete.[5] Its original date of composition has been much disputed. It seems to represent an early fourth-century recension, but the original text is earlier, perhaps Severan (although not necessarily Ulpianic), probably before the *Constitutio Antoniniana*. Its brief and summary style of 'rules' makes it an accessible digest of law, arranged according to the 'institutional' scheme, and it provides numerous references to Latins, including informative titles dedicated to freedmen ('I. De libertis') and to Latins ('III. De latinis').[6] The work was certainly longer, as it terminates suddenly with succession to freedmen, but with no title on succession to Latins (discussed, of course, in Gaius), and with whole areas of law missing (obligations, actions). One of the most interesting passages is clearly corrupt: 'preterea et senatus consulto uulgo quaesit te re nexa' (Vat. Reg. Lat. 1128 f. 192rb; *Epitome* 3.1), which is variously emended to mean that a female Latin, who has given birth three times, can upgrade to full citizenship in accordance with a *senatus consultum*,[7] although one editor suggested that the problematic *vulgo* be emended to *ingenua*, giving a rare reference to a freeborn Latin.[8]

The 290s saw the compilation of two of the most important collections of legal material of the later empire: the Gregorian and Hermogenian codes.[9] Each contained overwhelmingly private rescripts, representing imperial responses impetrated by petitioners coming from a wide cross-section of the empire's citizens, and so generated out of real litigation and authentic situations.[10] However, most of the material only

---

[3] *P.Lips.* II 151 (AD 246/7): Techosis, aged thirty-three; *P.Oxy.* IX 1205 (AD 291) [= *C.Pap.Jud.* III 473 (AD 291); Kloppenborg 2020, no. 276]: Paramone, aged forty-five (with two children); *P.Mich. Inv.* 5688c (AD 212/250): Sarapous, aged thirty-nine (or twenty-nine); also a pre-Caracalla example at *P.Oxy.* LXXXVI 5556 (AD 184). See generally Scholl 2001.

[4] Harper 2011, 369–78, with the document listed in n. 2 above.

[5] Vat. Reg. Lat. 1128 ff. 190v–202v. Modern editions disambiguate material on sources of law out of the first title ('de libertis'). On the manuscript, see Kaiser 2010; Coma Fort 2014, 173–9. For a recent summary of views on the date and author of the original work, see Johnston 2020, 305–7.

[6] Latins appear in the following places: 1.5, 10, 12, 16 (manumission); 3.1–6 (how Latins become Romans); 5.4, 9 (marriage and status of children); 7.4 (*patria potestas* in marriages of mixed status made in error); 11.16, 19 (Latins and *tutela*); 17.1 (legacies to Latins as *caduca*); 19.4 (Latins have capacity for mancipation); 20.8, 14 (Latins can participate in others' testamentary processes, but cannot make wills); 22.3 (Latins not institutable as heirs); 25.7 (on Latins taking under *fideicommissa*). *Dediticii* occur at *Epitome* 1.5, 11, 14; 7.4; 20.14; 22.2.

[7] Avenarius 2005, 221–4; Lucchetti 2012, 30. Legally significant *senatus consulta* are almost unknown after Severus, whose reign must provide a *terminus ante quem* for this change. See the list in Talbert 1984, 438–58 (the SC in question is no. 207); cf. Volterra 1969, no. 158 (Hadrianic).

[8] Muirhead 1880, 368; cf. *Pauli Sent.* 4.9.8 = *Breviary Paulus* 4.9.1.

[9] Liebs 1987, 134–43; Corcoran 2013.

[10] See Corcoran 2000, 95–122; Connolly 2010; Harper 2011, 378–90; Evans Grubbs 2013.

survives as redacted in the Justinian Code, whence Latins were excised (see further below), nor are Latins mentioned anywhere in fragments surviving via other routes. A potential light upon the life of Latins is therefore lost. Sometimes the status of a person as a Latin may be inferred, as in the case of Firma, whose manumission by Saturninus when under the age of thirty concludes Chapter 4 by Rodríguez Garrido.[11] Generally, however, Latins are rendered invisible.

Across the fourth and fifth centuries, this Latin invisibility as a social reality continues, but the survival of several pre-Justinianic legal works does give glimpses of the presence of Latins in normative materials throughout this period. Since classical juristic texts were still being copied, read, taught and excerpted, the legal status would have been understood by those who engaged to any extent with these materials, irrespective of how vital or relevant this was for them. Gaius' *Institutes*, of course, are pre-eminent for their late antique copies, although only the substantially preserved sixth-century Verona palimpsest contains the passages dealing with the Latins.[12] Other surviving copies of juristic works are mere traces. Nonetheless, there is a fourth-century fragment of a possibly Ulpianic work, which mentions Latins in one column and *dediticii* in the next.[13] Latins also appear in a newly published fourth-century fragment of Aelius Marcianus,[14] while Latins and the *lex Iunia* appear in a recently edited fifth-century fragment tentatively ascribed to Callistratus.[15] There may also be some allusion to Latinity among fifth- or sixth-century fragments of Papinian's *Responsa*.[16]

In addition, there are teaching materials in the form of lemmatised commentaries or lectures on Gaius (*Institutes*) in Latin[17] and Ulpian (*Ad Sabinum*) in Greek,[18] which mention Latins. It is also worth mentioning here the tract *De Manumissionibus*.[19] This is an elementary language-learning text in parallel Latin and Greek versions.[20] These

---

[11] *CJ* 4.57.3 (AD 224). As explored in greater depth in Chapter 4, Firma's son would also have been freeborn, but Latin; the status of the father (Fulcinius Maximus, addressee of the rescript) is unknown. Note also speculation on Polla and her mother in *CJ* 7.21.6 (AD 260) at Evans Grubbs 2013, 68, n. 144.

[12] Verona: *Codices Latini Antiquiores* IV 488; Briguglio 2012; Ammirati 2020. Oxyrhynchus: *P.Oxy.* XVII 1203 (third century). Antinoopolis: *PSI* XI 1182 (fifth century); a draft re-edition by M. Fressura and M. Wibier (REDHIS project, Pavia) is available at http://papyri.info/dclp/59956.

[13] Previously entitled *Fragmenta Berolinensia de iudiciis* (*FIRA* II, 625–6; Girard and Senn 1967, 458–9; *CPL* no. 75). See Marotta 2018 and the new draft edition by M. Fressura and V. Marotta (from the Pavia REDHIS project) available at http://papyri.info/dclp/62941.

[14] Fressura and Mantovani 2018, 665; online edition available at http://papyri.info/dclp/64631.

[15] *P.Vindob.* L 26 = *Codices Latini Antiquiores* X 1524; a draft of a new edition by S. Ammirati, D. Mantovani and P. Mitchell (from the Pavia REDHIS project) is available at http://papyri.info/dclp/64818.

[16] Bk 9 frag. 9 (*FIRA* II, 445; Girard and Senn 1967, 273).

[17] Thus the Autun Gaius commentary [CLA VI 726; fifth century]: *Frag. Aug.* 14 (*FIRA* II, 210; Girard and Senn 1967, 222), mentioning Latins and *dediticii*. On this work, see most recently Rodríguez Martín 2020; Ferri 2020, esp. 567–8. The *Liber Gai*, included in the Breviary of Alaric in AD 506 (see further below), may have been a pre-existing teaching summary of the fourth or fifth centuries, but this is far from clear: Mantovani 2020.

[18] *Scholia Sinaitica* 17 and 20 (Krüger 1890, 280, 282; *FIRA* II, 650, 652; Girard and Senn 1967, 603–4). Both passages deal with *tutela*.

[19] Goetz 1892, 48–56 (Leiden), 102–7 (Paris); Girard and Senn 1967, 464–8 (Latin only); Flammini 2004, 92–103 (Leiden).

[20] See discussion by Dickey 2012, 28–30.

sorts of elementary texts tended to be adapted and repurposed so variously that they could at different times have been used for learning either language, but it does appear that this was probably composed originally with Latin as the base text, perhaps as early as AD 200 or even before. The aim, however, would be to provide a crib to introduce Greek-speaking law students to the language they needed to learn so as to engage with their key texts. Although legal matters appear at various points in other *hermeneumata* for language teaching,[21] it is interesting that manumission was considered appropriate as a suitable introduction to the Latin language and technical legal terminology. But then this is part of the law of persons, one of the first topics encountered by any reader of Gaius' *Institutes* or the pseudo-Ulpianic Rules. Whatever the reason for choice of material, Latins or Junian Latins are mentioned in nine chapters,[22] the *lex Iunia* in four.[23] There is a certain bizarre irony, perhaps, in Roman Greek-speakers learning Latin by reading about Latins who were not Romans. Nonetheless, it is a reminder about the range of teaching needed to facilitate legal training for speakers of Greek, which will have expanded greatly after AD 212 along with the development of the law school at Beirut, and which remained vibrant into the sixth century.

Of the few surviving new juristic works, which even so tend to be largely *catenae* of quotations, three include material on the Latins. The *Sententiae* of Paulus are a pseudonymous work from circa AD 300,[24] attributed to the Severan jurist and soon accepted as genuine and authoritative by Constantine (*CTh* 1.4.2), just as Ulpian's name was attached to the early fourth-century recension of the *Regulae* (as discussed above). For the *Sententiae* there is limited direct manuscript attestation and the work is incompletely reconstructed from later quotations, especially those comprising the version in the Breviary of Alaric (see further below).[25] Several surviving chapters discuss Latins and the implications of their status,[26] including the sole explicit reference to a freeborn Latin woman (*Latina ingenua*).[27]

Next, the *Fragmenta Vaticana* comprise a juristic work, possibly composite, arranged under headings, which may have been composed originally in the earlier part of the fourth century, but whose surviving version, known from a fifth-century palimpsest, must post-date AD 372 (*Frag. Vat.* 37).[28] The *Fragmenta* contain quotations

---

[21] Dickey 2014. Another section based on rulings by Hadrian (the so-called *Sententiae Hadriani*) also provide legal style material: see Dickey 2012, 28.

[22] *Tractatus de manumissionibus* 4, 6, 7, 9, 11–14, 16 (Girard and Senn 1967, 466–8).

[23] *Tractatus de manumissionibus* 6–8, 12 (Girard and Senn 1967, 466–7).

[24] Liebs 2005, 46–50.

[25] I give the standard references from *FIRA* II (also Girard and Senn 1967), but there is an alternative reconstruction in Liebs 1996.

[26] *Pauli Sent.* 2.21a.1 (freeborn Latin woman and SC Claudianum) [from a lost Besançon ms]; *Pauli Sent.* 2.27.6 (on *tutela*) [from *Frag. Vat.* 172]; *Pauli Sent.* 4.10.3 (no intestate succession for Latins [freeborn] to their mothers) [from *Appendices Legis Romanae Wisigothorum* I.19]; *Pauli Sent.* 4.12.1 (jointly owned slave cannot be freed by one owner as Latin or Roman) [from *Brev. Paul.* 4.11.1]; *Pauli Sent.* 4.12.6–7 (a slave cannot become *dediticius* from having been bound while pledged, or by a *furiosus* or a ward) [*Brev. Paul.* 4.11.6–7].

[27] *Pauli Sent.* 4.9.8 [from *Brev. Paul.* 4.9.1]. This passage suggested the possible emendation to *Epitome Ulpiani* 3.1 (see p. 133 above).

[28] Liebs 1987, 150–62.

from Ulpian on Latins undertaking *tutela*, Papinian on a donation to a Latin, as well as a lacunose fragment of the *Pauli Sententiae*.[29] On the other hand, the *Lex Dei* or *Mosaicarum et Romanarum Legum Collatio* (c. AD 390) is a short work of comparative law, whose primary purpose is probably Christian or Jewish apologetic.[30] This quotes Paulus on who may kill whom with impunity when an adulterer is caught *in flagrante*, mentioning variously Latin freedmen and *dediticii* as possible adulterers.[31]

All these texts show some degree of engagement with existing writing about the Latins. By contrast, there is only one legal source that preserves evidence of more active use of the status. The Theodosian Code was made public by Theodosius II at Constantinople in AD 437 during the wedding celebrations for his daughter's marriage to his cousin Valentinian III, and it was promulgated across the empire east and west the following year.[32] Although Theodosius never completed a more comprehensive collection of Roman legal materials as he originally intended (*CTh* 1.1.5), the *Codex* was still substantial. It contains extracts from laws issued by emperors between Constantine and Theodosius (i.e. from AD 313 to 437), all arranged under thematic titles across sixteen books. However, the editing process has generally removed explanatory or justificatory prefaces. The code was to leave a significant imprint on the Roman legal legacy in the successor kingdoms, primarily through the Breviary of Alaric (AD 506), which contained much material taken directly from it, making it also an important witness to the text. However, the existence of the Breviary was a key reason that the full code was not copied much beyond the sixth century and the bulk of its content is known to us from only a handful of very early manuscripts. In particular, the first five books are imperfectly preserved (perhaps only one third), precisely the books where private law was treated, including topics such as manumission and succession.[33] In what follows therefore, this loss of evidence must be borne in mind. Nonetheless, in the code as it survives and has been reconstructed, only one emperor is shown as taking account of Latin status in the legislation he issued, namely Constantine. Four of his measures mention Latins, which I will discuss briefly in chronological order of their original issue, as far as that can be ascertained.

Constantine and Latinity

First, in AD 320, Constantine clarified the succession to Roman citizen freedmen, who died after suffering degradation to Latin status.[34] Their status at death is what counts and their property is treated as *peculium* subject to patronal right. It is likely that this loss

---

[29] *Frag. Vat.* 193, 221 (Ulpian, *De officio praetoris tutelaris*), 259 (Papinian's *responsa*), 172 (*Pauli Sent.* 2.27.6).
[30] See Liebs 1987, 162–74; Frakes 2011.
[31] *Coll.* 4.3.3–4. The issue is primarily whose freedmen they were.
[32] East: Theodosius II, *Novel* 1 (February 438); west: *Gesta senatus* (December(?) 438). On the promulgation and the early manuscripts, see Salway 2012.
[33] For brief discussion of the reconstruction of books 1–5, see Matthews 2000, 101–18.
[34] *CTh* 2.22.1 (from Serdica; AD 320 [Seeck]; on the date, see also Corcoran 2000, 311). On the text, see the full discussion by Falchi 1990; see also Harper 2011, 487–8; Buckland 1908, 423. Note that this text only survives via the Breviary tradition [*Breviary Theodosianus* 2.22.1], where the *interpretatio* makes it clear that the Roman citizen is a freedman.

of status was a punishment under Constantine's reform of the *actio liberti ingrati*, where re-enslavement became possible. However, since we only have the Justinian Code version of what is probably another part of this same law (*CJ* 6.7.2), which discusses Roman citizen status alone, any gradations in penalties will have been erased in later editing.[35] Perhaps originally a citizen freed citizen was Latinised, and a Latin re-enslaved.

Constantine also repeatedly modified the rules of the *Senatus Consultum Claudianum*, which regulated relationships between free women and enslaved men.[36] In one of these measures, probably part of a major reforming edict issued from Serdica about the same time as the previous item, he ameliorates the degradation of status involved for a woman cohabiting with an imperial slave (of the *fiscus*, *patrimonium* or *res privata* or on emphyteutic estates), whereby the woman remained free, while her children were born free also, although illegitimate and bearing a 'middle' status as Latins, subject to the patronal rights of the emperor and his financial administration.[37] The text also states that the change is not to apply in the case of the slaves of cities, while the situation regarding private owners is not discussed. In a later law, where a woman has children with a slave (likely her own), their children are to be left with *nuda libertas*, stripped of *dignitates*, which seems to envisage their being without claim to their mother's rank or property, rather than their being assigned a degraded status like a *dediticius* (or Latin).[38]

Next (i.e. in AD 326), in his edict against *raptus* or abduction-marriage,[39] Constantine exploits gradations of status in the rewards offered for informers in such cases. Thus, a slave is to be granted freedom with Latin status, while a Latin gains an upgrade to full citizenship.[40] The latest and final text (of AD 336) reflects a reform, which regulated whom not just senators, as under the old Augustan rules, but a range of men of high rank could marry. The long list of the unsuitable includes both freed and freeborn Latins ('liberta vel libertae filia, sive Romana facta seu Latina').[41] It is perhaps pertinent to note that the law and the preceding one (*CTh* 4.6.2; AD 336) in the code both deal also with a particularly notorious recent case of usurped status, that of the son of Licinianus at Carthage, which may have been the immediate occasion for this legislation.[42] It should also be noted that

---

[35] *CJ* 6.7.2 (AD 320 [Seeck]; posted at Rome); cf. *CTh* 4.10.1 (from Cologne; AD 332 [mss], AD 313 [Seeck]).

[36] *CTh* 4.12.1–4.

[37] *CTh* 4.12.3 (from Serdica; AD 320 [Seeck]). See Evans Grubbs 1995, 263–7; Harper, 2011, 435–8. The text survives in a single manuscript excerpt of this title (Vat. Reg. Lat. 520 f. 95; Coma Fort 2014, 241–3) and has appended to it a later *interpretatio* (although this text was not in the Breviary), which also picks up the mention of Latin status. Note that Mommsen emended the text to refer also to *originarii*, but this seems doubtful (Harper 2010, 625, n. 91).

[38] *CTh* 9.9.1 (AD 326?); see Evans Grubbs 1995, 273–7; Harper 2011, 438–40.

[39] *CTh* 9.24.1 (at Aquileia; AD 326 [Seeck]). For a full discussion of this law, see Evans Grubbs 1989; cf. Evans Grubbs 1995, 183–93. This law was taken into the Breviary.

[40] *CTh* 9.24.1.4. This gradation of reward does not appear at *CTh* 9.9.1pr., nor at *CTh* 9.21.2.1 (= *CJ* 7.13.2) (counterfeiting coinage), which latter specifies Roman citizenship as the slave's reward.

[41] *CTh* 4.6.3 (read out at Carthage; AD 336). Strictly interpreted, the daughter of a freeborn Latin woman would be an acceptable spouse. For detailed discussion, see Evans Grubbs 1995, 283–92; Harper 2011, 448–51. This law is omitted from the Breviary.

[42] Licinianus is sometimes thought a son of the deposed and disgraced emperor Licinius, but there is no need to make such a connection. See Corcoran 2000, 291; *contra* Evans Grubbs 1995, 285–6.

we only know the Theodosian Code version of this law from its survival by the slender route of the now burnt Turin palimpsest.[43]

This is the sum total of references to Latin status from the Theodosian Code and they show that it was a status of which the emperor and his palatine *magistri* still took active notice, utilising or regulating it as they deemed fit. Is Constantine's monopoly here an accident of textual survival or a genuine reflection of his activity relative to other emperors? It does appear that he was particularly engaged with areas connected to status, including issues of status dissonance; and, of the emperors prior to Justinian, Constantine seems to have been the one to tamper with the Augustan social legislation most significantly and to attempt to stamp his own views across various related areas of law.[44] These references may not be unrepresentative therefore, despite the fact that Constantine's legislation, as the oldest material in the Theodosian Code, is that most subject to uneven and unreliable transmission. Indeed, it is notable that the only other fourth- or fifth-century emperor to mention Latins is Marcian (*Nov.* 4.1, 4.3; AD 454), but precisely because he is modifying Constantine's marriage law to clarify that women are not ineligible for elite marriage simply on account of poverty, although otherwise he confirms the existing list of prohibited categories (including Latins).[45]

In the light of the above, it is no surprise that Constantine had a far-reaching effect also upon manumission law, much of which had been based upon Augustan legislation. According to Sozomen (*Historia Ecclesiastica* 1.9.6), relying on the Theodosian Code or more likely fuller pre-Theodosian texts, Constantine issued three laws easing the path to freedom with Roman citizenship (called 'the better freedom', perhaps a Constantinian term) by allowing manumission in church before bishops to achieve this.[46] The full Theodosian Code text for the relevant title is not extant. However, two laws survive in edited versions in the Justinian Code, for one of which we have its source in a near identical version from the *Breviary Theodosianus*. This law, the latest (AD 321), is addressed to bishop Hosius (of Cordoba), stating that Roman citizenship can be granted in church before the bishop, whilst also relaxing formalities for manumissions under clerics' last wishes.[47] The other law is earlier (AD 316), addressed to a bishop Protogenes, which confirms an existing provision that freedom may be granted in church before the bishop and congregation, but requires the creation of a witnessed deed of manumission.[48] It also allows easier manumission by clerics for their own slaves. Given what is stated in the rescript to Protogenes, there must have been at least one previous law, probably an early measure issued in favour of Christians following Constantine's victory over Maxentius

---

[43] Krüger 1880, 29–30.
[44] Evans Grubbs 1995, esp. 103–39, 261–316; Harper 2011, 443–55.
[45] Evans Grubbs 1995, 292–4; Harper 2011, 451. Marcian's full Novel only survives via the Breviary tradition.
[46] For Sozomen, see Harries 1986, 48–9. For the fullest discussion of Constantine's laws on this topic, see Fabbrini 1965, 48–89; cf. Buckland 1908, 449–51; Harper 2011, 471–85; Lenski 2012, 247–52.
[47] *CTh* 4.7.1 (from the Breviary) = *CJ* 1.13.2. The copy known from the late sixth-century *Sacra Privilegia Concilii Vizaceni* appears to derive from the Justinian Code: see Kaiser 2007, 427–30.
[48] *CJ* 1.13.1. If Protogenes is the bishop of Serdica (active between the councils of Nicaea and Serdica itself), the manuscript date (June 316) should perhaps be emended to December to allow issue by Constantine, who was in Serdica that month, rather than Licinius: for discussion, see Barnes 1981, 50; Corcoran 2000, 307. More sceptical are Harper 2011, 475–6; Lenski 2012, 248.

in AD 312 and appointment as senior emperor by the senate (thus Theodosian Code material appears to start with the year 313). Which of these measures in their original forms discussed Latins is unclear. Interpretation is tricky as both letters deal with two separate topics (manumission in church [Sozomen's focus] and clerical manumission of various types), neither letter is complete, and one (to Protogenes) is only known from the Justinian Code, so that references to Latins, if ever present, would have been omitted or emended.[49] They are also clearly rescripts responding to requests, whose nature is unknown.[50] Either bishop may have been asking for confirmation or for clarification of existing rules, or for new and extended privileges, perhaps dovetailed to their individual circumstances, in respect of either aspect of manumission. Thus, the imperial replies need not represent planned and coherent development in the law. If Protogenes is the bishop of Serdica, he may have been seeking application of Constantine's existing provisions in the newly acquired Balkan provinces.[51] Hosius, by contrast, is often seen as a 'court bishop', so that his request could have been closer to an official proposal (*suggestio*), made by someone both well informed and influential, that he hoped would then be reflected back to him.[52] The Hosius letter does specifically mention Roman citizenship, which might suggest that doubts had been expressed as to the type of liberty granted. In addition, this is dated only a year after there had already been enacted a general simplification of testamentary formalities.[53]

Given the relative ease of informal manumission, the freeing of slaves in a church *inter amicos* seems likely to have been of long standing,[54] without needing to invoke 'sacred manumissions' as a precedent, although these also were confirmed as valid after AD 212.[55] Thus, while Constantine may have started by settling doubts as to the validity of previous church manumission (which gave Latin status) and then extended its effect (and geographical scope), he might instead have intended to turn it into formal manumission from the start, emphasising and then developing the quasi-magistral role of the bishop.[56] The personal manumission capacity of clerics is even more uncertain to untangle. Justinian, in abolishing the age limit of thirty for a slave to be freed with citizenship by any means, notes this had already been relaxed for ecclesiastical manumissions (*CJ* 7.15.2), but whether this went back to Constantine is unknown. One thing is clear: before Constantine, manumission in church can only have given Latin

---

[49] Fabbrini 1965, 54–60 is sceptical of reading 'Junian' church manumission into the text, considering Protogenes was requesting clarification of the process to be followed rather than a change in the outcome, which was already citizenship.

[50] Millar 1992, 591.

[51] Barnes 1981, 50–1; *contra* Lenski 2012, 248.

[52] Hosius was clearly advising Constantine in AD 313 and 325 (Euseb., *Hist. Eccl.* 10.6.2; *Vit. Const.* 2.63, 73; Socrates, *Hist. Eccl.* 1.7, 13) and remained a key figure long into the reigns of his sons. Harper 2011, 479 associates the Hosius letter also with a law on bequests to churches (*CTh* 16.2.4 = *CJ* 1.2.1) [posted up at Rome, AD 321]; see also Corcoran 2000, 196.

[53] *CJ* 6.9.9, 6.23.15 (dated to AD 339 in mss, but generally ascribed to a Constantinian reforming edict of AD 320: Corcoran 2000, 194; see also Evans Grubbs 1995, 119–20; Harper 2011, 479).

[54] Buckland 1908, 450; Fabbrini 1965, 58–9.

[55] Fabbrini 1965, 150–93; Harper 2011, 369–78.

[56] Lenski 2012, 250: bishops as a 'new class of officials'.

status, while clerics were bound by the same manumission restrictions as other slave-owners. During Constantine's reign, these rules were relaxed or simplified for clergy and bishops, while manumission in church came to give Roman citizenship. In the long run this last probably did more than anything to reduce the incidence of Latin status.[57] Constantine provided a new and arguably easier route for granting manumission with citizenship, indeed also allowing manumissions (a legal act) on Sundays,[58] while the Christianisation fostered by him and most of his successors provided an increasing pool of manumitters and locations for manumission.

From Constantine to Abolition

The previous discussion is not intended to provide a definitive answer as to what Constantine's ecclesiastical manumissions rules were or how and why they developed. Rather it seeks to show how the accidents of survival of the Constantinian enactments constrain what can be known about precisely where and how Latin status appeared or was discussed in these legal texts. The problem of evidence becomes even more notable in the ensuing period. Thus, whereas we have manumission documents *inter amicos* in the third century, such clear evidence of Latin manumissions does not survive for the period after Constantine. For instance, in a copy of a deed of manumission of AD 355 from Kellis, in the western desert of Egypt, Aurelius Valerius writes to his slave Hilaria and frees her 'because of my exceptional Christianity, under Zeus, Earth and Sun' and allows her to take her *peculium*.[59] He also acts with the help of the priest(?) Psekes.[60] If it is a manumission *per epistulam*, it should give Latin status, and the *peculium* would revert to the patron on Hilaria's death. However, given the rare, but explicit, Christian aspect and the involvement of a possible priest, does Valerius think he has granted Roman citizenship under the Constantinian rules, however imperfectly followed? Another potential manumission *per epistulam* from the same year only releases a share, which simply transfers the manumitter's portion to the other owners, and does not create Latin freedpersons, unless the other owners had likewise written letters of manumission.[61]

Outside the legal sources, there is one fifth-century text suggesting that Latin status was more than legal theory. The text in question is fully discussed by de Wet in Chapter 10: for this reason, I merely indicate it here.[62] Thus, Salvian of Marseilles, in a diatribe against greedy parents, makes an analogy with masters of slaves, who may grant to the less deserving not freedom with Roman citizenship but the 'yoke of Latin liberty'. Thus, the bad father, like a master, denies full property rights to their monkish children and, like Latins, they 'live as if *ingenui*, but die as slaves' (i.e. with no property

---

[57] Corcoran 2011, 138; Harper 2011, 467.
[58] *CTh* 2.8.1 (AD 321). For discussion, see Corcoran 2000, 312. This, of course, did not only apply to manumission in church.
[59] *P.Kellis Gr.* 48 with the editor's discussion at Worp 1995, 140–3; cf. Glancy 2002, 92.
[60] For an alternative interpretation of a Manichaean context, see Teigen 2021, 249–50.
[61] *M.Chr.* 361 = *P.Oxy.* IV pp. 202–3 = *P.Edmonstone* (Porten 1996, 438–40, D18).
[62] For other recent significant discussions, see Nicosia 2007; Masi Doria 2018, 563–6.

to bequeath to the church).⁶³ Whatever the deeper issues, explored by de Wet, while Salvian's purpose is polemical and his language chosen more for rhetorical effect than legal nicety, his chosen parallel would have had little force, if in his mid-fifth-century Gaul there were not still slave-owners who strategised their manumission practices and actively sought to create freed Latins by design rather than accident.

And so we reach the sixth century and the legal activity of Justinian, which brings Latin status to its formal end within the empire. Justinian began his reign by commissioning a new codex of imperial constitutions, which was to recompile and update the three existing collections (Gregorian, Hermogenian, Theodosian) together with later enactments into a single code bearing his name, which was published in April 529.⁶⁴ However, with the appointment of Tribonian as quaestor (the emperor's chief legal officer) in the autumn of that year, legal activity became more intense. Tribonian seems to have been more proactive, than reactive, in matters of legislation, conducting what must in essence have been a wide-ranging review of current law. Vexed legal questions, unresolved in classical jurisprudence, were a particular focus. This led to a series of enactments known as the Fifty Decisions (*Quinquaginta Decisiones*) issued over the period from the summer of 530 to the spring of 531,⁶⁵ with even further constitutions passed subsequently, whereby many aspects of the law were tidied or consolidated. It is this remodelled law that is reflected in the next big project, the Digest, initiated in December 530, published in December 533, in which the writings of the classical jurists were edited and consolidated into an authoritative collection, both harmonised and up to date. At the same time the law schools and legal syllabus were reformed (December 533), associated with the publication of a new first-year text-book, the *Institutes*, which subsumed and superseded Gaius (November 533). One of the most notable results of this was that the whole edifice of manumission legislation as largely constructed in the era of Augustus was dismantled. Even before the issue of the new code, the restriction on numbers freed by will under the *lex Fufia Caninia* (2 BC) had been abolished in AD 528.⁶⁶ Next, in AD 530, came the abolition of the status of *dediticius* (deriving from the *lex Aelia Sentia* of AD 4, discussed in detail by Pellecchi in Chapter 2).⁶⁷ This is specifically attributed to the initiative of Tribonian as part of the Fifty Decisions, and it seems to be a tidying measure, since the status is regarded as having become an empty name. Existing discussions of *dediticii* in the writings of the jurists or in the code were thus rendered obsolete.⁶⁸ The age limit whereby formal manumission could only confer freedom with citizenship on a slave over thirty was also abolished (*CJ* 7.15.2; AD 530). Later on, one key post-Augustan measure, the *Senatus Consultum Claudianum*, was in addition abrogated (*CJ* 7.24.1; AD 533(?)).

---

[63] Salv. *Eccl.* 3.7.31–4. For discussion, see Lagarrigue 1971, 262–4.
[64] On Justinian's codification activities and their published outputs between AD 528 and 534, see Kaiser 2015; Corcoran 2016, xcviii–cxvii.
[65] Russo Ruggeri 1999.
[66] *CJ* 7.3.1; cf. *Inst.* 1.7.
[67] *CJ* 7.5.1; cf. *CJ* 7.6.1pr. and *Inst.* 1.5.3.
[68] Scheltema 1984, 3; Weber 2015, 97–8.

The longest surviving enactment in this area of law came in November 531, also on the initiative of Tribonian, although not forming part of the Fifty Decisions.[69] This was the law which, following the precedent set by the abolition of the *dediticii*, dealt with Latin status. It opens with Justinian, in words crafted by Tribonian, castigating Latinity as 'imperfecta Latinorum libertas incertis vestigiis titubans' ('incomplete Latin liberty tottering with unsteady footsteps', *CJ* 7.6.1pr.). There follows some typically Tribonianic historical background, including identifying the three key enactments from which most of the features of Latinity stemmed – i.e. the *lex Iunia*, of uncertain date (discussed with different results by both Pellecchi and López Barja, in Chapters 2 and 3 respectively); the *Senatus Consultum Largianum*, of AD 42; and an edict of Trajan – which are abrogated, since there is stated to be a mismatch between the ubiquity of the legal rules and the rarity of their application.

Thus, no grant of liberty will henceforth give Latin status (*CJ* 7.6.1pr.–1a). Justinian then goes on to enumerate and describe all the ways in which freedom and Roman citizenship can now be conferred, listing various 'informal' methods or other circumstances, which had previously conferred Latinity: *per epistulam* (*CJ* 7.6.1.1c); *inter amicos* (*CJ* 7.6.1.2); the Claudian freedom for abandoned slaves (*CJ* 7.6.1.3–3a);[70] slave-women prostituted in contravention of a covenant (*CJ* 7.6.1.4); slaves wearing the *pilleus* at the master's funeral (*CJ* 7.6.1.5); cases of formal manumission, where masters have tried explicitly to confer only Latinity(!) (*CJ* 7.6.1.6); slaves freed by an external heir before fulfilment of a testamentary condition (*CJ* 7.6.1.7); those freed by a third party after losing a *causa liberalis* (*CJ* 7.6.1.8); a slave-woman given formally in marriage by the owner to a free person (*CJ* 7.6.1.9); a slave recorded as a son by the owner in official acts (*CJ* 7.6.1.10); the owner publicly destroying or giving to a slave documents proving their status (*CJ* 7.6.1.11–11a). This long sequence is followed by a general statement that any other situations, which might in the past have created a Latin, will now be entirely ineffective, thus leaving the slave in bondage (*CJ* 7.6.1.12). Finally, after an emphatic repetition of the abrogation of all previous legislation relating to Latinity (*CJ* 7.6.1.12a), it is made clear that, while all future manumissions are to be governed by the new law, this will not be retrospective for the estates of already freed Latins, which are to be subject to the old law, thus passing entirely to the patron (*CJ* 7.6.1.13). It is notable that the following month (December 531) Justinian enacted a comprehensive new law in Greek on succession to freedpersons and the rights of patrons.[71]

Reading the law of abrogation closely, it is clear that the focus is entirely on manumission and the creation of freed status. Indignance is expressed at a status 'whence at the very time of death liberty and slavery exist concurrently in the same person and one, who has lived as if free, is snatched not only into death, but also into slavery' (*CJ* 7.6.1.1b). This rhetoric of the enigma of Latinity is not dissimilar to the sentiments of Salvian, noted above.[72] However, nowhere is it suggested that there are freeborn Latins, but neither is there any explicit statement that the law functions

---

[69] *CJ* 7.6.1; cf. *Inst.* 1.5.3, 3.7.4.
[70] Cf. *CJ* 6.4.4.2. On the Claudian edict on abandoned slaves, see Chapter 4, pp. 105–7.
[71] *CJ* 6.4.4; cf. *Inst.* 3.7.3.
[72] Masi Doria 2018, 566–7.

as an instant upgrade for existing Latins, freed or freeborn. Yet Latin status is to be expunged as a class of liberty and any references in existing legal texts or laws are to be interpreted as denoting Roman citizenship. This would hardly be compatible with the continued existence even of freeborn Latins. However, long though it is, the law is only known in the version edited for the Code, which does not necessarily preserve the full original text. A comprehensive upgrade must have been effected, since, in the *Institutes*, promulgated only two years later in November 533, all people are either free or slave. While slaves are of one condition only, the free are of two, namely freeborn or freed, but neither is further subdivided.[73] There is no room here for freeborn Latins. Indeed, the tenor of both the law of AD 531 and the discussion in the *Institutes* is that persons freed with Latinity are themselves rarities.[74] This could well be true, if two hundred years of manumissions in church had significantly tipped the balance in favour of manumissions as more routinely conferring Roman citizenship rather than Latinity.

Memories of Latinity in the Justinianic Afterglow

Thus, Latin status in the empire, even if already limited and moribund, came to an end in AD 531, although it might have been many years before the last patron, invoking the terms of the earlier legal situation, took over the estate of the last freedman, who had already been of Latin status when the law was issued. Some knowledge of Latin status as a historical curiosity remained in the legal texts, but very unevenly. The editing of texts for the Digest meant that any passages referring to Latin status, or indeed the *dediticii*, will have been either excluded or emended, and no explicit reference to either appears anywhere in that work.[75] Occasionally, however, it is possible to see where mentions could have been, as, for instance, in a passage of Modestinus referring to Claudius' measure for the freeing of sick and abandoned slaves.[76] In the *Institutes*, Latins (and *dediticii*) are mentioned only in relation to their abolition,[77] although this does include the sole reference to the original law as being called the *lex Iunia Norbana*.[78]

What of the Code? Justinian's original Code of AD 529 had been superseded by a revised edition in AD 534, which incorporated edited texts of the legislation of the intervening years, whilst also adapting existing content to reflect this legislation through emendation, omission or relocation of material. Thus, Latins and Latinity are only explicitly noted in the long law of abolition (*CJ* 7.6.1), as likewise *dediticii* (*CJ* 7.5.1; cf. *CJ* 7.6.1pr.). However, some parallel passages do exist in the pre-Justinianic material, which give an idea of the editing process which must have taken place between the two editions of the

---

[73] *Inst.* 1.3–5.
[74] *CJ* 7.6.1.1a; *Inst.* 1.5.3.
[75] I am not aware of any parallel passages in pre-Justinian sources which explicitly demonstrate this.
[76] Digest 40.8.2; cf. *CJ* 7.6.1.3–3a, 6.4.4.2. See also n. 70 above.
[77] *Inst.* 1.5.3, 3.7.4. These passages effectively replaced the extensive discussions of status, marriage and succession in Gaius' *Institutes* Books I and III.
[78] Given the vexed debates over dating the *lex Iunia* – illustrated in this volume in and by Chapters 2 and 3, as already observed – it is possible that this reference may be an over-historicising error on the part of one of the authors of the *Institutes*, Tribonian, Dorotheus or Theophilus. The latter kept the term *Iunia Norbana* in his Greek lecture course (Theophilus, *Paraphrasis Institutionum* 1.5.3; Lokin et al. 2010, 34–5). For further comment, see Balestri Fumagalli 1985, 203.

Code.[79] Thus, Latins have been removed from the Justinianic versions of Constantine's and Marcian's marriage laws,[80] as also from Constantine's offer of reward for denouncing *raptus*, which is now simply freedom (i.e. Roman citizenship).[81] In other cases, the elision of Latinity may be inferred.[82]

Justinian continued to legislate about freed status and, in his Novel of AD 539 granting all freedpersons notional free birth (*ingenuitas*), he placed this measure in the context of his earlier reform of manumission law and the abolition of Latinity (and of *dediticii*).[83] The creation of Greek course materials for the law school syllabus designed to aid teaching Justinian's new codified corpus meant that, even though Greek superseded Latin as the language of law and administration, some information about Latins survived on into the Byzantine period.[84] Theophilus, himself one of the co-authors of the *Institutes*, prepared lectures on them for the Constantinople law school probably in AD 533/4, and included discussion of Latins, greater in extent than in the source text.[85] This detailed treatment of Latins and *dediticii* shows his tendency to recycle material from his previous lectures on Gaius.[86] It also seems to be from Theophilus' use of the term that *dediticius* appears in some later Byzantine lexica, if not exactly helpfully defined.[87] A recently published fragment of a sixth-century Greek teaching text for the Digest, combining translation and lemmatised commentary, mentions *Latinoi*.[88] This occurs in a passage apparently commenting on Digest 1.3.32, where the corollary to custom acquiring the force of law through use is that the inverse may happen, with law being abrogated through desuetude. Although highly lacunose, the editors of the papyrus suggest that something akin to Theophilus' comments on obsolete *dediticii* (not present in the surviving text) and rare Latins is here invoked to illustrate a point about the fate of unused statutes.[89]

Thalelaeus, a contemporary of Theophilus, lectured on the Code and produced literal word-for-word ('kata poda': step-by-step) crib translations, including one for the relevant law abolishing Latin status.[90] However, when the *Basilica* was compiled in

---

[79] For comparison of the two editions in general, see Corcoran 2008.

[80] Compare *CTh* 4.6.3 with *CJ* 5.27.1pr.; and Marcian, *Nov.* 4.3 with *CJ* 5.5.7.2.

[81] *CJ* 7.13.3, adapted from *CTh* 9.24.1.4.

[82] Thus possibly excised from *CJ* 6.7.2 or from the church manumission laws; cf. the Latin freedwoman inferred at *CJ* 4.57.3.

[83] Justinian, *Novel* 78pr. The later summaries do not mention the abolition of Latinity: Athanasius, *Epitome Novellarum* 18.2 (Simon and Troianos 1989, 434); Theodore, *Breviarium Novellarum* 78 (Zachariae von Lingenthal 1843, 78). On the Novel, see Miller and Sarris 2018, I, 541–6.

[84] On sixth-century law teaching and associated texts, see Scheltema 1970; Corcoran 2017.

[85] Theophilus, *Paraphrasis Institutionum* 1.5.3, 1.8pr., 3.7.4. For discussion, see Lokin et al. 2010, 34–41, 58–9, 566–9. This is the only substantial intact law school work to survive.

[86] Nelson and David 1981, 279–84; Stolte 2020.

[87] See Burgmann 1984, p. 42 Δ6; 1990, p. 266 Δ11. There are also scholia on the relevant passages in some of the later manuscripts (esp. Par. Gr. 1366), although these are fairly slight (on the basis of consulting Alexander Falconer Murison's draft edition of the Paris scholia: UCL Special Collections MS ADD 22, Scholia Theophilina pp. 16–17, 19, 159).

[88] *P.Oxy.* LXXXV 5495, with translation of Digest 1.2.2.37–43 and commentary on Digest 1.3.32–3, 1.3.36–9. Although mostly in Greek, the lemmata and some technical terms are in Latin.

[89] *P.Oxy.* LXXXV p. 67.

[90] *Basilica scholia* 48.14.1.2 (Scheltema and Holwerda 1963, 2964–70).

the reign of Leo VI (c. 900), it contained no references to Latins and its abbreviated summary of the Code law, taken from Theodore of Hermopolis' *Breviary of the Code*, simply states that all slaves lawfully freed in any manner are considered Romans.[91] Perhaps this absence is no surprise, given that Leo also had a preference for formally abolishing and excluding the obsolete.[92] This did not, however, stop one scholiast from copying into his *Basilica* manuscript (Paris Gr. 1349, from the eleventh century) Thalelaeus' entire version of Justinian's abolition law, which is our only witness for his translation. Its most unusual feature is that it calls the *lex Iunia* the *lex Iulia* and sometimes replaces mentions of Trajan with Hadrian.[93]

Therefore, Justinian's definitive act of legislation marked a clear and formal end to Latin status. The situation in those territories which had ceased to be under imperial rule in the fifth century was rather different. The successor kings took over much of the apparatus of Roman law, at least for their Roman subjects. However, in Italy, there is no sign of Latins, for instance, in the Edict of Theoderic (c. AD 500),[94] where Latin status is missing from the rewards for denouncing *raptus* in measures derived from Constantine's law.[95] In any case, the reconquest meant that Justinian's legal changes should in due course have been applied in Italy, so that any vestigial Latin status would have disappeared anyway. This would also have been true of Africa, where Latins are reflected in texts of neither the Vandal nor Byzantine period.[96]

However, some knowledge that Latins had once existed would survive for anyone who knew the Justinian Code or the *Institutes* (or came across pre-Justinian materials[97]). In Italy, there may have been some legal teaching in Rome in the sixth or early seventh centuries, although it has been disputed how far various apparatuses of glosses represent teaching of this period and whether these originated from Constantinople or could at least in part have been generated in Italy.[98] Thereafter there was some limited copying of the *Institutes*, and indeed surviving fragments of a rare ninth-century manuscript

---

[91] *Basilica* 48.14.1 (Scheltema and van der Wal 1969, 2240); *Basilica scholia* 48.14.1.1 (Scheltema and Holwerda 1963, 2964); see also Scheltema 1972, 27. Note that the preface of *Nov.* 78, mentioning Latinity, is excluded from *Basilica* 48.26.1 (Scheltema and van der Wal 1969, 2266–7; cf. scholia at Scheltema and Holwerda 1963, 3019).

[92] For example, abolition of *senatus consulta* and the consulate (Leo VI, *Novels* 78, 94; Noailles and Dain 1944, 270–1, 308–11). For discussion, see Lokin 1997.

[93] For a similar error, note the Leiden version of Pseudo-Dositheus (derived from a Latin–Greek language teaching text), although that may be due to the *lex Iulia et Papia* mentioned in the same work: Pseudo-Dositheus, *De manumissionibus* 2, 6, 7, 8, 12 (Flammini 2004, 94–9). See Balestri Fumagalli 1985, 157–8.

[94] On the Edict, see Liebs 1987, 191–5; König 2018.

[95] *Ed. Theod.* 19 [*FIRA* II, 687], adapted from *CTh* 9.24.1.4. König 2018, 74 suggests that the status differentiation had disappeared (note that Lafferty 2013, 181–3, 255 does not comment on this aspect). However, the edict's wording is closer to Justinian at *CJ* 7.13.3, which might suggest later textual contamination. Note that the text essentially relies on sixteenth-century printed editions, with minimal earlier manuscript attestation (and not of this passage).

[96] The church manumission law in the African *Sacra Privilegia Concilii Vizaceni* derives from the Justinian Code (*CJ* 1.13.2), whether or not added later in Italy: see Kaiser 2007, 444 (with n. 47 above).

[97] Italian manuscripts sometimes include items deriving from the Theodosian tradition, including mentions of Latins; for example, the Aegidian Epitome of the Breviary in the *Collectio Gaudenziana* (British Library Add. Ms. 47676), dating to the tenth century; see Kaiser 2004, 655–846; Trump 2021, 60–6.

[98] Loschiavo 2015 gives a good account of the evidence and the debates.

from Verona include *Inst.* 1.5.3, although this section is not quoted or used anywhere else.[99] For the Code, there is the *Summa Perusina*, a curious text, which survives in an early eleventh-century manuscript but represents essentially one long catena of seventh-century scholia to the Code woven into a single work, probably in the tenth century.[100] *Summa Perusina* 7.6.1 gives the title from the Code (7.6.1), but the comments do not use the term *Latinus* or explain the *libertas Latina* of the title.[101] Rather, there is a pronounced interest in the routes to freedom described in the constitution, with eight of them being noted in turn. Similarly, one ninth-century ecclesiastical collection, the *Lex Romana canonice compta* (surviving in Par. Lat. 12448, c. 900), which contains a miscellany of Justinianic law, gives the title of *CJ* 7.6 but under it quotes only the section about the freeing of a sick, abandoned slave.[102] This passage was also recycled into the near contemporaneous *Collectio ad Anselmo Dedicata*.[103] Elsewhere in the *Summa Perusina*, the only explicit mention of a Latin is an anomalous case at *SP* 8.51.1, where there is a bizarre reference to an owner's right to the child of an *ala* or *latina*. The Code text (*CJ* 8.51.1) mentions an *ancilla* (presumably then miscopied from a cryptic scholion as 'ala') or *adscripticia*. This last must be a Justinianic generalising update of and interpolation into the Gregorian Code version of the emperor Alexander's original rescript.[104] How a *Latina* was then substituted for an *adscripticia* is unknown. Could the mention of the Latin be an inadvertent survival of such a reference in Alexander's rescript from the first Code (before Justinian's reform)? It has been speculated on the basis of a passage of Gaius that a Latin freedwoman living with a male slave (perhaps her continuing *contubernalis*) would bear slaves, so that it is just possible that this was the context of Alexander's constitution.[105] However, this is a slim basis for explaining the *Summa*'s text and the presence of the *Latina* remains a curiosity.

For the Novels of Justinian, the Latin translation of Novel 78 in the version later known as the *Authenticum*, originally a sixth-century interlinear student crib to help Latin-speaking students (probably in Constantinople) to understand the Greek, does not seem to have been much known until the twelfth century.[106] Instead, the *Epitome* of Julian, a sixth-century Constantinopolitan Latin lecture course, was the main source for knowledge of the Novels in the early medieval west. Julian's summary of Novel 78 does not pick up the mention of Latins.[107] However, there exists a set of sixth-century *paratitla* to the *Epitome*, essentially providing navigational cross-references across Justinian's corpus (especially regarding confirmations or innovations of law) and perhaps deriving ultimately from teaching at Constantinople. One of these cross-references points the

---

[99] Verona, Bibl. Cap. XXXVIII(36); see Moschetti 2006, 49–52; Macino 2008, 30–1, n. 2.
[100] Edition: Patetta 1900. For discussions, see Liebs 1987, 276–82; Kaiser 2004, 335–46; Ciaralli 2010.
[101] Patetta 1900, 219–20.
[102] *Lex Romana canonice compta* 240 (Mor 1927); cf. *CJ* 7.6.1.3–3a. On the *Capitula legis Romanae*, as he calls this, see Kaiser 2004, 493–508.
[103] *CAD* 7.72 (Russo 1980, 197). On the relationship between the collections, see Kaiser 2004, 556–9. Anselm, bishop of Milan, died in AD 896.
[104] Patetta 1900, 289. On the interpolation, see Weiss 1915, 173, n. 1; Broggini 1969, 139–40; Evans Grubbs 2013, 92, n. 229.
[105] Gai. *Inst.* 1.86; Crook 1967.
[106] *Nov.* 78pr. = *Authenticum* 79pr. (ed. Schöll-Kroll, *Corpus Iuris Civilis III*, 383).
[107] *Epitome Iuliani* Const. LXXII, kp 258 (Hänel 1873, 95–6).

reader of Justinian's Novel on marriages to the Code law on abolition of Latin status, since both discuss the rule about liberty for sick and abandoned slaves.[108]

Beyond the Empire: the Theodosian Legacy and the Fading of Latinity

While this was the situation in Italy, matters were different, of course, in territories where Justinian's writ never ran. For the Burgundian kingdom, there is one reference to Latins in the *Lex Romana Burgundionum* (44.5).[109] This is not part of a general exposition of manumission rules, which is to be found in chapter 3, where there are included manumission by will, in church (with clerically witnessed documents), and by the *princeps* (of his own slaves). Rather it appears in relation to freedmen's *operae*. Following mention of the duty of a freedman to support a needy patron (*LRBurg.* 44.4), the text goes on to say that a master who invites his slave to dine with him (*in convivio*) thereby frees him *inter amicos* with Latin status; but that this does not apply when the master is so poor that he dines with his slaves anyway! The Burgundian codes survived the fall of the independent kingdom in AD 534, but, although manumission after Roman fashion continued to be recognised in the normative texts and formulae of Frankish Burgundy, there is nothing to show that Latins were a reality.[110]

The presence of Latins is slightly more extensive in the Breviary of Alaric, issued by the Visigothic king Alaric II at Toulouse (in AD 506). This contained texts selected, but left largely unedited, from the Theodosian Code and post-Theodosian Novels, from the works of three jurists (an epitome of Gaius' *Institutes*, the *Pauli Sententiae* and a fragment of Papinian), and from the Gregorian and Hermogenian Codes.[111] Although texts were generally taken over unchanged, most had an explanatory *interpretatio* appended, often clearer and shorter than the original.[112] In the Breviary, the principal passage to note is the title at the beginning of the Gaius epitome, which sets out modes of manumission and statuses of the freed, including both Latins and *dediticii*.[113] There is no section corresponding to Gaius' discussion of succession to Latins (*Inst.* 3.55–76).[114] There are some further details in the *Pauli Sententiae* on manumission of jointly owned slaves or slaves held as pledges,[115] as well as the statement that

---

[108] *Paratitlon* at Hänel 1873, 204 = van der Wal 1985, 111 = Liebs 1987, 250 (cf. Kaiser 2004, 283) in relation to *Epitome Iuliani* Const. XXXVI, kp 134 (Hänel 1873, 59) [deriving from Just. *Nov.* 22.12], and referring to *CJ* 7.6.1.3–3a; cf. cross-reference to the same passage from a scholion to *CJ* 6.4.4 surviving in an eleventh-century Code manuscript (see Chiappelli 1885, 37).

[109] Bluhme 1863, 622–3; cf. *FIRA* II, 748.

[110] On Burgundian texts, see Chevrier and Pieri 1969; Liebs 2002, 163–6, 176–9; Rio 2017, 79, n. 14.

[111] The only 'modern' edition is Hänel 1849. The individual components are usually consulted in editions of their constituent works (Mommsen and Meyer for the Theodosian Code and Novels, and the various ante-Justinianic collections [*FIRA* II, Girard and Senn 1967] for the other works). On the Breviary, see Gaudemet 1965, 3–41; Liebs 2002, 109–11, 166–76.

[112] Matthews 2001; Liebs 2002, 146–8.

[113] *Breviary Gaius (Liber Gai)* 1.1–4 (Hänel 1849, 314–16; *FIRA* II, 232–3).

[114] Besson 2020, 661, 664. It remains unclear whether the epitome was created or adapted for the Breviary or was a pre-existing work directly imported; see Mantovani 2020; cf. Liebs 2002, 127–32.

[115] *Breviary Paulus* 4.11.1 [= *Pauli Sent.* 4.12.1] plus *interpretatio* (Latin); *Breviary Paulus* 4.11.6–7 [= *Pauli Sent.* 4.12.6–7] (*dediticius*).

a *Latina ingenua* can upgrade by giving birth three times.[116] Some scholars have seen the use of *ingenua* here as a sign of the terminological looseness of the early medieval period, where *ingenua* often simply means free.[117] But the usage in the Breviary's *Epitome* of Gaius is clear, stating that there is only one class of *ingenuus* but three of *libertus* (Roman citizen, being the 'better status' as termed also in Sozomen, Latin, *dediticius*). The Paulus passage is explicit that the Latin woman has not been manumitted and so clearly is freeborn, as was noted above.[118] The other Breviary examples are Constantine's references to Latin status as reward or punishment, where this aspect of the original text is reflected also in the *interpretationes*.[119] Constantine's marriage law is not present, but Marcian's response to it is.[120] The *interpretatio* to the church manumission law (*Breviary Theod.* 4.7.1 = *CTh* 4.7.1) does not mention Latin status, but it does refer to freedom with Roman citizenship as 'complete and full'.

Finally, later Breviary manuscripts sometimes had further material (of much earlier date) appended to them. This is how the *Tituli ex corpore Ulpiani* survive, since in Vat. Reg. Lat. 1128 they appear to be just the next juristic section following on from the Papinian fragment that would usually conclude the Breviary. Otherwise, in the so-called first *Appendix to the Breviary* there occurs a fragment of the *Pauli Sententiae* on Latins excluded from intestate succession to their mothers.[121] The influence of the Breviary can also be seen in the chance preservation of Constantine's legislation on the SC Claudianum, since, although not original to the Breviary, *interpretationes* were added to a copy of the constitutions from that title.[122] The *interpretatio* to *CTh* 4.12.3 includes mention of Latin status.

When we look for the presence of Latins in the Visigothic kingdom outside the Breviary, we look in vain. Partly this is owing to a lack of suitable literary and documentary evidence from Spain, the main component of the kingdom after the defeat at Vouillé (in AD 507). Isidore of Seville mentions both Latins and *dediticii*, but his aetiology is severely confused and inaccurate.[123] Certainly he knows more than could have been gleaned from the Breviary alone, so that, if not using Gaius directly, he must have used some legal miscellany or other source fuller than the Breviary.[124] He is important also as his work was widely read and copied outside Spain and served as a significant transmitter of legal knowledge in the Latin west.[125] The only Visigothic

---

[116] *Breviary Paulus* 4.9.1 [= *Pauli Sent.* 4.9.8]; cf. the derivative scholion to *Brev. Theod.* 5.1.1 (= *CTh* 5.1.1) in Par. Lat. 4413 (Hänel 1849, 462–3; Liebs 2002, 114, 210).
[117] Conrat 1907, 97.
[118] Liebs 1996, 199.
[119] *Breviary Theod.* 9.19.1 (= *CTh* 9.24.1) plus *interpretatio*; *Breviary Theod.* 2.22.1 (= *CTh* 2.22.1) plus *interpretatio*. This last is only known from the Breviary.
[120] Marcian, *Nov.* 4.1, 4.3 (no Latins in the *interpretatio*). The Novels of Marcian are preserved through the Breviary tradition.
[121] *Appendices Legis Romanae Wisigothorum* I.19 (*FIRA* II, 672–3) = *PS* 4.10.3. On the Breviary Appendices, see Liebs 2002, 141–5; Wibier 2020.
[122] Hänel 1849, 118 erroneously included *CTh* 4.12 in his Breviary edition. On these *interpretationes*, see Liebs 2002, 148–56.
[123] Isid. *Etym.* 9.4.49–51.
[124] Laistner 1921.
[125] Loschiavo 2012, 2016.

manumission formulae to survive make no mention of Latins.[126] Indeed, they talk of making the manumitted slave an *ingenuus et civis Romanus*.[127] This is not the law of the Breviary, but, by a strange coincidence, reflects the position in the empire after Justinian's Novel 78 (AD 539). This collection of *formulae*, datable to the early seventh century, probably originated from Cordoba, which had previously been independent of royal control for over twenty years from about AD 550 until reconquered by Leovigild in AD 572. Imperial intervention in Spain began around the same time as the revolt of Cordoba, but the area reconquered never extended much beyond Cartagena and probably never as far as Cordoba, so that any direct influence of Justinianic law seems improbable.[128] The change in the use of *ingenuus* seems to be an independent development. It is also found in the will of Vincent, Bishop of Huesca, dating to c. AD 575.[129] This includes several manumissions described in a variety of ways, the recipient becoming either *civis Romanus*, or *ingenuus*, or just *liber*, which are likely synonyms. Since this is a will and Vincent is a cleric, he could hardly grant Latin status, even if he so wished. In the end, even the theoretical presence of Latins in the Visigothic kingdom via the Breviary ceased, when it was rendered invalid under the unified legal system created by the *Lex Visigothorum* after AD 654. In fact, freed status became hereditary, so that a permanent subject class was created.[130] In its own way therefore, the Visigothic kingdom abolished any vestiges of the Augustan freed statuses.

In the Frankish kingdoms, by contrast, the Merovingian rulers did not issue any new codes for their Roman subjects, with the result that the Breviary of Alaric, originally issued in Gaul, enjoyed a long afterlife, either in its full form or as further epitomised. Such epitomes were created mostly in the eighth and ninth centuries and tended to comprise *catenae* of the *interpretationes*, with varying degrees of intervention.[131] Some are apparently *sui generis* in single copies, others form more widespread and stable texts (such as the Aegidian Epitome). Hänel's old (yet still the most recent) Breviary edition conveniently shows the parallels between the original text and several derivatives, making it easy to see which retained mentions of Latins.[132] Some epitomes now have better editions, such as St. Gall. 731[133] or the *Lex Romana Curiensis*.[134] There was certainly a clear textual presence of Latins in normative works.

---

[126] *Formulae Visigothicae* edited by Zeumer 1886, 572–95; Liebs 2002, 196–9. For some later Spanish examples, see the details in Rio 2009, 186.
[127] *Formulae Visigothicae* 2–6 (Zeumer 1886, 576–8).
[128] On the revolt, see Collins 2004, 48–9, allowing for the possibility of an imperial connection.
[129] Discussion of the document, and the manumissions recorded therein, is in Corcoran 2003; Roth 2016c. Note that a large part of the will may be missing and the manumissions could even belong to a separate document; see further Faci 2017, 309–10.
[130] Claude 1980; Rio 2017, 89–92.
[131] For a survey of the versions and their manuscripts, see Coma Fort 2014, 299–343, plus now Trump 2021 for the Aegidian Epitome (he is preparing a full edition); cf. Liebs 2002, 183–4, 202–30, 249–64.
[132] Hänel 1849, 60–1 and 192–3 (Theodosian passages), 302–5 (Marcian's Novel), 314–17 (Gaius passages), 406–7 and 410–11 (Paul passages).
[133] Liebs 2012, 20 and 58 (Theodosian passages), 91–2 (Paul passages), 100–1 (Gaius passages).
[134] Meyer-Marthaler 1968. Note *LRC* 2.22.1 and 9.19.1 (Theodosian passages), 22.1.1–4 (Gaius), with Meyer-Marthaler 1968, 93, 283–5, 417–19. For the *LRC* generally, see Liebs 2002, 230–5; Siems 2008.

Yet it is harder to assess any relation outside their pages to the reality of manumission and freed status in Frankish territories.[135] Certainly the language of bondage and status becomes very fluid. The fact that Latin was the typical language of normative texts and legal documents across a wide area with different and evolving social systems and ties of dependence means that terms such as *servus*, *colonus* and *ingenuus* can be protean.[136] Outside the Breviary, glossaries take *dediticius* as referring to surrendered barbarians,[137] the alternative late antique meaning of this term.[138] In this mix, *Latini* are seldom encountered beyond the Theodosian/Breviary tradition.

As regards documents, deeds of manumission now routinely refer to *ingenui*, matching the usage in the Spanish Visigothic material discussed above. This can be seen in a Rhaetian charter of AD 784 granting *ingenuitas*, reflecting the fact that the *Lex Romana Curiensis*, of similar date and region, manages in its version of Gaius to use *ingenuus* in both senses.[139] Indeed, it is in the Frankish formulae collections[140] that we may see Latin status becoming obsolete. Out of all the many surviving formulae, only one contains any explicit reference to Latins (*Formulae Arvernenses* 3).[141] This is in fact a charter of *manumissio in ecclesia* and gives full Roman citizenship without further obligation, but in a rather obscure sentence it mentions that liberty is being given in accordance with Roman law (as set out in the *Breviary Gaius* 1.1), which allows for three grades of liberty: '*Latina, dolitia* [sic], *et cives Romana*'. This formulae collection, with its material sourced ultimately from the Auvergne (the manumission is located in Clermont-Ferrand) and with a strong Roman flavour, is often taken as being extremely early and reflecting sixth-century events, although other interpretations are possible.[142] This reference implies the theoretical possibility of Latin manumission, but not its practice in Merovingian Gaul, let alone Carolingian Francia. Indeed, down to the eleventh century, charters and formulae granting Roman citizenship in church sometimes describe it with the Breviary phrase *meliorem libertatem*, 'the better form of freedom', but without naming the others.[143] Thus, Latin status is alluded to obliquely as something being avoided. However, an early ninth-century manuscript of the so-called *Formulae Turonenses*[144] has an index listing one formula as '*Ingenuitas*

---

[135] See generally Grieser 1997, 135–57; Rio 2017, 93–114.
[136] Davies 1996; Hammer 2002.
[137] Goetz 1889, 51 (from Vat. Lat. 3321, ff. 38v–39r; two different definitions nearby, neither a freedman); Hessels 1890, p. 40 D15; Lindsay 1917, 127.
[138] *CTh* 7.13.16. For issues surrounding barbarians as *dediticii*, see, for instance, Wirth 1997; Kerneis 2008; Bjornlie 2018.
[139] *Chartae Latinae Antiquiores* I 106, with n. 134 above.
[140] Extensively analysed in Rio 2009.
[141] Zeumer 1886, 30 (from the ninth-century Par. Lat. 4697; Rio 2009, 258).
[142] Rio 2009, 80–1; cf. Jeannin 2005.
[143] For example, *Formulae Bituricenses* 9 (Leiden BPL 114, c. 800; Rio 2009, 111–12, 245–6) at St Stephen's, Bourges (Zeumer 1886, 172; cf. Liebs 2016, 465), referring also to *CTh* 4.7.1 probably via *LRBurg.* 3.1. For Saint Maixent (Poitou) charters: Richard 1886, nos. 92 [1031/1033], 104 [1040/1044], 111 [1047/1049]. For the context of these late documents, see Rouche 1980.
[144] On the *Formulae Turonenses*, see Rio 2009, 112–17. For their reflection of Breviary content, see Liebs 2002, 241–7.

Latina' (Warsaw UB 1 f. 226v),[145] although no such formula exists at the matching point in the main text.[146] The source for this manuscript seems to have contained three documents of '*ingenuitas*', the others being one for a *civis Romanus* in church and one *sub patrono*, but only the church manumission remained relevant. At some point Latin manumission had been a reality – and then no longer.

However, recently one ninth-century copy of the Aegidian Epitome (Par. Lat. 4416 f. 50v) has revealed a surprise, since at the beginning of its *Epitome* of Gaius have been added glosses assigning wergilds (unknown to Roman law) to persons with Roman law statuses, including Latins and *dediticii*.[147] This at least suggests an attempt to correlate with contemporary conditions. Nonetheless, this document aside (although it deserves greater attention than can be given here), Latin status, as a reflection of anything genuinely derivative from the *lex Iunia*, fades away in our early medieval evidence.

Conclusion

This survey concludes by noting that the two streams of Roman legal normative sources that contained references to Latins experienced contrasting but related fates. The one dried up even as (and indeed because) the other came to be in spate. Thus, on the one hand, the Theodosian legacy, as principally transmitted in the Breviary, in which Latins were in theory a 'live' status, finds one of its latest manifestations in the famed Selden manuscript (Bodleian Arch. Selden B.16), written by William of Malmesbury in 1129.[148] This contains the various Breviary mentions of Latins.[149] However, for William the Breviary is not a source of relevant law, but rather a supplement about emperors and their activities designed to form part of a historical miscellany.[150] On the other hand, from the eleventh century in Italy, the *Institutes* and the Code of Justinian start to be copied, used and studied again in an increasingly active fashion. Thus, the earliest intact *Institutes* manuscript dates to the early eleventh century,[151] while the mid-eleventh-century Pistoia manuscript of the Code is the earliest surviving to contain the law abolishing Latin status (although not that on the *dediticii*).[152] These manuscripts are often heavily glossed, showing a combination of new comments and possibly ancient tralatician scholia.[153] Certainly, the development of the teaching and glossing of Justinianic

---

[145] On the Warsaw manuscript, see Rio 2009, 113, 270–1.
[146] *Formulae Turonenses cap.* 35 (Zeumer 1886, 134; cf. 155, 159–60 the replacement texts). See Zeumer 1881, 52–5; Bloch 1975, 132; Liebs 2016, 464.
[147] Liebs 2016; Bothe 2018, 362; Trump 2021, 267–8.
[148] Coma Fort 2014, 188–95.
[149] Bodl. Arch. Selden B.16, ff. 147rb, 168va, 205ra, 208rb, 218ra–b; cf. *Epit. Seld.* re Gaius and Paulus only at Hänel 1849, 315, 317, 407, 411.
[150] Thomson 2003, 63–70, 91; Corcoran (forthcoming).
[151] Bamberg Jur. 1 (olim D.II.3); Macino 2008, 64–8.
[152] Pistoia Arch. Cap. 106: Ciaralli 2000; Corcoran 2016, clii.
[153] For example, Pistoia Code: Chiappelli 1885, 36–7, Pistoia no. 94 (scholion based on the Greek of *CJ* 6.4.4 with cross-reference to *CJ* 7.6.1.3), nos. 100–3 on *CJ* 7.6.1 (quoting Isid. *Etym.* 5.16). Turin Institutes (Turin Bibl. Naz. Univ. D.III.13; see Macino 2008, 47–8, 68–73): Krüger 1868, 71, n. 312 on *Inst.* 3.7.4. For a summary of the debate over the Turin glosses, see Loschiavo 2015, 86–90.

materials developed apace and this included comment upon the passages mentioning Latins, which ended up part of the teaching at Bologna and elsewhere,[154] including the gold standard of the 'Glossa Ordinaria' of Accursius (d. c. 1263).[155] This new phase, however, represents engagement with the echoes of a long defunct status, and need not be discussed further here.[156] Thus, with the dawn of the Justinianic revival, we can indeed close our survey of the textual remains discussing Latins and Latinity.

---

[154] For the development of legal teaching, see Pennington 2020. For examples of comments on Latins in late eleventh- and twelfth-century material, note *Brachylogus* c.5 (Boecking 1829, 8–9); *Epitome exactis regibus* 2.13–14 (Conrat 1884, 22–3); Crescenzi 1990, 50–3 (glosses on *Inst.*).

[155] For *Inst.* 1.5 with the Accursian gloss, see Torelli 1934, col. 39–44.

[156] But note the use made of such material by Masi Doria 2018, 567–8.

II.

Junian Latins in the Latin Literary Sources

Second Prologue: The Latin Literary Universe of Junian Latinity

Ulrike Roth

The first port of call in the study of Junian Latinity has time and again been the relevant lines in Gaius' *Institutes*. More broadly, as both this volume's Introduction and the preceding part have underlined, the rich discussion of Junian Latinity in our legal sources is in many ways an extraordinarily lucky circumstance for the modern quest to understand the condition. Junian Latinity features of course also in writings that are quite different in nature to the legal sources. Besides the texts preserved in epigraphical and papyrological sources that offer the odd window into the lives of individuals endowed with Junian Latin status, there is the body of material commonly referred to in English as the literary sources, i.e. texts that are not, in their widely used form today, of an epigraphical or papyrological nature and that do not offer sustained legal exposition or form part of one or other legal compilation.[1] Outside the study of Junian Latinity, these literary sources have long benefited from sustained efforts at philological analysis as well as rich literary interpretation in the context of explorations of diverse topics in Roman social history, employing diverse approaches. Within the study of Junian Latinity, many of the texts in question have also been duly consulted – although primarily to illustrate one or other aspect of the condition, its gestation or application. Already Buckland, in his voluminous 1908 publication of the legal dimensions of Roman slavery, had recourse to the literary sources in his discussion of Junian Latinity. It is instructive to see how Buckland utilised the type of text in question, for instance on the issue of informal manumission:

> it is obvious that occasions must have arisen under which the intention to free a man, there and then, was expressed in less formal ways. Two such are in fact recorded. They are the declaration, *inter amicos*, that the man is free, and writing him a letter of enfranchisement.[7]
>
> [7] See e.g. G. 1. 44. *Amici* are *testes*. See G. 2. 25, and Bruns, Syro-Roman Law-book, 195. See also Suetonius, de Rhet. 1. As to manumission *in convivio*, *post*, p. 446.[2]

---

[1] This analytical separation of the literary sources from other textual evidence does not deny the regular overlap in subject matter between these bodies of evidence, nor does it seek to question the literary dimensions of many inscriptional and papyrological texts, or indeed of juridical discussion. For examples of overlaps and discussion, see Agosti 2020 and Kruschwitz 2020 (epigraphy, esp. poetical); Johnson 2009 and Renner 2009 (papyri); Mantovani 2018 (legal discourse).

[2] Buckland 1908, 444, with n. 7 (emphasis added).

The contention that informal modes of manumission existed is here documented with the help of a number of legal sources, before a passage in Suetonius is cited in addition. As this single example shows, Buckland made occasional, yet sparse use of the literary evidence, focusing instead on the juridical texts, and employing the literary material primarily for purposes of illustration – 'See also . . .' – especially as and when this evidence brought legal dimensions of additional interest to the table: Buckland's cited case will be in focus in Chapter 9. Buckland's approach is not surprising given that his aim was to understand the legal framework and juridical nature of the condition, and that, once clearly illustrated by a legal text, there was little or no need to add further references to other types of texts to explicate any particular aspect under scrutiny.

The rise in interest in the study of Junian Latinity in the last few decades, regularly concerned with the broader topic of the role of citizenship in Roman society, has, perhaps oddly, not significantly diverted from the method employed by Buckland with regard to the literary sources. Thus, while numerous recent studies make copious reference to several literary texts, these texts are typically utilised to illustrate in brief a particular piece of information or fact. A good example is constituted by Koops' study of (what he calls) the struggle for citizenship for Junian Latins, for instance in his discussion of the apparent challenges in effecting *manumissio vindicta*, which Koops supports inter alia as follows:

> Pliny wrote to his wife's grandfather that he was sure he could entice a friend to drop by who was on his way to a proconsular station, if his *prosocer* still wished to formally manumit those whom he had recently manumitted *inter amicos*.[83]

[83] Plin., *Ep.* 7.16.4. Lopez Barja de Quiroga 1998, op. cit. (n. 55), 157–159; P.R.C. Weaver, 'Where have all the Junian Latins gone? Nomenclature and status in the early Empire', *Chiron* 20 (1990), 279–281.[3]

As is self-evident, the Plinian evidence is summarised, without further interrogation of Pliny's text; the approach is supported by reference in a footnote to other modern studies that have offered discussion on the topic, utilising the literary sources in similar fashion. Put the other way round, like other scholars, Koops has employed the Latin literary sources primarily as *evidence* – i.e. the texts in question have in the first instance been ploughed for information that enhances our understanding of the historical development of the condition under scrutiny, with particular regard to the social, economic, cultural and political dimensions of Junian Latinity.[4] As a result of the many studies that subscribe to this approach to the Latin literary sources, our understanding of Junian Latinity is factually much improved, not least because the texts in question offer insights into aspects of the topic that the legal, epigraphical and papyrological materials do not articulate or articulate only in a partial or cryptic manner: the cited

---

[3] Koops 2014, 117, with n. 83, with Weaver 1990 (for example, 279, n. 12, regarding Plin. *Ep.* 8.16.1) and López Barja 1998 (for example, 152, n. 43, regarding Plin. *Ep.* 7.16.4).
[4] Recent examples include Koops 2012, esp. 228–32; López Barja 1998, 2018b; Rawson 2010; Roth 2010b.

example of the potential complexities involved in effecting *manumissio vindicta* that to all accounts frames the specific Plinian letter exchange is a case in point.

But as a consequence of the prominence of the just illustrated approach to the literary sources in the study of Junian Latinity, this evidence has not received the kind of detailed exploration and introspective critique that the legal and epigraphical source materials that speak to the topic have attracted. Conversely, the *literary* analyses of texts that pertain to Junian Latinity regularly omit serious engagement with the condition. The classic example is the scholarly handling of the type of status awarded in three manumission scenes in the so-called *Cena Trimalchionis* of Petronius' *Satyricon*: notwithstanding the fictional dimension of the text, all three manumissions are informal and, hence, lead to the award of Junian Latinity – with all the limitations attached to that status.[5] The scenes in question – one of which will also play a role in Chapter 9 – have for a long time escaped due historical or juridical comment.[6] Moreover, when scholars *read* those texts, they regularly stress the seemingly unrestricted liberality that the narrated actions appear to celebrate – ignoring outright the consequences of the informal nature of the manumissions in their literary interpretations.[7] Junian Latinity does not fare much better with regard to the study of texts that have long been central to the historical debate on the condition: notable in this context is the authorial universe constituted by the already mentioned correspondence of Pliny the Younger. Our modern appreciation of the world Pliny made has profoundly changed since the fundamental socio-historical exploration of Sherwin-White from 1966, thanks to a wave especially of recent cultural analyses of the Plinian correspondence.[8] Nevertheless, despite the long-standing scholarly engagement with several of his letters in historical discussions of Junian Latinity – as illustrated above on the work of Koops – the focus in literary and cultural studies of freedpersons in Pliny's correspondence is on individuals whose status includes Roman citizenship.[9] On the other hand, the socio-historical investigations into distinct authorial universes undertaken under the remit of ISTA – the *Index thématique des références à l'esclavage et à la dépendance* – have produced discussion of Junian Latinity as part of a broader inquiry into Roman slavery in precisely Pliny's correspondence:[10] Gonzalès' 2002 study details several passages in

---

[5] Petr. *Sat.* 40.3–41.4, 41.6–7, 54.1–5.

[6] Fuller discussion of all three scenes is in Roth 2016a, with earlier bibliography; see also n. 11 below.

[7] For example, Plaza 2000, 84–164, arguing for a complete reversal of traditional social hierarchies; Slater 1990, 62–4, 67, 83, arguing for a growing sense of loss of control that accompanies the narrated actions' seeming air of liberality; further examples are given in Roth 2016a.

[8] Instrumental have been Marchesi 2008 (followed by Marchesi 2015); Noreña 2007; Stadter 2006; Woolf 2006, 2015.

[9] A good example (surveying key examples) is the discussion offered in Leach 2012; notably, Leach comments on what she calls 'a borderland between slavery and citizenship' (p. 199) even for enfranchised freedpersons, emphasising just how characteristic the noted borderland was for those liberated from slavery, regardless of their more precise legal status; the same notion is also expressed in Strong 2016, speaking of the 'liminal space between slave and citizen in the Roman world'. For a historical investigation focused on enfranchised freedmen in Pliny, see Gonzalès 2017.

[10] An overview of the publications produced under the auspices of ISTA for the *Index thématique* is given at the Institute's website: https://ista.univ-fcomte.fr/bdd/esclaves-dependants.

his analysis of the freed individuals in Pliny's letters that include Junian Latins, even if he does not provide a sustained, differentiated discussion of the complexities arising from the Plinian depiction of the diverse freed statuses.[11] The situation does not change significantly regarding texts from later periods that mention Junian Latinity. Indeed, pride of place in the study of the condition in the later Roman Empire and through late antiquity is typically given to the relatively rich evidence provided especially in the Theodosianic and Justinianic legal sources, as Corcoran's 2011 survey illustrates, and to which the seemingly sparse non-legal textual material from that period – including such intriguing texts as Salvian's *Ad ecclesiam* – plays typically second fiddle: the relevant lines of Salvian's comments pertaining to Junian Latinity have been integrated in legally oriented studies, as, for instance, by Masi Doria, but still lack a fuller, historical contextualisation.[12]

Notwithstanding, then, the extensive use made of the Latin literary sources by historians and jurists alike, these texts have regularly been reduced to the status of 'mere' evidence, not seldom made use of *en passant*: in a way, the scholarly approach to these sources resembles the seemingly fleeting nature of Calestrius Tiro's involvement in the formal manumission of the three Junian Latins in Comum, featured above in the quotation from Koops (and to be returned to in detail in Chapter 8). Unsurprisingly therefore, the value of this body of evidence – whether from the early or the late Roman Empire or beyond – has even been regarded as inconsequential for the modern understanding of the condition, in comparison especially with the legal and epigraphic sources: in the context of a discussion of Salvian's *Ad ecclesiam*, Harper noted that '[w]ithout Gaius, the *Digest*, and the corpora of inscriptions from Rome, we would know little about Junian Latins.'[13] Thus, while there is unanimous agreement on the existence of Junian Latinity in the Latin literary sources, combined with these sources' regular use by historians and lawyers alike, their value for our appreciation of the condition can, quite evidently, be questioned. In brief, existence of evidence – yes; wide-reaching meaning – no. It is at this impasse that the present volume part is located. We seek to offer fresh investigations into the *literary* universe of Junian Latinity. The aim is twofold. First, as Chapter 7 demonstrates, there is in fact scope for new discoveries in well-known texts that enlarge our evidential basis for the study of the condition and, hence, for our comprehension of Junian Latinity in the wider web of slavery and freedom in Roman imperial society. Such new readings entail, naturally, repercussions for our appreciation of the texts themselves, even if the present volume is not the place

---

[11] Gonzalès 2002, for example, 127–9 (but note that several of Gonzalès' identifications of Junian Latins are contentious). The work on the *Index thématique* of Petronius' *Satyricon* appears to omit Junian Latinity altogether: Brunet 2008; Garrido-Hory 2008. The omission is the result of the terminological focus and mechanical treatment of the texts in this project: the database, analysis and index, and graphic analysis are at https://ista.univ-fcomte.fr/bdd/esclaves-dependants. Of the three informal manumission scenes that are staged during the *Cena Trimalchionis* (see n. 5 above), producing (or playing on the status of) Junian Latins, the two pertaining to humans are classed in the 'Analyse et indexation du corpus' solely under 'esclave' (pp. 77, 122–6), the one pertaining to the boar under 'métaphore', noting otherwise the mention of '*libertus*', but not offering any further differentiation of the freed status (p. 76).

[12] Salv. *Eccl.* 3.7.32–4, with Masi Doria 2018, 565–6. Harper 2011, 467 is extremely brief on this text.

[13] Harper 2011, 467.

to pursue that route any further. Second, as Chapter 8 shows, focused study of Junian Latinity in a single author whose work has long been recognised as important for the modern understanding of the topic – namely our friend the younger Pliny – can offer new insights into both the authorial universe under scrutiny as well as the socio-cultural approach to the condition, from the perspective of one with powers over Junian Latins. But even shorter, seemingly less valuable passages that speak to the condition constitute more than just handy means to illustrate what we seem to know already from the study of other source bodies: Chapter 9 explores how such texts can be employed to challenge scholarly approaches to the wider context in which the hunt for Junian Latins sits, namely the identification of civic status more broadly. Chapter 10 offers on the other hand an in-depth contextualisation of the seemingly cryptic reference to Junian Latinity in Salvian's *Ad ecclesiam* – to show that there is more to be got from this text than the scholarly headaches that it has caused so far.

In combination, the chapters presented in this volume's second part seek to encourage further, in-depth explorations of texts already known for portraying Junian Latinity as well as of texts hitherto left out of the equation: it is our contention that scholarship has only just scratched the (literary) surface of Junian Latinity in 'old' and 'new' authorial universes. Indeed, the texts and authors here presented display a striking pattern of engagement with *manumissio minus iusta*, for a range of purposes, from Columella's mid-first-century depiction of his agricultural paradise to Salvian's late antique recommendation to the unstinting faithful. The pattern is highly suggestive; if it holds, informal manumission and Junian Latinity emerge as staple ingredients of the surviving Latin literary discourse, rather than as rare occurrences – if only we look hard enough. There can, then, not be any doubt that future work will add to the list of texts that speak to the topic, thus to challenge further the notion that we would know little about Junian Latins were it not for the legal and epigraphic source materials.

But the type of analysis undertaken in the following chapters is in any case a necessary – if badly delayed – *first* step in the search for Junian Latinity in the literary source material: detailed, contextualised exploration of the passages that speak to the condition is a *sine qua non* to gain a firmer handle on the mentions of Junian Latinity in these sources in the first place, one that is fundamental to any ensuing historical interpretation: it is not possible to take this evidence places before understanding what makes it move.[14] If then, as we hope, the present part leads to fresh readings in other Latin authors (and indeed to further new readings in the present set of authors), thus discovering both 'new' evidence for Junian Latinity and reinterpreting 'old' evidence, it will have fully accomplished its mission – much like Calestrius Tiro en route to Baetica: *¡vamos!*

---

[14] This point was also made by Scheidel 1994, 514, in his study of the text discussed in Chapter 7: 'Die isolierte Analyse eines Testimoniums wie I, 8, 19 erklärt sich aus der Notwendigkeit, den Aussagegehalt und insbesondere auch die Unsicherheiten und Mehrdeutigkeiten eines Textes im Rahmen der Möglichkeiten zu klären oder zumindest deutlich zu machen, *ehe er sinnvoll als – potentiell tragendes – Element weiterreichender Rekonstruktionen und Modelle herangezogen werden kann*' (emphasis added).

7

Promoting Junian Latinity: Columella, *De re rustica* 1.8.19

Ulrike Roth

Introduction

What did Columella know about slavery? A lot, one would think, given his direct involvement in the exploitation of other human beings as slaves, documented through his substantial literary contribution to the management of rural estates – the *De re rustica*.[1] Originally from near modern Cadiz in southern Spain – ancient Gades – where his uncle owned and managed rural estates worked by enslaved labour, Columella became a landowner in central Italy, at Ardea, Carseoli and Alba, and probably also in southern Etruria, at Caere.[2] Columella's work, the *De re rustica*, was likely produced late in his life, around AD 65, combining 'practical experience of farming estates with an extensive knowledge of the work of previous Punic, Greek, and Latin agronomists'.[3] The period in which Columella's work falls means that it was conceived and written when the consequences of the *leges Aelia Sentia et Iunia* for those freed from slavery had firmly taken root. In fact, it is one of the earliest surviving, sizeable texts after the passing of these laws in which slavery plays a central role. For this reason, the *De re rustica* is potentially of great significance for the study of Junian Latinity, and the role of manumission in Roman slavery more broadly.

The Columellan rural universe has indeed long been an important source for the student of Roman, especially agricultural slavery, as much as it has been a treasure trove for the study of Italian agriculture, and the rural economy more widely, typically in tandem with the comparable works of Columella's republican 'predecessors', Cato and Varro.[4] The *De re rustica* has also long been of interest to those studying ancient

---

The idea for this chapter arose in post-paper discussion at the conference in Santiago de Compostela in September 2019 that brought most of the contributors to this volume together to discuss Junian Latinity: special thanks are therefore due to all my fellow Junian-*aficionados*, and particularly to Pedro López Barja for conceiving of, and organising, the gathering. The text of Columella is taken from the Oxford Classical Texts (Rodgers 2010); the English translation is mine.

[1] A brief introduction to the *De re rustica* is in Reitz 2013. For much modern bibliography, see Diederich 2015.
[2] See Col. *Rust*. 8.16.9 and 10.185 (Spanish origins), 3.9.2 (estates in Latium), 3.3.3 (his 'Carentum', in Etruria).
[3] Von Stackelberg 2013, 1679.
[4] For example, Roth 2007 (slavery; rural economy); Spurr 1986 (arable cultivation); White 1970 (arable cultivation; labour organisation, incl. slavery; animal husbandry; etc.).

Fachliteratur, regularly combined with the analysis of the work's relationship with earlier Greek and Latin writers, its poetical didacticism and literary qualities, besides Columella's socio-political stance, moral outlook and self-representation.[5] By contrast, the text has been all but ignored in the study of Junian Latinity. Given the lack of any explicit mention of the condition in the text, this is perhaps not surprising. But to ignore Columella's work in an exploration of the literary universe of Junian Latinity means to miss an important source and insight – for Columella *does* engage with Junian Latinity in his treatise, as this chapter will show. In brief, this chapter analyses a passage that has not hitherto been brought into the discussion of Junian Latinity, demonstrating its relevance to the topic, thereby also enriching our understanding of the text itself. My broader aim is to show that and how long-known texts can yield new evidence for the study of Junian Latinity. By so doing, this chapter seeks to encourage further, searching investigation into the Roman literary corpus to unearth other, 'new' evidence for the study of what has for far too long appeared as a condition that is for all practical purposes elusive to the modern scholarly eye.

The Reward of Liberty

In his discussion of labour force management, Columella offers several considerations regarding the managerial benefits arising from the use of a reward system for the enslaved estate population. As a benchmark, Columella recommends to 'reward those who conduct themselves with energy and diligence'; importantly for present purposes, for Columella, the reproductive success of enslaved women falls squarely into this rubric:

> Feminis quoque fecundioribus, quarum in subole certus numerus honorari debet, otium, nonnumquam et libertatem dedimus, cum complures natos educassent; nam cui tres erant filii, vacatio, cui plures libertas quoque contingebat.

> Also to more fertile women – in whom a certain number of off-spring ought to be honoured – I have given leave from work and sometimes also freedom, when they had reared several children. For to someone who had three children, exemption from work, for someone with more, freedom came their way.[6]

The passage is well known, and has received abundant treatment. Apart from noting the Columellan reward scheme as a means to increase the obedience and loyalty of the servile labour force vis-à-vis the estate owner, and thus the estate's profitability,[7] the passage is widely taken as a key piece of evidence for the occurrence of so-called

---

[5] For example, Connolly 1998, 138–40 (Latin authors); Diederich 2007, 209–58, 270–1, 368–95 (literary qualities; political stance); Doody 2007 (Latin authors); Fögen 2009, 171–82 (technical literature); Martin 1971, 311–42 (Greek sources; socio-political outlook); Fögen 2009, 189–96 and Milnor 2005, 254–5 (moral outlook); Pomeroy 1994, 70–2 (Greek authors); Reitz 2017 (poetical didacticism).

[6] Col. *Rust.* 1.8.19.

[7] So plainly stated by Columella (*Rust.* 1.8.19): 'Haec et iustitia et cura patris familiae multum confert augendo patrimonio' ('Such justice and consideration on the part of the master contributes greatly to the increase of his estate'). For discussion, see Bradley 1987 [1984], 21–30.

natural slave reproduction on rural estates: it is, as Phillips has put it, 'one of the strongest pieces of evidence that Roman masters allowed even their slaves on the rural estates opportunities to reproduce themselves'; or, as Phang has commented from a different perspective, evidence for the fact that '[m]asters may have encouraged slave-breeding'.[8] Others have seen in the passage evidence for the valuation of child labour on a Roman rural estate.[9] Some have employed the passage in broader discussions on the sexual relations among, and the family lives of, the enslaved.[10] There exists, moreover, some considerable debate on a couple of details of the recommended reward: the sex of the children (do only male children count?); and whether the women need to *raise* the children (to what age?) in addition to giving birth.[11] Despite these diverse analytical avenues that the debate on the passage has pursued, modern scholars have, however, not asked after the nature of the women's new status. Somehow, scholarship has tacitly treated the reward of liberty as a self-explanatory element of the Columellan text; as a result, the reward has fallen outside the broader discussion of the consequences of different modes of manumission, thereby implying that the women whom Columella recommends to liberate would have achieved the utmost with regard to, and as a consequence of, manumission.

Some examples are in order. For instance, Champion stated that Columella 'recommended exemption from work or even freedom for slave women who produced children'.[12] Bradley has commented similarly that Columella 'recommends time off from work or even manumission for prolific slave mothers and says that he himself released a mother of three from work and even set free a woman who had born more children'; in other words, 'Columella admits the prospect of freedom for the slave, the ultimate incentive and reward.'[13] The same interpretative take is visible in the study of ideal models of slave management by Dal Lago and Katsari: 'Columella also wrote that particular rewards, in the form of exemption from work or even freedom, went to female slaves who managed to provide their master with three or more children.'[14] As these examples illustrate, 'even freedom' appears as the apex of the rewards imaginable for the women in question. The underlying stance has also affected the translation of the passage – as, for instance, in an article by Harris:

> Columella 1.8.19: even mothers of three are classified as *feminae fecundiores* . . . 'nonnumquam et libertatem dedimus, cum complures natos educassent' ('sometimes we have even given them freedom, when they have raised several sons').[15]

The Columellan text, by contrast, *adds* freedom to the list of possible rewards, '*et libertatem*', best translated with '*and* freedom' – or, to be precise, in the concoction

---

[8] Phillips 1985, 22; Phang 2008, 229. For wider discussion of the Columellan evidence for our understanding of natural slave reproduction in the early imperial period, see generally Roth 2007.
[9] For example, Horn and Martens 2009, 168.
[10] For example, Joshel 1992, 44–6; Roth 2007, 12–20; cf. Bradley 1978, 248–9.
[11] Discussion of evidence and arguments is in Scheidel 1994, 514–17 and 522–5 (sex of children), 518–22 (age of children).
[12] Champion 1997, 175.
[13] Bradley 1978, 248; 1987 [1984], 23.
[14] Dal Lago and Katsari 2008, 198.
[15] Harris 2011, 66, n. 34 = Harris 1980, 135, n. 34 (there without translation); see also the cautionary comment in Harris 2011, 94, n. 28 = Harris 1999, 66, n. 28, regarding the effects of the potential gender

presented in Columella's text with 'and sometimes also freedom', as suggested in the English rendering given above – to avoid the ambiguity carried by '*even* freedom': the latter rendering, heavily re-used in modern interpretations, as seen, carries a sense of a final, ultimate reward – erroneously so, as will presently be shown.

To be sure, Columella *does* recommend the award of freedom, *libertas*, to the women in question: this is not in doubt. My point here is, rather, that beyond noting this fact, modern scholars have not probed more deeply into the meaning of the award of liberty. Instead, the Columellan evidence has readily been seen as illustrating the hope for freedom on the part of the enslaved – despite the fact that the text was, evidently, not written by an enslaved person, nor does it even purport to represent the voice of the enslaved and, hence, the latter's hopes.[16] Commenting on the prescription laid down in our passage, Bradley foregrounded the importance of giving 'something for which to hope, particularly the hope of one day being set free', noting in conclusion that 'this was the most devious method of manipulating emotions'.[17] Hopes aside, real or construed, for the time being: what was actually 'on offer'? This is the question that scholarship has not yet seriously asked – and to which we must now turn.

The obvious needs stating first: it is actually quite difficult to see how the award of liberty could have been utilised to their benefit by the women in question. As is evident, Columella does not mention the provision of any assets for the women upon manumission, with significant repercussions for the women's enjoyment of the value of the promised freedom. As Córcoles Olaitz has put it in her exploration of a later text that deals with comparable private manumissions, i.e. the *Formulae Visigothicae*, traditionally dated to the seventh century AD, 'without the existence of an own patrimony, the recently obtained freedom has no sense: without wealth there is no real autonomy'.[18] Moreover, the implication given by the passage is, obviously, that the women's children will remain in slavery, thus to be separated, at least in a legal sense, from their mothers by the latter's liberation. What the women's future relationship with the children's father(s) is envisaged to be, assuming that they too were members of the enslaved labour force on the estate (which, of course, need not have been the case, just as it need not have been the case that these women had a say in any sexual partnerships or engagements, or that any partnership was still ongoing), is not even alluded to by Columella.[19]

---

bias expressed by Columella, if the desired children are expected to be males only: on this point see also above, with n. 11.

[16] Interpretation of the voice of slavers as that of the enslaved is still common practice in ancient slavery studies; a recent example is Vlassopoulos 2021, 147–65, citing repeatedly texts produced by slavers about the enslaved, without confrontation of the issue or indeed an argument for the possibility of extracting the enslaved voice from these texts: for example, 148–50 (citing Artemidorus' *Interpretation of Dreams*), or 153–4 (citing Tacitus' *Annals*).

[17] Bradley 2015, 156; see also Scheidel 1994, 519.

[18] Córcoles Olaitz 2006, 346. Pedro López Barja reminds me that freedom by itself is not a meaningless good. Against this view in the type of setting here discussed, see further below and my own analysis of grants of freedom in a rural context in a Visigothic document, the so-called donation and will of Vincent of Huesca, pertaining specifically to enslaved men, in Roth 2016c.

[19] As already noted by Joshel 1992, 45. The identification of the fathers of children born into slavery is generally difficult: see, for example, the discussion of epigraphically attested fathers of children born into slavery – the so-called *vernae* – in Herrmann-Otto 1994, 42–6.

Second, what Columella offers through liberating the women is, as he plainly states, freedom – i.e. *libertas*. At no point does Columella suggest that he endeavours to reward the women with *libertas* and *civitas*, through *manumissio iusta*. Indeed, one would be hard pushed to argue that despite Columella's silence on the possibility of *manumissio iusta* he intended to endow the women with both – i.e. freedom *and* citizenship – and this despite the fact that we can tentatively assume on the basis of the number of children born (and raised) that the women were probably thirty years or older, and therefore capable of being endowed with Roman citizenship (unlike some of the cases discussed in Chapter 9).[20] Instead, the envisaged manumission mode is, evidently, *inter vivos*, excluding testamentary manumission from the list. If an award of freedom with *civitas* were to be envisaged, this reduces the options for all practical purposes to manumission 'by the rod' (*vindicta*), given the irregularity that we must assume manumission 'by the census' (*censu*) to have been subject to. Manumission 'by the rod' was of course made famous by the Plinian request to his friend Calestrius Tiro to undertake a detour to assist in the process of effecting *manumissio iusta* – which features in some considerable detail in the ensuing chapter. As far as Columella is concerned, however, even though his (known) estates are close to Rome and, hence, within reach of a magistrate with *imperium*, it requires more than a significant stretch of the imagination to see the passage as a prelude to the just cited Plinian enterprise to award *civitas*. Put simply, it is not credible that Columella's recommendation encapsulated the idea that Columella-the-estate-owner travelled with the women in question to see the magistrate, or that this ideal estate owner massaged his friendship ties to have a magistrate visit the estate to manumit the enslaved mothers, with or without the kind of pompous ceremonial clap-trap that Pliny was likely to have envisaged. It follows that an understanding of Columella's recommended reward as an award of liberty – and liberty only – through *manumissio minus iusta* is the natural reading of the text. This suggestion can be strengthened through an additional contextualisation of the passage.

Thus, as has long been pointed out, the Columellan recommendation plays on the Augustan *ius liberorum*: this right offered freedom from tutelage to freeborn women who gave birth to three children, and to freedwomen who gave birth to four.[21] The recommendation is, in other words, a private calque of a public right, without, however, constituting a right. As De Martino has already noted:

> Si tratta, com'è chiaro, di un precetto di opportunità, non di un obbligo giuridico, anche se l'analogia con le norme augustee sul diritto delle liberte con quattro figli di ottenere l'esenzione dalla tutela del patrono (*ius quattuor liberorum*) è evidente.[22]

In a way, Columella models his own ideal estate household on that of the state at large, putting himself by analogy in the role of the lawgiver and legal executive. This model is reminiscent of one proposed a few decades later by the already mentioned Pliny the Younger: in one of his letters to Plinius Paternus, Pliny states that he permits the enslaved in his household to make wills that will be warranted by him, as long as no property

---

[20] On the demographic implications, see Scheidel 1994, 522–5.
[21] For discussion of a documented claim, see Kelly 2017.
[22] De Martino 1979, 264–5.

passes outside of the household; Pliny explains his approach noting that for the enslaved, the household is the state: 'nam servis res publica quaedam et quasi civitas domus est'.[23] Evidently, Columella does not go to the same length as Pliny in elaborating the 'private state model' behind his manumission scheme.[24] But the allusion to such a model is sufficiently clear: Scheidel therefore speaks of 'Columellas privates *ius liberorum*'.[25] The consequence, however, of the private remit that frames Columella's reward scheme is, plainly, that the state does not get involved in the award of the promised liberty: the grant is Columella's, not that of the *res publica*. Indeed, the strength of Columella's self-fashioning as the stately head of his household 'empire' would be lost if the underlying idea were for the (real) state to become formally involved.

This point can be thrown into greater relief by way of a simple comparison. Thus, in his published correspondence with the emperor Trajan, our friend the younger Pliny showcases a letter that depicts him as instrumental in the award of the benefits of the real *ius liberorum*, to the childless Suetonius, described by Pliny alluringly as his constant companion – *in contubernium assumpsi*.[26] Trajan grants the request, and Pliny is thereby portrayed as effecting the benefits of this state-driven reward scheme (in this case without the need for reproductive successes), thus setting himself up more generally as an efficient imperial, i.e. public agent – even with regard to what is in essence a private matter.[27] Seen in this later light, Columella's private *ius liberorum* is put into a lesser place through Pliny's successful public engagement with the real thing. But once viewed in this way, and in combination with the earlier considerations regarding the emphasis on the award of *libertas* (only) to the multiple mothers, it is quite clear that what Columella recommends when speaking of the award of freedom to enslaved women with a certain number of offspring is, plainly, *manumissio minus iusta*. In consequence, in *Rust.* 1.8.19, Columella engages in promoting Junian Latinity.

Conclusion

The foregoing discussion has shown that a text hitherto ignored in the study of Junian Latinity constitutes in fact evidence for it. This result was achieved by contextualising a passage that quite obviously deals with manumission with an eye to the implied manumission mode and outcome: it is my contention that the same approach will yield further, interesting attestations of ancient engagement with the seemingly nebulous condition in the Roman literary universe, and that these attestations have, in their totality, the potential to add new insights to our understanding of Junian Latinity – as well as of the respective

---

[23] Plin. *Ep.* 8.16; see also Sen. *Ep.* 47.14; with Sherwin-White 1966, 467, and pp. 105–7 above.
[24] My emphasis on the brevity of Columella's remarks vis-à-vis the (comparative) length of Pliny's elaboration is inspired by, and responds in brief to, Whitton 2019, 245–8 (with n. 212). As the discussed overlap in theme between Columella and Pliny suggests, there is work to be done by the historian of slavery in unpicking Pliny's exchange with the other Pliny.
[25] Scheidel 1994, title and *passim*.
[26] Plin. *Ep.* 10.95.
[27] Plin. *Ep.* 10.96. On Plinian self-fashioning, see the discussion in Chapter 8. Note also Pliny's play on *contubernium*, which is 'metaphorical', as Sherwin-White 1966, 690 notes, 'of literary friendships', but also the denominator of emotional partnerships among the enslaved.

texts themselves. For the time being, however, suffice it to note two things as regards the particular text under scrutiny here.

First, the identification of the role played by *manumissio minus iusta* in Columella's reward scheme focuses attention on the benefits derived from the scheme by the owner of the estate, rather than the enslaved-cum-freedwomen: 'even freedom' was not what it may seem to be at first sight if awarded to enslaved individuals through a manumission that led to Junian Latinity, especially in the kinds of contexts adduced by the text under scrutiny. How the women may have supported themselves after the award of freedom is anyone's guess. It is equally unclear how (and indeed whether) they could have been perceived as capable of accumulating the resources necessary to finance iteration, should they have seen a benefit in this at all (and should they have been aware of this possibility in the first instance). It is worth emphasising in this context that the women's age and (therefore) reduced reproductive capacity at the point of the envisaged manumission appear to block the way to an award of citizenship through *anniculi probatio*: a bit like in the case of modern academic promotion practices, 'credit' once used for a promotion was no longer employable for future promotion applications – here with regard to the women's children that led to the mothers' award of *libertas* in the first instance. All in all, the Junian Latin dimension here foregrounded amplifies the problematic demographic, social and emotional aspects of Columella's ideal manumission scheme.

Second, the argument here presented opens up the passage for intertextual analysis with other works that (are already known to) explore Junian Latinity. The above brief aside on the correspondence of Pliny the Younger is a case in point that is likely to merit detailed further scrutiny.[28] Moreover, as I have argued elsewhere, the text known as Petronius' *Satyricon* critiques sharply the self-gratifying impetus behind the self-fashioning of members of the upper echelons in awarding freedom without citizenship to enslaved members of their households.[29] Columella needs to be included in the list of potential targets for Petronius' pen, and analysed accordingly. Generally speaking, there is scope for further introspective critique of the Roman literary universe to get to the bottom of the finely graded and diverse representations of freedom contained therein, with particular regard to freedom's complex relationship with slavery, at an individual level. What we can say with certainty already, however, is that the one surviving Latin agricultural treatise from the early imperial period is actively promoting Junian Latinity – irrespective of the women's odds in gaining that status (or desire to do so):[30] the seemingly elusive Junian condition was central enough to Columella's mindset to be given pride of place in what are really only very few lines concerned with the management of his ideal estate's enslaved population. Logically, it should be equally central to our investigations into other surviving texts from the Roman imperial period concerned with the interplay between slavery and freedom.

---

[28] See also the comment in n. 24 above.
[29] Roth 2016a.
[30] The likely contemporaneous Greek treatise on estate management by Bryson, which survived mostly in a medieval Arabic translation, does not mention manumission or freed status; the only 'improvement' envisaged on the part of the estate owner for the enslaved is to be elevated 'from one grade to the next' in a differentiated reward scheme that Bryson does not flesh out: *Oikonomikos* 73 (ed. Swain 2013).

8

READING PLINY'S JUNIAN LATINS

Ulrike Roth

Introduction

THE STUDY OF JUNIAN LATINITY, as far as it has attracted the attention of scholars at all, has been firmly in the hands of historians and epigraphers, besides its exploration by Roman lawyers.[1] This is perhaps not surprising, given that, on the one hand, some of the most exciting evidence for Junian Latinity is epigraphic in nature, addressing intriguing aspects of the social history of Rome, while, on the other hand, the status that we call Junian Latinity was created by force of law. The chapters in the first part of this book, as well as those featured in its partner volume, illustrate well the significance of historical, epigraphic and legal approaches to the topic.[2] At the same time, it is somewhat bewildering that in the light of the clear occurrence of Junian Latinity and Junian Latins – whether real or fictional – in the literary evidence from the Roman Empire, little effort has been expended on exploring how Junian Latinity is portrayed in the relevant texts.[3] What, to be more precise, does Junian Latinity *do* in these texts? To address this question is the primary task of this chapter.

To this end, the present contribution will concentrate on a handful of letters from the correspondence of Pliny the Younger. My chosen focus on a single author has three reasons. First, such a focus is essential to work out the conceptual image embedded in, and articulated through, a given matter – here, Junian Latinity – in any one specific authorial universe. This author-focused approach prevents the creation of a composite picture that is based on premature synthesis of different authors' subtle and often diverse perspectives on a subject: because of its innate hybridity, such a synthesis can no longer be securely anchored in a *particular* social or cultural context,

---

Thanks for comments on earlier chapter drafts are due to Pedro López Barja and Myles Lavan, as well as to Michael Crawford. Unless otherwise stated, the English translations of Pliny's letters are adapted from those given in the LCL; the text is taken from the Teubner edition (Schuster 1952).

[1] Besides the fundamental studies by Weaver (1986, 1990, 1997) and Sirks (1981, 1983), and Camodeca's (2006a, 2006b, 2002) detailed discussions of the material relating to what must be the most famous Junian Latin in modern scholarly thought – i.e. L. Venidius Ennychus – recent contributions include Corcoran 2011; Garnsey and De Ligt 2012; Hirt 2018; Koops 2014; López Barja 2018b, 1998; Pferdehirt 1998; Rawson 2010; Roth 2016a, 2010b; Scholl 2001.
[2] López Barja, Masi Doria and Roth forthcoming.
[3] For a first attempt, see Roth 2016a, primarily concerned with the image of Junian Latinity in Petronius' *Satyricon*, with brief counter-positioning to the Plinian approach in *Ep.* 10.104–5.

thereby weakening its usefulness for meaningful interpretation. Second, there exists, in my view, considerable doubt over the identification of Junian Latinity in some of the passages cited by modern scholarship in the study of the topic; quite obviously, focusing on ambiguous passages in a synthetic approach is likely to distort our appreciation of the story of Junian Latinity, instead of enhancing it. Broadly speaking, it would be methodologically unsound to offer a literary reading of Junian Latinity in texts that are not reliably identified as pertaining to the topic. Third, and by contrast, the Plinian correspondence offers demonstrable and sustained engagement with Junian Latinity, enabling meaningful discussion of the condition. This is not to suggest that all of the Plinian passages cited by modern scholars in their analyses of Junian Latinity are beyond doubt, but that there are *some* that are – and it is with those that any such investigation as the present one must start. In what follows, then, my primary attention is to the Plinian text, and on passages within that text that *clearly* attest the status of interest here. In practice, this means that this chapter's main concern is initially with just two letter exchanges, before contextualising the findings from this investigation through another two such exchanges that also raise the issue of Latinity, even if not securely of *Junian* Latinity. The journey starts in Pliny's northern Italian home town Comum, before heading into the wider imperial orbit, as seen from the geographically distant, but in epistolary terms rather close, Pontine shores.

Not Quite a Journey Round the World: *manumissio Comensis*

The first occasion in Pliny's published letter exchange on which Junian Latinity is given a prominent role is in Book 7. There, in a well-known and often cited letter from AD 107 to Calpurnius Fabatus, the grandfather of his wife, Pliny showcases his excellent relations with his friend Calestrius Tiro, the newly appointed governor of the province of Baetica. The two men's profoundly emphasised friendship serves in the second half of the letter to provide the basis for Pliny's suggestion to ask Calestrius Tiro to visit Comum,[4] Calpurnius Fabatus' home town and residence, to enable, in his role as magistrate with *imperium*,[5] the liberation 'by the rod', i.e. *vindicta*, of an unspecified number of individuals whom Calpurnius Fabatus had previously manumitted from slavery 'among friends', i.e. *inter amicos*, and thus through manumission *minus iusta*:

> [C. Plinius Fabato Prosocero Suo S.]
> Calestrium Tironem familiarissime diligo et privatis mihi et publicis necessitudinibus implicitum. Simul militavimus, simul quaestores Caesaris fuimus. ille me in tribunatu liberorum iure praecessit, ego illum in praetura sum consecutus, cum mihi Caesar annum remisisset. ego in villas eius saepe secessi, ille in domo mea saepe convaluit.

---

[4] In several earlier letters, Pliny established a link between Calestrius Tiro and the Calpurnii, via his wife Calpurnia, Fabatus' granddaughter, thus metaphorically preparing Calestrius Tiro's physical reunion with (a member of) the Calpurnii in Book 7: discussion of the 'Calpurnia–Tiro nexus' is in Gibson and Morello 2012, 101.

[5] The use of a proconsul's jurisdiction outside his own *provincia* was permitted in non-contentious matters: Digest 1.16.2pr. (Marcian).

Hic nunc pro consule provinciam Baeticam per Ticinum est petiturus. spero, immo confido facile me impetraturum, ut ex itinere deflectat ad te, si voles vindicta liberare, quos proxime inter amicos manumisisti. nihil est quod verearis ne sit hoc illi molestum, cui orbem terrarum circumire non erit longum mea causa.

Proinde nimiam istam verecundiam pone teque, quid velis, consule! illi tam iucundum, quod ego, quam mihi, quod tu iubes. vale.

[To Calpurnius Fabatus, his Wife's Grandfather]
Calestrius Tiro is one of my dearest friends, and we have been closely associated in both personal and official relations. We did our military service together and were both quaestors serving the Emperor. He held the office of tribune before me, through the privilege granted to fathers of children, but I followed him in the praetorship when the Emperor gave me a year's remission. I have often visited him in his country houses, and he has often spent times of convalescence in my home.

He is now setting out for Baetica as governor of the province, and will pass through Ticinum. I hope, in fact I am sure, that I can easily persuade him to leave his direct route to pay you a visit, if you intend to liberate 'by the rod' those you recently manumitted among your friends. You need not fear that this will be a trouble to a man who would not find a journey round the world too far on my behalf.

So be rid of your usual diffidence and consult your own inclinations! He will be as pleased to do my bidding as I am to do yours. Farewell.[6]

The proposed detour may not quite resemble a journey round the world, but it is not negligible: some 70 kilometres as the crow flies, but more like 100 kilometres for Calestrius Tiro and his entourage on the routes available; and that is just one way. In short, what Pliny proposes amounts to around one week of travelling for Calestrius Tiro: clearly, the purpose needed to be bracketed under the label *mérite le détour*. And that purpose is, as the letter openly states, to liberate formally, 'by the rod', some individuals whom Calpurnius Fabatus had previously freed informally – i.e. some Junian Latins.

Quite obviously, the proposed Plinian request vis-à-vis Calestrius Tiro has not one but multiple purposes, including the maintenance and advancement of friendship ties, beyond making a considerable contribution to Pliny's self-fashioning as a member of the upper crust, both through the actual letter exchange at the time and subsequently through the medium of the published correspondence.[7] But whatever these other purposes, it would be rather odd (albeit, admittedly, not impossible) for Pliny

---

[6] Plin. *Ep.* 7.16; see Sherwin-White 1966, *ad loc.* (pp. 419–21) for historical commentary.

[7] Pliny's self-fashioning has been the subject of intense debate in recent years; its study goes hand in hand with the increasing appreciation of the literary character of the Plinian correspondence, including Book 10: on Books 1–9, see, for example, Ash 2013; Carlon 2009; Hoffer 1999; Marchesi 2008; Riggsby 1995; Tzounakas 2015. On Book 10, see, for example, Noreña 2007; Stadter 2006; Woolf 2006, 2015. Brief discussion of Pliny's epistolary activity as reflecting a 'community-oriented ethic' is in Riggsby 1998, 92. The letter also offers the reader important information about Pliny's career, providing *en passant* the basis for a biographical perspective on Pliny's smooth advancement; brief comment on Pliny's 'autobiography' is in Gibson and Morello 2012, 13–19 (and more generally 9–35).

to request the services of Calestrius Tiro in the formal manumission of the individuals concerned had there been a significantly easier way for Calpurnius Fabatus to liberate the Junian Latins 'by the rod' or through another means that bestowed Roman citizenship.[8] Understandably therefore, the letter has regularly been taken as evidence for the difficulties involved in accomplishing formal manumission away from the centres of power and, consequently, as indicative of the spread of Junian Latinity especially in political backwaters.[9] But there is another element that needs spelling out for present purposes, namely the seemingly self-evident fact that the formal manumission is depicted as entirely owner-cum-patron driven. It is Calpurnius Fabatus – and not the informally freed individuals – who is active in securing the formal manumission of those previously freed without the franchise. To say so borders on stating the obvious. But it is important to be absolutely clear about the documented motor behind the proposed changes in status, to put the image of Junian Latinity created by Pliny in due course in its proper place.

The correspondence between Pliny and Calpurnius Fabatus is continued in a later, shorter exchange between the two men in which Calestrius Tiro's preparedness to undertake a journey round the world for Pliny appears significantly compromised, i.e. limited to reaching Mediolanum, not Comum, on his way to Baetica, as a lesser concession to satisfy Pliny's request:

[C. Plinius Fabato Prosocero Suo S.]
Gaudeo quidem esse te tam fortem, ut Mediolani occurrere Tironi possis, sed ut perseveres esse tam fortis, rogo, ne tibi contra rationem aetatis tantum laboris iniungas. quin immo denuntio, ut illum et domi et intra domum atque etiam intra cubiculi limen exspectes. etenim, cum a me ut frater diligatur, non debet ab eo, quem ego parentis loco observo, exigere officium, quod parenti suo remisisset. vale.

[To Calpurnius Fabatus, his Wife's Grandfather]
I am delighted to hear that you are feeling well enough to meet Tiro at Mediolanum, but I must ask you to conserve your strength and not take upon yourself a burden too heavy for your years. In fact, I insist that you wait for him at home, indoors and without leaving your bedroom; for as I love him like a brother, he must not demand from one I honour as a father an attention which he would not expect his own father to show. Farewell.[10]

---

[8] The sustained concern for due practical considerations behind Pliny's requests for assistance from other office holders, as well as from the emperor, is discussed in Morbidoni 2019, 83–95 on the example of several requests for citizenship featured in Book 10 (on which more below).

[9] For example, by Weaver 1990, 280, noting that '[t]he procedure for converting Junian Latin to Roman citizen status was formal and required the presence of a Roman magistrate with *imperium* i.e. praetor or consul or a provincial governor. The opportunities for such conversion were evidently far greater in the city of Rome than in the rest of Italy or in the provinces where only one day of the *conventus* was set aside for such applications.' See also López Barja 1998, 159; Buckland 1908, 444; and see Treggiari 1969, 29 from a republican perspective.

[10] Plin. *Ep.* 7.23.

Whatever Pliny's affection for his grandfather-in-law, and his concomitant insistence on Plan A – i.e. Calestrius Tiro's visit to *Comum*, not Mediolanum, there is a blatant omission in the letter: there is no mention of any of the Junian Latins who are the subject of the arrangement. They too, evidently, would need to travel to Mediolanum from Comum, where we must assume them to be located, to be manumitted 'by the rod' through Calestrius Tiro, should the latter not be prepared to head further north.

The focus on those with power over enslaved and (informally) manumitted individuals, and the simultaneous relegation of the latter to the margins of the image that Pliny creates in his correspondence is also evident in a third letter that confirms (for us) that Calestrius Tiro indeed accomplished the requested task, i.e. to undertake several formal manumissions for Calpurnius Fabatus, and that he may actually have been pressed successfully to do so in Comum itself:

[C. Plinius Fabato Prosocero Suo S.]
Delector iucundum tibi fuisse Tironis mei adventum; quod vero scribis oblata occasione proconsulis plurimos manumissos, unice laetor. cupio enim patriam nostram omnibus quidem rebus augeri, maxime tamen civium numero; id enim oppidis firmissimum ornamentum.

Illud etiam me, non ut ambitiosum, sed tamen iuvat, quod adicis te meque et gratiarum actione et laude celebratos. est enim, ut Xenophon ait, ἥδιστον ἄκουσμα ἔπαινος, utique si te mereri putes. vale.

[To Calpurnius Fabatus, his Wife's Grandfather]
I am glad you enjoyed my friend Tiro's visit, and particularly pleased to hear that you took the opportunity of his presence with a governor's authority to undertake several manumissions. I am always anxious for the advancement of our native place, and above all through the increasing numbers of her citizens, for that is a tribute which sets a town on the surest of foundations.

One other thing pleases me I confess, not that I am courting popularity; you go on to say that you and I were both warmly praised in a vote of thanks, and, as Xenophon says, 'praise is the sweetest thing to hear', especially if it is felt to be deserved. Farewell.[11]

In this later letter on the subject, the formality of the manumissions is clarified through the comment on the increase in the number of the citizens of Comum. And while Pliny does not actually say so, it is reasonable to infer that these manumissions functioned to iterate the manumissions of the previously informally manumitted individuals.[12]

---

[11] Plin. *Ep.* 7.32.

[12] Gonzalès 2002, 335 (no. 197) classifies the letter under his 'slave' label ('Esclave'), while *Ep.* 7.16.3–4 is given the 'freed' label ('Affranchi'), at 327 (no. 171); *Ep.* 7.23 does not feature in his analysis at all, given there is no direct talk of any enslaved or freed individuals, or such a process as manumission. This classification is analytically consistent, given that *Ep.* 7.32 can be read as dealing with manumissions other than those of the informally freed individuals previously mentioned in *Ep.* 7.16.3–4; but this seems to me an overly mechanical reading of the correspondence. The singular classification of 'slave' motivated by the discussion of manumissions illustrates, moreover, a monochrome perspective on manumission that omits,

Intriguingly, the Plinian depiction of (former) slavery and (newly gained) citizenship in the urban universe of Comum is a harmonious one. Indeed, it is striking that the former enslavement of the newly made citizens does not appear to dilute their capacity to enrich Pliny's home town: in contrast to the notion that formerly enslaved individuals are not normally welcomed warmly by freeborn Roman citizens, entertained in both ancient and modern thought, because they are assumed to have carried a defamatory mark as a result of their prior enslavement, Pliny relates the men's civic advancement in an entirely positive fashion, concentrated on the unreserved benefit the new citizens bring to the city.[13] As Shelton has put it, 'Pliny praises the manumission on the grounds that it increased the number of citizens in the area.'[14] In short, the formerly enslaved Junian Latins-made-Roman citizens *improve* Pliny's home town.

The contrast in Pliny's depiction of Roman citizens with a servile past with other texts from the early imperial period has been duly noted before. In language and thought not unusual still in the 1960s, Sherwin-White commented that 'Pliny does not object to the increase of the foreign element within the Roman community, which', he contends nonetheless, 'was the purpose of the Augustan legislation on manumission to hold in check.'[15] Pliny's lack of objection is shared by the good people of Comum if one understands the source of the praise for him and Calpurnius Fabatus to be found in the local council, publicly commending the two benefactors, probably in the form of a decree (as suggested by Sherwin-White).[16] Seen this way, the focus is quite generally on the positive contribution that the former Junian Latins bring to their community, not on the identification of any potential negative traits or consequences carried or brought by them as a result of their prior subjection to slavery. Moreover, Sherwin-White observed in commenting on the correspondence that these 'three notes can hardly be other than genuine, if rewritten, documents'.[17] The documentary dimension of this letter triad powerfully underscores, then, the arrestingly refreshing approach championed in Pliny's epistolary universe towards the civic value of the enfranchisement of Junian Latins, suggesting an echo in real life, in contradistinction to the hostile image projected onto formerly enslaved individuals in several other authors of the imperial period.

quite plainly, the notion that manumissions can be associated with (already) freed individuals, rather than just with the enslaved. Furthermore, the ties created by Pliny between the letters in question strongly supports the identification of the manumissions in *Ep.* 7.32 with those of the Junian Latins in focus here. The concern with enslaved individuals, rather than (informally) freed individuals, in this cluster of letters is also evident in Gibson and Morello 2012, 49, noting that Calestrius Tiro headed up north 'to officiate at the manumission of *some slaves*' (my emphasis).

[13] The idea of a defamatory mark as a result of a person's prior enslavement is widespread in both ancient and modern thought. For discussion of the negative effects of the *macula servitutis* on freed individuals, see Mouritsen 2011, 10–35; a refreshingly different case is argued in Vermote 2016.

[14] Shelton 2013, 333.

[15] Sherwin-White 1966, §7.32.1 (p. 443); citing negative portrayals of the enslaved and freed by Tacitus and Juvenal, Sherwin-White sought to reconcile the contrast with Pliny's appreciation of the new citizens geographically: 'these refer to Rome itself – postulating a difference between the Empire's largest city and the other urban agglomerations, especially those further afield. But note also the wider context of Pliny's depiction of Comum as a place full of civic harmony: brief summary is in Gibson 2020, 175–6.

[16] Sherwin-White 1966, §7.32.2 (p. 444): 'The context suggests that this refers to a decree of the Council [. . .] Compare I.8.17.'

[17] Sherwin-White 1966, §7.23.2 (p. 430).

However, despite the seeming universal embrace of the new Roman citizens by the city and its prominent son, the individuals in question remain once again on the sidelines of the epistolary activity; their names are not given, nor even their number. In fact, the perspective adopted in the letter is entirely external to those directly affected by the requested acts of enfranchisement: Pliny does not engage with the consequences of the process on the persons undergoing it. Instead, as noted above, the manumissions are cast as a means for the advancement of the town, i.e. for the advancement of *Comum*, not the newly enfranchised persons, through the enlargement of the town's citizen body. What, conversely, the acquisition of Roman *civitas* may have meant to those awarded it is left out of the equation. In a sense, then, the provisioning of Comum with new citizens is in line with other gifts bestowed on the town by Pliny – typically in the form of financial support for construction work: the new citizens *are given* to Comum, by Pliny, exposing them as a means to an end.[18] In turn, the advancement of Comum is thus underpinned by, and in many ways competes with, Pliny's self-fashioning as the keenest of supporters of his home town.

The theme of municipal progress through individual support was indeed carefully prepared by Pliny in the preceding letter, to Pompeius Saturninus; in this letter, Pliny unmistakably emphasises the great merit of 'managing the affairs of one's city'.[19] All told, the former Junian Latins and their newly gained civic status have all but disappeared from sight by the end of the letter under discussion: it is the actions of Pliny and Calpurnius Fabatus that conclude the exchange under the rubric 'subject to praise'. In fact, if the reference to *gratiarum actio* is taken to evoke the formal praise offered by a newly elect consul to the emperor of the type previously delivered by Pliny to Trajan, in the *Panegyric*,[20] Pliny's usage of the term for himself and Calpurnius Fabatus conceptually parallels both men with the apex of imperial power, thus creating an image of their own civic perfection. And in Pliny's immodest shade, with the spotlight unambiguously directed at himself and his grandfather-in-law and *their* commendable civic action, the importance of which Pliny had explored at greater length already in an earlier exchange with Calpurnius Fabatus,[21] the former Junian Latins appear ever more thoroughly eclipsed. Consequently, much as these new Roman citizens are likely to have been made to offer services by and to Calpurnius Fabatus during their enslavement, they continue to be dominated also following manumission and enfranchisement in the only sources surviving of their existence, being allocated a mere ancillary function in the much larger civic game played by Pliny.

This perspective on the focus on Pliny and *his* world, and on the simultaneous disregard for the manumitted individuals *qua* individuals does not change even if one assumes, perhaps perversely, that the voice behind the praise is that of the former Junian Latins themselves – i.e. what Sherwin-White has called 'the spokesman of the freedmen'[22] – and that Pliny does not just conceptually advance his own role

---

[18] Pliny's financial support for Comum was notable; see Nicols 1980 for discussion (including on the role in which Pliny offered his support).
[19] Plin. *Ep.* 7.15.
[20] On the *gratiarum actio*, see Paladini 1961.
[21] Plin. *Ep.* 5.11.
[22] Sherwin-White 1966, §7.32.2 (p. 444).

by paralleling it to that of the emperor, but assimilated the role of the newly made Roman citizens to that of consuls praising emperors: the Plinian microcosm is thereby made to correspond to the imperial macrocosm. In *that* scenario, the newly made citizens are sketched appropriately (if somewhat loftily) in their new civic persona, contributing to the exchange of civic dues and rewards. Simultaneously, however, the letter then also contributes to the idea of the Plinian household as a state, entertained by Pliny elsewhere explicitly with regard to testamentary provisions by members of his enslaved *familia*.[23] Either way – and there need not of course be a single, exclusive meaning at play in the first instance – the (former) Junian Latins emerge as a mere means to Pliny's much grander designs: in the Plinian text, *manumissio comensis* is not carried out for the benefit of those manumitted; rather, the Junian Latins who are awarded Roman citizenship through formal manumission *serve a purpose* in Pliny's epistolary universe.

This last point can be contextualised further. Thus, Riggsby's analysis of Pliny's discussion of the orator as an engaged public figure concentrates attention on (recommended) behaviour that is 'consequential for the community'; and, like this orator, Pliny appears in the present letter exchange 'judged ultimately by concrete effects he will have on those around him', fully fitting with Pliny's view that 'virtue is constructed under (perhaps even by) the gaze of the community' – as the town council of Comum seems to have understood well.[24] Thus, while the Junian Latins whose earlier manumission Calpurnius Fabatus chose to iterate with the help of Calestrius Tiro appear in broad historical terms as civic assets to the community of Comum, they only just scrape onto the backbenches in Pliny's epistolary self-fashioning, set to implement and advance his own constitution as 'an element of a larger community',[25] not theirs. In brief, these men (and there is little reason to think that women were involved) and their enfranchisement *serve* Pliny to advance *his* persona, commensurate with how Pliny is known to have acted in other spheres of life too – not least on the seemingly distant Pontine shores, which now call for their own exploration.

Not Really Asking for Too Much: *modicum Plinianense*

Perhaps the most cited occasion in Pliny's published correspondence that gives centre stage to Junian Latinity is a pair of letters between Pliny and the emperor, Trajan, from around AD 110.[26] Although the exchange in question is well known (and will benefit from further discussion in the ensuing chapter), it is imperative to take full account of the wording, besides the narrated action, to gain further insight into Pliny's approach to Junian Latinity. First, Pliny's letter to Trajan:

---

[23] Plin. *Ep.* 8.16.1–2: 'res publica [. . .] et quasi civitas domus est'.
[24] Riggsby 1998, 77, citing Picone 1978, 151–3 for discussion of the communal aspect of the Plinian construction of virtue. Evaluation of a person and their achievements by the community was of course the norm in ancient Rome: brief elaboration is in Riggsby 1998, 77–80, with 80–90 for an exploration of Pliny's embrace of that norm outside the oratorical sphere.
[25] Riggsby 1998, 95.
[26] See Sherwin-White 1966, 80–1 for discussion of the likely period of Pliny's governorship in Bithynia.

[C. Plinius Traiano Imperatori]
Valerius, domine, Paulinus excepto Paulino ius Latinorum suorum mihi reliquit. ex quibus rogo tribus interim ius Quiritium des: vereor enim, ne sit immodicum pro omnibus pariter invocare indulgentiam tuam, qua debeo tanto modestius uti, quanto pleniorem experior. sunt autem, pro quibus peto: C. Valerius Astraeus, C. Valerius Dionysius, C. Valerius Aper.

[Pliny to the Emperor Trajan]
Valerius Paulinus, Master, having passed over his son Paulinus, (in his will) has bequeathed to me his right over his (Junian) Latins. I ask you to confer on three of them meantime the *ius Quiritium*, for I fear that it may be going too far to invoke your generosity on behalf of all of them. I must exploit that generosity all the more moderately as I experience it more fully. Those for whom I entreat it are C. Valerius Astraeus, C. Valerius Dionysius, and C. Valerius Aper.[27]

Second, Trajan's reply to Pliny:

[Traianus Plinio]
Cum honestissime iis, qui apud fidem tuam a Valerio Paulino depositi sunt, consultum velis, mature per me, iis interim, quibus nunc petisti, dedisse me ius Quiritium referri in commentarios meos iussi idem facturus in ceteris, pro quibus petieris.

[Trajan to Pliny]
Since you most honourably wish thought to be taken promptly by me for those who have been placed in your trust by Valerius Paulinus, I have ordered it to be placed in my records that I have for now granted the *ius Quiritium* to those for whom you have now asked it, and I will do the same for those for whom you ask it in the future.[28]

Starting at the end, the pair of letters documents, at base, a request by Pliny, for three Junian Latins to be granted the *ius Quiritium*, and thus full emancipation; Trajan's reply documents that the request fell on fertile ground, and that all three men gained Roman *civitas*. As Pliny observes at the beginning of his letter, the three men came under his patronage through a testamentary disposition by his friend Valerius Paulinus, who opted to pass over his own son, Paulinus, in doing so.[29] As the exchange also documents, the three men in question – whose names are given by Pliny at the end of his letter – were not the only ones over whom he thus acquired patronal rights, even if the correspondence does not provide any information on either the number or the names of the others. That the three men – all of whom carry the *tria nomina* – are Junian Latins, while labelled by Pliny merely as 'Latins' ('Latinorum'), is clear from

---

[27] Plin. *Ep.* 10.104; the translation is adapted from Morbidoni 2019, 37.
[28] Plin. *Ep.* 10.105; the translation is mine, while the punctuation of the text has been slightly amended from that given in the Teubner edition.
[29] The technical juridical details are not of interest to the present inquiry. For discussion, see Sherwin-White 1966, *ad loc.* (pp. 714–15).

the contextual details, including the men's names (documenting the patronal role of Valerius Paulinus) and the juridical transfer of patronage. The purpose of providing the full names of the three individuals in Pliny's request is contextualised through Trajan's reply: the onomastic details were essential for the recording of the men's transfer of status in the imperial records; these details are more fully discussed in the subsequent chapter, and have in any case no further bearing on the present inquiry. In sum, having previously exercised his good relations with his friend Calestrius Tiro, in this later exchange with Trajan, Pliny steps up the game of enfranchising Junian Latins by having direct recourse to the *emperor* – successfully so. But this is not the only feat that this slim correspondence accomplishes.

Quite obviously, apart from the act of enfranchisement enabled by the letter exchange, the correspondence contributes to Pliny's literary self-fashioning, in multiple ways. There is, perhaps most notably, the stress on Pliny's modesty – what I have frivolously called the *modicum Plinianense*: notwithstanding the evident window for future requests, underscored by the play on the term *interim*, asking for citizenship for three men only, out of an unspecified pool, is put into words that operate to cast Pliny as perfectly measured while giving centre stage to – and deliberately creating a contrast with – imperial generosity ('Vereor enim, ne sit immodicum pro omnibus pariter invocare indulgentiam tuam'). Pliny's exploitation of the emperor's largesse is, moreover, specifically labelled as moderate ('modestius'), underscoring the noted contrast further. Trajan replies accordingly, emphasising Pliny's restraint – his 'maniera molto signorile', as Bracci has termed it – at the outset of the response ('Cum honestissime').[30] Within the epistolary context, the letter plays, as Bracci observes, on 'la dialettica fra ostentazione del favore imperiale e riservatezza nelle lettere di raccomandazione'.[31] In combination, the restrained governor and the charitable emperor make, unsurprisingly, a perfect pair, as elsewhere in Pliny's correspondence.

But whatever the literary self-fashioning, Pliny's request for an imperial grant of citizenship for three men only, out of a larger number, is once more real and need not be doubted.[32] The selective approach has been seen as an indication of Pliny's lived respectability: 'La *honestas* di P.', is how Bracci has summarised the matter.[33] This view indeed makes sense *within* the world that Pliny made, i.e. it springs from and simultaneously reinforces a particular type of rapport between members of the elevated social echelons to which our two correspondents belong; Bracci speaks even of a game, played well and voluntarily by both correspondents ('un gioco di cui entrambi conoscono bene le regole').[34] But a closer look at Pliny's literary treatment of the Junian Latins in question challenges that respectability on the larger plane, thereby also demonstrating that attention to Junian Latinity enhances modern understanding of our evidence beyond appreciation of the Junian condition itself.

---

[30] Bracci 2011, *ad loc.* (p. 281).

[31] Bracci 2011, *ad loc.* (p. 280).

[32] Brief comment is in Sherwin-White 1966, *ad loc.* (pp. 714–15). On the realism that characterises the correspondence between Pliny and Trajan, including its formal aspects, see the recent interventions by Lavan 2018; Coleman 2012.

[33] Bracci 2011, *ad loc.* (p. 281).

[34] Bracci 2011, *ad loc.* (p. 281), with reference to 10.8.1 ('honestissimo exemplo') and 7.14.1 ('tu quidem honestissime').

To begin with, the obvious needs stating first: just as at Comum, the Junian Latins in question are mute. There is no attempt at representing *their* voices, at indicating *their* desire for citizenship; instead, it is *Pliny* who asks ('rogo') for the *ius Quiritium* for the three men; and it is *Pliny* who expresses concern over the need to balance the request with due measure ('Vereor'). Pliny's position in the matter is replicated in Trajan's reply: *you wish* thought to be taken ('consultum velis'). And Pliny's role in any possible future requests is suitably acknowledged by Trajan in like fashion: 'I will do the same for those for whom you ask it in the future' ('idem facturus in ceteris, pro quibus petieris'). To be sure, the very real, beneficial role of an influential governor in the process of acquiring citizenship rights cannot be denied.[35] This fact is underscored on other occasions in Pliny's correspondence in which he asks Trajan to award citizenship to several individuals (to which attention will turn shortly). With regard to the three Junian Latins, Bracci has therefore commented that Paulinus deliberately sought the assistance of Pliny in making the enfranchisement process simpler, not least because of the Junian Latins: 'Paolino voleva probabilmente rendere piu semplice *per i liberti* l'acquisizione della cittadinanza romana, grazie alla raccomandazione di un personaggio influente come P.' (my emphasis).[36] Viewed in this manner, the desire to gain citizenship is understood as theirs, or at the very least approximated to their own, and plainly understood as in their interest – despite the silence in the letter on the views of the Junian Latins themselves.

Bracci's viewpoint is not an isolated one. Germerodt speaks even of patronal 'Fürsorge' vis-à-vis the informally manumitted men.[37] Kasten has similarly put the spotlight on Pliny's concern and care *for* the Junian Latins in his German translation of the text: 'Da Du den ehrenwerten Wunsch hast, *für die*, welche Valerius Paulinus Dir anvertraut hat, *zu sorgen*, darfst Du Dich, soviel an mir liegt, gern damit beeilen' (my emphases).[38] Indeed, the weight of this caring and charitable understanding comes full circle precisely in modern translations, such as the one offered by Radice in English for the Loeb Classical Library, or that by Durry for the French Budé edition (with my emphases):

Your desire to further *the interests of the freedmen* entrusted to you by Valerius Paulinus does you very great credit.

Puisque tu as le désir très honorable de veiller *aux intérêts de ceux* que Valerius Paulinus t'a confiés [. . .][39]

---

[35] Brief comment is in Mattern 1999, 3.
[36] Bracci 2011, *ad loc.* (p. 280), citing legal reasons: 'In caso di morte del patrono l'autorizzazione imperiale diventava indispensabile per dare il ius Quiritium ad un liberto iunianus (Gaio III, 72; Tituli ex corpore Ulpiani 3,2).'
[37] Germerodt 2015, 165.
[38] Kasten 1982, *ad loc.* (p. 649).
[39] Radice 1969, *ad loc.* (p. 297) = Radice 1963, *ad loc.* (p. 297); Durry 1959, *ad loc.* (p. 77). Other, more recent examples (throughout with my emphases): Williams 1990, *ad loc.* (p. 75): 'Since you most honourably wish to make prudent provision through me for *the interests of those* who were entrusted to your good faith by Valerius Paulinus [. . .]'; Walsh 2006, *ad loc.* (p. 281): 'Since you most honourably wish opportunely through me to promote *the interests of those* whom Valerius Paulinus has committed to your good faith [. . .]'.

That Roman citizenship was a desirable good, not least for the enslaved, is of course a widely shared view in modern scholarship. And it is of course undoubtedly true that many of those who experienced Roman slavery sought to exit slavery through manumission and the acquisition of *civitas*. But as I argue in Chapter 9 in this volume, this does not give us licence to *automatically* read every shred of evidence in this vein; indeed, we would likely be better served in our quest to understand the ancient Roman world if we did not. As things stand, we know nothing about the interests of those whose patronal oversight Valerius Paulinus passed to Pliny via his will. Crucially, as has been seen with Pliny's dealings in Comum, manumission that leads to the award of *civitas* is a matter that Pliny was already more than happy to exploit for his own purposes before becoming Rome's most perfect governor – to enrich the citizen body of his home town and thereby his own civic standing in it. Indeed, taking full account of the self-serving dimensions of the Plinian *manumissio Comensis*, discussed in the previous section, should prevent any rushed 'excavation' of the interests of those whom we are not allowed to hear in the Plinian text. More broadly, in the context of a society whose social hierarchies are grounded, at base, in violence and inequality, it is rash to assume without due evidence any scope for decision-making on the part of those who held the shorter straw in their hands – here the Junian Latins: would a lack of interest on their part in gaining *civitas* have made any difference to Pliny's action? At the same time, if the happenings in Comum are anything to go by, it is more likely than not that the desire to advance rapidly through imperial grant the civic status of the three Gaii Valerii must have been at least in *Pliny's* interest. To be clear: I am not arguing that the three Junian Latins would not have wanted Roman citizenship; perhaps they did, perhaps they did not. Nor am I suggesting that Pliny and his peers must unthinkingly be deemed tone-deaf to the interests of those over whom they exercised ownership and patronal powers: going by Pliny's own words, elsewhere, to be taken, evidently, with a large pinch of salt, the implication is that the fates of the enslaved and freed were not *categorically* disregarded.[40] Rather, I hold that it is high time to take note of the crucial silence cast over the men in question, by Pliny, in our discussion of the stakes and desires behind the requests for imperial grace. That being so, and notwithstanding the rules of the genre (which, however, Pliny after all *chose* in order to record for posterity the enfranchisements in question), the epistolary muzzling of the three Junian Latins is more likely than not a reflection of their silencing also in real life, including with regard to the role of civic status in their lives.

Leaving Pliny aside, *what about* the three Junian Latins? We know their names, i.e. those by which they were known in slavery – Astraeus, Dionysius, Aper – and the

---

[40] For instance, in an earlier exchange precisely with Valerius Paulinus (*Ep.* 5.19), or with regard to his reader Encolpius (*Ep.* 8.1), regularly given a positive write-up by modern scholars: see, for example, Lefèvre 2009, 181–94, including brief comment on other scholars' take on Pliny's 'gelebte *humanitas*' (p. 182). In the light of the literary purpose that the relevant passages serve, it is obviously naïve to take Pliny's words about his seeming care and attention for the enslaved in his household unreservedly at face value, or to challenge critical approaches to the slaving dimension of Pliny's *persona* and habitat through mere citation of the relevant lines in his letters, as trialled, for instance, in du Prey 1994, 228; see also the remarks at the end of the conclusion to this chapter.

onomastic conglomerates that drew on the *praenomen* (Gaius) and *nomen* (Valerius) of their owner-cum-patron under which they become known following their transition to *libertas*. But that is all. Evidently, this is more, in strict personal terms, than what we know of those manumitted in Comum, by Calpurnius Fabatus with the help of Calestrius Tiro. The letter exchange between Pliny and Calpurnius Fabatus of course culminates in the assertion that the enfranchisement of Fabatus' Junian Latins was greatly appreciated by the town, leading to praise being issued, and implying in turn, as discussed above, that the individuals in question were seen as of suitable personal and communal standing for joining the civic ranks. No such external acknowledgement is forthcoming in Pliny's exchange with Trajan, given the near complete contextual vacuum in which the correspondence sits. That said, Pliny's request to Trajan, framed by the governor's modesty and discernment, works to create an aura of selectivity and, hence, of distinction and merit pertaining to the few chosen ones. This is echoed – one may want to say: understood – by Trajan, in his response, who indeed encourages further requests from Pliny in consequence. But again: we need to be on the watch to avoid being taken in by this charming screen, because Trajan's response stresses first and foremost *Pliny*'s respectability behind the request ('honestissime'), as observed above. In this way, the selectivity functions to highlight the governor's ability to identify those worthy of civic advancement, rather than to draw attention to the chosen individuals themselves. Once again, we hear Pliny talking (or Trajan) – about Pliny, or rather about what Gibson has termed 'Pliny's privileged self'.[41] Moreover, the noted respectability is, plainly, locked into the social world that is so vividly depicted in the Plinian correspondence all round, i.e. the world of imperial Rome's public and political elites – and thus the world of elite slavers. And it is precisely the Roman slaver's respectability – a contradiction in terms from our modern perspective – that drives the silencing of the Junian Latins in the letters under scrutiny here.[42] In sum, for Pliny's modesty and discernment to take centre stage, the Junian Latins must take the back seat; they emerge, yet again, as a mere cog in the machine, i.e. as '[s]omeone or something that is functionally necessary but of small significance or importance within a larger operation or organization'.[43]

Not Actually Commending Libertine Merit:
ornatissimi patroni

The cases so far studied can be paired with another two that have traditionally been part of the study of Junian Latinity in the Plinian correspondence, even if the core of the letters in question is concerned with special requests to Trajan for individuals who

---

[41] Gibson 2020, 241.

[42] This is not the same as saying that the enslaved 'receive largely incidental attention, as in Pliny' (Gibson 2020, 244), but to point towards their use and usefulness for the kind of literary constructions here exemplified on Pliny's correspondence, however selective, and thus seemingly incidental. Note the attention to purpose, not incidence, in Gibson and Morello 2012, 216, regarding 'the scant attention given to accommodation for slaves and freedmen' in Pliny's description of his Laurentine villa in Book 2, geared to underpin the self-portrait thereby constructed of the villa's owner, i.e. Pliny himself.

[43] So defined by TheFreeDictionary.com ('a cog in the machine/wheel'); accessed 9 October 2021.

were *not* Junian Latins. Each of these exchanges arises from Pliny's debt to medical professionals who had been instrumental in improving his health, with their professional merit consequently underpinning Pliny's requests. Moreover, in both cases, Pliny ends by asking for further grants, for others, potentially including some Junian Latins. The first of these exchanges, from the end of the first century AD, is concerned with gaining Roman citizenship for an Egyptian physiotherapist called Harpocras who is of freed but peregrine status, having been manumitted by a peregrine; the request is followed by another seeking the *ius Quiritium* for two women – (Antonia?) Hedia and Antonia Harmeris – both of freed status, having been manumitted by a woman called Antonia Maximilla.[44] The second case to be discussed is headed by Pliny's request for citizenship for the relatives of his doctor, Postumius Marinus – four in total, all of whom are freeborn non-Romans: Chrysippus, son of Mithridates, his wife Stratonice, daughter of Epigonus, and Chrysippus' sons Epigonus and Mithridates; the letter concludes, however, with another set of requests for three further individuals – Lucius Satrius Abascantus, Publius Caesius Phosphorus and Pancharia Soteris – at the wish of their (otherwise unnamed) patrons, whose mention, however, illustrates the three persons' freed status.[45] Hedia, Harmeris, Abascantus, Phosphorus and Soteris are all widely regarded as Junian Latins, given their attested freed status combined with their lack of Roman citizenship, even if the contextual information provided in the letters that enables status identification is slim at best – a point to be returned to below. Moreover, Pliny's mention of the two medical professionals, although certainly not of Junian Latin status, has a perhaps surprisingly significant bearing on the present inquiry, further encouraging these letters' analysis here. As before, it is crucial to take full account of Pliny's rationale for, and the manner in which he made, the various requests. First, Harpocras et al.:

[C. Plinius Traiano Imperatori]
Proximo anno, domine, gravissima valetudine usque periculum vitae vexatus iatralipten adsumpsi; cuius sollicitudini et studio tuae tantum indulgentiae beneficio referre gratiam parem possum. quare rogo des ei civitatem Romanam. est enim peregrinae condicionis, manumissus a peregrina. vocatur ipse Harpocras, patronam habuit Thermuthin Theonis, quae iam pridem defuncta est.

Item rogo des ius Quiritium libertis Antoniae Maximillae, ornatissimae feminae, Hediae et Antoniae Harmeridi; quod a te petente patrona peto.

[Gaius Plinius to the Emperor Trajan]
Last year, Master, I was afflicted by an illness so serious that my life was in danger. So I called a physiotherapist, whose concern and attentiveness I can repay with equal gratitude only by your gracious kindness. I am therefore asking you to award him Roman citizenship, for he is a foreigner, having been manumitted by a foreign mistress. His name is Harpocras, and his patroness Thermuthis, wife of Theon, is long dead.

---

[44] Plin. *Ep.* 10.5, 10.6, 10.7, 10.10. See Sherwin-White 1966, *ad loc.* (pp. 566–71, 575–6) for historical commentary.
[45] Plin. *Ep.* 10.11.

I am also begging you to grant the *ius Quiritium* to Hedia and Antonia Harmeris, freedwomen of a most distinguished lady, Antonia Maximilla. I make this plea at the request of that patroness.[46]

As acknowledged above, the contextual information for the legal and civic statuses of the two women for whom Pliny asks for the *ius Quiritium* is slim: nevertheless, the fact that both women are explicitly referred to as freedwomen of Antonia Maximilla ('libertis Antoniae Maximillae') clearly documents their freed status, while their lack of Roman citizenship – the basis for the request to Trajan – has provided the impetus for identifying them as Junian Latins: Sherwin-White noted that they belong to the category of 'freedmen [sic] of the inferior grade known as *Latini Iuniani*'.[47] On the other hand, Morbidoni has suggested that the two women were *Latin* freedwomen, having been manumitted *before* their patroness had acquired the Roman franchise.[48] Leaving the precise status of the two women aside for the moment, what stands out from the few lines that deal with them is the same kind of silence cast over their views on their legal and civic statuses that has been characteristic of the cases studied in the previous two sections: whether Junian or other freed Latins, the letter does not document the women's own voices; instead, Pliny emphasises that he appeals to Trajan at the request of the women's patroness – a woman, as Pliny has not been remiss to point out, of distinction ('ornatissimae feminae'). Sherwin-White has in turn not been remiss to point out that Pliny's emphasis on Antonia Maximilla's take on the matter has a legal backdrop, stressing that her 'consent was essential, since the patron of Junians succeeded to their property'.[49] This is obviously correct; but in the lack of any evidence for the two freedwomen's own wishes (including *their* consent – an issue duly observed by Weaver in general terms),[50] the point about the *patroness*'s consent actively directs the gaze away from those who are directly affected by the request, adding from a modern vantage point to the epistolary muzzling of the two freedwomen themselves. It is only logical, if seen from the perspective here adopted, that the question of merit is on the other hand reserved for the patroness: she – not those freed – is identified as a most distinguished woman, *thereby* justifying the request.

It could be argued that the already cited rules of the game – here: the genre – obliged Pliny to compose his letters in the way he did, including the sidelining of those who were about to be gifted with the supposedly greatest *beneficium*. However one should interpret adherence to such rules, it is in any case precisely in the letter

---

[46] Plin. *Ep.* 10.5.
[47] Sherwin-White 1966, *ad loc.* (p. 567), followed since, for example, in Shelton 2013, 335–6; López Barja 2018b. Roth 2016a, 627, with n. 70 appears to have been incapable *auf drei zu zählen*, listing only one (not three) individuals of (supposed) Junian Latin status for *Ep.* 10.11; while Weaver 1997, 68 appears to exclude (Antonia?) Hedia from the list of (possible) Junian Latins in *Ep.* 10.5 without comment.
[48] Morbidoni 2019, 89–94. Apart from uncertainty about her civic status at the point of the manumission of Hedia and Harmeris, Antonia Maximilla's relationship with Pliny is equally obscure; she is called his *necessaria*, which can indicate kinship or friendship ties. Brief summary of the issues surrounding Antonia Maximilla is in Shelton 2013, 335–6.
[49] Sherwin-White 1966, *ad loc.* (p. 567).
[50] Weaver 1997, 67.

under scrutiny that a quite different approach is applied to the deserving physiotherapist Harpocras, of freed but peregrine status: Pliny specifically underlines *the man*'s accomplishments for which he wishes to thank him by way of facilitating an award of Roman citizenship, i.e. the therapist's 'concern and attentiveness' in Pliny's care – 'cuius sollicitudini et studio'. To be sure, Harpocras' own views remain equally unknown; but that is perhaps less startling in the context of a Plinian attempt to find a suitable thank-you present for the therapist. As things stand, otherwise than in the case of the Junian (or perhaps other) Latin freedpersons, Pliny contextualises, and thus justifies, his request to Trajan for *civitas* for Harpocras by reference to what in brief can be called the person's merits.

The noted contrast between Pliny's handling of the request for citizenship for Harpocras and the request stemming from Antonia Maximilla is substantiated by the letter that immediately follows the correspondence between Trajan and Pliny about Harpocras, already briefly summarised above. Again, it is essential to pay close attention to the patterns produced by Pliny's formulation of the requests made in this letter:

[C. Plinius Traiano Imperatori]
Proxima infirmitas mea, domine, obligavit me Postumio Marino medico; cui parem gratiam referre beneficio tuo possum, si precibus meis ex consuetudine bonitatis tuae indulseris. rogo ergo, ut propinquis eius des civitatem, Chrysippo Mithridatis uxorique Chrysippi, Stratonicae Epigoni, item liberis eiusdem Chrysippi, Epigono et Mithridati, ita ut sint in patris potestate utque iis in libertos servetur ius patronorum.

Item rogo indulgeas ius Quiritium L. Satrio Abascanto et P. Caesio Phosphoro et Panchariae Soteridi; quod a te volentibus patronis peto.

[Pliny to the Emperor Trajan]
My recent indisposition, Master, has put me under an obligation to my doctor, Postumius Marinus. Through your kindness I can do him an equal favour, if in accord with your usual good nature you are favourable to my requests. So I am asking you to grant the citizenship to his relatives Chrysippus, son of Mithridates, and to Chrysippus' wife Stratonice, daughter of Epigonus, and also to the sons of this Chrysippus, Epigonus and Mithridates, on condition that they remain under their father's authority though preserving their rights as patrons over their freedmen.

I am further asking that you grant the *ius Quiritium* to Lucius Satrius Abascantus, to Publius Caesius Phosphorus, and to Pancharia Soteris. I make this request of you in accord with the wishes of their patrons.[51]

There are two sets of requests to Trajan in this letter. The first arises from Pliny's debt to his doctor Postumius Marinus, who according to Pliny's words has been instrumental in curing him from a recent illness. The gift of gratitude that Pliny envisages is a grant of citizenship to five of the doctor's relatives, each of whom is identified by a single, Greek name, followed by a patronym or at the least patronymical information. The doctor's

---

[51] Plin. *Ep.* 10.11. For historical commentary, see Sherwin-White 1966, *ad loc.* (pp. 576–7).

own, Roman-sounding name, in combination with the request for Roman citizenship for his relatives only (i.e. not for him), implies that Postumius Marinus already held the Roman franchise.[52] More relevant for present purposes, as in the case of Harpocras, the request is based on, and justified through, the professional merit displayed by the medic vis-à-vis Pliny.[53] At the end of the letter, however, follows another request for Trajan, namely to bestow the *ius Quiritium* on three further individuals: Lucius Satrius Abascantus, Publius Caesius Phosphorus and Pancharia Soteris.[54] The request is underscored by the same kind of statement that concluded the preceding request for Hedia and Antonia Harmeris in the letter about Harpocras, i.e. the mention of the patrons' appeal. As Birley put it in brief, 'P. requests citizenship [. . .] at the desire of (the) patron.'[55] In short, and notwithstanding several differences between the two letters and the requests made in them, Pliny's approach is the same in both: first comes a request that arises from – and is explicitly ascribed to – personal accomplishment (in both cases of medical professionals); second comes a request that is explained entirely through the patronal wish.[56] Once again, we do not hear the views of those to be granted the *ius Quiritium* – Lucius Satrius Abascantus, Publius Caesius Phosphorus and Pancharia Soteris – nor do we hear the reasons for their selection for the grant.

Referring to these three individuals in his commentary on the letter, Sherwin-White stated plainly that '[t]hese persons are Junian Latins', a view widely shared.[57] In the lack of any details beyond their names, however, it is unsurprising that other possibilities have been raised as well, as did Morbidoni, arguing (much as in the case of Hedia and Antonia Harmeris) that they are Latin freedpersons.[58] The evidence at hand does not permit certainty. What *is* evident, however, is that Pliny's epistolary handling of these three individuals conforms to his handling of the *clearly* attested Junian Latins in the two letters discussed in the first two sections of this chapter, as does his handling of Hedia and Antonia Harmeris. In sum, these freedpersons, whether Junian or other Latins, are almost literally in the hands of their patrons, besides those of the smoothest of imperial operators – Pliny the Younger.

Conclusion

In his detailed study of both the enslaved and the freed in Pliny's correspondence, Gonzalès proposed a clear distinction between Pliny's approach to those in slavery in

---

[52] As already noted by Sherwin-White 1966, *ad loc.* (p. 576).

[53] Sherwin-White 1966, *ad loc.* (p. 576) suggests, without argument, that Postumius Marinus was the driving force behind the request, having been encouraged by Harpocras' success.

[54] The name 'Pancharia' is in dispute. For a brief summary of the salient issues, see Birley 2000, 36 ('Ancharia Soteris, P.').

[55] Birley 2000, 44 ('Caesius Phosphorus, P.'), with 36 ('Ancharia Soteris, P.') and 86 ('Satrius Abascantus, L.').

[56] Note also the request for citizenship in *Ep.* 10.106 (and Trajan's reply and confirmation of the grant: 10.107), for the daughter of a Roman soldier; Pliny's stress on the man's membership in the Roman army implies that here, too, merit is at play, i.e. the valued contribution of the centurion to the military, even if only on a general level. On the possible legal status of the centurion's daughter, see Sherwin-White 1966, *ad loc.* (p. 715).

[57] Sherwin-White 1966, *ad loc.* (p. 578), with the contributions listed in n. 47 above.

[58] Morbidoni 2019, 96.

rural settings and those freed (or of uncertain status) and (implicitly) of an urban derivation; for the latter, Gonzalès argued, individual competences, foremost intellectual, play out favourably:

> Si globalement les dépendants ruraux sont englobés dans des énumérations qui évoquent les grands traités d'agronomie de Caton, Varron et Columella, associant hommes, bêtes et matériel, la situation est totalement différente lorsque nous abordons les affranchis ou les individus au statut incertain. Ici les compétences, intellectuelles la plupart du temps, ont une reconnaissance réelle qui bénéficie à celui qui les possède et les met en œuvre, ce qui n'empêche pas qu'il y ait toute une hiérarchie de reconnaissances et de recompenses, mais nous sommes sur ce point mal renseignés: nous savons seulement que Pline, dans son cas, recourt à l'affranchissement et à l'octroi de la capacité de tester pour les esclaves.[59]

The fundamental 'merit-narrative' that underlies Gonzalès' contention regarding the freed is a general staple of modern – and ancient – discussions of slavery and the route to freedom through manumission: this hardly needs specific emphasis in the context of a volume concerned with Junian Latinity; suffice it, here, merely to recall the notion entertained by Suetonius that Augustus sought to keep the citizen body free of undesirable elements by legislating on manumission – cited already above, and more fully discussed in this volume's Introduction.[60] This being so, it is especially rewarding that, in contradistinction to the neat differentiation proposed by Gonzalès, the analysis undertaken in the present chapter has shown that the Plinian discourse ignores for all practical purposes individual competences, intellectual or otherwise, when the issue of Junian Latinity plays a role, be this in the urban context of Comum or in the provincial backwaters on the Pontine shore: Pliny does *not* have recourse in his portrayal of the individuals to personal capacities or the merits that arise from the demonstration of such capacities. Indeed, the persons in question do not exist as active agents at all in Pliny's literary treatment, irrespective of the massive detour undertaken by one of Pliny's chums for an act that may well have benefited them personally too. This image of Junian Latinity is maintained by Pliny also in his request to the emperor for citizenship for the three individuals over whom he acquired the rights of patronage through the will of his friend Valerius Paulinus. And the same holds also for the letters that deal with freedpersons of uncertain Latin derivation. What the Plinian discourse *does* foreground, in many ways unsurprisingly, is Pliny's own, active role in the process of enfranchisement. Viewed the other way, Pliny's portrayal implies that without his help, the Junian Latins (and possibly other Latins) in question would have had little chance of gaining the *magnum beneficium* – irrespective of personal competences. In short, the enfranchisement of the freed individuals here focused on serves to embellish the governor's own competences; the freedpersons do not appear in their own right.[61]

---

[59] Gonzalès 2002, 248.
[60] Suet. *Aug.* 40.3; see also the relevant discussions in the chapters by Garcia Fernández and López Barja in this volume.
[61] The contrast is especially stark with Pliny's depiction of the poorly Zosimus, whose numerous talents and accomplishments are duly enumerated by Pliny precisely for the purpose of documenting the man's serviceability (*Ep.* 5.19.1–4), but it is also notable in the description of the activities undertaken

Pliny's privileged self once more aside, it is notable on a broader plane that the letters establish a firm relationship between the acquisition of Roman citizenship and Junian Latinity – or, to be more precise, between Junian Latinity and Roman citizenship: Pliny's Junian Latins appear only in contexts that call up Roman citizenship, unlike the Columellan exploration of the manumission of women, discussed in the previous chapter, or the manumissions played out on the stage known as the *Cena Trimalchionis*, one of which features in the subsequent chapter.[62] On the other hand, in 'Pliny's Empire', manumission does not lead to Roman citizenship directly; instead, Junian Latinity emerges as a critical step on the road to full emancipation. Even in Comum, desperate for new citizens, the manumissions undertaken by Calpurnius Fabatus with the help of Calestrius Tiro are tied in the Plinian narrative to those recently manumitted among friends ('quos proxime inter amicos manumisisti'). Put differently, Pliny did not choose to paint a picture of individuals' direct elevation from servility to *civitas* – in clear contradistinction to the majority of modern scholars. Informal manumission, and its consequences for the legal status of those freed, is, then, a firm element of the Plinian approach to liberation from slavery and the acquisition of Roman citizenship.

Intriguingly, however, despite the Junian Latins' near complete erasure from sight, kicking *their* competences into the long epistolary grass, Pliny's depiction of Junian Latinity and the award of Roman citizenship promotes a considered and selective approach. More to the point, Pliny's depiction of Junian Latinity advocates exceptionality and selectivity in the award of Roman citizenship to informally freed individuals – a process that is, unsurprisingly really, firmly in the hands of Pliny-the-patron (or his associates, such as his grandfather-in-law): *he* desires, as Trajan put it – 'velis' – for the selected individuals to be granted *civitas*. To be sure, Pliny's grandfather-in-law undertook 'several manumissions' ('plurimos manumissos'), implying, moreover, that *all* those manumitted informally on a recent occasion were chosen to be manumitted formally with the help of Calestrius Tiro. As seen, this relative liberality on the part of Calpurnius Fabatus serves the Plinian self-representation as a devoted supporter of his home town, through the enlargement of its citizen body – even if the lack of data to back up Pliny's quantitative comment should make one at least a little bit suspicious as to the numerical impact of the suggested generosity. In any case, at no point does Pliny even allude to the individuals as individuals, let alone the reasons for their selection – and this despite the fact that Pliny's take on slavery is otherwise full of stories of individual fates.[63] Indeed, while in the letter from Pontus the names of those for

---

by Hermes, who is specifically commended for having acted just as Pliny would have done himself (*Ep.* 7.11.6). Note also, however, the silence over personal merit regarding several imperial freedmen (Maximus: *Ep.* 10.27–8; Lycormas: *Ep.* 10.63, 10.67), besides the scathing review of Pallas' supposed merits (*Ep.* 7.29).

[62] Petron. *Sat.* 40.3–41.4, 41.6–7, 54.4–5. For discussion, see Roth 2016a.

[63] Brief discussion is in Lefèvre 2009, 182–3. Note as an example the lavish description of the merits of one Zosimus, one of Pliny's *liberti*, in *Ep.* 5.19, designed as a justification for Pliny's request to Valerius Paulinus to host the man for a period of rehabilitation. Intriguingly, while it is not the case that all of Pliny's letters that deal with individuals who experienced slavery comment on individual fates and characteristics, Hoffer 1999, 49 explains the absence of interest in individual traits in the context of slavery precisely with Pliny's 'specific concerns about their individual personalities', which Pliny seeks to mask through the use of generalities.

whom citizenship is sought via imperial grant are given, the request is equally lacking in the kinds of individual details that one would expect from a narrative of manumission that advances the notion of servile merit and achievement. The noted omission is replicated in the cases of freedpersons whose Latinity cannot be further pinpointed, at least not by us. This omission is, on the one hand, powerfully thrown into relief by several requests for *civitas* put to Trajan by Pliny that foreground precisely personal merit – as in the case of Harpocras and Postumius Marinus.[64] The contrast is meaningful. It is here, in the maintenance of complete control, to the point of excluding even his readers from any knowledge about the rationale behind the selections, that Pliny-the-slaver comes most prominently to the fore: through their silencing, Pliny's Junian Latins help to celebrate the Roman slave-owner's powers, exercised with absolute discretion and culminating in unchallenged authority – only too hastily subsumed under the notion of respectability by modern scholars, as seen. It hardly needs stressing, on the other hand, that, in contrast to the few individuals for whom Pliny asked for Roman citizenship with Trajan, the majority went empty-handed; this conclusion is not weakened by acknowledging future requests from Pliny to Trajan, as noted. The same, we must assume, happened in Comum, regarding those not previously freed informally. What the correspondence under scrutiny in this chapter implies, then, in its emphasis on due selectivity, is that the Plinian Junian Latins by and large *remain* Junian Latins, challenging on a historical plane the notion of regularity regarding the acquisition of *civitas* upon manumission, at least within the elevated social circle to which Pliny belonged.[65] As a corollary, Pliny's epistolary exploration of Junian Latinity culminates in an image of the *managed* spread of Roman *civitas*: there was, to reiterate, no free-for-all regarding the acquisition of Roman *civitas*. One can only but wonder what Pliny would have made of Finley's 'astonishing rule' – discussed in the Introduction to this volume.[66]

Looked at in the other way, these letters testify, then, not so much to 'La *honestas* di P.', cited above, but to what Hoffer has called Pliny's 'disingenuous modesty'.[67] Notably, Pliny's approach to the matter under scrutiny has been shown to be consistent throughout, suggesting that his later, gubernatorial role in Pontus represents a

---

[64] Similar emphasis on personal merit is documented in epigraphy, as in the case of another physician, Gaius Calpurnius Asclepiades: *CIL* XI, 3943. For discussion of the social and civic advancement of physicians on the basis of their medical skills, see Mattern 1999.

[65] MacLean's 2021 analysis of the acquisition of citizenship through manumission at sub-elite levels, based on epigraphic evidence from the Danube, suggests a potentially marked contrast in manumission practices between the middle and the upper classes, with the former drawing more readily on manumission as a means of securing the passing of property and the maintenance of the 'family line' upon death. The widely assumed quantitative prevalence of Roman slaving at elite levels would, however, militate against the notion of a numerically significant impact on the spread of *civitas* through such a sub-elite practice.

[66] Finley 1980, 97, following Hopkins 1978, 116: 'Almost all ex-slaves freed by Roman masters received Roman citizenship.'

[67] Hoffer 1999, 51; note also Hoffer's broader argument for considerable anxiety on the part of Pliny-the-slave-owner, arising from his slaving (pp. 45–54). This is not to deny that the formulaic language used by Pliny for several of his requests from Trajan suggests that such requests were 'routine in nature': Mattern 1999, 3, with Millar 1977, 481–3. On mediators for provincials, see generally Saller 1982, 168–87 (with a focus on North Africa).

mere external layer of a much deeper, ingrained *modus operandi* – one characteristic of the elite slaver. In this way, too, there is much common ground between Pliny's so-called private letters and his public correspondence.[68] What, in turn, scholars should make of Pliny's 'maniera molto signorile' – the trademark of the slaver across the ages – has thus been thrown sharply into relief by an analytical focus on our friends the Junian Latins. Indeed, the focus on Junian Latinity in this chapter has emphasised the need to ask more probing questions about the Roman slaver's privileged self than hitherto done, with a view to confronting openly the wider socio-cultural practices that were the bedrock of Roman slaving.[69]

---

[68] For recent discussions of the nature of Pliny's correspondence, and the relationship between Books 1–9 and Book 10, see the contributions listed in nn. 7 and 32 above.

[69] The difficulty in approaching this issue, not least for scholars of the ancient, classical world, on the example of Pliny the Younger, is patent in Gibson 2020, 239–45, while earlier generations were still much more at ease with crediting positively the behavioural practices and habits of men like Pliny (for example, Dunham 1945, 26, suggesting that Pliny 'would do credit to any age'). The broader need to diverge from an approach that bases its interpretations of slavery on the Roman elite's viewpoints is emphasised in Walter's 2006 review of Knoch 2005; see also n. 42 above.

9

THE NAME, THE GARB, THE CAP: A PLEA FOR THE RENUNCIATION OF *CIVITAS*

Ulrike Roth

Introduction

THE PROBLEM WITH IDENTIFYING Junian Latins in our evidence is at the heart of much work on the subject, as summarised in the Introduction to this volume. This is perhaps most notable in the case of work focused on the epigraphic evidence: the chapters concerned with the inscriptional materials in the sequel to the present volume illustrate this well, as do the chapters in that volume concerned with diverse social settings that have left evidence for Junian Latins behind, especially in the familial realm. The problem looms so large in fact that the very question of how to identify Junian Latins in the epigraphic evidence was of central concern to Weaver's important contribution from 1990, tellingly titled 'Where have all the Junian Latins gone?' It has also been at the core of a recent study of the monumental dimensions of inscribed tombs: two decades after Weaver put the question as just cited, Emmerson courageously tackled the material remains of tomb complexes in Pompeii to associate several of the deceased who technically fall into the category of *incerti* with (former) holders of the Junian Latin status.[1] What all these contributions have in common is their careful attention to detail. But they also share a considerable level of ambiguity in their attempted status identifications – for both obvious and unavoidable reasons: as I noted myself a few years ago, '[s]cholarship currently lacks a means to distinguish freed slaves endowed with citizenship from freed slaves without.'[2] In the light of this methodological problem, it may not be entirely welcome to add more complexities to the mix. Still – this chapter foregrounds a couple of socio-cultural conventions that further muddy the waters of status identification in Roman society: naming and clothing. Both conventions have been duly noted and discussed previously in scholarly attempts at identification of legal status, especially in the epigraphic and visual realms. What has not been emphasised strongly enough is not only the extent to which

---

For uncountable, enjoyable discussions about diverse status 'diagnostics' pertaining to the Roman world I owe thanks to Michael Crawford, and to Pedro López Barja for specific comments on the present text. Details of the editions and translations of the texts discussed in this chapter are given with each text.

---

[1] Emmerson 2011.
[2] Roth 2016b, 106.

naming and clothing conventions complicate the differentiation of freedpersons with or without citizenship – *cives Romani liberti* and *Latini Iuniani* – but that these conventions obstruct the identification of the civic status *of any pedigree* in much of our evidence, whether held by individuals of freed *or* freeborn status. In giving centre stage to the broader problem with identification of civic status in the analysis of three short texts, this chapter calls for renewed attention to the centrality of free as opposed to freed status, in the sources that document the conventions under scrutiny here, necessitating greater caution in their employment in the hunt especially for the precise civic condition of the freed.

The Name, the Garb, the Cap

We can dispose of the first of the three cases without much ado, concerned with onomastic conventions, because it has been intensely discussed by previous scholarship with due reference to Junian Latinity, besides its detailed exploration in the preceding chapter.[3] The case in question is the letter exchange with Trajan in which Pliny the Younger asks the emperor to grant Roman citizenship to three Junian Latins. Importantly, Pliny names the three men in question:

[C. Plinius Traiano Imperatori]
Valerius, domine, Paulinus excepto Paulino ius Latinorum suorum mihi reliquit. ex quibus rogo tribus interim ius Quiritium des: vereor enim, ne sit immodicum pro omnibus pariter invocare indulgentiam tuam, qua debeo tanto modestius uti, quanto pleniorem experior. sunt autem, pro quibus peto: C. Valerius Astraeus, C. Valerius Dionysius, C. Valerius Aper.

[Pliny to the Emperor Trajan]
Valerius Paulinus, my Lord and Master, having passed over his son Paulinus, (in his will) has bequeathed to me his right over his (Junian) Latins. I ask you to confer on three of them meantime the *ius Quiritium*, for I fear that it may be going too far to invoke your generosity on behalf of all of them. I must exploit that generosity all the more moderately as I experience it more fully. Those for whom I entreat it are C. Valerius Astraeus, C. Valerius Dionysius, and C. Valerius Aper.[4]

As is self-evident, the three men of interest to both Pliny and us all carry *tria nomina*: Gaius Valerius Astraeus, Gaius Valerius Dionysius and Gaius Valerius Aper. Their relationship to one another, and to Pliny, is of no interest here. The sole criterion that matters for present purposes is the fact that these Junian Latins are documented with an onomastic signifier that is typical in the early Roman Empire for male enfranchised

---

[3] For example, Gonzalès 2002, 123, 127–31; Roth 2016a, 626–30; Sherwin-White 1966, §§104–5 (pp. 714–15); Weaver 1990, 279–81.
[4] Plin. *Ep.* 10.104. The text is taken from the Teubner edition (Schuster 1952); the translation is adapted from Morbidoni 2019, 37. On the Junian Latin status carried by the three men, see Sherwin-White 1966, *ad loc.* (p. 714).

referents – i.e. Roman citizens. But while the *tria nomina* were typical for male Roman citizens especially in the hundred years or so that span the late republican power struggles at one end and the consolidation of imperial rule in the Julio-Claudian period at the other, the *tria nomina* were not the sole onomastic identifier for a Roman citizen, even in the early imperial period, nor were the *tria nomina* used only by Roman citizens.[5] Indeed, the relevant discussion in Chapter 1 by García Fernández, in the context of an exploration of municipal Latinity, highlights just how complex and varied the matter is. Within the study of Junian Latinity, the complexity has been underlined by Weaver in his already mentioned contribution from 1990: 'use of the *tria nomina* without tribal indication does not necessarily imply Roman citizenship'.[6] A decade later, Weaver returned to the issue, explicating the onomastic situation even more forcefully. Thus, in his 2001 study of families belonging to the lower strata of Roman society, Weaver coined two hypothetical rules for the onomastic identification of legal status: the first was concerned with identifying enslaved individuals; the second with identifying Roman citizens, especially among the freed population. This second, 'Provisional Rule Two of Sepulchral Nomenclature' – thus called by Weaver – summed up the widespread belief that the *tria nomina* constitute evidence of the male referent's Roman civic status.[7] Weaver then proceeded to dissect this rule in front of his readers' eyes on a single inscriptional case. Weaver concluded, rightly, that '[i]t emerges from this simple case that Rule Two above (i.e. *tria nomina* = Roman citizenship) is defective, seriously so if Junian Latins lurk untraced in large numbers in the *sepulcrales*, as I think they must.'[8] Weaver fleshed out his exposition by direct reference to the text under scrutiny in the present analysis: 'The use of *tria nomina* by *Latini Iuniani* (and by extension by *Latini* in general) is already clear from Pliny, *Letters* 10.5.2, 10.11.2, and especially 10.104.'[9] In short, amidst widespread scholarly practice to treat the *tria nomina* as a proxy for *civitas*, Weaver's work plainly emphasised that the onomastic usage of the *tria nomina* by Roman citizens and non-citizens alike is not in doubt and that therefore the *tria nomina* cannot be used by themselves as the signifier of Roman *civitas*:[10] onomastically speaking, male Junian Latins may look like male Roman citizens, and male Roman citizens, like male Junian Latins. The crux of the matter that is reflected in the *tria nomina* is, simply, not *civitas* but freedom. As Salway

---

[5] A comprehensive overview of the relevant onomastic developments is in Salway 1994.

[6] Weaver 1990, 279.

[7] Weaver's 'Rule One' concerned the equation of 'single name = slave status'. As Weaver 2001, 104 commented, '[i]t is enough to observe that it is not always the case that a single name, even one of Greek derivation, implies slave status, nor should the rule be applied automatically.'

[8] Weaver 2001, 103.

[9] Weaver 2001, 103.

[10] The *tria nomina* continue to be used as a proxy for Roman citizenship, not least in scholarship concerned with the study of Roman freedmen: for example, Carroll 2006, 129, 146, 243; Hope 2009, 167–8; Petersen 2006, 109. The same confusion underlies Kleiner 1977, 18–20 (citing earlier bibliography in n. 16). The use of the *tria nomina* as an indicator for citizenship status is also found outside of a visual/epigraphic context: see, for example, Perkins 2005. The extended idea that the *tria nomina* document Roman *ingenuitas* has been articulated even in legal scholarship: Jakab 2014, 211 states that 'die freigeborenen Römer trugen traditionell drei Namen': cf. Salway 1994 (with n. 11 below) on the relatively brief period in which the *tria nomina* dominated Roman onomastics (of the free, not necessarily the freeborn).

has noted citing passages from Juvenal and Quintilian that play on the *tria nomina*, the 'phraseology contrasts possession of the *tria nomina* with servile status rather than as defining Roman citizenship', adding that the *tria nomina* were also borne by Latins and Latinised peregrines – as the already mentioned chapter by García Fernández brings home with force.[11] With regard to women, attempts at onomastic differentiation of freed female citizens from female Junian Latins end up in a similar kind of onomastic dead end. Indeed, where women do not sport either filiation or libertination, their precise legal and civic status is regularly impossible to identify at all.[12]

The ambiguity inherent in the socio-cultural convention of naming that frames the usage of the *tria nomina* by men of diverse civic statuses, and that enables Junian Latins to look like their enfranchised counterparts (and indeed like Roman citizens *tout court*), is also evident in another type of convention that pertains to Junian Latinity: clothing. This ambiguity is brilliantly staged in a debating exercise quoted by Suetonius in his treatise about illustrious rhetoricians:

> venalicius cum Brundusi gregem venalium e navi educeret, formoso et pretioso puero, quod portitores verebatur, bullam et praetextam togam imposuit; facile fallaciam celavit. Romam venitur, res cognita est, petitur puer quod domini voluntate fuerit [liber] in libertate.

> When a slave-dealer was putting his band of slaves for sale ashore at Brundisium, he fitted out one good-looking and valuable boy with the *bulla* and *toga praetexta*, because he feared the customs-officers. He carried off his deception without a hitch; but when they reached Rome, the matter was brought under investigation, and the boy's freedom was claimed on the ground that he had been at liberty by his master's conscious choice.[13]

As seen in the Prologue to this volume part, the scenario depicted by Suetonius was cited by Buckland as the only literary source to flesh out the desire to free an enslaved person away from the formal settings and modes for manumission.[14] The reason for Buckland's choice is to be found in the legal dimensions that the cited case displays. The scenario is pretty straightforward as such: for the purpose of tax avoidance, a slave-trader dressed an enslaved boy whom he hoped to sell for a steep price in the attire of the freeborn Roman child – the *toga praetexta*, and the *bulla*.[15] In this way, the trader sought to disguise the boy's subjection to slavery, thereby avoiding the

---

[11] Salway 1994, 129; the cited passages are Juv. 5.127 and Quint. *Inst.* 7.3.27.

[12] For an overview of the onomastics of women in the Roman world, especially in the early imperial period, see Salway 1994, 125–31. For discussion of female Junian Latins, see the chapter by Masi Doria in the sequel to this volume.

[13] Suet. *Gram. et rhet.* 25.5. The text is that given in Kaster 1995, *ad loc.* (pp. 32–3); the translation is adapted from that given there. On the deletion of 'liber' in Suetonius' text, see Kaster 1995, *ad loc.* ('petitur [. . .] in libertate'; p. 288).

[14] Above, p. 155, with Buckland 1908, 444.

[15] Female children are also known to have worn the *toga praetexta*: for example, Cic. II *Verr.* 1.112–13. Whether girls wore the *bulla* is debated: critical are Goette 1986, 143–5; Palmer 1989, 42–6.

tax due on his pricey import. How and why the matter was eventually discovered is not of interest here. What is of interest is the fact that once the truth was revealed, freedom was claimed for the boy on the ground that his master had chosen to set him free. Kaster sums up the general view of the case thus: 'The slave-dealer's attempt to smuggle the *puer* past the customs-collectors as an *ingenuus* results in an action [. . .] through which the *puer* is claimed as free'; and, Kaster adds, '[t]he background of the controversy is the practice of informal manumission.'[16] In brief, the trader's decision to dress the boy in garb that signalled freedom was interpreted as an expression of his intent to manumit him.

The kind of logical construction that underpins this interpretation is well known in Roman law, not least with regard to manumission, both informal and formal. For example, the decision to identify one's slave as one's heir in one's will is cited in Justinian's *Institutes* as evidence of the testator's intention to set free the enslaved, even if the will lacked any reference to manumission: 'where an owner appoints his own slave as heir and the man's position remains unchanged, the will operates to make him free and compulsory heir'; as Tribonian explained further, 'the appointment can be made even without a grant of freedom'.[17] The general principle underlying this approach is summed up in the *Minor Declamations* ascribed to Quintilian, in the course of exploring the very case cited by Suetonius: 'who shall have been at liberty by the will of the master, shall be free' ('qui voluntate domini in libertate fuerit, liber sit').[18] Intention – on the part of the owner – is what counted.

To be sure, there is little reason to think that the trader who dressed the enslaved boy in fancy Roman garb *intended* him to be liberated; instead, the trader's concern when dressing the boy accordingly was with avoiding tax, not effecting manumission. This point is made plain also in the discussion offered in the *Minor Declamations*.[19] For obvious reasons, the juridical gymnastics that this kind of case encouraged were central to the debates among rhetoricians and jurists, not least to sharpen their analytical minds and argumentation skills.[20] Viewed from this angle, it is equally easy to see why the case was of particular interest to Buckland, worthy of citation, given his concern with the legal dimensions of slavery, construction included. On the other hand, it is worth emphasising that at the heart of the episode sits, to speak with Knoch, the issue of status ambiguity: 'das [. . .] Problem der allgemeinen Statusunsicherheit',[21] which also constitutes the impetus for the present discussion.

The longer treatment of the episode in the *Minor Declamations* – alongside the parallel case of an enslaved female dressed in the stola to pass as freeborn – provides some insight into the kind of specific arguments that were advanced, at least by the

---

[16] Kaster 1995, §25.5 (p. 287).
[17] *Inst.* 2.14.1; the translation is that of Birks and McLeod 2001.
[18] [Quint.] *Decl. Min.* 340.1.
[19] [Quint.] *Decl. Min.* 340.8–9.
[20] On the fruitful interplay between declamation and (juridical) oratory, see Winterbottom 1982. On the important role of the 'hypothetical case' in the development and understanding of jurisprudence at Rome, see Frier 1985, 163–70; Schmidlin 1976, 104–5, with further bibliography.
[21] Knoch 2018, 149.

declaimers.[22] Notably, although the point is made that the boy's garb signalled not only freedom, but specifically the freedom of the freeborn child – 'this boy is not only quasi-free but quasi-freeborn: he wore a *praetexta*' – what was at stake for the boy was nevertheless freedom only.[23] Thus, and leaving the boy's fate aside, what matters for present purposes is that the toga and *bulla* were *not* construed to argue for the award of *civitas*, let alone *ingenuitas*, but merely *libertas*.[24] The stress on freedom (only) is also evident in Suetonius' text. In their approach, both the declaimers and Suetonius' rhetoricians took a different route to a part of modern scholarship that employs the toga in general, and the *toga praetexta* and *bulla* in particular, as generic signifiers of Roman citizenship (if not also of *ingenuitas*).[25] Now, the declaimers and rhetoricians are of course right: despite the regular association of toga and *bulla* with *civitas* and *ingenuitas* respectively in Roman society, the context in which the enslaved *praetextatus* found himself in Brundisium ruled these options out.[26] Notably, although a case could be made for the trader's intent to set the boy free by dressing him accordingly, the process of liberation was, plainly, informal: even the declaimers would not stretch the case beyond freedom. Thus, apart from the fact that the *puer* was depicted as a child, i.e. well below the age of thirty, his liberation, however construed, did not draw on any of the modes of manumission that led to the award of citizenship. What was left was the rudimentary equation of his garb with freedom – and freedom only.

We of course do not know the original date of the episode of the boy in toga and *bulla*. In Suetonius' account, the episode appears in the brief historical sketch of the development of rhetoric in ancient Rome, followed by discussion of several notable rhetoricians, many of whom operated during the republican period. That said, both the text in the *Minor Declamations* as well as in Suetonius emphasise strongly those who were '*in libertate*' by the will of their master – a figure that is central to the legal

---

[22] The case of the enslaved female who is dressed in the outfit of a Roman matron (*matronali habitu*; *habitu matronae*) is given in [Quint.] *Decl. Min.* 342; the specific identification of her dress as the *stola* is at [Quint.] *Decl. Min.* 342.6, 342.7. Although the *stola*, too, functions – as this case underlines – as a signifier of Roman citizenship and *ingenuitas*, it has been significantly less central to the debate on status identification compared with the toga-clad male. For this reason, this case, and women's dress more broadly, takes a back seat in the present investigation, which is concerned in the main with the dominant scholarly practice.

[23] [Quint.] *Decl. Min.* 340.6–7: 'hic puer non tantum pro libero sed etiam pro ingenuo est: praetextatus fuit'. A comprehensive discussion of the (semantic) history of *toga praetexta* and *bulla*, emphasising their role in denoting freeborn status, is in Palmer 1989.

[24] The distinction is obscured in Rothe 2020, 5, despite the acknowledgement that the claim was for the boy's *freedom*, including with regard to her comment on the possible existence of a law that regulated the wearing of the toga.

[25] For example, Carroll 2006, 146 (with 256–7), noting that 'the depictions [. . .] of freedmen in the toga, which only Roman citizens could wear [. . .] were visual confirmation of the newly acquired legal and social status of these individuals'. The same assumption about the essential civic meaning of a toga-clad figure is expressed in Petersen 2006, 109, in a discussion of the Tomb of the Baker. For a brief, correct summary in the context of Roman art history, see Goette 1990, 2 (and 7, n. 57). For a longer discussion in the context of Roman legal history, see Mommsen 1887, 215–23, esp. 222–3.

[26] The same holds for the toga-clad and bulla-wearing 'King of Veii': Plut. *Vit. Rom.* 25.6–7; a summary discussion is in Palmer 1989, 6–12.

discussion surrounding Junian Latinity (as is underlined by Pellecchi in Chapter 2). For this reason, Kaster has argued for an imperial context, specifically identifying the *lex Iunia* as 'a *term. p. q.* for the collection of *veteres controversiae*', quoted by Suetonius.[27] Whatever one's view on this matter, we can in any case be fairly confident that readers in the imperial period would have found no problem in interpreting the case in the context of manumission practices (and their consequences) framed by the enactments that created and refined Junian Latinity. It is helpful to cite in this context Gunderson's notion of a 'faux-wilderness' for declamations, in analogy with the idea of a zoo in the heart of the city, which is 'constructed and then fenced in so that one may behold dangerous animals not so much as they are but as we have staged them ourselves'; against this backdrop, Gunderson concludes, the 'wilderness comments on who *we are*' (emphasis added).[28] Applied to the episode of the *praetextatus* in the accounts here cited, the settings and circumstances that surround the case comment on approximations to freedom, citizenship and *ingenuitas* in Roman *imperial* society, irrespective of any possible republican dimensions of the case. What we are ending up with, then, is a simple, as such well-known, and yet quite unfortunate, consequence: depending on setting and circumstance, freedom acquired from slavery in an informal manner can be associated with clothing otherwise privileged in the representation of both *civitas* and *ingenuitas* in imperial Rome, including in the context of manumission. Logically, like the *tria nomina*, the Roman garb in which the boy was dressed to defy the tax inspectors is not a safe identifier of Roman civic status either. It follows that, conversely, the freedom that *is* associated with the toga, and *bulla*, includes that enjoyed by Junian Latins. In sum, both the socio-cultural naming convention discussed above and the socio-cultural dress convention in focus in this second case may document the informally or imperfectly freed besides the Roman citizen, freed or freeborn. The inclusive nature of these socio-cultural conventions, and the interpretative ambiguities arising from it, can be deepened in a third case, before tying together the chief repercussions for the study of the Junian Latin status.

The third and final case, then, moves the discussion firmly into the world of Latin fiction, somewhat increasing the inherent complexities for the argument here pursued. The case has, however, recently received focused discussion in an exploration of Junian Latinity; its exposition in this chapter can therefore be kept to the relevant essentials.[29] At the centre of attention is another *puer*, this time in Petronius' *Satyricon*, in the episode known as the *Cena Trimalchionis*. The relevant lines describe the seemingly inadvertent liberation of an enslaved performer at the dinner:

> dum haec loquimur, puer speciosus, vitibus hederisque redimitus, modo Bromium, interdum Lyaeum Euhiumque confessus, calathisco uvas circumtulit et poemata domini sui acutissima voce traduxit. ad quem sonum conversus Trimalchio 'Dionyse' inquit 'liber esto'. puer detraxit pilleum apro capitique suo imposuit.

---

[27] Kaster 1995, §25.5 (p. 288).
[28] Gunderson 2003, 19.
[29] I.e. in Roth 2016a. See Schmeling 2011, 161 (§§7–8) for a brief summary of the standard modern understanding of the *liber*-pun.

As we were speaking, a beautiful boy with vine-leaves and ivy in his hair brought round grapes in a little basket, impersonating Bacchus in ecstasy, Bacchus full of wine, Bacchus dreaming, and rendering his master's verses in a most shrill voice. Trimalchio turned round at the noise and said, 'Dionysus, be Liber/free.' The boy took the cap of freedom off the boar, and put it on his head.[30]

The elements that matter for present purposes are quickly summarised. First, Trimalchio utters an ambiguous command – 'liber esto' – that can be understood in the narrated context as either an instruction to impersonate Liber or a grant of liberty: 'be Liber' or 'be free'. Second, the *puer* interprets the ambiguous instruction (also) in the latter fashion, i.e. as a grant of liberty, grabbing the *pilleus* that had hitherto adorned the roast boar. Understood this way, the scene parodies an informal manumission, creating another Junian Latin. It is specifically the head gear that shall concern us further though.

The *pilleus*, which the *puer* put on, is said to have been worn by those manumitted through a will at the funeral of their former master; it was thus firmly associated with liberation from slavery.[31] In contrast, however, to the notion of the award of liberty *and* citizenship regularly entertained in discussions of funerary manumission, Trimalchio's Liber remains without the franchise, thereby also removing the *pilleus* from Roman *civitas* (or, rather, *civitas* from the *pilleus*). It is notable in this context that in the days of Justinian, who – as Corcoran reminds us in his chapter on late Roman and early medieval legal texts – abolished Junian Latinity, enslaved individuals who donned the *pilleus* at their master's funeral were to be given Roman citizenship irrespective of the testator's wish: 'if any slaves wearing a cap of liberty march in front of a funeral procession of their master [. . .] whether this be by the wish of the testator or of his heir, they shall immediately become Roman citizens'; Justinian's target was 'empty manumissions', i.e. attempts at presenting oneself as humane by pretending to manumit, but in effect deceiving the public and cheating the 'liberty-cap wearers'.[32] It is irrelevant that for Justinian, Junian Latinity was no longer an option, leaving citizenship (with freedom, naturally) as the only possible way of honouring the wearing of the *pilleus* by the enslaved at the funeral. In this way, Justinian reinforced the association of the *pilleus* with *civitas*. On the other hand, the episode highlights just how difficult it is to be clear about the legal status of those who appear with the *pilleus* in one or other source. Indeed, one just wonders how many *pilleus*-donning enslaved individuals presented at funerals in the hope of manumission only to find themselves cheated out of freedom thereafter. At base, the idea that enslaved persons may be wearing the *pilleus* without any manumission intention on the part of their owners is comparable to the case of the toga-clad *puer* at Brundisium: however corrupt the

---

[30] Petron. *Sat.* 41.6–7. The text is taken from the Teubner edition (Müller 2003); the translation is mine.
[31] Dion. Hal. *Ant. Rom.* 4.24.6.
[32] *CJ* 7.6.1.5: 'Sed et qui domini funus pileati antecedunt vel in ipso lectulo stantes cadaver ventilare videntur, si hoc ex voluntate fiat vel testatoris vel heredis, fiant ilico cives Romani. et ne quis vana liberalitate iactare se concedatur, ut populus quidem eum quasi humanum respiciat multos pileatos in funus procedentes adspiciens, omnibus autem deceptis maneant illi in pristina servitute publico testimonio defraudati: fiant itaque et hi cives Romani, iure tamen patronatus patronis integro servando.' Text and translation are from Frier 2016, *ad loc.*

depicted slave-owners, and however clear the relationship of the *pilleus* with Roman citizenship at one semantic level certainly in the case of Justinian's intervention, the scope for morally and legally debased practices underscores the relevance of context and detail for a correct understanding of the use of the conventions under scrutiny *at any single point* in our source material.

More critically, apart from the appearance of the *pilleus* in sources speaking about both formal and informal manumissions, besides empty manumission promises, the cap's semantic association with freedom can in any case not be reduced to manumission: the 'liberty cap' enjoyed a much more profound association with *libertas* in Roman society that throws further light on the matter at stake here.[33] Perhaps most famously, following the assassination of Caesar, Brutus put the *pilleus* on his coins in 42 BC, framed by two daggers (above the date of the assassination) on the reverse, to announce the return of political freedom at Rome (Figure 1).[34] Not dissimilarly,

Figure 1 Roman denarius from 42 bc, depicting on its reverse a *pilleus* between two daggers, above the date of the assassination of Caesar (EID MAR) celebrated by the coin. (Courtesy of Classical Numismatic Group, Inc., http://www.cngcoins.com, CC BY-SA 2.5, via Wikimedia Commons)

---

[33] Some other, related meanings associated with the *pilleus*: Gell. *NA* 6.4.1–3 records that a slave was sold wearing a *pilleus* to indicate that the seller gave no guarantee, while Roman authors regularly played with the image of the *pilleus* to denote slavishness or a lack of due (civic) liberality among the free (for example, Mart. 11.6.4, 14.1.1–2).

[34] *RRC* 508.3; Dio Cass. 47.25.3.

according to Suetonius, the plebs wore *pillei* after the death of Nero.[35] In both these instances, the celebrated freedom was that of Roman citizens, understood as an extension of the freedom of the Roman state.[36] Irrespective of their quite different historical contexts and dates, both cases recall the Ciceronian mantra that freedom is citizenship (*libertas id est civitas*).[37] But again, there are comparable contexts in which Roman citizenship did not matter.

Notably, there existed a republican precedent to the action of the plebs following Nero's death that adds another layer of meaning to the cap. Thus, in 197 BC, the cities of Cremona and Placentia were besieged by the Gauls, reported by Livy in Book 33 of the *Ab urbe condita*.[38] The Roman army under Gaius Cornelius Cethegus came to the rescue of both cities, successfully fighting off the Gauls. In his account of the triumph awarded to Cethegus, Livy states that beside the spoils and captives, the triumphal procession contained an unusual element: the colonists of Cremona and Placentia joined the procession wearing the *pilleus*, drawing considerable attention. As Livy comments, 'what especially attracted attention was the throng of colonists of Cremona and Placentia, following his car with caps of liberty upon their heads' (*pilleatorum*).[39] The interpretation of the colonists' action is, as such, fairly straightforward. As Arena writes in her discussion of the episode:

> The colonists wished to express their gratitude to the consul C. Cornelius Cethegus for having been freed by him from the peril of siege, and, for many of them, for having been rescued from their condition of slavery as prisoners in the hands of the enemy [. . .]
>
> The important metaphorical meaning of the ex-slave's cap was immediately intelligible within the set of social conventions and collective attitudes of Roman society. In defining the dichotomy between liberty and slavery, the *pilleus* designated those who wore it as non-slaves, and described their status as both devoid of someone else's *dominium*, in this case the Gauls, and as recognised members of the Roman community. Often exhibited to show gratitude to those who had spared them from the condition of slavery, the *pilleus* also acted as a symbol of belonging.[40]

By donning the *pilleus*, the colonists of Cremona and Placentia showed not only their gratitude to Rome, but also their membership in, and sense of belonging to, the

---

[35] Suet. *Ner.* 57.1.

[36] Arena 2012, 43 rightly points out that the meaning behind the imagery on the coin issued by Brutus concerns the liberty of the commonwealth, rather than the liberty of individual citizens. But this does not take away from the fact that the members of the commonwealth in question were of Roman civic status. Note also the *pilleus*' association with *virtus* discussed in López Barja 2019, in an exploration of the practice of 'calling the slave to the *pilleus*' (*servos ad pileum vocare*), i.e. to take up arms for the Roman commonwealth.

[37] Cic. *Balb.* 9.24; further exploration of the equation of liberty with citizenship in a republican context is in Humbert 1976.

[38] Livy 33.23.1–7.

[39] Livy 33.23.6.

[40] Arena 2012, 33.

Roman community. Intriguingly, the civic status of the colonists was that of Latin citizens, given the status of their cities in the Roman commonwealth – discussed at the beginning of Chapter 1 by García Fernández. Their self-declared membership in the Roman community in Cethegus' triumph was, plainly, not that of the Roman citizen. Besides its use by Roman citizens outside the context of manumission from slavery, illustrated in the preceding two cases, the *pilleus* is thus attested also as a symbol of liberty in relation to Latins, in republican Rome.

Further examples can be dispensed with. Whatever the precise nuances in its usage as a symbol of freedom, and the particular historical developments, the *pilleus* was known as a token of liberty that was drawn on by Roman citizens and those without the Roman franchise alike; and among the former featured both freeborn and freed. In short, the story is messy: the cap's base association was with liberty, rather than citizenship (let alone *ingenuitas*), even if the idea of the funerary procession of individuals freed from slavery in a testament, with which this discussion has begun, calls up the notion of citizenship, *leges Iunia*, *Aelia Sentia* and *Fufia Caninia* notwithstanding. By contrast, in the case of the *puer* who grabbed the cap off the boar in Trimalchio's fabulous dining room, the cap signified the freedom of the Junian Latin, not the enfranchised freedperson, given the informal nature of the manumission (apart from the likely young age of the *puer*): here, the *pilleus* is associated with the same legal status as the toga and *bulla* worn by the other *puer* who landed at Brundisium. The association with Junian Latinity of an element otherwise found with Roman citizens also applies, as seen, to the three Gaii Valerii – Astraeus, Dionysius, Aper – for whom Pliny sought the *ius Quiritium*, and whose *tria nomina* signalled the freedom (merely) of the Junian Latin, in Pliny's letter. There is little reason to doubt, in my view, that any visual representation of these men, on a tombstone, would have shown them in the toga, had they died before being granted *civitas*. Be that as it may, in all three cases, then, the liberty enjoyed by Junian Latins is signified through a socio-cultural convention that in other contexts signifies the freedom of the Roman citizen, at times including that of the freeborn among them. It is time to round up the consequences of the importance of context for our appreciation of the discussed signifiers in the study of Junian Latinity.

Conclusion

There is nothing new in pointing out that the *tria nomina*, toga (and *bulla*) and *pilleus* do not necessarily illustrate the status of a Roman citizen, freeborn or otherwise – even if, as already noted,[41] this is a fact that is regularly ignored in modern interpretations of both the textual and visual evidence. It is self-evident therefore that whenever these conventions are used in a generic fashion to identify Roman *cives*, the resulting argument can only be circular: the identification of Roman citizenship is made on the basis of a convention or conventions that are thereby reconfirmed as seemingly reliable signifiers for the status that they are meant to identify; as a result, these signifiers

---

[41] Above, with nn. 10 and 22–5.

are ever more firmly embedded in our conceptual universe of the signifiers for Roman citizenship, however mistaken in individual cases. It is also self-evident that the use of these conventions as generic signifiers of Roman citizenship closes, not opens, avenues for our broader understanding of the ancient world by building a bulwark around citizenship's role in Roman society. By contrast, the fact that Junian Latins (among other civic and legal status groups in Roman society) may appear identical to Roman citizens in outfit and by name sets up a more intriguing basis for the study of status in the Roman imperial world than the crude identification of the umpteenth togate figure or commemorated carrier of the *tria nomina* with Roman *civitas*. Some of the chapters in the sequel to the present volume illustrate powerfully notable differences in the interpretation of a distinct source body if greater care is taken and an open mind maintained in studying specifically onomastic conventions, opening in consequence new windows on the Junian Latin status as well as the roles of Junian Latins in their communities.

But the onomastic and 'dressy' overlap also serves as a wake-up call for a deeper reconsideration of the value attached to citizenship (and *ingenuitas* in the next generation) among Rome's freed population. Representations of freedmen in the toga, and their sons with the *bulla*, on tomb monuments have repeatedly been seen as evidence for the pride that freedpersons took in their citizenship, and in the freeborn status of their children. But as Mouritsen rightly pointed out, 'while the toga on one level may have signalled citizen status, it was also the obvious costume for a funerary portrait'.[42] Context, not clothing, maketh the man.[43] It is notable, moreover, that the funerary realm is marked by significant temporal and regional differences: from the second century AD onwards, freedmen are repeatedly portrayed in the tunic, rather than the toga; and funerary 'dress codes' not least in the northern provinces regularly defy the metropolitan and Italian role models that have been at the centre of the modern scholarly debate and its togate fetish.[44] There are also several representations of enslaved individuals in the precious Roman outfit, and not only in contexts that occupy special niches within Roman slavery.[45] Given that the vast majority of togate

---

[42] Mouritsen 2011, 282.
[43] For the marginalisation of female dress in this chapter, see the comment in n. 22 above.
[44] Examples of the different 'fashions' especially in the northern provinces of the Roman Empire are discussed (in the context of slavery) in several chapters in Binsfeld and Ghetta 2019; especially notable is the contribution by Kremer (pp. 157–72) on funerary monuments from the Danube regions that illustrates the irrelevance of legal and civic status in local self-representation.
[45] Two public slaves are long acknowledged as wearing the toga:

Papi(as) (*servus publicus* in toga): *CIL* VI, 2365 (and 2366) = Benndorf and Schöne 1867, 21, no. 33. For discussion, see Kleiner 1987, no. 100 (= pp. 236–7) and plate LVII.1–2.
Helius Afinianus (*publicus augurum* in toga and with marriage contract): *CIL* VI, 2317 = Sinn 1987, no. 522 (= pp. 217–18) and plate 78b. Helius is also known from his daughter's tombstone: *CIL* VI, 2316.

See also the case of the depiction of a deceased boy in the *toga praetexta*, labelled as *verna* in his epitaph, on a funerary altar from Rome: *CIL* VI, 22972 = Goette 1990, C a 34. For discussion, see Lahusen 1989, no. 34 (= pp. 121–3) and plate 59.

figures, and the vast majority of those who sport the *tria nomina*, come without any clear status identifier,[46] it is obvious that relentless emphasis on the Roman civic meaning attached to these signifiers potentially obstructs on a significant scale the roles played by the many other meanings that these signifiers carried, thereby distorting – i.e. exaggerating – our appreciation of the value attached to Roman citizenship in the imperial age. In her recent study of the toga, Rothe underlined the diverse semantic uses to which that garment was put: besides the representation of Roman ideal masculinity (when not worn by women!), the toga served inter alia as a means to express social distinctions *among* Roman (male) citizens.[47] As with the three cases analysed in this chapter, the varied meanings that Rothe elaborates depend critically on context.

None of what has been said in this chapter denies the association of the analysed socio-cultural conventions with Roman *civitas* (and in the case of the *bulla* with *ingenuitas*). But it is instructive to take a second look at the arc sketched by the three discussed textual examples to challenge more clearly the centrality allocated by modern scholars to Roman *civitas* in the interpretation of these conventions in individual cases. What stands out, then, in the case of the Gaii Valerii, the togate boy from Brundisium, and the *pilleus*-donning performer at Trimalchio's dinner table is the lack of an association of their names-cum-garb with Roman *civitas*. Seen the other way, the three texts do *not* associate Junian Latinity with any particular socio-cultural convention that is distinct for this status. More critically still, these texts document a complete lack of tension regarding the association of Junian Latinity with socio-cultural conventions that convey in other circumstances what Carroll has called 'clear messages about status and citizenship'.[48] By so doing, however, these examples challenge outright the modern scholarly reduction of the analysed naming and clothing conventions to the semantics of enfranchised status. What all three examples *do* show is an association with Roman *libertas* – i.e. an association with freedom, in a Roman context: they portray (and parody in one case) what Arena has referred to in her above cited discussion of the good people of Cremona and Placentia as 'members of the Roman community' – albeit without the Roman franchise. For the three Gaii Valerii to get anywhere near Roman *civitas* required the combined bother of the best of emperors and his most devoted governor, while the declaimers wisely stopped precisely at the point at which Pliny mobilised the imperial power. There is little reason to think that in the dreams of Encolpius the wee Bacchus was given more than his freedom either. If, on the contrary, as is currently widely cherished

---

[46] Leaving aside representations that are fragmentary – themselves the vast bulk of the surviving evidence – the range of visual examples included in Goette 1990 illustrates well the prolific use of togate figures in reliefs of different types. The volume of so-called *incerti*, for instance, in Solin's 2003 catalogue of Greek personal names from the city of Rome is overwhelming.

[47] Rothe 2020, 37–100. Note, however, that Rothe also contends that a 'reason for the central importance of the toga in Roman society – and its near ubiquity in funerary portraits – was its association with citizenship' (p. 81). For discussion of the toga as a 'gendered garment' that increasingly embodied 'Roman maleness', see Rothe 2020, 37–42, including a brief overview of its use by women.

[48] Carroll 2012, 142.

practice, modern scholars gloss over the complexities of (and in) our evidence by way of semantic reduction, the role of statuses that do not encompass Roman *civitas* will by definition be marginalised, both in the interpretation of individual cases and, as a result, in our wider conceptualisation of society in the Roman Empire. Is it really so unimaginable that individuals without Roman *civitas* were proud and valued members of their communities, and that they articulated this pride and recognition in presenting themselves appropriately clad, as a form of civil self-assertion rather than an expression of legal aspiration?

I noted above regional differences in funerary self-representation, especially between provincial areas on the one hand and much of Italy and the city of Rome on the other. But it does not follow that the point here made applies only to the provinces (or that there are no differences between the various Italian regions, let alone between urban and rural environments). Most scholars hold that the heartland of Roman slaving was Italy, quantitatively speaking, while Rome itself has been said to have taken up potentially as much as half of Italy's urban enslaved population.[49] It follows that Italy and Rome are also the numerical hubs for manumission – including both manumission that led to citizenship and manumission that did not. In fact, once account is taken of the socio-economic impetus for Roman slavers to operate a two-tier approach to manumission, as I have argued elsewhere, the scope for the creation of Junian Latins in Italy, and Rome, is vast, irrespective of geography or the manumitters' socio-political clout:[50] Junian Latinity was not the prerogative of the backwater known as Comum. For numerical reasons alone, it is therefore imperative not to sidestep our friends the Junian Latins in the study of the available onomastic and visual evidence from Italy, including Rome.

Junian Latinity, then, is good to think with, above and beyond the exploration of this particular condition: it reminds us of the complexity of Roman society, the diversity of individual statuses, and the need to avoid a historically teleological perspective. It must not be forgotten that the 'award' of citizenship is, in Roman legal terms, a means by which non-Romans could be incorporated *forcefully* into the Roman commonwealth.[51] In the study of Junian Latinity, in contradistinction, modern scholars have firmly privileged the notion of a strong *desire* for citizenship in the affected individuals' lives.[52] This notion of widespread civic desire among Junian Latins is more assumed than proven, regularly through the same kind of circular argumentation as is used in the identification of Roman citizens on the basis of the socio-cultural conventions discussed above.

In sum, by rehearsing what are admittedly well-known facts, this chapter makes a plea for the renunciation of *civitas*, as it were, urging a diversion from current practice to follow instead the path set by the declaimers, thus to withstand the temptation to

---

[49] See Scheidel 2005, 2011.
[50] See Roth 2010b.
[51] It is notable that even at the height of Roman expansion in the republican period, this option was not the preferred Roman approach: see Dahlheim 1965, 61–2.
[52] This is most clearly expressed in the sub-title of Koops 2014: 'Junian Latins and *the struggle* for citizenship' (emphasis added).

usurp the powers of the emperor to grant the *ius Quiritium* at will. Pliny was highly selective in his choice of individuals for whom he thought Roman *civitas* the more appropriate civic status – setting up a role model that, in our scholarly enterprises, is worthy of emulation. If we do, we will surely get a fuller understanding of the diverse civic statutes and their interplay in the Roman world. Moreover, we may well gain a better handle – by way of an ancient sounding board – on simplistic and simplifying approaches to the value, purpose and desirability of citizenship not just in antiquity, but also in contemporary society, thus to mobilise the ancient world in making the modern one a better, more inclusive – because diverse – place: the good people of Cremona and Placentia did not need Roman *civitas* to make the case for their belonging and contribution to the society whose citizenship they lacked.

10

'They live as freeborn, and die as slaves': Junian Latins and *filii religiosi* in Salvian's *Ad ecclesiam* 3

Chris L. de Wet

Introduction

ONE OF THE MOST COMMON and famous non-legal sources which refers to Junian Latins is Salvian of Marseilles' (c. AD 400–490) *Ad ecclesiam* 3.7.31–4, essentially a jeremiad against greed and a call to almsgiving to the church. In section 33, Salvian writes:

> More ergo illorum uteris qui servos suos non bene de se meritos, quia civitate Romana indignos iudicant, iugo Latinae libertatis addicunt: quos scilicet iubent quidem sub libertorum titulo agere viventes, sed nolunt quidquam habere morientes. Negato enim his ultimae voluntatis arbitrio, etiam quae superstites habent morientes donare non possunt.
>
> You [some rich Christian parents] employ the custom of those who sentence their contemptible slaves to the burden of Latin freedom, because they consider them unworthy of Roman citizenship. These are the slaves whom their masters allow to act under the title of freedpersons while they are alive, but whom their masters do not want to own anything when they die. Since the option of a last testament is denied to them, their inheritors, too, when dying, are not able to disperse that which they possess.[1]

As is well known, Salvian's statement is often used in reference to the presence of Junian Latins in late antique Gaul, and to show that Salvian considered Latin status to be close to that of enslavement.[2] But, to my knowledge, no study has fully contextualised and further

---

[1] Salv. *Eccl.* 3.7.33 (SC 176.262–3). For the Latin text, the critical edition of Lagarrigue 1971 (SC 176) is used. This source also contains useful information on the life and works of Salvian, with helpful, though now dated, bibliographical entries; see Lagarrigue 1971, 9–72. All translations of ancient texts are my own, although there is an English translation of Salvian's works by O'Sullivan 1962. In the translations, I have attempted to use inclusive and accessible language where possible and appropriate.

[2] See, among other studies, Balestri Fumagalli 1985, 210; López Barja 1998, 160; Weaver 1997, 58; Corcoran 2011, 139; Harper 2011, 466–7; Evans Grubbs 2013, 88.

explored this reference to Junian Latins in the broader framework of *Ad ecclesiam* 3. The purpose of this chapter is to address this gap in scholarship, which forms part of the greater 'black hole' with which this volume is concerned. My aim is therefore to contextualise and critically examine the reference to Junian Latins in *Ad ecclesiam* 3.7.31–4, asking what we can learn about Junian Latins from this broader context, especially their relation and similarity to another, seemingly disenfranchised group, whom Salvian calls *filii religiosi*, or 'children in religion'. By way of introduction, especially for readers unfamiliar with this elusive Christian writer, the chapter begins with a short overview of Salvian's life and works, especially that of *Ad ecclesiam*. Thereafter, the focus will shift firmly onto Junian Latins and *filii religiosi* in the text at hand, namely *Ad ecclesiam* 3. I will conclude by asking some questions on the presence and role of Junian Latins in early Christian communities. The importance of this analysis lies in the fact that, while there are numerous studies on the legal sources for Latins, we know less about their social aspects, especially in the context of late antique Christianity. This chapter aims to delineate some of the social perceptions and challenges that Junian Latins, in Salvian's time and place, may have faced.

Framing Salvian's Life and Works

Information about the life of Salvian is rather scant. Even in his own works, Salvian does not provide that much biographical information.[3] Salvian is included in Gennadius' *Catalogus virorum illustrium* 67, written around AD 480, in which he writes that Salvian 'lives even today in a good old age'.[4] Salvian would have been over eighty years old at the time, if we take the year of his birth to be around AD 400, somewhere in the northern parts of Gaul. This possible date of birth is inferred from his knowledge of the destruction of Trèves and Cologne at the beginning of the fifth century.[5] We do get some biographical details from his *Epistola* 4, written to his parents-in-law.[6] He took Palladia, who apparently grew up in a non-Christian household, as his wife. It seems her parents did later convert to Christianity, but remained in northern Gaul, some distance from where Salvian and his family would settle. They had a daughter, Auspiciola. As with many early Christian families,[7] Salvian and Palladia later separated to pursue a monastic life. He entered the monastery of Honoratus at Lérins and was most likely ordained to the priesthood while he was there. There, Salvian taught rhetoric and became a very popular teacher, a *magister episcoporum* ('master of bishops'), according to Gennadius.[8] It also seems as if he had studied law at an earlier age, as is evident from his extensive use of legal concepts – like Junian Latinity – in his writings. Salvian later left the monastery and became a presbyter at Marseilles.

---

[3] Some of the main studies on Salvian, more generally, include: Méry 1849; Pellegrino 1940; Lagarrigue 1971, 1975; Badewien 1980; Elm 2017.
[4] See PL 58.1099: 'Vivit usque hodie in senectute bona.'
[5] Grey 2006, 164–5.
[6] Salv. *Ep.* 4 (SC 176.88–107).
[7] See, more generally, Vuolanto 2015; see also several essays in Chin and Schroeder 2020.
[8] Genn. *Cat. vir. illus.* 67 (PL 58.1099).

Gennadius lists a number of works attributed to Salvian, although all that survive are *De gubernatione Dei*, *Ad ecclesiam* and nine letters. *De gubernatione Dei*, also known as *De praesenti iudicio*, is certainly the most well known of Salvian's works. It represents a harsh criticism against the vices of Christian-Roman society, attempting to then also explain, in religious terms, why the empire is slowly falling to the attacks of 'barbarians'.[9] Salvian probably wrote *De gubernatione Dei* while he was a presbyter in Marseilles. His four instructional letters *Ad ecclesiam*, 'to the church' – also perhaps more appropriately titled *Adversus avaritiam*, 'against greed' – was written before *De gubernatione*, most likely while he was at the monastery in Lérins. *Ad ecclesiam* was written under a pseudonym, Timothy. Salvian implicitly refers to his authorship of *Ad ecclesiam* in *De gubernatione Dei* 4.1 when he says, 'Nam, sicut ait quidam in scriptis suis [. . .]'.[10] Georges Lagarrigue, the editor of the critical text in the SC, comments, 'Le mot *quidam* désigne Salvien lui-même, auteur anonyme des "Livres de Timothée à l'Église".'[11] We are not exactly sure how much time passed between the writing of *Ad ecclesiam* and *De gubernatione Dei*; the former is usually dated between AD 435 and 440. The main purpose of *Ad ecclesiam* is to inspire Christians to almsgiving and donations to the church. Brown rightly notes:

> In fact, Salvian was a vivid person, with his own, idiosyncratic 'take' on the problems of his day . . . [I]n his writings we catch the hopes and fears of a particular group at a particular juncture in the crisis of the empire – what he calls the *Respublica* – and in a particular region.[12]

Salvian's statements about Junian Latins can therefore be dated between AD 435 and 440, and taken to have been composed while he was in a monastery, written to other Christians, or *sancti*, about their financial obligations towards the church, the poor and other Christians.

Contextualising *Ad ecclesiam* 3.7.31–4

Salvian's statements about Junian Latins function within a broader argument and vitriol against parents who do not wish their so-called *filii religiosi* to inherit property. More broadly, however, Salvian criticises testamentary customs of some Christians. His main thesis is this:

> Et ideo etiam ego minimus et indignissimus famulorum dei primum ac saluberrimum religionis officium esse dico, ut Christianus dives, dum in hac vita est, divitias mundi huius pro dei nomine atque honore consumat; secundum autem, ut si id

---

[9] Badewien 1980, 19–30; Elm 2017.
[10] 'For as one says in his writings . . .', with reference to Salv. *Eccl.* 2.37 (SC 220.232).
[11] Lagarrigue 1971, 30; see also the helpful introduction in Marotta 1997, 7–20.
[12] Brown 2012a, 3. Brown 2012b, 438 quotes the German church historian of the nineteenth century E. Loening, who called *Ad ecclesiam* 'a manual of the clerical art of extortion, a guide to legacy hunters'.

vel metu, vel infirmitate, vel necessitate aliqua praepeditus forte non fecerit, saltim moriens universa dispenset.

> Therefore, I, too, the lowliest and unworthiest of the servants of God, say that it is the first and the most appropriate duty of religion for the wealthy Christian, while such a person is in this life, to spend the riches of this world for the sake of the name and honour of God. Secondly, if such a person has not done this, either because of fear, or weakness, or any other necessity, such a person should at least dispense of all their wealth when they are dying.[13]

Salvian encourages Christians to bequeath their property, in whole, to the church for the distribution to the poor. The main incentive behind his reasoning is that by distributing one's goods, while alive or at the point of dying, to the church or to the poor, one secures an eternal treasure in heaven and safe harbour for one's soul. This type of rhetoric was very common in late antique Christian moral discourse.[14] In an off-hand interpretation of the parable of the talents in Matt. 25: 14–30, Salvian explains that the bankers mentioned in verse 27 (who will pay back the landowner's money with interest) actually signify the poor.[15] When one gives money to the poor, one secures heavenly interest on the money.

Yet, one of the main excuses such persons might give is that they have children, and that they have a natural obligation to leave their children an inheritance. 'A case can be made for this argument,' Salvian responds, 'but not for someone who wants to be saved.'[16] Thus, even the bonds of parenthood are no excuse for not distributing one's wealth; as Matt. 10: 37 states, someone should not love their children more than God.[17] What is even worse, however, is that some childless persons may actually go and adopt others in order to have someone to inherit their wealth.[18] The negative consequences are clear: in this way, rich Christians leave their children in a precarious position, because wealth has the tendency to corrupt, but they also condemn their own souls to judgement in the process. The management of inheritance, then, for Salvian, could have dire consequences for the afterlife. The first and best option is to either bequeath everything to the church or distribute one's goods to the poor.[19] Behind this reasoning lies the assumption, first, that the church also represents the kin of the rich person and, second, that all property a person could own truthfully belongs to God and should therefore be returned.

But Salvian does make one concession in this regard:

> sint quamvis interdum non filii tantum, quibus videtur naturaliter plus deberi, sed etiam pignora alia eius vel meriti vel condicionis ut eis ad inpertiendum quiddam ac

---

[13] Salv. *Eccl.* 3.1.5 (SC 176.242).
[14] See esp. the discussions of Brown 2015, 115–48; Grey 2006. More generally, see Holman 2001; Rhee 2012.
[15] Salv. *Eccl.* 3.1.4 (SC 176.242).
[16] Salv. *Eccl.* 3.2.8 (SC 176.244): 'Dici aliquid potest, tametsi salubriter dici non potest.'
[17] Salv. *Eccl.* 3.2.6 (SC 176.244).
[18] Salv. *Eccl.* 3.2.9–10 (SC 176.246).
[19] Brown 2015, 119.

largiendum iustitia ipsa ac dei cultus patrocinetur, et quibus non solum pie aliquid relinquatur sed etiam inreligiose non relinquatur: scilicet si aut parentes sint calamitosi, aut germani fideles, aut sanctae coniuges, aut, ut longius denique munus pietatis extendam, si aut propinqui inopes, aut adfines egestuosi, aut denique cuiuslibet necessitudinis indigentes, vel certe, quod super omnia est, deo dediti.

there may be at times not only children to whom, according to nature, more appear to be owed, but also other offspring who, because of their integrity or way of life, have a claim either by justice or because of religion, to a share in the inheritance. To bequeath something to them is an act of piety – to bequeath nothing to them is an act of impiety. Such instances include parents who have suffered loss, or genuine brothers, or holy spouses, or, if I may extend the effect of goodness, kin who are destitute or their relatives who are in need, or, at last, those who share any relationship at all, or most certainly, above all else, those who are dedicated to God.[20]

At this point then, Salvian provides clear and precise guidelines for wealthy Christians who are preparing a last will. They should not, by default, care for their natural children, but first and foremost distribute their wealth in a way that has eternal merit. If one does not want to bequeath everything to the church or the poor directly, one may help those who are close in kinship or religion only if they are loyal, faithful, in need and dedicated to God. Salvian therefore inverts the expectation of receiving an inheritance, placing the needy and the faithful at the top of the list.

The final and most pertinent issue Salvian addresses in this context is that of bequeathing to one's children in religion or children dedicated to God – *filii religiosi*. The question of who these *filii religiosi* might be deserves attention. In late antiquity, it often happened that families would devote a child or children to God, which usually implied giving the child to a monastery. This practice became known as *oblatio*. Vuolanto demonstrates that it was usually children in their teens who were given to monasteries, although there are some cases of children as young as three years of age being given to an ascetic community. *Oblatio* is not considered to have been an alternative to child exposure (*expositio*). The family still had an obligation to pay for the child's upbringing.[21] We should also not assume that all children given to ascetic communities would become monks or virgins. They may continue to live and work in the community as a labourer or, when older, leave the monastery. Of course, some of these children did indeed go on to become monks and virgins. A famous example of *oblatio* from the East is that of Theodoret, later becoming the bishop of Cyrus, who was given to an ascetic community at a young age.[22] On the one hand, *filii religiosi* probably refer to such children. But we also have children who decide, on their own account, to enter into the ascetic life, sometimes against the wishes of their parents. To cite another example from the East, John Chrysostom tells us of a case in which a

---

[20] Salv. *Eccl.* 3.4.18–19 (SC 176.252).
[21] Vuolanto 2015, 132–3; see also the important study of de Jong 1996.
[22] Price 1985, xi–xii.

young boy was entrusted to the pedagogy of a monk, by the wishes of his mother, to follow the ascetic life.[23] This was done surreptitiously without the father's knowledge. In Salvian's case, *filii religiosi* most likely refer to both children devoted in *oblatio* and those who chose the path on their own. But it seems clear that such *filii religiosi* were often not given any inheritance, as Salvian bemoans:

> At vero nunc diversissime et inpiissime nullis omnino a suis minus relinquitur, quam quibus ob dei reverentiam plus debetur, nullos pietas minus respicit, quam quos praecipua religio commendat. Denique si qui a parentibus filii offeruntur deo, omnibus filiis postponuntur oblati: indigni iudicantur hereditate, quia digni fuerint consecratione; ac per hoc una tantum re parentibus viles fiunt, quia coeperint deo esse pretiosi. Ex quo intellegi potest quod nullus paene apud homines vilior est quam deus, cuius utique fit despectione ut eos praecipue parentes filios spernant qui ad deum coeperint pertinere.

> But now, in the most different and unholy manner, those to whom the least is left by their parents are the people to whom most is owed, out of reverence for God. The persons whom parental affection regards the least are the ones most commended by religion. Therefore, if some children are offered to God by their parents, those offered in such a way are regarded after all the other children. They are judged unworthy of an inheritance, because they were worthy of consecration to God, and thus, by this one fact alone they are regarded worthless in the eyes of their parents, because they have begun to be of great worth to God. From this it can be surmised that almost no one is less valuable among men than God, in contempt of whom parents despise those children who have begun to belong to God.[24]

Salvian is not the only one who complains about this. 'Certainly', Jerome writes, 'those who consider themselves to be more religious, give to their virgin daughters allowances barely sufficient for their daily needs, and give the greater of their property to sons and daughters living in the world.'[25] Such *filii religiosi* seem to have been considered unworthy of an inheritance, most likely because parents believed they did not need it or would squander the inheritance among the poor. But Salvian's response to this underlines this exact point. By leaving *filii religiosi* an inheritance, the parents enable such children to show generosity and, as such, choose poverty. In early Christian monasticism, voluntary poverty was held in very high regard. Thus, a *filius religiosus* who receives a large inheritance and distributes it in the church and among the poor further amplifies their voluntary poverty.[26] Leaving an inheritance for such a purpose therefore holds numerous benefits both for the parents and the children.

---

[23] Chrys. *Adv. oppug.* 3.12 (PG 47.369); see also Hunter 1988, 152–3.

[24] Salv. *Eccl.* 3.4.21 (SC 176.254).

[25] Hieron. *Ep.* 130.6 (Hilberg 1918, 182): 'Certe qui religiosiores sibi videntur, parvo sumptu, et qui vix ad alimenta sufficiat, virginibus dato, omnem censum in utroque sexu, saecularibus liberis largiuntur'; see also Vuolanto 2015, 133–4.

[26] See esp. Brown 2012b, 438–41. On voluntary poverty more generally, see Brown 2016.

However, some parents insult their *filii religiosi* even more:

> 'Sunt enim, inquit aliquis, sunt ex parentibus multi, qui aequales filiis suis faciant portiones, nisi quod una tantum eos condicione discernunt quod in iis ipsis partibus quae religiosis videntur adscribi, usum iubent ad eos proprietatem ad alios pertinere.' At vero hoc multo est peius et infidelius! Tolerabilioris quippe inpietatis videtur esse cum proprietate aliquem filiis suis minus relinquere quam proprietatem his rerum penitus auferre.

> 'There are', some say, 'many parents who create equal portions for their children, except that they discern between them with this one stipulation: in those specific portions which appear to be bequeathed to those in religion, the parents provide for its use by those in religion, but its ownership for other children.' Truly, this is far worse and more unfaithful! It is more tolerable if a father leaves a scant portion, with ownership rights, to his children than for him to completely deny them the rights of property ownership.[27]

These parents also do not provide an inheritance to their *filii religiosi*, but they do allow them use of the property as long as they are alive. In other words, these children may use the land, houses and possessions of their parents, but they may not claim ownership, and thus cannot leave an inheritance. Such parents, once again, aim to secure their wealth after death from distribution to the church or the poor. It is then in this context that Salvian makes the comparison between the *filii religiosi* and Junian Latins. Thus, using the discourse of slavery and manumission, Salvian further castigates these impiously cunning parents:

> Quid agis, miserrima infidelitas et paganicae, ut ita dixerim, inreligiositatis error? Itane tantum odisti deum ut possis etiam filios tuos ob hoc tantum quia ad deum pertinent, non amare? Meliore enim condicione quidam relinquunt libertos suos quam tu relinquis filios tuos. In usu siquidem cotidiano est ut servi, etsi non optimae certe non inprobae servitutis, Romana a dominis libertate donentur, in qua scilicet et proprietatem peculii capiunt et ius testamentarium consequuntur, ita ut et viventes cui volunt res suas tradant, et morientes donatione transcribant. Nec solum hoc, sed et illa quae in servitute positi conquisierant, ex dominorum domo tollere non vetantur. Tantum eis interdum gratia patronae liberalitatis inpertit ut etiam iuri suo detrahat quod libertorum dominio largiatur. Quanto, o quisquis ille es infidelissime pater, quanto domini illi melius cum libertis agunt quam tu cum liberis! Illi quae donant perpetuo iure donant, tu temporario; illi testamenti faciendi arbitrium dant libertis, tu tollis liberis; illi postremo servos suos dant libertati, tu quasi addicis filios servituti. Nam quid est aliud quam servituti addicere quos non vis aliquid quasi ingenuos possidere?

> What are you doing, most miserable unbelief and, so to speak, error of pagan impiety? Do you hate God so much that you cannot even love your children because

---

[27] Salv. *Eccl.* 3.6.28–9 (SC 176.260).

they belong to God? Some leave their freedpersons in a better condition than you leave your children. For it is a daily practice that slaves, though not the best and certainly not in bad servitude, are awarded with Roman freedom by their masters, in which they both acquire possession of the ownership of private property and obtain testamentary rights, so that while alive they give their property to whom they want and when dying transfer it in a gift. Not only this, but they are not forbidden to take those things which they collected while enslaved from the home of their masters. Sometimes the favour of a generous patron awarded them so much that the patron even deprived from his own jurisdiction what he awarded to the proprietorship of the freedperson. O unfaithful father, whoever you are, how much better do these masters act towards their freedpersons than you towards your children! What they give, they give perpetually by right; you give with a temporary right. They give their freedpersons the choice of making a will; you take it away from the freeborn. In sum, they give freedom to their slaves; you, as it were, condemn your children to slavery. What else is it than to condemn to slavery those whom, as freeborn, you do not wish to possess anything?[28]

Seen from the angle adopted here, Salvian's remarks about Junian Latins should therefore be understood, first and foremost, in the context of what we might call the monastic crisis of inheritance. In *Ad ecclesiam* 3, Salvian aims to provide a new moral standard and guidelines for Christians on how to structure inheritance and execute a testament. In the process, he first addresses apparently incorrect and impious practices of bequeathment. Unlike common consensus, Christians should not necessarily bequeath everything to their natural children. The best option is to give one's possessions back to God by distributing them to the church and the poor. One could also distribute one's goods among poor relatives or friends, or to those in the church. A person should not adopt children simply to secure heirs for the inheritance. Most importantly, if parents have *filii religiosi*, they should be first in line for inheritance, so that they may further enhance their voluntary poverty by distributing their goods. We should remember that many *filii religiosi* would have been celibate, so they would not be able to keep the wealth in the family, which was probably another reason the parents denied them inheritance. Parents should not force their *filii religiosi* into poverty, it must be a choice. The most despicable practice Salvian highlights is when parents allow *filii religiosi* the use of their property but deny them ownership and the opportunity to bequeath their own wealth. This practice is then compared to the practice of (informally) manumitting slaves to become Junian Latins:

> Ita ergo et tu religiosos filios tuos quasi Latinos iubes esse libertos, ut vivant scilicet quasi ingenui et moriantur ut servi, et iuri fratrum suorum quasi per vinculum Latinae libertatis adstricti, etiamsi videntur arbitrii sui esse, dum vivunt, quasi sub illorum tamen positi potestate moriantur.

---

[28] Salv. *Eccl.* 3.7.31–2 (SC 176.262).

In this way, then, you order your children in religion to be free like Latins, so that they live as freeborn and die as slaves and are bound by the rights of their brothers as by the bond of Latin freedom. Even though they seem to have their own free will while they are alive, they die, however, placed, as it were, under the authority of their brothers.[29]

Thus, while criticising these practices, Salvian simultaneously criticises practices of slavery, manumission and Junian Latinity.

Slavery is of course a very common discourse in Salvian's works more generally.[30] In *De gubernatione Dei*, Salvian is especially aware of impious practices of Christians relating to slaveholding. In particular, he is acutely aware of how some impious believers treat their slaves, including punishing them harshly and sexually abusing them. For example, Salvian bemoans the fact that some married men had sexual relations with slaves, or with women of servile rank:

> Quotus enim quisque est divitum conubii sacramenta conservans, quem non libidinis furor rapiat in praeceps, cui non domus ac familia sua scortum sit, et qui non, in quamcumque personam cupiditatis improbae calor traxerit, mentis sequitur insaniam? secundum illud scilicet quod de talibus dicit sermo divinus: *Equi insanientes in feminas facti sunt*.

> What rich man guards his sacred marriage vows, who among them does not plunge headlong into frenzied lust, who does not abuse his household slaves as a prostitute, and pursue his insanity against anyone on whom the heat of his unconscionable desires may kindle? Accordingly, of such men the words of divine scripture says: 'They have become like horses madly pursuing the mares' [Jer. 5: 8].[31]

To be sure, Salvian is certainly not against the practice of slaveholding, but like many Christian authors of his time, he believes that Christians should treat their slaves well. In turn, many Christian masters resemble bad slaves of God. By examining this comparison more closely, we might delineate some important points about contemporary social perceptions of Junian Latins.

---

[29] Salv. *Eccl.* 3.7.34 (SC 176.264). With regard to the expression *ut vivant scilicet quasi ingenui et moriantur ut servi*, Nicosia 2007 argues (with reference to Gai. *Inst.* 3.56) that the phrase *moriantur ut servi* should be read in a limited sense, as not referring to Junian Latins but only to the *filii religiosi*. Nicosia's argument is not without merit and should be considered. However, we should remember that Salvian's text is a religious and spirited polemical exposition, and not a technical legal document such as that of Gaius (notwithstanding Salvian's knowledge of Roman law and legal terminology). It is equally plausible that Salvian does apply the phrase to both Junian Latins and *filii religiosi*, if only indirectly, precisely because his moral and conceptual scope of slavery is quite broad. Salvian aims to make a moral-religious point, and not a legal argument per se, and when one examines the broader comparison between Junian Latins and disinherited *filii religiosi*, he argues that both these groups depart this world without the dignity of leaving an inheritance, like slaves.

[30] On slavery in Salvian, see de Wet 2019, 2018.

[31] Salv. *Gub.* 4.5.24 (SC 220.250).

Slavery, Inheritance and Junian Latins in *Ad ecclesiam* 3.7.31–4

What can we then deduce from Salvian's comparison between *filii religiosi* and Junian Latins? As with most research on Junian Latins – who are aptly described as 'invisible' in the sources[32] – we sometimes need to argue based on inference and some implicit deductions. In the first instance, we should acknowledge that the Latins are *not* Salvian's primary concern. Rather, based on his former legal education, he considered Junian Latinity a good point of comparison with the status of *filii religiosi* in terms of inheritance and property rights. Yet, his main concern remains the *filii religiosi*. Considering the fact that Salvian probably wrote *Ad ecclesiam* from the monastery at Lérins, and that he and his family may themselves be considered mid-life *filii religiosi*, this concern is understandable. There were probably numerous other *filii religiosi* in that monastery. As seen above, the comparison with Junian Latinity was indeed useful for Salvian, clearly supporting his argument. More broadly, early Christian monasticism and asceticism were permeated with the discourse of slavery. The title 'slave of God' practically became synonymous with being a monk or a virgin in late antiquity.[33] Salvian himself uses this language throughout his writings. In some early Christian monastic contexts, especially in the East, the children given to monasteries shared the nomenclature of slavery, and monasteries also housed slaves and freedpersons.[34] We may even speculate that in the monastery at Lérins there were Junian Latins, making the comparison even more facile and relevant.

Second, Salvian's comments about Junian Latins function within the broader monastic problem of inheritance. If Salvian does critique the informal manumission of slaves towards Latinity, it is mainly because of the testamentary implications of the practice, which he deems unjust and shameful. What this may indicate, however, is that the Christian moral and religious restructuring of bequeathment practices in Christian families, as we find in Salvian and others, like Jerome, could have extended into the realm of slavery and manumission practices, especially regarding Junian Latins, albeit indirectly. It is also interesting, moreover, that although Salvian's argument in *Ad ecclesiam* 3 commences with a potent rhetoric of gathering treasure in heaven, this rhetoric begins to shift to the background when the issue of the inheritance of *filii religiosi* and, to a lesser extent, Junian Latins, comes to the fore. For Salvian, it is about the principle of allowing a freeborn person or freedperson the dignity of inheritance and property ownership, even if this would further enhance the voluntary poverty of said *filii religiosi* should they distribute their inheritance among the poor or in the church. In this regard, however, one of the main differences between *filii religiosi* and Junian Latins is that some *filii religiosi* would not have had children to whom they could leave an inheritance. *Filii religiosi* could, of course, have their own 'spiritual' children. Conversely, Junian Latins could gain citizenship and testamentary rights through *anniculi probatio*, that is, marrying and producing a child who lived to the age of one

---

[32] Discussion is in Corcoran 2011, 129.
[33] De Wet 2020, 2018.
[34] See, for instance, Papaconstantinou 2002, 92; Giorda 2009, 2020; Schroeder 2009, 335–6; de Wet 2015, 154; 2017.

year – as outlined in this volume's Introduction. *Filii religiosi* may also have had a better chance of gaining an inheritance from their parents if they married and had children (since the family wealth would then remain in the family). But for many *filii religiosi*, marriage and procreation were not an option. In turn, the early Christian preference for celibacy may have complicated matters for some Christian Junian Latins, who might have now reconsidered gaining citizenship through *anniculi probatio*. Salvian, of course, prefers for the sake of his argument to emphasise the similarities between *filii religiosi* and Junian Latins.

Third, despite his emphasis on heavenly treasure and the freedom of the soul, we witness that social and legal freedom, for Salvian, was defined via the eligibility to receive an (earthly) inheritance or to fully own and bequeath property. Roman liberty versus Latin liberty – i.e. the liberty of Junians – in the end did matter, even for a staunch Christian moralist like Salvian. It also highlights how far the carceral grip of the slaveholder may extend, even into the state of freedom beyond manumission, thereby destabilising perceived status distinctions between enslaved and free. As I have stated in a previous publication, '[f]reedom [through manumission] is quite relative, and also a carceral mechanism'.[35] Manumission in no way ameliorated the social ills of slavery; as a carceral mechanism, manumission sustained slaveholding practices by allowing slaves to accept their fate for a while until they may be freed (making enslavement *seem* less harsh) and by opening up positions for new slaves. Notwithstanding the relative longevity of some slaving systems that did not rely heavily on liberation from slavery, it seems obvious that, without manumission, Roman slavery would not have been so pervasive, resilient and long-lasting. The possibility of freeing slaves in Latin liberty even gave slaveholders a socio-economic incentive for manumission. Not only do such slaveholders appear to be benefactors, but they also get a return on their investment, so to speak. So, Junian Latins were technically free, but for Salvian they were still in the grip of slavery.[36]

We can then deduce, in the fourth place, that Salvian probably considered informal manumission practices leading to Junian Latin status as not being an ideal practice for Christian slaveholders. There are several reasons for this. Rendering a person as a Latin seems to blur the lines between being enslaved and free – as Salvian says, they live as if they are free, but die as if they are slaves. Such social status ambiguity does seem to bother Salvian, just as *filii religiosi* appear to have status as children but are treated like slaves when it comes to inheritance. He also explicitly states that slaveholders who formally manumit their slaves, bestowing on them Roman freedom, act in a better and more generous way than both slaveholders who create Latins and parents who deny their *filii religiosi* an inheritance. The fact that *manumissio in ecclesia* was rather accessible as a formal type of manumission was probably another implicit reason why Salvian does not endorse the making of Junian Latins through informal manumission. Furthermore, if we follow Salvian's reasoning, it seems that Junian

---

[35] De Wet 2015, 23.
[36] See esp. the astute analysis of Roth 2010b, in which she highlights the problems and ambiguities of manumission and freedom in the Roman slave system, with particular regard to the economic benefits gained by Roman slaveholders from manumitting into Latinity.

Latinity offered slaveholders an opportunity to cunningly satisfy their greed by appearing as good patrons but actually gaining more wealth through avaricious motives. By implication, if we speculate and develop Salvian's argument to a further extent, he might have thought it better to keep slaves under thirty years of age or seemingly 'unworthy' slaves in bondage rather than to bestow on them Latin freedom. Salvian does believe that slaveholders have the responsibility to treat their slaves well and to teach them virtue: rendering them Junian Latins may not always serve these purposes. As it is morally and religiously shameful for some parents to deny their *filii religiosi* an inheritance, so too may it have been considered shameful to bestow Latin liberty on one's freed slaves.

Finally, to a certain extent, Salvian seems to imply that bad masters with avaricious motives bestow Latin liberty on their slaves, but also that slaves who become Latins were bad slaves or slaves unworthy of 'true' freedom. Salvian's assessment of Junian Latinity in the context of *filii religiosi* and Christian testamentary practices is therefore a double-edged sword. It cuts on the side of the avaricious slaveholder and the delinquent slave. The type of rhetoric about Roman freedom versus Latin freedom we see in Salvian reinforced the practice of slaveholding in Christian society. Despite being a critique against some masters, the rhetoric also remains biased against the enslaved and accepts many of the typical Roman stereotypes about slaves. We should also be careful not to project Salvian's elite and Christian concerns onto Junian Latins or *filii religiosi*, for that matter. We are not sure how important the issue of citizenship was for Junian Latins at the time, particularly those outside of the main urban centres. Whether Junian Latins, in reality, were treated differently, socially, is difficult to surmise. But what we can say from Salvian's comments is that the ineligibility to receive inheritance or to own and bequeath property may not have been an insignificant issue for *filii religiosi* and Junian Latins.

Thus, Salvian's comments in *Ad ecclesiam* 3.7.31–4 do represent a critique of Junian Latinity. He does not approve of the practice of bestowing Latin liberty on one's slaves. But the argument is not against slavery and manumission per se. As with his comments about slavery in other works like *De gubernatione Dei*, it is about maintaining seemingly fair, just and, ironically, holy practices within the institution of slavery. It is rather a perchance comparison, and one of secondary importance, proving useful and expedient – like a good slave – for his argument. It might even be true that the type of negative assessment of Junian Latinity we see in Salvian laid part of the foundation for the eventual abolition of Junian Latin status later during the time of Justinian in AD 531.

Conclusion: Junian Latins and Early Christianity?

Our analysis of Salvian leaves us with one final question – one that takes us distinctly away from the literary universe of Salvian's writings, and one that is undoubtedly difficult to answer: what were the nature and implications of Junian Latinity in early Christian communities? At the outset, we should acknowledge that any answer to this question would be speculative because of the paucity of data concerning Junian Latins in Christian communities, and in particular outside the kind of legal sources discussed by Corcoran in Chapter 6. Laws promulgated by Constantine and other Christian emperors may give us some limited insight, but the actual nature and experience of Christian Latins elude us. But if we take seriously recent scholarship on Junian Latins, and especially the kind of work presented in the other chapters in this volume part by Roth, it means that scholars of early Christianity may at times need to *read* Junian Latinity into early Christian texts and concomitant social and cultural discourses and practices. As Harrill has shown, the earliest Christian communities did encourage the manumission of slaves.[37] And if Corcoran is correct, and I believe he is, then the earlier informal instances of *manumissio in ecclesia* would have resulted in many Junian Latins in the early Christian communities – a matter that comes to the fore also in his chapter that concludes the preceding volume part.[38] Early Christian communities, from the time of Paul the Apostle, may have had in their ranks more Junian Latins than we might expect, as Glancy seems to hint.[39] Moreover, ideologies of heavenly citizenship, gathering treasures in heaven, and having a spiritual inheritance would have been appealing to Junian Latins who could not change their status easily. Furthermore, as noted already above, the early Christian preference for celibacy could have dissuaded some Christian Junian Latins from transforming their status by means of *anniculi probatio*, further increasing their numbers in the early church. Lastly, what impact did the Christian ascetic programme of reform have on Junian Latins? Even if mass manumissions, like that of Melania, were few and far between (and we are even doubtful whether the numbers and historical accounts are accurate), the focus on the ascetic renunciation of property did, in some ways, influence Christian manumission practices. Some Christians, especially the more ascetically inclined, did free many or all their slaves (or communally only owned a few). For instance, when John Chrysostom tells his audience to manumit most of their slaves, and to keep only one or two,[40] what impact could this have had on the presence of Junian Latins in later Roman society? Did the call to distribute property and manumit slaves lead to the presence of more Junian Latins in this society? Or could the phenomenon of Latin liberty have caused that the 'one or two slaves' John Chrysostom allows his audience to keep were those, probably under thirty, who would have become Junian Latins upon manumission? These are the next important and pertinent questions that remain for scholars of Junian Latins and early Christian slavery – to address the invisibility, the 'black hole', of Junian Latins in the context of the rise of Christianity in late antiquity.

---

[37] Harrill 1995.
[38] Corcoran 2011, 137–8.
[39] Glancy 2002, 94–5.
[40] Chrys. *In ep. 1 Cor. hom.* 40.6 (Field 2.515); see also de Wet 2015, 55–7.

APPENDIX: LIST OF LEGAL ENACTMENTS (WITH KEY SOURCES)

Pedro López Barja and Jacobo Rodríguez Garrido

AUGUSTUS

Lex Iunia (17 BC?).
　Gai. *Inst.* 1.22–4, 1.31, 1.35, 1.167, 2.275, 3.55–62; Ulp. *Reg.* 1.10, 1.16, 11.16, 11.19, 20.14, 22.3, 22.8, 25.7; *Frag. Dos.* 3.5–8, 3.11–14; *CJ* 7.6.1.1a; *Inst.* 1.5.3, 3.7.4; *P.Vindob.* L 26 (Vienna, Österreichische Nationalbibliothek).

Lex Aelia Sentia (AD 4).
　Gai. *Inst.* 1.18, 1.21, 1.29, 1.31, 1.66, 1.68–71, 1.73; Ulp. *Reg.* 1.12, 1.14, 3.1, 3.3, 7.4; *Inst.* 1.6.1–2; Suet. *Aug.* 40.2; Cass. Dio 55.13.7; Riccardi Fragment (*RS* I, no. 34).

TIBERIUS

Lex Visellia (AD 24): Roman citizenship is granted to Junian Latins after six-year service in the *vigiles*.
　Gai. *Inst.* 1.32b; Ulp. *Reg.* 3.5.

CLAUDIUS

SC Largianum (AD 42): only by disinheriting his sons can the *patronus* bequeath his rights over a Junian's inheritance to a third party.
　Gai. *Inst.* 3.63–71; *Inst.* 3.7.4; *CJ* 7.6.1.1a.

Edict on the granting of *Latina libertas* to abandoned sick slaves (AD 46).
　Digest 40.8.2; *CJ* 7.6.1.3; Suet. *Claud.* 25.2; cf. Cass. Dio 61.29.7 (Xiph. 142, 26–9; Zonar. 11.9); Suda, s.v. 'Klaudios'.

Edict on the granting of Roman citizenship to Latins who charter a grain ship (AD 51).
　Gai. *Inst.* 1.32c; Ulp. *Reg.* 3.6; Suet. *Claud.* 18.2.19.

NERO

Constitution on the granting of Roman citizenship to Latins who build a house (AD 64–8?).
　Gai. *Inst.* 1.33.

VESPASIAN

SC of Pegasus and Pusio which opens the *anniculi probatio* procedure to all *Latini* (AD 75).
　Gai. *Inst.* 1.31; Ulp. *Reg.* 3.4.

SC on the freedwoman who commits *adulterium* with a *servus alienus* (Buckland 1908, 416, attributed it to Vespasian).
　Pauli Sent. 2.21a.7.

Constitution of Vespasian on the *ne serva prostituatur* covenant.
　CJ 7.6.4; Digest 37.14.7, 2.4.10.1, 40.8.6–7; *CJ* 4.56.1.

TRAJAN

Constitution on the granting of Roman citizenship to Latins who established a bakery in Rome.
　Gai. *Inst.* 1.34.

Constitution on the limits of the granting of Roman citizenship to Latins through *beneficium principis*.
　Gai. *Inst.* 3.72.

SC which reduced the service with the *vigiles* to obtain Roman citizenship down to three years (unknown date, attributed to Trajan because of the similar time-span in the case of the establishment of a bakery: three years).
　Gai. *Inst.* 1.32b; Ulp. *Reg.* 3.5.

HADRIAN

SC on the *erroris causae probatio*.
　Gai. *Inst.* 2.143; *Coll.* 16.3.7.

SC which reforms the constitution of Trajan on the granting of Roman citizenship to Latins through *beneficium principis*.
　Gai. *Inst.* 3.73.

SC on the concession of Roman citizenship to the Latin woman who has three children.
　Ulp. *Reg.* 3.1.

SC on the applicability of *lex Aelia Sentia* to *peregrini*.
　Gai. *Inst.* 1.47.

SC on the Roman children of a male Latin and a female Roman citizen.
　Gai. *Inst.* 1.30, 1.80; Ulp. *Reg.* 3.3–4.

Rescript on *erroris causae probationes* of unknown content (ms. unreadable in this part).
　Gai. *Inst.* 1.73.

ANTONINUS PIUS

Rescript which considered the *iustae causae* already accepted to be irrevocable.
Digest 40.2.9.1.

Constitution on the Junian Latin bequeathed to a colony.
Gai. *Inst.* 2.195.

MARCUS AURELIUS

Rescript on the duty of guardianship to the children of the first manumitter.
Frag. Vat. 221.

CARACALLA

Constitution on the irrevocable nature of the *iustae causae* (AD 211).
CJ 7.1.1.

SEVERUS ALEXANDER

Rescript on the slave sold on condition of being freed at the age of twenty-five (AD 224).
CJ 4.57.3.

Rescript on the recovery of an exposed child of a female slave (AD 224).
CJ 8.51.1 (mentioning *ancilla* or *adscripticia*); cf. *Summa Perusina* 8.51.1 (mentioning *a[ncil]la* or *Latina*); cf. also Gai. *Inst.* 1.86 (possible original reference to the child of a Latin freedwomen living with a male slave).

CONSTANTINE

Those manumitted *in ecclesia* or by clerics are granted Roman citizenship in all cases (AD 321).
CTh 4.7.1 = *CJ* 1.13.2; cf. Sozom. *HE* 1.9 = Cassiodorus, *Historia Tripartita* 1.9.20-1 (ἀμείνονος ἐλευθερίας, *melioris libertatis*; 'better freedom').

On the slaves who detected rape (AD 326).
CTh 9.24.1.4; cf. *CJ* 7.13.3 (Latinity excised).

On the sons of a freewoman who cohabits with a slave of the fisc (AD 320).
CTh 4.12.3.

Freedman (*civis Romanus*) reduced to Latin status: his *patronus* can claim his entire estate (AD 326).
CTh 2.22.1.

Men of high rank cannot marry a Latin freedwomen or her daughter (AD 336).
CTh 4.6.3.

MARCIAN

Reiteration of Constantine's ban on elite men marrying Latin women (AD 454).
Marcian, *Novel* 4.1, 3; cf. *CJ* 5.5.7.2 (Latinity excised).

JUSTINIAN

The condition of being at least thirty upon manumission to obtain Roman citizenship is abolished (AD 530).
  CJ 7.15.2.

Junian Latinity abolished (AD 531).
  CJ 7.6.1; *Inst.* 1.5.3.

UNKNOWN DATE

SC on the rules of marriage and *erroris causae probatio* (probably prior to the Hadrianic SC on the same subject).
  Gai. *Inst.* 1.67–71, 2.142, 3.73; Ulp. *Reg.* 7.4.

SC which considered the *manumissio matrimonii causa* as *iusta causa*.
  Digest 40.2.13.

SC which prevents Junian Latins ('quibus capere per legem non liceret') from receiving donations *mortis causa*.
  Digest 39.6.35pr.

SC by which a slave under the age of thirty could not be declared free and heir in a will.
  Gai. *Inst.* 2.276.

Imperial constitution on the female master who frees a slave through *manumissio inter amicos* with the permission of her guardian.
  Frag. Dos. 15.

Ancient rule by which a slave who had lost a *causa liberalis* against his master cannot be manumitted as a Roman citizen (but as a Latin). Probably enacted after Marcus Aurelius.
  CJ 7.6.8.

BIBLIOGRAPHY

Abascal Palazón, J. M. and Rabanal Alonso, M. A. 1985. 'Inscripciones romanas de la provincia de Alicante', *Lucentum* 4, 191–244.
Agosti, G. 2020. *Paideias eneken. Antologia di carmi epigrafici tardoantichi* (Alessandria).
Albanese, B. 1979. *Le persone nel diritto privato romano* (Palermo).
Alföldy, G. 1966. 'Notes sur la relation entre le droit de cité et la nomenclature dans l'Empire romain', *Latomus* 25, 37–57.
Alföldy, G. 1972. 'Die Freilassung von Sklaven und die Struktur der Sklaverei in der römischen Kaiserzeit', *Rivista storica dell'antichità* 2, 97–129.
Alföldy, G. 1986. 'Latinische Bürger in Brigantium und im Imperium Romanum', *Bayerische Vorgeschichtsblätter* 51, 187–222.
Ammirati, S. 2020. 'Il codice veronese delle Institutiones di Gaio. Paleografia e codicologia', in Babusiaux and Mantovani 2020, 321–58.
Ando, C. 2015. 'Fact, fiction, and social reality in Roman law', in Del Mar and Twining 2015, 295–323.
Andreu Pintado, J. 2004. *Edictum, Municipium y Lex: Hispania en época flavia (69–96 d.C.)* (Oxford).
Arena, V. 2012. *Libertas and the Practice of Politics in the Late Roman Republic* (Cambridge).
Armani, S. 2003. 'La transmission du gentilice maternel en Hispanie sous le Haut Empire', in Armani, Hurlet-Martineau and Stylow 2003, 75–92.
Armani, S., Hurlet-Martineau, B. and Stylow, A. eds. 2003. *Epigrafía y sociedad en Hispania durante el Alto Imperio: estructuras y relaciones sociales* [Acta Complutensia IV] (Madrid and Alcalá de Henares).
Ash, R. 2013. 'Drip-feed invective: Pliny, self-fashioning, and the Regulus letters', in A. Marmodoro and J. Hill eds. *The Author's Voice in Classical and Late Antiquity* (Oxford), 207–30.
Atkinson, K. M. T. 1966. 'The purpose of the manumission laws of Augustus', *The Irish Jurist* 1.2, 356–74.
Avenarius, M. 2005. *Der pseudo-ulpianische Liber Singularis Regularum* (Göttingen).
Babusiaux, U. and Mantovani, D. eds. 2020. *Le Istituzioni di Gaio: avventure di un bestseller. Trasmissione, uso e trasformazione del testo* (Pavia).
Badewien, J. 1980. *Geschichtstheologie und Sozialkritik im Werk Salvians von Marseille* (Göttingen).
Bagnall, R. S. ed. 2009. *The Oxford Handbook of Papyrology* (Oxford).
Balbo, M. 2016. 'La rivolta di Fregellae nel 125 a.C.', *Mediterraneo antico* 19, 253–61.
Balestri Fumagalli, M. 1985. *Lex Iunia de manumissionibus* (Milan).

Bandelli, G. 1990. 'Colonie e municipi delle regioni Transpadane in etá Repubblicana', in *La Cittá nell'Italia settentrionale in etá romana. Morfologia, strutture e funzionamento dei centri urbani delle Regiones X e XI* [Atti del convegno di Trieste, 13–15 marzo 1987] (Trieste and Rome), 251–77.

Barbati, S. 2012. 'Asc., *In Pis.* 3 Clark: sulle cosiddette "colonie latine fittizie" transpadane', *Revista General de Derecho Romano* 18, 1–44.

Barbati, S. 2013. 'Ancora sulle cosiddette "colonie latine fittizie" transpadane (Ascon. *In Pis.* 3 Clark)', *Quaderni Lupiensi di Storia e Diritto* 3, 59–106.

Barnes, T. D. 1981. *Constantine and Eusebius* (Cambridge, MA and London).

Battaglia, F. 2020. 'Strutture espositive in Gaio: per una morfologia delle Institutiones', in Babusiaux and Mantovani 2020, 205–78.

Bell, S. and Ramsby, T. eds. 2012. *Free at Last! The Impact of Freed Slaves on the Roman Empire* (London).

Bellen, H. 1982. 'Antike Staatsräson', *Gymnasium* 89, 449–67.

Bellen, H. and Heinen, H. eds. 2001. *Fünfzig Jahre Forschungen zur Antiken Sklaverei an der Mainzer Akademie 1950–2000* (Stuttgart).

Benndorf, O. and Schöne, R. 1867. *Die antiken Bildwerke des lateranensischen Museums* (Leipzig).

Ben Zeev, M. P. 2016, 'Philo on the beginning of the Jewish settlement at Rome', in Schaps, Yiftach and Dueck 2016, 69–90.

Besson, A. 2020. 'La succession ab intestat dans le Liber Gai', in Babusiaux and Mantovani 2020, 657–71.

Bettinazzi, M. 2014. *La legge nelle declamazioni quintilianee: una nuova prospettiva per lo studio della lex Voconia, della lex Iunia Norbana e della lex Iulia de adulteriis* (Saarbrücken).

Bianchi, E. 2012. 'Gai. 3.56. Alcune riflessioni in tema di ius Latii e delle fictiones legis Iuniae Norbanae', *Revista General de Derecho Romano* 18, 1–33.

Binsfeld, A. and Ghetta, M. eds. 2019. *Ubi servi erant? Die Ikonographie von Sklaven und Freigelassenen in der römischen Kunst* (Stuttgart).

Birks, P. and McLeod, G. tr. 2001. *Justinian's Institutes. Translated with an Introduction by Peter Birks and Grant McLeod. With the Latin Text of Paul Krueger* (London).

Birley, A. R. 2000. *Onomasticon to the Younger Pliny* (Leipzig).

Bisio, E. 2020. *La lex Aelia Sentia de manumissionibus* (PhD thesis, Universitá degli studi di Pavia) [OpenAccess: http://hdl.handle.net/11571/1321851].

Bispham, E. 2007. *From Asculum to Actium: The Municipalization of Italy from the Social War to Augustus* (Oxford).

Bjornlie, M. S. 2018, 'Romans, barbarians and provincials in the *Res Gestae* of Ammianus Marcellinus', in Pohl et al. 2018, 71–89.

Bloch, M. 1975. *Slavery and Serfdom in the Middle Ages: Selected Essays* (Berkeley).

Bluhme, F. 1863. 'Lex Romana Burgundionum', in G. H. Pertz ed. *Monumenta Germaniae Historica: Legum tomus III* (Hanover), 579–624.

Blume, F. H. 1952. *Annotated Justinian Code* [2nd ed. 2008, T. G. Kearley] (University of Wyoming, College of Law) [http://www.uwyo.edu/lawlib/blume-justinian/].

Boecking, E. 1829. *Corpus Legum sive Brachylogus Iuris Civilis* (Berlin).

Bothe, L. 2018. 'From subordination to integration: Romans in Frankish law', in Pohl et al. 2018, 345–68.

Bracci, F. 2011. *Plinio il Giovane, Epistole, Libro X. Introduzione, traduzione e commento* (Pisa).

Bradley, K. R. 1978. 'The age at time of sale of female slaves', *Arethusa* 11, 243–52.

Bradley, K. R. 1987 [1984]. *Slaves and Masters in the Roman Empire: A Study in Social Control* (New York and Oxford).

Bradley, K. R. 2015. 'The bitter chain of slavery', *Dialogues d'histoire ancienne* 41, 149–76.

Bravo Bosch, M. J. 2009. 'Latium maius versus Latium minus en la Hispania flavia', *Anuario da Facultade de Dereito da Universidade da Coruña* 13, 39–56.
Briguglio, F. 2012. *Il codice veronese in trasparenza. Genesi e formazione del testo delle Istituzioni di Gaio* (Bologna).
Briguglio, F. 2020. 'Il codice veronese delle Istituzioni di Gaio e gli interventi editoriali. Analisi multispettrale e formazione del testo', in Babusiaux and Mantovani 2020, 391–408.
Broggini, G. 1969. *Index Interpolationum quae in Iustiniani Codice inesse dicuntur* (Cologne and Vienna).
Broughton, T. R. 1952. *The Magistrates of the Roman Republic.* 3 vols (New York).
Brown, P. R. L. 2012a. *Salvian of Marseilles: Theology and Social Criticism in the Last Century of the Western Empire* [Dacre Lecture 2010] (Oxford).
Brown, P. R. L. 2012b. *Through the Eye of a Needle: Wealth, the Fall of Rome, and the Making of Christianity in the West, 350–550* (Princeton).
Brown, P. R. L. 2015. *The Ransom of the Soul: Afterlife and Wealth in Early Western Christianity* (Cambridge, MA).
Brown, P. R. L. 2016. *Treasure in Heaven: The Holy Poor in Early Christianity* (Charlottesville).
Brunet, C. 2008. 'La vision de l'affranchi chez Pétrone: terminologie et discours', in Gonzalès 2008, 263–72.
Brunt, P. A. 1962. 'The army and the land in the Roman Revolution', *The Journal of Roman Studies* 52, 69–86.
Brunt, P. A. 1971. *Italian Manpower* (Oxford).
Brunt, P. A. 1988. *The Fall of the Roman Republic and Related Essays* (Oxford).
Buckland, W. W. 1908. *The Roman Law of Slavery: The Condition of the Slave in Private Law from Augustus to Justinian* (Cambridge).
Burgmann, L. 1984. 'Das Lexikon ἀδετ', in *Fontes Minores VI* (Frankfurt), 19–61.
Burgmann, L. 1990. 'Das Lexikon αὐσηθ', in *Fontes Minores VIII* (Frankfurt), 249–337.
Caballos Rufino, A. 2006. *El nuevo bronce de Osuna y la política colonizadora romana* (Seville).
Caballos Rufino, A. 2009. 'Publicación de documentos públicos en las ciudades del Occidente romano: el ejemplo de la Bética', in R. Haensch ed. *Selbstdarstellung und Kommunikation. Die Veröffentlichung staatlicher Urkunden auf Stein und Bronze in der römischen Welt* [Vestigia 61] (Munich), 131–72.
Caballos Rufino, A. 2018. '*Monumenta fatiscunt*. Meaning and fate of legal inscriptions on bronze: the Baetica', in A. Kolb ed. *Literacy in Ancient Everyday Life* (Berlin and Boston), 289–317.
Camodeca, G. 2002. 'Per una riedizione dell'archivio ercolanese di L. Venidius Ennychus', *Cronache Ercolanesi* 32, 257–80.
Camodeca, G. 2006a. 'Cittadinanza romana. *Latini Iuniani* e lex Aelia Sentia. Alcuni nuovi dati dalla riedizione delle *Tabulae Herculanenses*', in L. Labruna ed. *Tradizione romanistica e costituzione I* (Naples), 887–904.
Camodeca, G. 2006b. 'Per una riedizione dell'archivio ercolanese di L. Venidius Ennychus. II', *Cronache Ercolanesi* 36, 189–211.
Camodeca, G. 2017. *Tabulae Herculanense: edizione e commento* (Rome).
Cantarelli, L. 1882. 'I Latini Iuniani: contributo alla storia del diritto latino, I', *Archivio giuridico* 29, 3–31.
Cantarelli, L. 1883. 'I Latini Iuniani: contributo alla storia del diritto latino, II', *Archivio giuridico* 30, 41–117.
Cantarelli, L. 1885. 'La data della legge Junia Norbana, nuovi studi e nuove osservazzione', *Archivio giuridico* 34, 38–55.
Cappelletti, L. 2011. *Gli statuti di Banzi e Taranto nella Magna Graecia del I secolo a.C.* (Frankfurt).

Carlon, J. M. 2009. *Pliny's Women: Constructing Virtue and Creating Identity in the Roman World* (Cambridge and New York).
Carroll, M. 2006. *Spirits of the Dead: Roman Funerary Commemoration in Western Europe* (Oxford).
Carroll, M. 2012. 'The Roman child clothed in death', in M. Carroll and J. P. Wild eds. *Dressing the Dead in Classical Antiquity* (Stroud), 134–47.
Castello, C. 1951. *L'acquisto della cittadinanza e i suoi riflessi familiari nel diritto romano* (Milan).
Cavalieri Manasse, G. 2000. 'Un documento catastale dell'agro centuriato veronese', *Athenaeum* 88, 5–48.
Cavalieri Manasse, G. 2004. 'Note su un catasto rurale veronese', *Index* 32, 49–81.
Cavalieri Manasse, G. 2008. 'Il frammento di catasto rurale', *L'area del Capitolium di Verona. Ricerche storiche e archeologiche* (Verona), 289–91.
Cavalieri Manasse, G. and Cresci Marrone, G. 2015. 'Un nuovo frammento di forma dal Capitolium di Verona', in Cresci Marrone 2015, 21–54.
Cavalieri Manasse, G. and Cresci Marrone, G. 2017. 'Due frammenti di formae dal Capitolium di Verona', in S. Segnni and M. Bellomo eds. *Epigrafia e politica. Il contributo della documentazione epigrafica allo studio delle dinamiche politiche nel mondo romano* (Milan), 65–94.
Cels-Saint-Hilaire, J. 2002. 'Le sens du mot *libertinus*: quelques réflexions', *Latomus* 61, 285–94.
Champion, C. 1997. 'Columella's *De re rustica*', in J. P. Rodriguez ed. *The Historical Encyclopedia of World Slavery*, Vol. 1 (Santa Barbara, Denver and Oxford), 174–5.
Chastagnol, A. 1987a. 'À propos du droit latin provincial', *Iura* 28, 1–24.
Chastagnol, A. 1987b. 'Considérations sur les municipes Latins du premier siècle apr. J.C.', in *L'Africa dans l'Occident romain. I a.C.–IV d.C.* (Rome), 351–65.
Chastagnol, A. 1990. 'L'onomastique de tipe pérégrine dans les cités de la Gaule Narbonnaise', *Mélanges de l'École française de Rome – Antiquité* 102.2, 573–93.
Chastagnol, A. 1995. *La Gaule romaine et le droit latin. Recherches sur l'histoire administrative et sur la romanisation des habitants. Scripta varia* III (Lyons and Paris).
Cherry, D. 1990. 'The Minician law: marriage and the Roman citizenship', *Phoenix* 44, 244–66.
Chevrier, G. and Pieri, G. 1969. *La loi romaine des Burgondes* (Milan).
Chiappelli, L. 1885. *La glossa pistoiese di Codice Giustinianeo tratta dal manoscritto capitolare di Pistoia* (Turin) [= *Memorie della Reale Accademia delle Scienze di Torino*^{2} 37].
Chin, C. M. and Schroeder, C. T. eds. 2020. *Melania: Early Christianity through the Life of One Family* (Oakland).
Christol, M. 1989. 'Le droit latin en Narbonnaise: l'apport de l'epigraphie (en particulier celle de la cité de Nîmes)', in *Les inscriptions latines de Gaule Narbonnaise* (Nîmes), 87–100.
Christol, M. 1999. 'La municipalisation de la Gaule Narbonnaise', in M. Dondin-Payre and M.-T. Raepsaet-Charlier eds. *Cités, municipes, colonies. Les processus de municipalisation en Gaule et en Germanie sous le Haut Empire romain* (Paris), 1–27.
Christol, M. and Deneux, C. 2001. 'La latinisation de l'anthroponymie dans la cité de Nîmes à l'époque impériale (début de la seconde moitié du Ier siècle av.J.-C.-111e siècle ap.J.-C.): les données de la dénomination pérégrine', in Dondin-Payre and Raepsaet-Charlier 2001, 39–54.
Christol, M. and Goudineau, C. 1987–8. 'Nîmes et les Volques Arécomiques au Ier siècle avant J.-C.', *Gallia* 45, 87–103.
Ciaralli, A. 2000. 'Ancora sul manoscritto pistoiese del *Codex* (Arch. Cap. C. 106): note paleographice e codicologiche', *Scrittura e civiltà* 24, 173–225.
Ciaralli, A. 2010. 'Per le *Adnotationes Codicum Domini Iustiniani (Summa Perusina)*, Perugia, Bibl. dell.'Archivio Capitolare Ms. 32', *Studia et Documenta Historiae et Iuris* 76, 861–9.

Claude, D. 1980. 'Freedmen in the Visigothic kingdom', in E. James ed. 1980. *Visigothic Spain: New Approaches* (Oxford), 159–88.
Coleman, K. 2012. 'Bureaucratic language in the correspondence between Pliny and Trajan', *Transactions of the American Philological Association* 142.2, 189–238.
Collins, R. 2004. *Visigothic Spain 409–711* (Malden, MA and Oxford).
Coma Fort, J. M. 2014. *Codex Theodosianus: Historia de un texto* (Madrid).
Connolly, J. 1998. 'Mastering corruption: constructions of identity in Roman oratory', in S. R. Joshel and S. Murnaghan eds. *Women and Slaves in Greco-Roman Culture: Differential Equations* (London and New York), 130–51.
Connolly, S. 2010. *Lives Behind the Laws: The World of the Codex Hermogenianus* (Bloomington and Indianapolis).
Conrat, M. 1884. *Die Epitome Exactis Regibus* (Berlin).
Conrat, M. 1907. *Der westgothische Paulus. Eine rechtshistorische Untersuchung* (Amsterdam).
Cooley, A. E. 2009. *Res Gestae Divi Augusti* (Cambridge).
Corbier, M. 2008. 'Famille et intégration sociale: la trajectoire des affranchi(e)s', in Gonzalès 2008, 313–27.
Corbino, A., Humbert, M. and Negri, G. eds. 2010. *Homo, caput, persona. La costruzione giuridica dell'identità nell'esperienza romana* (Pavia).
Córcoles Olaitz, E. 2006. 'The manumission of slaves in the view of the *Formulae Visigothicae*', *Veleia* 23, 339–49.
Corcoran, S. 2000. *The Empire of the Tetrarchs: Imperial Pronouncements and Government AD 284–324* [rev. ed.] (Oxford).
Corcoran, S. 2003. 'The donation and will of Vincent of Huesca. Latin text and English translation', *Antiquité Tardive* 11, 215–21.
Corcoran, S. 2008. 'Justinian and his two codes. Revisiting *P. Oxy.* 1814', *Journal of Juristic Papyrology* 38, 73–111.
Corcoran, S. 2011. '"Softly and suddenly vanished away": the Junian Latins from Caracalla to the Carolingians', in K. Muscheler ed. *Römische Jurisprudenz – Dogmatik, Überlieferung, Rezeption: Festschrift für Detlef Liebs zum 75. Geburtstag* (Berlin), 129–52.
Corcoran, S. 2013. 'The Gregorianus and Hermogenianus assembled and shattered', *Mélanges de l'École française de Rome – Antiquité* 125.2, 285–304.
Corcoran, S. 2016. 'The Codex of Justinian: the life of a text through 1,500 years', in Frier 2016, I, xcvii–clxiv.
Corcoran, S. 2017. 'Roman law and the two languages in Justinian's empire', *Bulletin of the Institute of Classical Studies* 60.1, 96–116.
Corcoran, S. forthcoming. 'William of Malmesbury and the Novels in the Selden Breviary', in P. Jaillette and D. Moreau eds. forthcoming. *De legibus novellis ad Theodosianum pertinentibus: promulgation, réception, compilation des Novelles post-Théodosiennes* (Bari).
Cornell, T. J. 1995. *The Beginnings of Rome: Italy and Rome from the Bronze Age to the Punic Wars (c. 1000–264 BC)* (London and New York).
Courrier, C. 2014. *La plèbe de Rome et sa culture* (Rome).
Crawford, M. H. 1996. *Roman Statutes*. 2 vols (London).
Crawford, M. H. 1998. 'How to create a *municipium*. Rome and Italy after the Social War', *Bulletin of the Institute of Classical Studies* 42, 31–46.
Crawford, M. H. 2008. 'The text of the Lex Irnitana', *The Journal of Roman Studies* 98, 182.
Crescenzi, V. 1990. *La glossa di Poppi* (Rome).
Cresci Marrone, G. ed. 2015. TRANS PADUM . . . VSQUE AD ALPES. *Roma tra il Po e le Alpi: dalla romanizzazione alla romanità* (Rome).
Crook, J. 1967. 'Gaius, *Institutes*, i. 84–86', *Classical Review* 17, 7–8.

Daalder, E. forthcoming. 'The Ulpianic *Liber singularis regularum* or *Tituli ex corpore Ulpiani*', in Mantovani and Wibier forthcoming.

Dahlheim, W. 1965. *Deditio und societas: Untersuchungen zur Entwicklung der römischen Aussenpolitik in der Blütezeit der Republik* (Inaugural-Dissertation, Ludwig-Maximilians-Universität München).

Dal Lago, E. and Katsari, C. 2008. 'Ideal models of slave management in the Roman world and in the ante-bellum American South', in E. Dal Lago and C. Katsari eds. *Slave Systems: Ancient and Modern* (Cambridge), 187–213.

Dalla Rosa, A. 2018. 'Gli anni 4–9 d.C.: riforme e crise alla fine dell'epoca augustea', in S. Segenni ed. *Augusto dopo il bimillenario: un bilancio* (Milan), 84–100.

Dardaine, S. 1999. 'Les affranchis des cités dans les provinces de l'Occident romain: statut, onomastique et nomenclature', in González 1999, 213–28.

Dardaine, S. 2003. 'Citoyenneté, parenté, conubium dans les réglements des municipes flaviens de Bétique', in Armani, Hurlet-Martineau and Stylow 2003, 93–106.

Daube, D. 1946. 'Two early patterns of manumission', *The Journal of Roman Studies* 36, 57–75.

Davies, W. 1996. 'On servile status in the early Middle Ages', in M. L. Bush ed. *Serfdom and Slavery: Studies in Legal Bondage* (London and New York), 225–46.

de Dominicis, M. 1973. 'Les Latins Juniens dans la pensée du législateur romain', *Revue internationale des droits de l'Antiquité* 20, 310–24.

de Jong, M. 1996. *In Samuel's Image: Child Oblation in the Early Medieval West* (Leiden).

De Martino, F. 1979. *Storia economica di Roma antica* (Florence).

de Wet, C. L. 2015. *Preaching Bondage: John Chrysostom and the Discourse of Slavery in Early Christianity* (Oakland).

de Wet, C. L. 2017. 'Slavery and asceticism in John of Ephesus' *Lives of the Eastern Saints*', *Scrinium* 13, 84–113.

de Wet, C. L. 2018. 'The great Christian failure of mastery: slavery and Romanness in Salvian of Marseilles's *De gubernatione Dei*', *Religion and Theology* 25.3/4, 394–417.

de Wet, C. L. 2019. '"The barbarians themselves are offended by our vices": slavery, sexual vice and shame in Salvian of Marseilles' *De gubernatione Dei*', *HTS Theological Studies* 75, 1–8.

de Wet, C. L. 2020. 'Modelling *Msarrqūtā*: humiliation, Christian monasticism, and the ascetic life of slavery in late antique Syria and Mesopotamia', in K. Cooper and J. Wood eds. *Social Control in Late Antiquity: The Violence of Small Worlds* (Cambridge), 105–30.

de Zulueta, F. 1946. *The Institutes of Gaius* (Oxford).

Del Mar, M. and Twining, W. eds. 2015. *Legal Fictions in Theory and Practice* (Cham).

Dickey, E. 2012. *The Colloquia of the Hermeneumata Pseudodositheana Volume I* (Cambridge).

Dickey, E. 2014. 'New legal texts from the *Hermeneumata Pseudodositheana*', *Tijdschrift voor Rechtsgeschiedenis* 82, 30–44.

Diederich, S. 2007. *Römische Agrarhandbücher zwischen Fachwissenschaft, Literatur und Ideologie* (Berlin and New York).

Diederich, S. 2015. 'Columella', *Oxford Bibliographies Online* [https://www.oxfordbibliographies.com/].

Dixon, S. ed. 2001. *Childhood, Class and Kin in the Roman World* (London), 205–20.

Dondin-Payre, M. 2001. 'L'onomastique dans les cités de Gaule centrale (Bituriges Cubes, Éduens, Senons, Carnutes, Turons, Parisii)', in Dondin-Payre and Raepsaet-Charlier 2001, 193–341.

Dondin-Payre, M. 2011a. 'La diffusion des processus d'adaptation onomastique: comparaison entre les Gaules et l'Afrique', in Dondin-Payre 2011b, 177–96.

Dondin-Payre, M. ed. 2011b. *Les noms de personnes dans l'Empire romain. Transformations, adaptation, évolution* (Bordeaux).

Dondin-Payre, M. and Raepsaet-Charlier, M.-T. eds. 2001. *Noms, identités culturelles et romanisation sous le Haut-Empire* (Brussels).
Doody, A. 2007. 'Virgil the farmer? Critiques of the *Georgics* in Columella and Pliny', *Classical Philology* 102, 180–97.
du Prey, P. de la Ruffinière. 1994. *The Villas of Pliny: From Antiquity to Posterity* (Chicago).
Duff, A. M. 1928. *Freedmen in the Early Roman Empire* (Oxford).
Dunham, F. S. 1945. 'The Younger Pliny. Gentleman and citizen', *The Classical Journal* 40, 417–26.
Durry, M. 1959. *Pline le Jeune. Tome IV. Lettres. Livre X. Panégyrique de Trajan* [Budé] (Paris).
Eck, W. 2007. *The Age of Augustus* (Oxford).
Eck, W. 2016. 'Die *lex Troesmensium*: ein Stadtgesetz für ein *municipium civium Romanorum*', *Zeitschrift für Papyrologie und Epigraphik* 200, 565–606.
Edwards, C. 2008. *Suetonius: Lives of the Caesars* (Oxford).
Eisele, F. 1912. *Studien zur römischen Rechtsgeschichte*, II. *Nochmals zur Zivilität der Cognitur* (Tübingen).
Elm, S. 2017. '2016 NAPS presidential address: New Romans: Salvian of Marseilles *On the governance of God*', *Journal of Early Christian Studies* 25, 1–28.
Emmerson, A. L. C. 2011. 'Evidence for Junian Latins in the tombs of Pompeii?', *Journal of Roman Archaeology* 24, 161–90.
Espinosa-Espinosa, D. 2014. *Plinio y los 'oppida de antiguo Lacio'. El proceso de difusión del Latium en Hispania Citerior* (Oxford).
Espinosa-Espinosa, D. 2016. 'Reflexiones sobre la probable promoción de Cesse/Tarraco a colonia latina', *Klio* 98, 570–604.
Espinosa-Espinosa, D. 2018. 'The question of the *oppida veteris Latii* in Pliny the Elder's *Naturalis Historia*', *The Classical Quarterly* 68, 232–45.
Euzennat, M. and Marion, J. 1982. *Inscriptions Antiques du Maroc, vol. II, Inscriptions Latines* (Paris).
Evans Grubbs, J. 1989. 'Abduction marriage in antiquity. A law of Constantine (*CTh* IX.24.1) and its social context', *The Journal of Roman Studies* 79, 59–83.
Evans Grubbs, J. 1995. *Law and Family in Late Antiquity: The Emperor Constantine's Marriage Legislation* (Oxford).
Evans Grubbs, J. 2013. 'Between slavery and freedom: disputes over status and the Codex Justinianus', *Roman Legal Tradition* 9, 31–93.
Fabbrini, F. 1965. *La manumissio in ecclesia* (Milan).
Fabre, G. 1981. *Libertus. Recherches sur les rapports patron-affranchi à la fin de la République romaine* (Rome).
Faci, G. T. 2017. 'The transmission of Visigothic documents in the Pyrenean monastery of San Victorián de Asán (6th to 12th centuries)', *Antiquité Tardive* 25, 303–14.
Falchi, G. L. 1990. 'Osservazioni sulla situazione giuridica dei liberti latini nel Codice Teodosiano. A proposito del CTh. 2,22,1', in *Atti dell'Accademia Romanistica Costantiniana VIII* (Naples), 567–77.
Favory, F. 1978/9. 'Clodius et le péril servile: fonction du thème servile dans le discours polémique cicéronien', *Index. Quaderni camerti di studi romanistici* 8, 173–205.
Fear, A. T. 1990. '*Cives Latini, servi publici* and the Lex Irnitana', *Revue international des droits de l'antiquité* 37, 149–66.
Fernández Gómez, F. and del Amo y de la Hera, M. 1990. *La lex Irnitana y su contexto arqueológico* (Seville).
Ferrary, J.-L. 1996. '*Princeps legis et adscriptores*: la collégialité des magistrats romains dans la procédure de proposition des lois', *Revue de philologie, de littérature et d'histoire anciennes* 70, 217–46.

Ferrary, J.-L. 2012a. 'La législation augustéenne et les dernières lois comitiales', in Ferrary 2012b, 569–92.
Ferrary, J.-L. ed. 2012b. *Leges publicae. La legge nell'esperienza giuridica romana* (Pavia).
Ferretti, P., Fiorentini, M. and Rossi, D. eds. 2017. *Il governo del territorio nell'esperienza storico-giuridica* (Trieste).
Ferri, R. 2020. 'Teaching Roman law in an ancient Western school', in Babusiaux and Mantovani 2020, 565–76.
Fezzi, L. 2001a. 'In margine alla legislazione frumentaria di età repubblicana', *Cahiers du Centre Gustave Glotz* 12, 91–100.
Fezzi, L. 2001b. 'La legislazione tribunizia di Publio Clodio Pucro (58 a.C.) e la ricerca del consenso a Roma', *Studi Classici e Orientali* 47.1, 245–340.
Field, F. ed. 1854–62. *Ioannis Chrysostomi interpretatio omnium epistularum Paulinarum* (Oxford).
Finley, M. I. 1975. 'The necessary evil', *Times Literary Supplement* 14, 1348.
Finley, M. I. 1980. *Ancient Slavery and Modern Ideology* (London).
Flammini, G. 2004. *Hermeneumata Pseudodositheana Leidensia* (Munich and Leipzig).
Fögen, T. 2009. *Wissen, Kommunikation und Selbstdarstellung. Zur Struktur und Charakteristik römischer Fachtexte der frühen Kaiserzeit* (Munich).
Frakes, R. 2011. *Compiling the 'Collatio Legum Mosaicarum et Romanarum' in Late Antiquity* (Oxford).
Frank, T. 1916. 'Race mixture in the Roman Empire', *American Historical Review* 21, 689–708.
Fressura, M. and Mantovani, D. 2018. 'P.Vindob. L 59 + 92. Frammenti delle Institutiones di Elio Marciano', *Athenaeum* 106, 619–90.
Frier, B. W. 1985. *The Rise of the Roman Jurists: Studies in Cicero's Pro Caecina* (Princeton).
Frier, B. W. ed. 2016. *The Codex of Justinian: A New Annotated Translation, with Parallel Latin and Greek Text, based on a translation by Justice Fred H. Blume*, 3 vols (Cambridge).
Gagliardi, L. 2006. *Mobilità e integrazione delle persone nei centri cittadini romani: aspetti giuridici. I. La classificazione degli incolae* (Milan).
Gagliardi, L. 2016. 'Droit romain et droits locaux dans les municipes italiques', *Revue historique de droit français et étranger*, 94.3, 369–91.
Gagliardi, L. 2020. 'Niebuhr, l'isopoliteia e il ius migrandi arcaico', *Ius-online* 4, 160–99.
Galsterer, H. 1976. *Herrschaft und Verwaltung im republikanischen Italien. Die Beziehungen Roms zu den italischen Gemeinden vom Latinerfrieden 338 v. Chr. bis zum Bundesgenossenkrieg 91 v. Chr.* (Munich).
García Fernández, E. 2001. *El municipio latino. Origen y desarrollo constitucional* (Madrid).
García Fernández, E. 2009. 'Reflexiones sobre la latinización de Hispania en época republicana', in J. Andreu Pintado, J. Cabrero Piquero and I. Rodà de Llanza eds. *Hispaniae. Las provincias hispanas en el mundo romano* (Tarragona), 377–90.
García Fernández, E. 2010. 'Latinidad y onomástica en el Noroeste', in I. Sastre and A. Beltrán eds. *El bronce de El Picón (Pino de Oro). Procesos de cambio en el occidente de Hispania* (Junta de Castilla y León), 145–55.
García Fernández, E. 2012. 'Sobre la condición latina y su onomástica: los ediles de Andelo', *Espacio, tiempo y forma* (Serie II, Historia antigua) 25, 423–36.
García Fernández, E. 2015. 'Client relationships and name diffusion in Hispania. A critical review and interpretation proposal', in M. Jehne and F. Pina Polo eds. *Foreign clientelae in the Roman Empire: A Reconsideration* (Stuttgart), 107–18.
García Fernández, E. 2018. 'La condición latina provincial: el derecho de *conubium* y la *lex Minicia de liberis*', in García Fernández and López Barja 2018, 379–99.
García Fernández, E. 2020. 'El *ius Latii* y la legislación municipal', in F. Russo ed. *Municipal Structures in Roman Spain and Roman Italy: A Comparison*. Proceedings of the Colloquium Vienna, 3 July 2018 [WBAGon 3], 65–81.

García Fernández, E. and López Barja, P. eds. 2018. *De latinitate definienda. Sobre la condición / ciudadanía latina* [*Gerión* 36.2] (Madrid).
Gardner, J. F. 1991. 'The purpose of the *lex Fufia Caninia*', *Echos du monde classique / Classical Views* 35, 21–39.
Gardner, J. F. 1996. 'Hadrian and the social legacy of Augustus', *Labeo* 42, 83–100.
Gardner, J. 2001. 'Nearest and dearest: liability to inheritance tax in Roman families', in Dixon 2001, 205–20.
Gargola, D. J. 1990. 'The colonial commissioners of 218 BC and the foundation of Placentia and Cremona', *Athenaeum* 78, 465–73.
Garnsey, P. 1981. 'Independent freedmen and the economy of Roman Italy under the Principate', *Klio* 63, 359–71.
Garnsey, P. 1988. *Famine and Food Supply in the Graeco-Roman World: Responses to Risk and Crisis* (Cambridge).
Garnsey, P. and De Ligt, L. 2012. 'The Album of Herculaneum and a model of the town's demography', *Journal of Roman Archaeology* 25, 69–94.
Garrido-Hory, M. 2008. 'Les affranchis chez Pétrone: comportements et mentalités', in Gonzalès 2008, 251–62.
Gaudemet, J. 1965. *Le Bréviaire d'Alaric et les Epitome* (Milan).
Genovese, M. 2010. '*Duarum civitatum civis noster esse iure civili nemo potest* (*Balb.* 11.28): visione ciceroniana e sua rispondenza al contesto storico-giuridico della tarda repubblica', in *Studi in onore di Luigi Arcidiacono*, vol. IV (Catania), 1591–638.
Germerodt, F. 2015. *Amicitia in den Briefen des jüngeren Plinius* (Speyer).
Gibson, R. K. 2020. *Man of High Empire: The Life of Pliny the Younger* (New York and Oxford).
Gibson, R. K. and Morello, R. 2012. *Reading the Letters of Pliny the Younger: An Introduction* (Cambridge).
Giménez Candela, T. 1984. 'Una contribución al estudio de la ley Irnitana: la manumisión de esclavos municipales', *Iura* 32, 37–56.
Giorda, M. C. 2009. 'De la direction spirituelle aux règles monastiques: Péchés, penitence et punitions dans le monachisme pachômien (IVe–Ve siècles)', *Collectanea Christiana Orientalia* 6, 95–113.
Giorda, M. C. 2020. 'Disciplining the slaves of God: monastic children in Egypt at the end of antiquity', in K. Cooper and J. Wood eds. *Social Control in Late Antiquity: The Violence of Small Worlds* (Cambridge), 151–70.
Giovannini, A. 2004. 'Die *Tabula Heracleensis*: neue Interpretationen und Perspektiven. Teil I: die *frumentationes*', *Chiron* 34, 187–204.
Girard, P. F. and Senn, F. 1967. *Texts de droit romain*, Tome 1 [7th ed.] (Paris).
Glancy, J. A. 2002. *Slavery in Early Christianity* (Oxford) [repr. Minneapolis, 2006].
Goette, H. R. 1986. 'Die Bulla', *Bonner Jahrbücher* 186, 133–64.
Goette, H. R. 1990. *Studien zu römischen Togadarstellungen* (Mainz).
Goetz, G. 1889. *Corpus Glossariorum Latinorum IV* (Leipzig).
Goetz, G. 1892. *Corpus Glossariorum Latinorum III: Hermeneumata Pseudodositheana* (Leipzig).
Gonzalès, A. 2002. *Pline le Jeune. Esclaves et affranchis à Rome* (Paris).
Gonzalès, A. ed. 2008. *La fin du statut servile? Affranchissement, libération, abolition* [Actes GIREA XXX] (Besançon).
Gonzalès, A. 2017. '*Scripsit mihi, domine, Lycormas, libertus tuus*: Pliny the Younger, the governor and Lycormas, freedman of Trajan, and project manager', *Dialogues d'histoire ancienne* 17, 773–98.
González, J. ed. 1999. *Ciudades privilegiadas en el Occidente Romano* (Seville).
González, J. and Crawford, M. H. 1986. 'The Lex Irnitana. A new copy of the Flavian municipal law', *The Journal of Roman Studies* 76, 147–243.

González Román, C. and Mangas Manjarrés, J. 1991. *Corpus de Inscripciones latinas de Andalucía. Jaén (CILA III)*, vol. 1 (Seville).
Gordon, W. M. and Robinson, O. F. tr. 1988. *The Institutes of Gaius. Translated with an Introduction by W. M. Gordon and O. F. Robinson. With the Latin Text of Seckel and Kuebler* (London).
Grey, C. 2006. 'Salvian, the ideal Christian community and the fate of the poor in fifth-century Gaul', in M. Atkins and R. Osborne eds. *Poverty in the Roman World* (Cambridge), 162–82.
Grieser, H. 1997. *Sklaverei im spätantiken und frühmittelalterlichen Gallien (5.–7. Jh.). Das Zeugnis der christlichen Quellen* (Stuttgart).
Gunderson, E. 2003. *Declamation, Paternity, and Roman Identity: Authority and the Rhetorical Self* (Cambridge).
Hammer, C. 2002. *A Large-Scale Slave Society of the Early Middle Ages: Slaves and their Families in Early Medieval Bavaria* (Aldershot).
Hanard, G. 1987. 'Note à propos des leges Salpensana et Irnitana. Faut-il corriger l'enseignent de Gaius?', *Revue internationale des droits de l'antiquité* 34, 173–9.
Hänel, G. 1849. *Lex Romana Visigothorum* (Leipzig).
Hänel, G. 1873. *Iuliani Epitome Latina Novellarum Iustiniani* (Leipzig).
Harper, K. 2010. 'The *SC Claudianum* in the *Codex Theodosianus*: social history and legal texts', *The Classical Quarterly* 60, 610–38.
Harper, K. 2011. *Slavery in the Late Roman World*, AD 275–425 (Cambridge).
Harries, J. 1986. 'Sozomen and Eusebius. The lawyer as Church historian in the fifth century', in C. Holdsworth and T. P. Wiseman eds. *The Inheritance of Historiography 350–900* (Exeter), 45–52.
Harrill, J. A. 1995. *The Manumission of Slaves in Early Christianity* (Tübingen).
Harris, W. V. 1980. 'Towards a study of the Roman slave trade', in J. H. D'Arms and E. C. Kopff eds. *The Seaborne Commerce of Ancient Rome: Studies in Archaeology and History* [Memoirs of the American Academy at Rome 36] (Rome), 117–40.
Harris, W. V. 1999. 'Demography, geography, and the sources of Roman slaves', *The Journal of Roman Studies* 89, 62–75.
Harris, W. V. 2011. *Rome's Imperial Economy: Twelve Essays* (Oxford).
Hawkins, C. 2016. *Roman Artisans and the Urban Economy* (Cambridge).
Herrmann-Otto, E. 1994. *Ex ancilla natus. Untersuchungen zu den 'Hausgeborenen' Sklaven und Sklavinnen im Westen des römischen Kaiserreiches* (Stuttgart).
Herrmann-Otto, E. 2009. *Sklaverei und Freilassung in der griechisch-römischen Welt* (Hildesheim).
Hessels, J. H. 1890. *An Eighth-Century Anglo-Saxon Glossary preserved in the Library of Corpus Christi College, Cambridge (ms. no.144)* (Cambridge).
Hilberg, I. ed. 1918. *Sancti Eusebii Hieronymi: Epistulae* (Vienna).
Hirt, M. 2018. 'In search of Junian Latins', *Historia* 67, 288–312.
Hoffer, S. E. 1999. *The Anxieties of Pliny the Younger* (Atlanta).
Holman, S. R. 2001. *The Hungry Are Dying: Beggars and Bishops in Roman Cappadocia* (Oxford).
Hope, V. M. 2009. *Roman Death: The Dying and the Dead in Ancient Rome* (London and New York).
Hopkins, K. 1978. *Conquerors and Slaves* (Cambridge).
Horn, C. B and Martens, J. W. 2009. *'Let the little children come to me': Childhood and Children in Early Christianity* (Washington DC).
Huemoeller, K. P. 2020. 'Freedom in marriage? Manumission for marriage in the Roman world', *The Journal of Roman Studies* 110, 123–39.
Humbert, M. 1976. '*Libertas id est civitas*: autour d'un conflit négatif de citoyennetés au IIe s. avant J.-C.', *Mélanges de l'École française de Rome – Antiquité* 88, 221–42.
Humbert, M. 1978. *Municipium et civitas sine suffragio. L'organisation de la conquête jusqu'à la guerre sociale* (Paris).

Humbert, M. 1981. 'Le droit latin impérial: cités latines ou citoyenneté latine?', *Ktema* 6, 207–26.
Humbert, M. 2006. '*Municeps et municipium; définition et histoire*', in L. Capogrossi Colognesi and E. Gabba eds. *Gli statuti municipali* (Pavia), 3–29.
Humbert, M. 2010. 'Le *status civitatis*. Identité et identification du *civis Romanus*', in Corbino, Humbert and Negri 2010, 139–73.
Hunter, D. G. tr. 1988. *A Comparison between a King and a Monk; Against the Opponents of the Monastic Life: Two Treatises by John Chrysostom* (Lewiston).
Impallomeni, G. 1963. *Le manomissioni mortis causa. Studi sulle fonti autoritative romane* (Padua).
Incelli, E. 2017. 'Le rapport maître–esclave et les modalités de manumission dans l'empire romain', in M. Dondin-Payre and N. Tran eds. *Esclaves et maîtres dans le monde romain. Expressions épigraphiques de leurs relations* (Rome), 31–43.
Jakab. E 2014. 'Methoden der Identifikation in lateinischen *tabulae*', in M. Depauw and S. Coussement eds. *Identifiers and Identification Methods in the Ancient World* (Leuven, Paris and Walpole, MA), 209–31.
Jeannin, A. 2005. 'La persistance du droit romain dans le centre de la Gaule à travers l'exemple des formules d'Auvergne', in A. Dubreucq ed. *Traditio Iuris* (Lyons), 45–55.
Johnson, W. A. 2009. 'The ancient book', in Bagnall 2009, 256–81.
Johnston, D. 1999. *Roman Law in Context* (Cambridge).
Johnston, D. 2020. 'Gaius and the Liber singularis regularum attributed to Ulpian', in Babusiaux and Mantovani 2020, 303–18.
Joshel, S. 1992. *Work, Identity, and Legal Status at Rome: A Study of the Occupational Inscriptions* (Norman and London).
Kaiser, W. 2004, *Die Epitome Iuliani* (Frankfurt).
Kaiser, W. 2007. *Authentizität und Geltung spätantiker Kaisergesetze: Studien zu den 'Sacra privilegia concilii Vizaceni'* (Munich).
Kaiser, W. 2010. Review of M. Avenarius, *Der pseudo-ulpianische liber singularis regularum* (2005) and *Die pseudo-Ulpianische Einzelschrift über die Rechtsregeln* (2005), *Zeitschrift der Savigny-Stiftung für Rechtsgeschichte* 127, 560–603.
Kaiser, W. 2015. 'Justinian and the Corpus Iuris Civilis', in D. Johnston ed. *The Cambridge Companion to Roman Law* (Cambridge), 119–48.
Kaser, M. 1971. *Das römische Privatrecht* (Munich).
Kasten, H. 1982. *Plinius der Jüngere. Briefe* (Berlin).
Kaster, R. A. 1995. *C. Suetonius Tranquillus, De Grammaticis et Rhetoribus* (Oxford).
Kelly, B. 2017. 'Proving the *ius liberorum*: *P.Oxy.* XII 1467 reconsidered', *Greek, Roman and Byzantine Studies* 57, 105–35.
Kerneis, S. 2008. '*Francus ciuis, miles Romanus*. Les barbares de l'Empire dans le *Code Théodosien*', in J.-J. Aubert and P. Blanchard eds. *Droit, religion et société dans le Code Théodosien* (Geneva), 377–99.
Kienast, D. 1999. *Augustus. Prinzeps und Monarch* (Darmstadt).
Kleijwegt, M. ed. 2006. *The Faces of Freedom: The Manumission and Emancipation of Slaves in Old World and New World Slavery* (Leiden).
Kleiner, D. E. E. 1977. *Roman Group Portraiture: The Funerary Reliefs of the Late Republic and Early Empire* (New York).
Kleiner, D. E. E. 1987. *Roman Imperial Funerary Altars with Portraits* (Rome).
Kloppenborg, J. S. 2020. *Greco-Roman Associations: Texts, Translations, and Commentary III: Ptolemaic and Early Roman Egypt* (Berlin).
Knoch, S. 2005. *Sklavenfürsorge im Römischen Reich. Formen und Motive* (Hildesheim).
Knoch, S. 2018. *Sklaven und Freigelassene in der lateinischen Deklamation. Ein Beitrag zur römischen Mentalitätsgeschichte* (Hildesheim, Zurich and New York).

Kondratieff, E. J. 2003. *Popular Power in Action: Tribunes of the Plebs in the Roman Republic* (PhD thesis, University of Pennsylvania).
König, I. 2018. *Edictum Theodorici Regis* (Darmstadt).
Koops, E. 2012. 'Second-rate citizens: Junian Latins and the *Constitutio Antoniniana*', *Maastricht Journal of European and Comparative Law* 19, 223–39.
Koops, E. 2014. 'Masters and freedmen: Junian Latins and the struggle for citizenship', in S. Benoist and G. de Kleijn eds. *Integration in Rome and in the Roman World* (Leiden and Boston), 105–26.
Kremer, D. 2006. *Ius Latinum. Le concept de droit latin sous la république et l'empire* (Paris).
Krüger, P. 1868. 'Die Turiner Institutionenglosse', *Zeitschrift für Rechtsgeschichte* 7, 44–79.
Krüger, P. 1880. *Codicis Theodosiani Fragmenta Taurinensia* (Berlin).
Krüger, P. 1890. *Collectio librorum iuris anteiustiniani III* (Berlin).
Kruschwitz, P. 2020. 'Poetry on the advance: the emergence and formation of a poetic culture in Roman Britain', *Greece & Rome* 67.2, 177–202.
Lafferty, S. 2013. *Law and Society in the Age of Theoderic the Great: A Study of the Edictum Theoderici* (Cambridge).
Laffi, U. 2007. 'La struttura costituzionale nei municipi e nelle colonie romane. Magistrati, decurioni, popolo', in *Colonie e Municipi nello stato romano* (Rome), 49–79 [= L. Capogrossi Colognesi and E. Gabba eds. 2006. *Gli statuti municipali* (Pavia), 109–32].
Lagarrigue, G. ed. 1971. *Salvien de Marseille: Œuvres* 1 [SC 176] (Paris).
Lagarrigue, G. ed. 1975. *Salvien de Marseille: Œuvres* 2 [SC 220] (Paris).
Lahusen, G. 1989. '34. Grabaltar für Nicon und Eutyches', in P. C. Bol ed. *Forschungen zur Villa Albani. Katalog der antiken Bildwerke I* (Berlin).
Laistner, M. L. W. 1921. '*Dediticii*. The source of Isidore (*Etym.* IX, 4, 49–50)', *The Journal of Roman Studies* 11, 267–8.
Lamberti, F. 1993. *Tabulae Irnitanae. Municipalità e ius Romanorum* (Naples).
Lamberti, F. 2016. 'La giurisdizione nei municipia dell'occidente romano e il cap. 84 della lex Irnitana', in R. Haensch ed. *Recht haben und Recht bekommen im Imperium Romanum* (Warsaw), 183–211.
Last, H. A. 1934. 'The social policy of Augustus', *Cambridge Ancient History* X, 425–64.
Lavan, M. 2018. 'The empire of letters: Book 10 of Pliny's Letters and imperial correspondence', in A. R. König and C. L. Whitton eds. *Roman Literature under Nerva, Trajan and Hadrian: Literary Interactions, AD 96–138* (Cambridge), 280–301.
Le Roux, P. 1986. 'Municipe et droit latin en Hispania sous l'Empire', *Revue historique de droit français et étranger* 64, 325–50.
Le Roux, P. 2017. 'Le *ius Latii* d'Auguste aux Flaviens. Histoire d'une expansion provinciale', *Revue des études anciennes* 119.2, 585–608.
Leach, E. W. 2012. 'What has Pliny to say?', in Bell and Ramsby 2012, 196–210.
Lebek, W. D. 1993. 'La *lex Lati* di Domiziano (lex Irnitana): le strutture giuridiche dei capitoli 84 e 86', *Zeitschrift für Papyrologie und Epigraphik* 97, 159–87.
Lefèvre, E. 2009. *Vom Römertum zum Ästhetizismus. Studien zu den Briefen des jüngeren Plinius* (Berlin and New York).
Lemmonier, H. 1887. *Étude historique sur la condition privée des affranchis aux trois premiers siècles de l'Émpire romain* (Paris).
Lenel, O. 1927. *Das Edictum perpetuum: Ein Versuch zu seiner Wiederherstellung* [3rd ed.] (Leipzig).
Lenski, N. 2012. 'Constantine and slavery; *libertas* and the fusion of Roman and Christian values', in *Atti dell'Accademia Romanistica Costantiniana XVIII* (Rome), 235–60.
Letta, C. 2005. 'Da Segusio ad Augusta Praetoria. La creazione del municipio segusino e i rapporti con la valle d'Aosta nelle iscrizioni dei liberti delle dinastia cozia', *Studi Trentini di Scienze Storiche A* 84 (sezione I-4-S), 858–62.

Letta, C. 2006. 'La creación del municipio de Segusio (Alpes Cottiae) y el problema de los *municipia Latina* en el Occidente romano', *Florentia Iliberritana* 17, 121–30.
Lewis, N. 1991. '*Hadriani sententiae*', *Greek, Roman, and Byzantine Studies* 32, 267–80.
Liebs, D. 1987. *Die Jurisprudenz im spätantiken Italien (260–640 n. Chr.)* (Berlin).
Liebs, D. 1996. 'Die pseudopaulinischen Sentenzen II', *Zeitschrift der Savigny-Stiftung für Rechtsgeschichte* 110, 132–242.
Liebs, D. 2002. *Römische Jurisprudenz in Gallien (2. bis 8. Jahrhundert)* (Berlin).
Liebs, D. 2005. *Römische Jurisprudenz in Africa* [2nd ed.] (Berlin).
Liebs, D. 2012. 'Legis Romanae Visigothorum Epitomen Sangallensem', *Zeitschrift der Savigny-Stiftung für Rechtsgeschichte* 129, 1–112.
Liebs, D. 2016. 'Vier Arten von Römern unter den Franken im 6. bis 8. Jh.', *Zeitschrift der Savigny-Stiftung für Rechtsgeschichte* 133, 459–68.
Liebs, D. 2017. 'La protezione degli schiavi contro maltrattamenti dei loro padroni in età precristiana, cristiana e nell'Alto Medioevo', in G. Bassanelli Sommariva ed. *Dopo il Teodosiano. Il diritto pubblico in Occidente nei secoli V–VIII* (Bologna), 19–40.
Ligios, M. A. 2018. 'Note sul regime successorio dei *dediticii Aeliani* in Gai. 3.74–76', *Jus: Rivista di scienze giuridiche* 69, 283–308.
Lindsay, W. M. 1917. 'The Abstrusa Glossary and the Liber Glossarum', *The Classical Quarterly* 11, 119–31 [repr. in M. Lapidge ed. 1996. *Studies in Early Medieval Latin Glossaries* (Aldershot), VII].
Lo Cascio, E. 1997. 'Le procedure di recensus della tarda repubblica al tardo antico e il calcolo della popolazione di Roma', in C. Virlouvet ed. *La Roma impériale. Démographie et logistique* (Rome), 3–76.
Lokin, J. H. A. 1997. 'The Novels of Leo and the decisions of Justinian', in S. Troianos ed. *Analecta Atheniensia ad ius Byzantinum spectantia I* (Athens), 131–40 [repr. in *Analecta Groningana ad ius graeco-romanum pertinentia*, ed. Th.E. van Bochove (Groningen, 2010), 175–82].
Lokin, J. H. A., Meijering, R., Stolte, B. H. and van der Wal, N. eds. 2010. *Theophili antecessoris paraphrasis Institutionum* (Groningen).
López Barja, P. 1986/7. 'Latinus Iunianus. Una aproximación', *Studia Historica* 4–5, 125–36.
López Barja, P. 1991a. 'La dependencia económica de los libertos en el Alto Imperio romano', *Gerión* 9, 163–74.
López Barja, P. 1991b. 'Latini y Latini Iuniani. De nuevo sobre IRNI, 72', *Studia Historica. Historia Antigua* 9, 51–60.
López Barja, P. 1998. 'Junian Latins: status and numbers', *Athenaeum* 86.1, 133–63.
López Barja, P. 1999. 'Latinidad municipal y latinidad juniana', in González 1999, 411–16.
López Barja, P. 2002–3. 'Relaciones entre el *ius Latii* y el *ius personarum* (ley Flavia caps. 21–23 y 97)', *Memorias de Historia Antigua* 23/24, 59–75.
López Barja, P. 2007. *Historia de la manumisión en Roma. De los orígenes a los Severos* (Madrid).
López Barja, P. 2008. 'Las leyes augusteas sobre manumisión', in Gonzalès 2008, 219–27.
López Barja, P. 2010. 'Empire sociology: Italian freedmen, from success to oblivion', *Historia* 59.3, 321–41.
López Barja, P. 2018a. 'Independent freedmen in the "album" of Herculaneum', *Index. Quaderni camerti di studi romanistici* 46, 255–78.
López Barja, P. 2018b. 'La onomástica de los Latini Iuniani: una primera aproximación', in García Fernández and López Barja 2018, 573–92.
López Barja, P. 2019. '*Seruos ad pileum uocare*: violencia y libertad', in A. Gonzalès ed. *Praxis e ideologías de la violencia. Para una anatomía de las sociedades patriarcales esclavistas desde la Antigüedad* [Actes GIREA XXXVIII] (Besançon), 417–28.
López Barja, P. 2020. 'Patronage and slavery in the Roman world: the circle of power', in S. Hodkinson, K. Vlassopoulos and M. Kleijwegt eds. *The Oxford Handbook of Greek and Roman Slaveries* (e-publication).

López Barja, P. 2022. 'On freedom and citizenship. Freedmen as agents and metaphors of Roman political culture', in V. Arena and J. R. W. Prag eds. *A Companion to Roman Republican Political Culture* (New York), 374–86.

López Barja, P., Masi Doria, C. and Roth, U. eds. forthcoming. *Junian Latinity in the Roman Empire. Volume 2: Epigraphy, Papyrology, Society* (Edinburgh).

Loposzko, T. 1978/9. 'Gesetzentwürfe betreffs den Sklaven in Jahre 53 v.u.Z.', *Index. Quaderni camerti di studi romanistici* 8, 154–66.

Loposzko, T. 1979. 'La famine à Rome en 57 av. J.Chr.', *Quaderni di storia* 9, 101–22.

Loschiavo, L. 2012. 'L'impronta di Isidoro nella cultura giuridica medievale: qualche esempio', in G. Bassanelli Sommariva and S. Tarozzi eds. *Ravenna Capitale. Uno sguardo ad Occidente* (Santarcangelo di Romagna), 39–55.

Loschiavo, L. 2015. 'Was Rome still a centre of legal culture between the 6th and 8th centuries?', *Rechtsgeschichte* 23, 83–108.

Loschiavo, L. 2016. 'Isidore of Seville and the construction of a common legal culture in early medieval Europe', *Clio@Themis* 10, 1–21.

Lucchetti, G. 2012. 'Tituli ex corpore Ulpiani XXVIII', in G. Purpura ed. *Revisione ed integrazione dei Fontes Iuris Romani Anteiustiniani (FIRA): Studi preparatori*, II (Turin), 23–84.

Luraschi, G. 1976. 'Sulla data e sui destinatari della lex Minicia de liberis', *Studia et Documenta Historiae et Iuris* 42, 431–43.

Luraschi, G. 1979. *Foedus, ius Latii, civitas: aspetti costituzionali della romanizzazione in Transpadana* (Padua).

Luraschi, G. 1983. 'Sulla magistrature nelle colonie latine fittizie (a proposito di Frag. Atestinum ll. 10–12)', *Studia et Documenta Historiae et Iuris* 49, 261–329.

McGinn, T. A. J. 1998. *Prostitution, Sexuality, and the Law in Ancient Rome* (New York).

McGinn, T. A. J. 2004. 'Missing females? Augustus' encouragement of marriage between freeborn males and freedwomen', *Historia* 53, 200–8.

Macino, F. 2008 *Sulle tracce delle Istituzioni di Giustiniano nell'alto medioevo: i manoscritti dal VI al XII secolo* (Vatican City).

MacLean, R. 2018. *Freed Slaves and Roman Imperial Culture: Social Integration and the Transformation of Values* (Cambridge).

MacLean, R. 2021. 'Manumission, citizenship, and inheritance: epigraphic evidence from the Danube', in M. Lavan and C. Ando eds. *Roman and Local Citizenship in the Long Second Century* CE (Oxford), 140–63.

Maganzani, L. 2015. 'Il nuovo catasto di Verona. Profili giuridici', in Cresci Marrone 2015, 93–117.

Maganzani, L. 2017. 'Per una revisione del concetto di "colonia fittizia" in Transpadana: nuovi dati da Verona', in Ferretti, Fiorentini and Rossi 2017, 57–85.

Major, A. 1994. 'Claudius' edict on sick slaves', *Scholia: Studies in Classical Antiquity* 3.1, 84–90.

Mancini, G. 1997. *Cives Romani, Municipes Latini* (Milan).

Manni, E. 1940. 'L'utopia di Clodio', *Rivista di Filologia e di Istruzione Classica* 18, 161–78.

Mantovani, D. 2018. *Les juristes écrivains de la Rome antique. Les œuvres des juristes romains comme literature* (Paris).

Mantovani, D. 2020. 'Sul Liber Gai. Trasmissione, forma, contenuti e storia degli studi', in Babusiaux and Mantovani 2020, 577–638.

Mantovani, D. and Wibier, M. eds. forthcoming. *The Circulation, Use, and Reception of Classical Juristic Literature in Late Antiquity* (Cambridge).

Marchesi, I. 2008. *The Art of Pliny's Letters: A Poetics of Allusion in the Private Correspondence* (Cambridge).

Marchesi, I. ed. 2015. *Pliny the Book-Maker: Betting on Posterity in the Epistles* (Oxford).

Marotta, E. ed. 1997. *Salviano di Marsiglia: Contro l'avarizia* (Rome).

Marotta, V. 2012. 'I diritti degli stranieri', in A. Giardina and F. Pesando eds. *Roma Caput Mundi. Una città tra dominio e integrazione* (Milan), 201–9.

Marotta, V. 2016. 'Doppia cittadinanza e pluralità degli ordinamenti. La *Tabula Banasitana* e le linee 7–9 del Papiro di Giessen 40 col. I', *Archivio giuridico* 236, 461–91.

Marotta, V. 2018. 'P. Berol. inv. P 6757: Fragmenta Berolinensia incerti auctoris de iudiciis', in D. Mantovani and S. Ammirati eds. *Giurisprudenza romana nei papyri. Tracce per una ricerca* (Pavia), 137–44.

Martin, R. 1971. *Recherches sur les agronomes latines et leurs conceptions économiques et sociales* (Paris).

Masi Doria, C. 1993a. *Civitas Operae Obsequium. Tre Studi sulla condizione giuridica dei liberti* (Naples).

Masi Doria, C. 1993b. 'Zum Bürgerrecht der Freigelassenen', in M. J. Schermaier and Z. Végh eds. *Ars boni et aequi. Festschrift für Wolfgang Waldstein zum 65. Geburtstag* (Stuttgart), 231–60.

Masi Doria, C. 1996. *Bona libertorum. Regimi giuridici e realtà sociali* (Naples).

Masi Doria, C. 2013. '*Ancilla efficitur . . . In eo statu manebit*. Le conseguenze del Sc. Claudianum per le donne di status libertino', in R. Rodríguez López and M. J. Bravo Bosch eds. *Mulier: algunas historias e instituciones de derecho romano* (Madrid), 157–78.

Masi Doria, C. 2016. 'Tracce del Senatuconsultum Claudianum nella legislazione di Giustiniano', in I. Piro ed. *Scritti per Alessandro Corbino*, vol. 4 (Tricase), 597–618.

Masi Doria, C. 2018. 'La Latinitas Iuniana. Aspetti patrimoniali', in García Fernández and López Barja 2018, 555–71.

Mattern, S. P. 1999. 'Physicians and the Roman imperial aristocracy: the patronage of therapeutics', *Bulletin of the History of Medicine* 73.1, 1–18.

Matthews, J. F. 2000. *Laying Down the Law: A Study of the Theodosian Code* (New Haven and London).

Matthews, J. F. 2001. 'Interpreting the *interpretationes* of the Breviarium of Alaric', in R. W. Mathisen ed. *Law, Society, and Authority in Late Antiquity* (Oxford), 11–32 [repr. in *Roman Perspectives* (London, 2010), 343–60].

Melchor Gil, E. 2013. 'Quattuorviri y aediles en los municipios de constitución cuatorviral a fines de la república y en época altoimperial', *Rivista storica dell'antichità* 43, 133–52.

Méry, L. 1849. *Études Sur Salvien, Prêtre de Marseille* (Marseille).

Meyer-Marthaler, E. 1968. *Römisches Recht in Rätien im frühen und hohen Mittelalter* (Zurich).

Millar, F. 1977 [rev. 1992]. *The Emperor in the Roman World (31BC–AD337)* (London).

Miller, D. and Sarris, P. 2018. *The Novels of Justinian*, 2 vols (Cambridge).

Milnor, K. 2005. *Gender, Domesticity, and the Age of Augustus: Inventing Private Life* (Oxford).

Mirabella Roberti, M. 1990. 'Milano e Comum', in *La Città nell'Italia settentrionale in età romana. Morfologia, strutture e funzionamento dei centri urbani delle Regiones X e XI* [Atti del convegno di Trieste, 13–15 marzo 1987] (Trieste and Rome), 479–98.

Mitchell, P. forthcoming. 'Fragmentum Dositheanum', in Mantovani and Wibier forthcoming.

Mommsen, T. 1887. *Römisches Staatsrecht*, 3 vols [3rd ed.] (Leipzig).

Mommsen, T. 1889 [tr. 1887]. *Le droit public romain* (Paris).

Mor, C. G. 1927. *Lex Romana canonice compta. Testo di leggi romano-canoniche del sec. ix, pubblicato sul Ms. Parigino Bibl. Nat. 12448* (Pavia).

Morbidoni, P. L. 2019. *Freedom and Citizenship in the Roman Empire: Legal and Epigraphic Approaches to Status Identification* (PhD thesis, University of Edinburgh).

Moreau, P. 2014. 'Loi Aelia traitant de procédure administrative ou judiciaire dans une colonie', *Lepor* no. 890 [http://www.cn-telma.fr/lepor/notice890/].

Moreau, P. 2017. 'Loi *Iulia de maritandis ordinibus*', *Lepor* no. 449 [http://www.cn-telma.fr/lepor/notice449/].

Morley, N. 2013. 'Population size and social structure', in P. Erdkamp ed. *The Cambridge Companion to Ancient Rome* (Cambridge), 29–44.
Moschetti, G. 2006. *Frammenti veronesi del secolo IX delle Istituzioni di Giustiniano* (Rome).
Mourgues, J.-L. 1987. 'The so-called letter of Domitian at the end of the Lex Irnitana', *The Journal of Roman Studies* 77, 78–87.
Mouritsen, H. 2011. *The Freedman in the Roman World* (Cambridge).
Mouritsen, H. 2016. 'Manumission', in P. J. du Plessis, C. Ando and K. Tuori eds. *The Oxford Handbook of Roman Law and Society* (Oxford), 402–15.
Muirhead, J. 1880. *The Institutes of Gaius and the Rules of Ulpian* (Edinburgh).
Müller, K. ed. 2003. *Petronius. Satyricon Reliquiae* (Munich).
Nelson, H. L. W. and David, M. 1981. *Überlieferung, Aufbau und Stil von Gai Institutiones* (Leiden).
Nicolet, C. 1976. 'Le temple des Nymphes et les distributions frumentaires à Rome à l'époque républicaine d'après des découvertes récentes', *Comptes rendus des séances de l'Académie des Inscriptions et Belles-Lettres* 120.1, 29–51.
Nicols, J. 1980. 'Pliny and the patronage of communities', *Hermes* 108.3, 365–85.
Nicosia, E. 2000. '*Manumissio per epistulam*', *Revue internationale des droits de l'antiquité* 42, 221–34.
Nicosia, E. 2007. '*Moriuntur ut servi*? Un aspetto rilevante della condizione giuridica dei *Latini Iuniani*', in F. M. d'Ippolito ed. φιλία. *Scritti per G. Franciosi III* (Naples), 1829–46.
Noailles, P. and Dain, A. 1944. *Les Novelles de Léon VI le Sage* (Paris).
Noreña, C. F. 2007. 'The social economy of Pliny's correspondence with Trajan', *American Journal of Philology* 128, 239–77.
O'Sullivan, J. F. tr. 1962. *The Writings of Salvian, the Presbyter* (Washington DC).
Paladini, M. L. 1961. 'La *gratiarum actio* dei consoli in Roma attraverso la testimonianza di Plinio il Giovane'. *Historia* 10, 356–74.
Palmer, R. E. A. 1989. '*Bullae insignia ingenuitatis*', *American Journal of Ancient History* 14, 1–69.
Panciera, S. 1998. 'L. Plotius Liberalis, *ingenuus frumento publico*', in *La mémoire perdue. Recherches sur l'administration romaine* [Actes des tables rondes de Rome (mai 1994–mai 1995)] (Rome), 267–70.
Papaconstantinou, A. 2002. 'Notes sur les actes de donation d'enfant au monastère thébain de Saint-Phoibammon', *Journal of Juristic Papyrology* 32, 83–105.
Patetta, F. 1900. *Adnotationes Codicum Domini Iustiniani* (Rome).
Pellecchi, L. 2015. 'Loi *Iunia Norbana* sur l'affranchissement', *Lepor* no. 490 [http://www.cn-telma.fr/lepor/notice490/].
Pellecchi, L. forthcoming. 'Loi *Aelia Sentia* sur l'affranchissement', *Lepor* (forthcoming).
Pellegrino, M. 1940. *Salviano di Marsiglia: Studio Critico* (Rome).
Pennington, K. 2020. 'The beginnings of law schools in the twelfth century', in C. Giraud ed. *A Companion to Twelfth-Century Schools* (Leiden), 226–49.
Perkins, J. 2005. 'Trimalchio: naming power', in S. Harrison, M. Paschalis and S. Frangoulidis eds. *Metaphor and the Ancient Novel* (Groningen), 139–62 [repr. in *Roman Imperial Identities in the Early Christian Era* (London and New York, 2009), 127–43].
Perry, M. J. 2014. *Gender, Manumission, and the Roman Freedwoman* (New York).
Petersen, L. H. 2006. *The Freedman in Roman Art and Art History* (Cambridge).
Pferdehirt, B. 1998. 'Fragment eines neuen Militärdiploms aus Thrakien vom Jahr 138 n. Chr.', *Archäologisches Korrespondenzblatt* 28, 445–50.
Phang, S. E. 2008. *Roman Military Service: Ideologies of Discipline in the Late Republic and Early Principate* (New York and Cambridge).
Phillips, W. D. 1985. *Slavery from Roman Times to the Early Transatlantic Trade* (Manchester).
Picone, G. 1978. *L'eloquenza di Plinio: teoria e prassi* (Palermo).

Pina Polo, F. 2021a. 'Frumentary policy, ideology and welfare state in the late Roman Republic', in G. Urso ed. *Popularitas: ricerca del consenso e 'populismo' in Roma antica* (Rome), 127–62.

Pina Polo, F. 2021b. 'Sallust's *Epistulae ad Caesarem*: A *popularis* proposal for the Republican crisis?', *Hermes* 149, 185–6.

Piper, D. J. 1988. 'The *ius adipiscendae civitatis Romanae per magistratum* and its effect on Roman–Latin relations', *Latomus* 47, 59–68.

Plaza, M. 2000. *Laughter and Derision in Petronius' Satyrica: A Literary Study* (Stockholm).

Pohl, W., Gantner, C., Grifoni, C. and Pollheimer-Mohaupt, M. eds. 2018. *Transformations of Romanness: Early Medieval Regions and Identities* (Berlin).

Pomeroy, S. B. 1994. *Xenophon, Oeconomicus: A Social and Historical Commentary* (Oxford).

Porten, B. 1996. *The Elephantine Papyri in English: Three Millennia of Cross-Cultural Continuity and Change* (Leiden).

Price, R. M. tr. 1985. *A History of the Monks of Syria by Theodoret* (Trappist).

Radice, B. 1963. *The Letters of Pliny the Younger* (Harmondsworth).

Radice, B. 1969. *Pliny: Letters and Panegyricus* (London).

Raepsaet-Charlier, M.-T. 2001. 'Caractéristiques et particularités de l'onomastique trévire', in Dondin-Payre and Raepsaet-Charlier 2001, 343–98.

Raepsaet-Charlier, M.-T. 2011. 'Les noms germaniques: adaptation et latinisation de l'onomastique en Gaule Belgique et Germanie inférieure', in Dondin-Payre 2011b, 203–34.

Raggi, A. 2006. *Seleuco di Rhosos: cittadinanza e privilegi nell'Oriente greco in età tardo-repubblicana* (Pisa).

Rainbird, J. S. 1976. *The Vigiles of Rome* (PhD thesis, Durham University).

Rawson, B. 1966. 'Family life among the lower classes at Rome in the first two centuries of the Empire', *Classical Philology* 61.2, 71–83.

Rawson, B. 2010. 'Degrees of freedom: *vernae* and Junian Latins in the Roman *familia*', in V. Dasen and T. Späth eds. *Children, Memory, and Family Identity in Roman Culture* (Oxford), 195–221.

Reiner, J. M. 2021. '*Latinitas Aeliana* und *Latinitas Iuniana*', *Annali del Seminario Giuridico di Palermo (AUPA)* 64, 73–96.

Reitz, C. 2013. 'Columella, *De Re Rustica*', in E. Buckley and M. T. Dinter eds. *A Companion to the Neronian Age* (Chichester and Malden, MA), 275–87.

Reitz, C. 2017. '*Auctoritas* in the garden: Columella's poetic strategy in *De re rustica* 10', in M. Formisano and P. van der Eijk eds. *Knowledge, Text and Practice in Ancient Technical Writing* (Cambridge), 217–30.

Renner, T. 2009. 'Papyrology and ancient literature', in Bagnall 2009, 282–302.

Rhee, H. 2012. *Loving the Poor, Saving the Rich: Wealth, Poverty, and Early Christian Formation* (Grand Rapids).

Richard, A. 1886. *Chartes de Saint Maixent* [Archives Historiques du Poitou 16] (Poitiers).

Richardson, J. S. 2012. *Augustan Rome 44 BC to AD 14* (Edinburgh).

Riggsby, A. M. 1995. 'Pliny on Cicero and oratory: self-fashioning in the public eye', *American Journal of Philology* 116, 123–35.

Riggsby, A. M. 1998. 'Self and community in the younger Pliny', *Arethusa* 31, 75–98.

Rio, A. 2009. *Legal Practice and the Written Word in the Early Middle Ages: Frankish Formulae c. 500–1000* (Cambridge).

Rio, A. 2017. *Slavery After Rome, 500–1100* (Oxford).

Rising, T. 2019. 'Bread and bandits. Clodius and the grain supply of Rome', *Hermes* 147, 189–203.

Robleda, O. 1976. *Il diritto degli schiavi nell'antica Roma* (Rome).

Rodgers, R. H. ed. 2010. *L. Iuni Moderati Columellae: Res Rustica; Incerti Auctoris: Liber de Arboribus* (Oxford).

Rodríguez Álvarez, L. 1978. *Las leyes limitadoras de las manumisiones en época augustea* (Oviedo).
Rodríguez Garrido, J. 2017. 'Latini y Latini Iuniani. El problema del *conubium*', in M. Carrero-Pazos, M. Díaz Rodríguez, A. A. Rodríguez Novoa and B. Vilas Estévez eds. *Re(escribindo) a Historia* (Santiago de Compostela), 261–78.
Rodríguez Garrido, J. 2018. '*Iustum matrimonium* e *ius conubii*. Las uniones matrimoniales y el derecho de los latinos', in García Fernández and López Barja 2018, 593–609.
Rodríguez Garrido, J. 2020. '*Ne serva prostituatur*. Esclavitud, prostitución y los límites de la *dominica potestas* en la Roma Antigua', *Dialogues d'histoire ancienne* 46, 173–96.
Rodríguez Martín, J.-D. 2020. 'Gayo a través de los Fragmenta Augustodunensia: cuestiones exegéticas', in Babusiaux and Mantovani 2020, 531–64.
Roselaar, S. 2013. 'The concept of *conubium* in the Roman Republic', in P. J. du Plessis ed. *New Frontiers: Law and Society in the Roman World* (Edinburgh), 102–22.
Roth, U. 2007. *Thinking Tools: Agricultural Slavery between Evidence and Models* (London).
Roth, U. ed. 2010a. *By the Sweat of Your Brow: Roman Slavery in its Socio-Economic Setting* (London).
Roth, U. 2010b. 'Peculium, freedom, citizenship: golden triangle or vicious circle? An act in two parts', in Roth 2010a, 91–120.
Roth, U. 2011. 'Men without hope', *Papers of the British School at Rome* 79, 71–94.
Roth, U. 2016a. 'Liberating the *Cena*', *The Classical Quarterly* 66, 614–34.
Roth, U. 2016b. Review of Perry 2014, *Ancient History Bulletin Online Reviews* 6, 104–7.
Roth, U. 2016c. 'Slavery and the Church in Visigothic Spain: the donation and will of Vincent of Huesca', *Antiquité Tardive* 24, 433–52.
Rothe, U. 2020. *The Toga and Roman Identity* (London and New York).
Rotondi, G. 1912. *Leges publicae populi Romani* (Milan).
Rouche, M. 1980. 'Survivances antiques dans trois cartulaires du Sud-Ouest de la France aux Xe et XIe siècles', *Cahiers de civilisation médiévale* 23, 93–108 [repr. in *Le choc des cultures: Romanité, Germanité, Chrétienté durant le Haut Moyen Âge* (Villeneuve d'Ascq, 2003), 59–83].
Ruffing, K. 1993. 'Ein Fall von politischer Getreidespekulation im Jahr 57 v. Chr. In Rom?', *Münstersche Beiträge zur antiken Handelsgeschichte* 12, 75–93.
Ruggiero, I. 2017. 'Una breve nota sulla condizione dei liberti latini e dei loro discendenti in età tardoantica', *Koinonia* 41, 461–74.
Russo, F. 2018. 'Sullo *ius adipiscendae civitatis Romanae per magistratum* nella Lex Irnitana', in García Fernández and López Barja 2018, 481–505.
Russo, G. 1980. *Tradizione manoscritta di leges romanae nei codici dei secoli ix e x della Biblioteca Capitolare di Modena* (Modena).
Russo Ruggeri, C. 1999. *Studi sulle Quinquaginta decisiones* (Milan).
Sablayrolles, R. 1996. *Libertinus miles: les cohortes de vigiles* (Paris).
Saddington, D. B. 2004. 'C.L. in the titulature of the Coh. II Tungrorum', *Britannia* 35, 244–8.
Saller, R. P. 1982. *Personal Patronage under the Early Empire* (Cambridge).
Salmon, E. T. 1969. *Roman Colonization under the Republic* (London and Southampton).
Salway, B. 1994. 'What's in a name? A survey of Roman onomastic practice from c. 700 B.C. to A.D. 700', *The Journal of Roman Studies* 84, 124–45.
Salway, R. W. B. 2012. 'The publication of the Theodosian Code and transmission of its texts: some observations', in P. Jaillette and S. Crogiez-Pétrequin eds. *Sociéte, économie, administration dans le Code Théodosien* (Lille), 21–61.
Sandon, T. forthcoming. *The Lives of Roman Freedwomen: Epigraphic Evidence from the Latin West* (Edinburgh).
Schaps, D. M., Yiftach, U. and Dueck, D. eds. 2016. *When West Met East. The Encounter of Greece and Rome with the Jews, Egyptians, and Others. Studies Presented to Ranon Katzoff in Honor of his 75th Birthday* (Trieste).

Scheidel, W. 1994. 'Columellas privates *ius liberorum*: Literatur, Recht, Demographie. Einige Probleme', *Latomus* 53, 513–27.
Scheidel, W. 2004. 'Human mobility in Roman Italy I: the free population', *The Journal of Roman Studies* 94, 1–26.
Scheidel, W. 2005. 'Human mobility in Roman Italy, II: the slave population', *The Journal of Roman Studies* 95, 64–79.
Scheidel, W. 2007. 'A model of real income growth in Roman Italy', *Historia* 56, 322–46.
Scheidel, W. 2011. 'The Roman slave supply', in K. Bradley and P. Cartledge eds. *The Cambridge World History of Slavery, Vol. 1: The Ancient Mediterranean World* (Cambridge), 287–310.
Scheltema, H. J. 1970. *L'enseignement de droit des antécesseurs* (Leiden) [repr. in Scheltema 2004, 58–110].
Scheltema, H. J. 1972. 'Fragmenta breviarii Codicis a Theodoro Hermopolitano confecti e Synopsi erotematica collecta', in *Studia Byzantina et Neohellenica Neerlandica* (Leiden), 9–35 [repr. in Scheltema 2004, 371–94].
Scheltema, H. J. 1984. 'Subseciva XVIII. Les Quinquaginta Decisiones', *Subseciva Groningana* 1, 1–9 [repr. in Scheltema 2004, 158–62].
Scheltema, H. J. 2004. *Opera Minora ad iuris historiam pertinentia* (Groningen).
Scheltema, H. J. and Holwerda, D. 1963. *Basilicorum Libri LX, Series B Volumen VII* (Groningen).
Scheltema, H. J. and van der Wal, N. 1969. *Basilicorum Libri LX, Series A Volumen VI* (Groningen).
Schipp, O. 2017. 'Der grosszügige Patron Gajus Seccius. Eine Fallstudie zur *lex Aelia Sentia* und ihren Folgen für unter 30-jährige Freigelassene', *Mainzer Zeitschrift* 112, 15–27.
Schmeling, G. 2011. *A Commentary on the* Satyrica *of Petronius* (Oxford).
Schmidlin, B. 1976. '*Horoi, pithana* und *regulae* – Zum Einfluß der Rhetorik und Dialektik auf die juristische Regelbildung', *ANRW* 2.15, 101–30.
Schmitt, G. and Rödel, V. 1974 'Die kranken Sklaven auf der Tiberinsel nach dem Edikt des Claudius', *Medizinhistorisches Journal* 9, 106–24.
Scholl, R. 2001. '"Freilassung unter Freunden" im römischen Ägypten', in Bellen and Heinen 2001, 159–69.
Schroeder, C. 2009. 'Children and Egyptian monasticism', in C. B. Horn and R. R. Phenix eds. *Children in Late Ancient Christianity* (Tübingen), 317–38.
Schulz, F. 1990. *Principios del derecho romano* (Madrid) [tr. *Prinzipien des Römischen Rechts* (Munich, 1934)].
Schumacher, L. 2001. *Sklaverei in der Antike. Alltag und Schicksal der Unfreien* (Munich).
Schuster, M. ed. 1952. *C. Plini Caecili Secundi Epistularum libri novem, Epistularum ad Traianum liber, Panegyricus*. Editio altera aucta et correctior (Leipzig).
Shelton, J.-A. 2013. *The Women of Pliny's Letters* (London and New York).
Sherwin-White, A. N. 1966. *The Letters of Pliny: A Historical and Social Commentary* (Oxford).
Sherwin-White, A. N. 1972. 'The date of the *lex repetundarum* and its consequences', *The Journal of Roman Studies* 62, 83–99.
Sherwin-White, A. N. 1973a. *The Roman Citizenship* [2nd ed.] (Oxford).
Sherwin-White, A. N. 1973b. 'The Tabula of Banasa and the *Constitutio Antoniniana*', *The Journal of Roman Studies* 63, 86–98.
Sicari, A. 1991. *Prostituzione e tutela giuridica della schiava* (Bari).
Siems, H. 2008. 'Zur Lex Romana Curiensis', in H. Eisenhut, K. Fuchs, M. Graf and H. Steiner eds. *Schrift, Schriftgebrauch und Textsorten im frühmittelalterlichen Churrätien* (Basel), 109–36.
Simon, D. and Troianos, S. 1989. *Das Novellensytagma des Athanasios von Emesa* (Frankfurt).
Sinn, F. 1987. *Stadtrömische Marmorurnen* (Mainz).
Sirks, A. J. B. 1980. 'A favour to rich freed women (*libertinae*) in 51 A.D. On Sue. *Cl.* 19 and the Lex Papia', *Revue internationale des droits de l'antiquité* 27, 283–94.

Sirks, A. J. B. 1981. 'Informal manumission and the Lex Junia', *Revue internationale des droits de l'antiquité* 28, 247–76.
Sirks, A. J. B. 1983. 'The *lex Junia* and the effects of informal manumission and iteration', *Revue internationale des droits de l'antiquité* 30, 211–91.
Sirks, A. J. B. 1995. 'A decision of the emperor Hadrian', *The Journal of Legal History* 16.3, 318–27.
Sirks, A. J. B. 2005. 'Der Zweck des *Senatus Consultum Claudianum* von 52 n. Chr.', *Zeitschrift der Savigny-Stiftung für Rechtsgeschichte* 122, 138–49.
Sirks, A. J. B. 2012. 'The purpose of the Lex Fufia Caninia', *Zeitschrift der Savigny-Stiftung für Rechtsgeschichte* 129, 549–53.
Sisani, S. 2016. 'Le istituzioni municipali: legislazione e prassi tra il I secolo a.C. e l'età Flavia', in L. Capogrossi Colognesi, E. Lo Cascio and E. Tassi Scandone eds. *L'Italia dei Flavi* [Acta Flaviana 3] (Rome), 9–55.
Sisani, S. 2018a. 'Latinità non latina: lo *ius Latii* come strumento di integrazione delle comunità provinciali in età repubblicana', in García Fernández and López Barja 2018, 331–78.
Sisani, S. 2018b. 'Le magistrature locali delle comunità municipali di ambito provinciale. Uno studio sulla diffusione del quattuorvirato e del duovirato tra l'età tardo-repubblicana e l'età imperiale', *Gerión* 36.1, 41–78.
Slater, N. W. 1990. *Reading Petronius* (Baltimore and London).
Solin, H. 2003. *Die griechischen Personennamen in Rom: ein Namenbuch* (Berlin and New York).
Spichenko, N. 2018. 'El estatus legal del liberto municipal', in García Fernández and López Barja 2018, 611–25.
Spurr, M. S. 1986. *Arable Cultivation in Roman Italy, c. 200 BC–c. AD 100* (London).
Stadter, P. A. 2006. 'Pliny and the ideology of Empire: the correspondence with Trajan', *Prometheus* 32, 61–76.
Stagl, J. F. 2014. 'Das didaktische System des Gaius', *Zeitschrift der Savigny-Stiftung für Rechtsgeschichte* 131, 313–48.
Stolte, B. H. 2020. 'Gaius in the Paraphrase of Theophilus', in Babusiaux and Mantovani 2020, 683–714.
Strong, A. K. 2016. Review of Perry 2014, *Bryn Mawr Classical Review* 2016.08.18.
Swain, S. 2013. *Economy, Family, and Society from Rome to Islam: A Critical Edition, English Translation, and Study of Bryson's Management of the Estate* (Cambridge).
Talamanca, M. 1991. 'I mutamenti della cittadinanza', *Mélanges de l'École française de Rome – Antiquité* 103, 703–33.
Talbert, R. A. 1984. *The Senate of Imperial Rome* (Princeton).
Tarpin, M. 2002. *Vici et pagi dans l'Occident romain* (Rome).
Teigen, H. F. 2021. *The Manichaean Church in Kellis: Social Networks and Religious Identity in Late Antique Egypt* (Leiden).
Terreni, C. 1999. 'Gaio e l'"erroris causae probatio"', *Labeo* 45, 333–67.
Thomson, R. D. 2003. *William of Malmesbury* [2nd ed.] (Woodbridge).
Tibiletti, G. 1953. 'La politica delle colonie e delle città latine nella guerra sociale', *Rendiconti dell'Istituto Lombardo di Scienze e Lettere (RIL)* 86, 45–63.
Torelli, P. 1934. *Accursii Florentini Glossa ad Institutiones Iustiniani Imperatoris* (Bologna).
Torrent, A. 1970. *La iurisdictio de los magistrados municipales* (Salamanca).
Treggiari, S. 1969. *Roman Freedmen during the Late Republic* (Oxford).
Treggiari, S. 1996. 'Social status and social legislation', *Cambridge Ancient History* X, 873–904.
Troiano, A. 2019. 'Sul *fragmentum* Riccardi e la *lex Aelia Sentia* in TH^2 89', *Journal of Juristic Papyrology* 49, 281–7.
Trump, D. 2021. *Römisches Recht im Karolingerreich: Studien zur Überlieferungs- und Rezeptionsgeschichte der 'Epitome Aegidii'* (Ostfildern).

Tuori, K. 2016. *The Emperor of Law: The Emergence of Roman Imperial Adjudication* (Oxford).
Tzounakas, S. 2006. 'Clodius' projected manumission of slaves in Cicero's *Pro Milone*', *Arctos* 40, 167–74.
Tzounakas, S. 2015. 'Pliny as the Roman Demosthenes', in O. Devillers ed. *Autour de Pline le Jeune: en hommage à Nicole Méthy* (Bordeaux), 207–18.
van Berchem, D. 1939 [reprint 1975]. *Les distributions de blé et d'argent à la plèbe romaine sous l'Empire* (Geneva).
van der Wal, N. 1985. 'Die Paratitla zur Epitome Juliani', *Subseciva Groningana* 2, 93–137.
Veldman, E. 2020. *The Lex Iunia, lex Fufia Caninia and lex Aelia Sentia: Impact and Motives of the Augustan Manumission Laws* (PhD thesis, Utrecht).
Venturini, C. 1995/6. 'Latini facti, peregrini e civitas: note sulla normativa adrianea', *Bullettino dell'Istituto di Diritto Romano* 98/9, 219–42.
Vermote, K. 2016. 'The *macula servitutis* of Roman freedmen. *Neque enim aboletur turpitudo, quae postea intermissa est?*', *Revue belge de philologie et d'histoire* 94.1, 131–64.
Vervaet, F. 2020. 'No grain of salt. Casting a new light on Pompeius' *cura annonae*', *Hermes* 148, 149–72.
Virlouvet, C. 1995. *Tessera frumentaria: les procédures de la distribution de blé public à Rome* (Rome).
Virlouvet, C. 2009. *La plèbe frumentaire dans les témoignages épigraphiques* (Rome).
Vlassopoulos, K. 2021. *Historicising Ancient Slavery* (Edinburgh).
Voci, P. 1963. *Diritto ereditario romano. II. Parte speciale: successione ab intestato, successione testamentaria* (Milan).
Vogt, J. 1965. *Sklaverei und Humanität. Studien zur antiken Sklaverei und ihrer Erforschung* (Wiesbaden).
Volterra, E. 1957. 'Le affrancazioni di schiavi nei documenti aramaici del V secolo a.C.', *Rivista degli Studi Orientali* 32, 675–96.
Volterra, E. 1969. 'Senatus consulta', in *Novissimo Digesto Italiano* (Turin), 1047–78 [repr. in *Scritti giuridici V: Le fonti* (Naples, 1994), 193–297].
von Stackelberg, K. T. 2013. 'Columella', in R. S. Bagnall, K. Brodersen, C. B. Champion, A. Erskine and S. R. Hübner eds. *The Encyclopedia of Ancient History* (Oxford), 1679–80.
Vuolanto, V. 2015. *Children and Asceticism in Late Antiquity: Continuity, Family Dynamics and the Rise of Christianity* (London).
Wacke, A. 1989. '*Manumissio matrimonii causa*: le mariage d'affranchies d'après les lois d'Auguste', *Revue historique de droit français et étranger* 67, 413–28.
Wacke, A. 2001. '*Manumissio matrimonii causa*: Die Freilassung zwecks Heirat nach den Ehegesetzen des Augustus', in Bellen and Heinen 2001, 133–58.
Waldstein, W. 1986. *Operae libertorum. Untersuchungen zur Dienstpflicht freigelassener Sklaven* (Stuttgart).
Walsh, P. G. 2006. *Pliny the Younger: Complete Letters* (Oxford).
Walter, U. 2006. 'Drückende Humanität', *Frankfurter Allgemeine Zeitung* 114, 34.
Watson, A. 1985 [1998]. *The Digest of Justinian: Latin Text Edited by Theodor Mommsen with the Aid of Paul Krueger; English Translation Edited by Alan Watson*, 4 vols (Philadelphia).
Weaver, P. R. C. 1972. *Familia Caesaris: A Social Study of the Emperor's Freedmen and Slaves* (Cambridge).
Weaver, P. R. C. 1986. 'The status of children in mixed marriages', in B. Rawson ed. *The Family in Ancient Rome: New Perspectives* (London), 145–69.
Weaver, P. R. C. 1990. 'Where have all the Junian Latins gone? Nomenclature and status in the early Empire', *Chiron* 20, 275–305.
Weaver, P. R. C. 1997. 'Children of Junian Latins', in B. Rawson and P. Weaver eds. *The Roman Family in Italy: Status, Sentiment, Space* (Oxford), 55–72.
Weaver, P. R. C. 2001. 'Reconstructing lower-class Roman families', in Dixon 2001, 101–14.

Weber, H. 2015. 'A hypothesis regarding Justinian's *decisiones* and the Digest', *Roman Legal Tradition* 11, 92–117.
Weiler, I. 2001. 'Eine Sklavin wird frei. Zur Rolle des Geschlechts bei der Freilassung', in Bellen and Heinen 2001, 113–32.
Weiler, I. 2003. *Die Beendigung des Sklavenstatus im Altertum: Ein Beitrag zur vergleichenden Sozialgeschichte* (Stuttgart).
Weiss, E. 1915. 'Zwei Bittschriften aus Lydien', *Zeitschrift der Savigny-Stiftung für Rechtsgeschichte: Romanistische Abteilung* 36, 157–76.
White, K. D. 1970. *Roman Farming* (Ithaca, NY).
Whitton, C. 2019. *The Arts of Imitation in Latin Prose: Pliny's Epistles/Quintilian in Brief* (Cambridge).
Wibier, M. 2020, 'The so-called *Appendices* to the *Lex Romana Visigothorum*: compilation and transmission of three late Roman private legal collections', *Athenaeum* 108, 150–80.
Wiedemann, T. E. J. 1985. 'The regularity of manumission at Rome', *The Classical Quarterly* 35, 162–75.
Wiedemann, T. E. J. 1988. 'Review: "The Duties of Freedmen". *Operae libertorum: Untersuchungen zur Dienstpflicht freigelassener Sklaven* by Wolfgang Waldstein', *The Classical Review* 38, 331–3.
Wilinski, A. 1963. 'Zur Frage von Latinern *ex lege Aelia Sentia*', *Zeitschrift der Savigny-Stiftung für Rechtsgeschichte* 80, 378–92.
Williams, W. 1990. *Pliny the Younger: Correspondence with Trajan from Bithynia* (Epistles X) (Warminster).
Winterbottom, M. 1982. 'Schoolroom and courtroom', in B. Vickers ed. *Rhetoric Revalued* (Binghamton, NY), 59–70.
Wirth, G. 1997. 'Rome and its Germanic partners in the fourth century', in W. Pohl ed. *Kingdoms of the Empire: The Integration of Barbarians in Late Antiquity* (Leiden), 13–55.
Woolf, G. 2006. 'Pliny's province', in T. Bekker-Nielsen ed. *Rome and the Black Sea Region: Domination, Romanisation, Resistance* (Aarhus), 93–108.
Woolf, G. 2015. 'Pliny/Trajan and the poetics of empire', *Classical Philology* 110, 132–51.
Worp, K. A. 1995. *Greek Papyri from Kellis I* (Oxford).
Zachariae von Lingenthal, K. E. 1843. *Anekdota III* (Leipzig).
Zeumer, K. 1881. 'Ueber die älteren fränkischen Formelsammlungen', *Neues Archiv der Gesellschaft für ältere deutsche Geschichtskunde* 6, 9–115.
Zeumer, K. 1886. *Formulae Merowingici et Karolini Aevi* [Monumenta Germaniae Historica Legum V] (Hanover).

Index Locorum

AE = Année Epigraphique (L')
  1922, 14, 53n
  1989, 456, 50n
  1995, 1066, 53n
  1995, 1067, 53n
  1998, 285, 95n
Appendices Legis Romanae Wisigothorum
  I, 19, 135n, 148n
Appian
  Bella civilia
    2.98, 29n, 39n
    2.102, 88n
Asconius
  In Pisonem, 3, 22n, 27, 29n, 39n
Athanasius
  Epitome Novellarum, 18.2, 144n
Aulus Gellius
  Noctes Atticae
    6.4.1–3, 196n
    16.16.6, 33n

Bryson, *Oikonomikos* (ed. Swain 2013), 73, 166n

Cassius Dio
  37.9.5, 50n
  39.24.1, 85n
  41.36.3, 25n
  43.21.4, 88n
  47.25.3, 196n
  48.33.5, 99n
  53.24.4–6, 90n
  54.10.1–2, 90n
  54.16.7, 92n
  54.30.2, 92n
  55.9.10, 93n
  55.13.3, 99n
  55.13.4, 99n
  55.13.7, 98n
  55.25.5, 45n
  55.26.2, 97n
  55.31.4, 97n
  56.7.6, 98n
  56.33.3, 98n
  61.29.7, 105n
Chartae Latinae Antiquiores
  I 106, 150n
  XI 496, 102n
Codices Latini Antiquiores
  IV 488, 134n
  X 1524, 134n
Collatio Legum Mosaicarum et Romanarum
  3.3.4, 76n
  4.3.3, 125n, 126n
  4.3.3–4, 136n
Collectio Anselmo dedicata 7.72, 146n
Columella
  De re rustica
    1.8.19, 161, 161n, 161n, 162, 165
    3.3.3, 160n
    3.9.2, 160n
    8.16.9, 160n
    10.185, 160n
Corpus Inscriptionum Latinarum
  II
    834, 41n
    1610, 34n

1631, 34n
1967, 50n
2096, 34n
3008, 46n
3251, 46n
II²
  5, 324, 55
  5, 832, 55
  5, 976, 55
III
  4870, 51n
  5227, 51n
V
  532, 29n
  5050, 48n, 50n
VI
  2316, 199n
  2317, 199n
  2365, 199n
  2366, 199n
  2584, 95n
  10220, 95n
  10221, 95n
  10223, 95n
  10224b, 95n
  10225, 95n
  10228, 95n
  22972, 199n
XI, 3943, 186n
XII
  95, 41n
  516, 41n
  523, 51n
  4190, 50n, 53n, 55
XIII
  2726, 53n
  2912, 53n
Corpus papyrorum Latinarum (Cavenaile ed.)
  74, 102n
  75, 134n
  148, 102n
  172, 132n, 133n
  174, 102n
Corpus Provincial de Inscripciones Latinas
  (Cáceres), 818, 41n

Dionysius of Halicarnassus
  Antiquitates Romanae
    4.24.5–6, 90n

    4.24.6, 99n, 195n
    4.24.8, 92n
    55.4.1, 92n

Edict of Theoderic, 19, 145n
Eusebius
  Historia Ecclesiastica, 10.6, 139n
  Vita Constantini
    2.63, 139n
    73, 139n

Fontes iuris Romani anteiustiniani
  (FIRA)
  II
    210, 134n
    232–3, 147n
    445, 134n
    625–6, 134n
    650, 134n
    652, 134n
    672–3, 148n
    748, 147n
  III
    625–6, 134n
    no.11, 132n
Fragmenta Berolinensia de iudiciis,
  134n
Fragmenta Vaticana
  172, 124n, 136n
  193, 136n
  221, 117n, 125n, 136n
  259, 136n
Fragmentum Pseudo-Dositheanum
  2, 145n
  4, 135n
  5, 57n, 57n, 85n, 107
  5–6, 84n
  6, 57n, 58n, 124n, 135n,
    145n
  6–8, 60n, 135n
  7, 57n, 135n, 145n
  8, 58n, 145n
  9, 135n
  9–11, 58n
  11–14, 135n
  12, 60n, 135n, 145n
  13, 62n
  15, 58n, 109
  16, 58n, 76n, 135n

Gaius
   Epitome, 147n
   Fragmenta Augustodunensia
      1.6–7, 29n
      14, 134n
   Institutiones
      1.12, 115
      1.13, 62n
      1.14, 62n
      1.15, 62n, 62n, 110n
      1.17, 2n, 62n
      1.18, 59n
      1.19, 119
      1.20, 3n, 130n
      1.22, 2n, 57n, 124, 124n
      1.22–3, 60n
      1.23, 68n, 68n
      1.25, 62n
      1.27, 62n
      1.28, 28n
      1.28–34, 128n
      1.29, 2n, 26n, 44n, 64n, 103n, 124n
      1.30, 114
      1.31, 26n, 113n
      1.32b, 110n
      1.32b–35, 28n
      1.32c, 111
      1.33, 112n
      1.35, 6n, 117n, 128n
      1.37, 76n
      1.38, 62n
      1.38–40, 2n
      1.39, 118
      1.40, 62n, 101n
      1.41, 3n
      1.42, 7n
      1.43, 8n
      1.44, 3n, 155
      1.46, 102n
      1.55, 44n
      1.65–6, 69n
      1.66, 26n, 128n
      1.67–8, 62n
      1.67–73, 116n
      1.68, 26n, 124n
      1.70, 26n
      1.73, 113n
      1.77, 115
      1.78–9, 71n
      1.79, 29n, 47n, 114n
      1.80, 26n, 60n, 64n, 71n, 114, 114n
      1.84, 113n
      1.85, 113n
      1.86, 146n
      1.91, 107
      1.95, 28n, 38n, 128n
      1.95–6, 29n, 29n
      1.96, 40n, 40n
      1.131, 27n
      1.167, 60n
      2.25, 155
      2.110, 60n
      2.195, 117
      2.275, 60n, 68n
      3.39–53, 123
      3.42, 101n
      3.56, 4–5, 4n, 27n, 47n, 58n, 59n, 74n, 85n, 107, 115n, 123n, 124, 124n, 211n
      3.56–7, 60n
      3.56–66, 123
      3.63, 126n
      3.70, 60n
      3.72, 115n, 131n
      3.73, 116n
      3.74–6, 63n
      3.75, 62n
      3.100, 113n
Gennadius
   Catalogus virorum illustrium, 67, 204n
   Gnomon of the Idios Logos, 19, 68n

Heidelberg Epigraphische Datenbank, HD007878, 125n
Hermeneumata (Sententiae Hadriani),
   2, 96n
   3.10, 127n
Hieronymus
   Chronicon
      ad ann. 42 (p.152 Helm), 99n
   Epistulae, 130.6, 208n

Isidor of Seville
   Etymologiarum sive originum libri, 9.4.49–51, 148n
Iulianus
   Epitome
      36, 147n
      72, 146n

INDEX LOCORUM

Iulius Caesar, C.
   De bello civili, 1.14.4, 88n
   De Bello Hispaniensi, 31.9, 88n

John Chrysostom
Adversus oppugnatores vitae monasticae, 3.12, 208n
In ep. 1 Cor. hom, 40.5, 215n

Justinian
   Codex Iustinianus
      1.2.1, 139n
      1.13.1, 138n
      1.13.2, 138n, 145n
      4.57.3, 119n, 134n, 144n
      5.27.1pr., 144n
      6.1.5, 99n, 195n
      6.3.7, 76n
      6.4.4, 142n, 151n
      6.4.4.2, 142n, 143n
      6.7.2, 137, 137n, 144n
      6.9.9, 139n
      6.23.15, 139n
      6.51.19, 113n
      7.1.1, 118
      7.3.1, 141n
      7.4.4, 57n
      7.5.1, 141n
      7.6, 6n
      7.6.1, 56n, 142n, 151n
      7.6.1pr., 141n
      7.6.1.1a, 60n, 143n, 125
      7.6.1.3, 125, 151n
      7.6.1.3–3a, 143n
      7.6.1.4, 74n
      7.6.1.5, 59n, 195n
      7.6.1.6, 59n
      7.6.1.8, 123n, 125
      7.6.1.9, 59n
      7.6.1.11, 125n
      7.6.1.12a, 60n
      7.6.3, 107n
      7.6.3–3a, 147n
      7.6.4, 108
      7.6.8, 109
      7.9.1, 130n
      7.9.2, 130n
      7.9.3, 131n
      7.13.3, 144n, 145n
      7.21.6, 134n

      7.54.3.1, 113n
      11.48.22.3, 113n
   Digesta Iustiniani Augusti
      1.2.2.37–43, 144n
      1.3.32–3, 144n
      1.5.22, 119n
      1.16.2pr., 168n
      2.4.8.2, 76n
      2.4.10, 119n
      2.4.10.1, 74n
      5.1.52.1, 95n
      18.7.6, 108
      24.1.7.8, 119n
      25.3.6, 75n
      26.4.3.2, 119n
      28.5.43, 113n
      28.5.85.1, 119n
      30.1.20, 121n
      31.66.1, 113n
      34.2.2, 113n
      36.1.69, 113n
      37.14.5.1, 75n
      37.14.7, 108
      37.14.13, 78n
      37.14.15, 76n
      38.1.13pr.–1, 119n
      38.1.25, 76n
      38.1.41, 75n
      38.2.24, 76n86
      38.2.33, 75n, 94n
      38.5.11, 76n
      38.16.3.5, 76n
      39.5.7pr., 78n
      40.1.10, 119n
      40.2.9.1, 118
      40.2.11, 120n
      40.2.12, 120n
      40.2.13, 118n, 120n
      40.2.15.1, 60n, 118
      40.2.16pr., 121n
      40.2.20.1, 119n
      40.8.1, 119n
      40.8.2, 105n, 143n
      40.8.6, 119n
      40.8.8, 120n
      40.8.9, 119n
      40.9.30, 76n
      40.9.32.1–2, 76n
      40.12.9.2, 76n

Justinian (cont.)
    40.12.24.3, 57n
    40.12.38pr.–1, 119n
    40.12.44pr. 118
    50.1.1.1, 33n
    50.16.53pr., 75n
    50.16.70, 76n
  Institutiones Iustiniani
    1.3–5, 143n
    1.5.3, 60n, 141n, 142n, 143n, 143n
    1.7, 141n
    1.20pr., 61n
    2.6.2, 61n
    2.14.1, 192
    3.7.3, 142n
    3.7.4, 60n, 142n, 143n
  Novellae Constitutiones
    22.12, 147n
    78pr., 144n, 146n
Juvenal 5.127, 191n

Leo VI
  Novels
    78, 145n
    94, 145n
lex Irnitana
  19, 33, 34n, 35, 35n
  20, 33, 34n
  21, 31, 36, 38–45, 40n
  22, 31, 36, 38, 45, 46n, 129n
  23, 31, 36, 46n, 129n
  28, 26n, 31, 103
  31, 34, 37, 43
  40, 34n
  50, 34
  72, 26n, 31, 36, 51n, 72, 130, 130n
  81, 34, 34n
  84, 35, 35n
  86, 43, 46
  93, 48
  97, 31, 43, 46n
  Epistle of Domitian, 36–8
lex Malacitana
  52, 33
  53, 29n, 31, 43, 53n, 129
  54, 43
Lex Romana Burgundionum
  44.4, 147
  44.5, 147

lex Salensana
  21, 31, 40n
  22, 31
  23, 31
  28, 31, 103, 129
Livy
  9.34, 130n
  21.25.2–5, 22n
  32.2.6–7, 28n
  33.23.1–7, 197n
  33.23.6, 197n
  33.24.8, 28n
  43.3.1–4, 22n
  45.15.1–2, 98n

Periochae, 115, 88n
Martial
  11.6.4, 196n
  14.1.1–2, 196n
Mitteis, *Chrestomathie*
  361 (= *P.Edmonstone*), 140n
  362 (= *P.Amherst Lat.*), 132n, 133n
Papiri della Societá Italiana (*PSI*) XI 1182, 134n
Papyrus Amherst Latinus, 132n, 133n
Papyrus Edmonstone, 140n
Papyrus Hamburgensis, 1, 72, 102n
Papyrus Kellis, Gr.48, 140n
Papyrus Lipsius, II 151, 133n
Papyri Michigan
  3.169, 102
  7.436, 102n
Papyri Oxyrhynchus
  IV pp.202–3, 140n
  IX 1205, 133n
  XVII 1203, 134n
  LXXXV
  5495, 144n
  p. 67, 144n
Papyrus Vindobonensis, L 26, 60n, 70n, 125n, 134n
Paulus
  Pauli Sententiae
  2.21a.1, 52n, 107, 126n, 128n, 135n
  2.21a.7, 108n
  2.27.6, 124n, 135n, 136n
  3.2.5, 75n
  4.9.8, 52n, 127n, 133n, 135n, 148n
  4.10.3, 52n, 127n, 135n

4.12.1, 126n, 135n, 147n
4.12.2, 59n
4.12.6–7, 135n, 147n
Breviary Paulus
  4.11.1, 147n
  4.11.6–7, 147n
  4.9.1, 133n, 148n
Persius
  5, 73–6, 94
  Scholia Persius, 94n
Petronius
  Satyricon
    40.3–41.4, 157n, 185n
    41.6–7, 157n, 185n, 194–8
    54.1–5, 157n
    54.4–5, 185n
Philo
  Legatio ad Gaium 23.155–8, 96n
Pliny the Elder
  Naturalis Historia
    3.7, 30n
    3.18, 30n
    3.20, 53n
    3.30, 29n, 30n
    3.91, 29n, 36n
    3.135, 29n
    4.117, 30n
Pliny the Younger
  Epistulae
    5.11, 173.21
    5.19, 178n, 185n
    5.19.1–4, 184n
    7.11.6, 184n
    7.14.1, 176n
    7.15, 173n
    7.16, 168–70, 169n
    7.16.3–4, 171n
    7.16.4, 156
    7.23, 170–1, 170n, 171n
    7.32, 171–4, 171n, 171n
    8.1, 178n
    8.16, 106n, 165n
    8.16.1, 156
    8.16.1–2, 174n
    10.5, 111, 180–2, 180n, 181n, 181n
    10.6, 123n, 180n
    10.7, 180n

10.8.1, 176n
10.10, 180n
10.11, 111, 180n, 181n, 182–3, 182n
10.27–8, 185n
10.63, 184n
10.67, 184n
10.95, 165n
10.96, 165n
10.104, 26n, 117, 126n, 167, 174–9, 175n, 189–191, 189n
10.105, 167, 174–9, 175n
10.106, 183n
10.107, 183n
Panegyricus
  37.5–6, 45n
  38.7, 44n
  39, 39n
  39.1, 45n
Plutarch
  Vita Romuli, 25.6–7, 193n
  Vita Caesaris
    29, 39n
    55.5–6, 88n
Polybius 3.40.3–5, 22n

Quintilian
  Declamationes minores
    340, 59n
    340pr., 57n
    340.1, 192n
    340.6–7, 193n
    340.8–9, 192n
    342, 59n, 193n
    342pr., 57n
  Institutio oratoria, 7.3.27, 191n

Res Gestae Divi Augusti (RGDA)
  8, 99n
  15.2, 93n
  15.4, 93n
Riccardi fragment, 102–3
Roman Statutes (ed. M. Crawford)
  I
    n. 24 (*tabula Heracleensis*), ll. 89–93, 100n
    n. 34 (Riccardi fragment), 102n
  II, plate X, 102n

[Sallust]
   Epistulae ad Caesarem Senem, 1.7.2, 87n

Salvian of Marseille
   Ad ecclesiam
      2.37, 205n
      3.1.4, 206n
      3.1.5, 206n
      3.2.6, 206n
      3.2.8, 206n
      3.2.9–10, 206n
      3.4.18–19, 207n
      3.4.21, 208n
      3.6.28–9, 209n
      3.7.31, 126n
      3.7.31–2, 210n
      3.7.31–4, 140–1, 203–14
      3.7.32–4, 158n
      3.7.33, 65n, 203n
      3.7.34, 123n, 126n, 211n
   De gubernatione Dei
      4.1, 205
      4.5.24, 211n
   Epistulae, 4, 204n

Scholia Bobiensia
   175, 50n
   De aere alieno Milonis, fragm. XVII, 86n

Scholia Sinaitica
   17, 125n, 134n
   20, 134n

Seneca
   De beneficiis, 3.21.2, 76n
   Epistulae, 47.14, 165n

Socrates
   Historia ecclesiastica
      1.7, 139n
      13, 139n

Sozomen
Historia Ecclesiastica 1.9.6, 138

Strabo, 4.1.12, 29n

Suetonius
   De Grammaticis et Rhetoribus
      1, 155
      25.5, 191–4, 191n
   Divus Iulius
      41.3, 88n
      42.1, 89n
   Divus Augustus
      19.1, 90n
      32.3, 100n
      37.1, 99n
      40.1, 93n
      40.2, 97n
      40.3, 184n
      42.2, 90n, 93n
   Divus Claudius
      15, 111n
      18.2–19.1, 111n
      19, 125n, 128n
      25.2, 105n
      25.7, 50n
   Nero
      38.3, 111
      57.1, 197n
   Divus Vespasianus
      3, 126n
      11.1, 107n

Tabula Heracleensis, ll. 89–93, 100n

Tabulae Herculanenses (ed. Camodeca) 2.89, 28n, 64n

Tabula Siarensis, II A II. 8–9, 29n, 129n

Tacitus
   Annales
      4.17, 110n
      12.43, 111n
      13.26.2, 77n
      13.27.2, 59n
      15.32, 29n

Theodore
   Breviarium Novellarum, 78, 144n

Theodosius II
   Breviary Theodosianus
      2.22.1, 136n, 148n
      5.1.1, 148n
      9.19.1, 148n
   Codex Theodosianus
      1.1.5, 136
      1.4.2, 135
      2.8.1, 140n
      2.22.1, 124n, 136n, 148n
      4.6.2, 137
      4.6.3, 124n, 137n, 144n
      4.7.1, 138n, 148, 150n
      4.12, 148n
      4.12.1–4, 137n
      4.12.3, 124n, 137n, 148
      5.1.1, 148n
      6.13.2, 75n

    7.13.16, 150n
    9.9.1, 137n, 137n
    9.24.1, 137n
    9.24.1.4, 125n, 137n, 144n, 145n
    16.2.4, 139n
  Gesta senatus, 136n
  Novel 1, 136n
Theophilus
  Basilica
    48.14.1, 145n
    48.26.1, 145n
  Basilica scholia
    48.14.1.1, 145n
    48.14.1.2, 144n
  Paraphrasis Institutionum
    1.5.3, 56n, 60n, 143n, 144n
    1.8.pr., 144n
    3.7.4, 144n
Tullius Cicero, M.
  De domo sua
    10.25, 85n
    10.26, 85n
    78, 27n, 41n
  De haruspicum responso, 27.57, 86n
  De lege agraria (contra Rullum), 1.131, 50n
  De officiis, 3.11.47, 50n
  De oratore, 1.38, 86n
  Epistulae ad Atticum
    4.3.2, 87n
    5.11.2, 39n
    14.12.1, 29n
  Epistulae ad familiares, 11.8.2, 88n
  Epistulae ad Quintum fratrem, 2.6.1, 85n
  In M. Antonium orationes Philippicae
    10.21, 88n
    11.29, 130n
  Pro A. Caecina
    98, 27n, 41n
    100, 41n
    102, 72n
  Pro Archia poeta
    4.7, 23n
    10, 50n
  Pro L. Balbo
    9.24., 197n

    24, 29n
    28, 41n
    28.30, 27n
    30, 41n
    52, 50n
  Pro M. Caelio
    78, 86n
    89, 86n
  Pro T. Annio Milone
    73, 86n
    87, 86n
  In Verrem actio prima, 1.112–13, 191n

Ulpian
  Regulae Ulpiani
    1.5, 123n, 124n
    1.10, 3n, 57n, 60n, 84n
    1.12, 57n, 59n, 62n
    1.13, 62n
    1.15, 76n
    1.18, 3n
    3.1, 128, 133
    3.2, 128
    3.3, 60n, 64n, 91n, 128
    3.3–4, 114
    3.4, 113n
    5.4, 26n, 47n, 127n
    5.6, 115
    7.4, 26n, 64n
    11.2, 63n
    11.16, 60n, 68n, 124n
    11.19, 60n
    17.1, 68n, 124n
    19.4, 47n, 68n, 124n
    20.8, 124n
    20.14, 60n, 62n, 68n, 124n
    22.2, 62n
    22.3, 60n, 68n, 124n
    25.7, 68n, 124n
Valerius Maximus, 3.4.5, 50n
Velleius Paterculus
    2.20.2, 33n
    2.91.3, 90n
    2.92.4, 90n

General Index

Aelius Marcianus, jurist, 134
age requirements, manumission, 2–3, 101, 121
   Justinian, 139, 141
   lex Aelia Sentia, 59, 61–2, 99, 100
agriculture, 160
Alaric II, 147
anniculi causae probatio, 6–7, 64, 71, 77, 81, 103, 110, 112–15, 126, 128, 166, 212–13
Antoninus Pius, Emperor, 117, 118, 119, 218
archaeological remains, 12
Asconius, 22–3, 27, 86
Augustan laws, 81–3, 101–2; *see also lex Aelia Sentia*; *lex Fufia Caninia*; *lex Iunia (Norbana)*
Augustus, Emperor, 26–32, 93, 96–7, 99–100, 216
Aurelius Ammonion, M., 132–3
Aurelius Valerius, 140

Baetica, 35, 50–1, 53, 168
bonitary rights, 59
Breviary of Alaric, 135, 136, 147–8, 149, 151
Breviary Theodosianus, 138, 148
Brutus *see* Junius Brutus, M.
Brundisium, 191, 193
bulla, 191–4, 198–9
Burgundian codes, 147

Caesar *see* Iulius Caesar, C.
Caligula, Emperor, 96, 104
Callistratus, 134

Calpurnius Fabatus, L., 168–74, 179, 185
Caracalla, Emperor 118, 132, 218
Calestrius Tiro, 156–8, 159, 164, 168–71, 174, 185
Cassius Dio, 85, 93, 97–8, 216
Catalogus virorum illustrium (Gennadius), 204–5
censuses, 86, 89, 99
   recensus, 87–8, 89, 90, 93–4
children
   enslaved, 162–5
   freeborn, 191
   inheritance and, 77, 127, 205–11
   intermarriage (*conubium*) and, 46, 114–15
   manumission, 2
   rewards for, 98, 147–8
   Roman citizenship and, 67
   natural slave reproduction, 162, 163
   see also anniculi causae probatio; *iura patronatus*; *patria potestas*
Christianity, 140, 204, 214–15
   filii religiosi, 205–9: comparison with Junian Latins, 209–11, 212–14
   manumission by clerics, 138–9, 150 *see also* manumission (*in ecclesia*)
Cicero *see* Tullius Cicero, M.
citizenship
   dual citizenship, 41–3
   see also Latin citizenship; Roman citizenship
Civil War, 87, 88
Claudius, Emperor, 50, 105–7, 111, 125, 216
Clodius Pulcher, P., 84–7, 89–90
Cloelius, Sextus, 84–5

clothing, 188–9, 191–8, 199
Collatio Legum Mosaicarum et Romanarum, 136, 217
colonial Latins (*Latini coloniarii*), 5, 57, 66, 72–3, 74
  fictitious colonial Latins, 71
  link with Junian Latins, 26–9, 92
  Roman citizenship, 52, 58
  see also municipal Latin rights; provincial Latinity
Columella, Lucius Junius Moderatus, 160–6
  De re rustica, 160–6
commercium, 46, 48, 68, 118
Comum, 168, 171–3, 174, 179, 185
Constantine, Emperor, 6, 124, 135, 136–40, 144, 215, 218
Constitutio Antoniniana, 29, 123, 132, 133
conubium (intermarriage), 46–8, 68, 71, 114–15, 127
Cordoba, 149
corn dole, 89, 93–7; *see also* grain distribution
Cornelius Cethegus, G., 197
Cremona, 197

dediticii, 62–3, 110, 143–4, 148, 150–1
denarius, 196
Dionysius of Halicarnassus, 61, 90, 92, 98–9
Domitian, Emperor 36–8
duo nomina, 53–4

ecclesiastical manumission *see* manumission (*in ecclesia*)
Edict of Theoderic, 145
Egnatius Rufus, M., 90
enslaved women, 10, 119–22, 162–5
Epitome Iuliani, 146
Epitome Ulpiani see Ulpian, Rules
erroris causae probatio, 113

family relationships, 45, 163
Fifty Decisions (*Quinquaginta Decisiones*), 141
filii religiosi, 205–9
  comparison with Junian Latins, 209–11, 212–14
Firma (manumission of), 119–22
Flavia Domitilla, 126
Flavian municipal legislation, 30–1, 32–6, 40, 42, 43, 129–31; *see also* lex Irnitana

Formulae Arverneses, 150
Formulae Turonenses, 150–1
Formulae Visigothicae, 149, 163
Fragmenta Vaticana, 117, 135–6, 218
Fragmentum Dositheanum, 68–9, 84, 107, 109, 124, 216, 219
Frankish kingdoms, 149–50
freedom, 97, 161–5, 193; *see also libertas*
freedpersons, 63, 66, 67, 73–6, 78–9; *see also liberti*
bona libertorum, 115, 116
frumentationes, 5, 90, 93, 94; *see also* grain distribution

Gaius, *Institutes*, 2, 134, 216–19
  anniculi causae probatio, 128
  colonial Latins, 27, 66
  formal manumission, 2–3, 6
  inheritance rights, 4, 107
  intermarriage, 114, 115
  iusta causa manumissionis, 118, 119
  Latin freedwomen, 146
  Latin rights (*ius Latii*), 40
  libertas Latina, 66–7, 69–70, 74
  liberti, 123–4
  municipal Latins, 131
  origin of Junian Latinity, 83
  Roman citizenship, 110, 112, 116
  testamentary manumission, 7–8
Gaius Caesar (Augustus' grandson), 99
Gallia Cisalpina, 23, 25, 27
Gallia Transalpina (Narbonensis), 25, 26, 27
Gallia Transpadana, 22–6, 27, 28
grain distribution, 84–9, 93–7; *see also frumentationes*
Gregorian Code, 133–4

Hadrian, Emperor, 35, 96, 113, 114–15, 116, 217
Sententiae Hadriani, 96
Harpocras, 180–1, 182, 186
Hermogenian Code, 133–4
Hispania, 26, 30, 31, 37
Hosius of Cordoba, 138, 139

informal manumission, 1, 3–4, 73, 159, 164, 165, 166, 213
  grain distribution and, 84–9, 90, 93–4

inheritance
  filii religiosi, 205–9: comparison with Junian Latins, 209–11, 212–14
  see also testamentary manumission; wills
inheritance rights, 4–5, 65–7, 68, 94n57, 100–1, 107, 115–18, 127; *see also* testamentary manumission
insula Aesculapii, 105
intermarriage (*conubium*), 46–8, 68, 71, 114–15, 127
Index thématique des références à l'esclavage et à la dépendance, 157
Isidore of Seville, 148
iteration (*iteratio*), 6, 17, 128, 168–71; *see also* formal manumission
Iulius Caesar, C., 85, 87–9, 90, 91, 93, 196
iura patronatus, 115–18; *see also* patronage
ius Latii see Latin rights (*ius Latii*)
ius liberorum, 164, 165
ius Quiritium, 48, 109–12, 127, 128, 129
  Pliny's letters to Trajan, 175, 177, 180–1, 183
  see also Roman citizenship

Jerome, 208
Jewish community, 96
John Chrysostom, 207–8, 215
Junian Latinity
  abolition, 141–3, 195
  definition, 1
  historical and legal context, 15–20
  legal foundation, 5l; *see also lex Aelia Sentia*; *lex Iunia (Norbana)*
  legal status, 19, 68–70: as 'black hole', 9, 12, 70–8
  in literary sources, 155–9
  longevity, 6
  Republican background, 83–9
  social and civic disadvantages, 3–4
  time of Augustus, 26–32, 81–3
Junian Latins
  bona Latinorum, 115–7
  comparison with *filii religiosi*, 209–11, 212–14
  creation of, 105–9
  problems with identification: clothing, 188–9, 191–8, 199; naming, 11, 55, 188–91 *see also* Firma
  as proportion of population, 9–10
  textual references: scholarly approach to, 155–8; AD 212 onwards, 132–6; beyond the Empire, 147–51; under Constantine, 136–40; after Constantine, 140–3; as historical curiosity, 143–7
Junius Brutus, M., 196
Justinian, 141–2, 145, 195, 218
  Code, 134, 143, 146, 151, 216–19
  Digest, 74n, 95, 105, 108, 118, 119–20, 141, 144, 216–19
  corn dole, 95
  prostitution, 108
  sale of slaves, 119–20
  sick slaves, 105
  Firma (manumission of), 119
  Institutes, 60, 61, 141, 143, 145–6, 147, 151, 192, 216, 218
  Latin status, 142
  Latina / Latinus, 2, 125, 146
  manumission, 99, 139, 141
  Novellae, 144, 146–7, 149
  prostitution, 108
  sick slaves, 106–7, 109

labour force management, 161
labour hoarding, 17
Latins
  fictitious colonial Latins, 71
  freeborn Latins, 25, 26, 52, 126–7, 128, 143
  freed Latins (*libertas Latina*), 57–60
Latin citizenship, 42–3, 46, 123–31, 198
Latin rights (*ius Latii*), 21, 21n, 40–1, 71; *see also* municipal Latin rights
Latin status, 2, 5, 15–16, 54–5, 123–31
  abolition, 140–1, 142–3, 145
  Constantine, 135–40
  Formulae Turonenses, 150–1
  as historical curiosity, 143–7
  see also colonial Latins; freeborn Latins; freed Latin status (*libertas Latina*); provincial Latinity
Latini (Latina / Latinus), 2, 26, 125, 146, 150
Latini coloniarii see colonial Latins (*Latini coloniarii*)
Latini ingenui, 28, 38, 95, 127, 129
Latini Iuniani / Latinus Iunianus, 26, 27, 29, 124, 190; *see also* Junian Latins
Latinus Aelianus, 124
Latinus libertinus, 130; *see also* freed Latin status

Leo VI, 145
lex Aelia Sentia, 56, 83, 102; *see also* Riccardi fragment
  anniculi causae probatio, 6–7, 103, 113
  Columella, *De re rustica* and, 160
  Patron's duties, 94n
  Latinus Aelianus, 124
  manumission, 2, 59, 61–3, 92, 99–100, 118, 130
  patronage, 73–8
  relationship with *lex Iunia*, 61–4, 67–8, 91
lex Clodia
  on grain distribution, 85
lex Cornelia Caecilia, 85
Lex Dei see Collatio Legum Mosaicarum et Romanarum
lex frumentaria, 87, 89; *see also* grain distribution
lex Fufia Caninia, 7–8, 83, 98–9, 102, 141
lex Irnitana, 30
  conubium (intermarriage), 46, 47
  dual citizenship, 42–3
  Latini, 26
  letter of Domitian, 36–8
  manumission, 51, 130–1
  marriage, 43
  municipal government, 33, 34, 35
  municipal Latins, 45
  patria potestas, 44
  Roman citizenship, 40, 41
lex Iulia de civitate, 25, 52
lex Iunia (Norbana), 4–5, 56, 60, 61, 91, 143, 194
  aims, 65–8, 82, 82–3, 84
  authorship, 60–1: and relationship with *lex Aelia Sentia*, 61–4, 67–8
  'black hole' of Junian Latinity, 9, 12, 70–3: patronage, 74–5, 77, 78
  Columella, *De re rustica* and, 160
  corn dole and, 93–7
  date, 60–4, 89–92
  freed Latin status, 57–60
  inheritance rights, 94n, 100–1
  operae, 17–18, 73–5
  precedent for, 86
lex Lati(i), 36–8, 43–4
lex Malacitana, 33, 34, 43, 129
lex Minicia, 47, 114
lex municipii Troesmensium, 92

lex Papia Poppaea, 75, 77, 101, 102
lex Porcia, 85
lex Quinctia de aquaeductibus, 91
lex rogata domitiana, 37
Lex Romana Burgundionum, 147
Lex Romana canonice compta, 146
Lex Romana Curiensis, 149, 150
lex Salpensana, 40
lex Terentia Cassia, 85
lex Visellia, 110
Lex Visigothorum, 149
libertas, 161–6, 196–8; *see also* freedom; Gaius, *Institutes (libertas Latina)*
libertas Latina see freed Latin status (*libertas Latina*)
liberti, 123–4; *see also* freedpersons
literary sources, 155–9
Livy, 197

magistrates, 23, 31, 33–5, 39–41, 43
manumission
  Augustan laws and, 81–3
  and citizenship, 92
  and slaving, 10–11, 164–5, 183–7, 191–2, 213
  censu (by the census), 2–3
  construed, 191–6
  Firma (manumission of), 119–22
  formal, 1–3, 6, 90, 170, 171
  Frankish kingdoms (manumission in), 149–50
  imperial grant, 175–6, 189–90
  in ecclesia, 138–40, 150, 213, 215
  informal, 1, 3–4, 73, 159, 164, 165, 166, 213: grain distribution, 84–9, 90, 93–4; Pliny the Younger, 185
  inter amicos (among friends), 2–3, 59–60, 64, 194–5
  inter vivos (among the living), 2–3
  iusta causa, 2, 118–19, 164
  lex Aelia Sentia, 2, 59, 61–3, 92, 99–100, 118, 130
  lex Irnitana, 51, 130–1
  modes, 2–3, 6–7
  per epistulam (by letter), 140, 142
  role, 8–11, 163
  testamento (testamentary), 3, 7–8, 98–9, 192
  vindicta (by the rod), 2–3, 164, 169–70
Visigothic kingdom, 148–9

Marcian, Emperor, 138, 144, 148
Marcus Aurelius, Emperor, 109, 117, 121, 218
marriage, 43–9, 77, 113–14
　letter of Domitian, 36–7
　manumission and, 2, 64, 118–19
　Marcian, 138
　see also intermarriage (*conubium*)
matrimonium ex lege Aelia Sentia see anniculi causae probatio
medical professionals, 180–1, 182–3
mothers (motherhood), 162–5
municipal Latin rights, 21–55
　access to Roman citizenship, 39–43
　Flavian municipal legislation and *ius Latii*, 32–6
　ius Latii, 32–6, 38
　lex Lati(i) and letter of Domitian, 36–8
　marriage, 43–9
　onomastic identification of municipal Latins, 49–54
　origin, 22–6
　provincial Latinity, 38–9
　in time of Augustus, 26–32

naming, 54–5, 188–91; *see also* onomastics
natural slave reproduction, 162
Nero, Emperor, 111–12, 128, 197, 216
Nerva, Emperor, 45

oblatio, 207–8
obsequium, 17, 117–18
onomastic identification, 49–54, 189–91
onomastics, 11, 39, 46, 54–5, 176; *see also* naming
operae, 17, 17n, 18, 73–6, 94n, 117, 147

Papinian, *Responsa*, 134, 136
patria potestas, 44, 69, 113, 127
　laws limiting, 97–101
　municipal Latins and, 38, 39, 44, 45
patronage, 73–8, 175–6, 179–83, 189
　iura patronatus, 115–18
Pauli Sententiae, 107, 124, 126, 128, 135, 136, 147–8, 217
peculium, 4–5, 78, 140
Persius, 94
Petronius, *Satyricon*, 157, 166, 194–5
Philo, 96

pilleus (liberty cap), 195–8
Placentia, 22, 22n5, 197
plebs frumentaria, 89, 93, 96–7, 98
Pliny the Younger, 126, 156
　humanitas, 106
　letters, 157–8, 167–87: to Calpurnius Fabatus, 168–74, 179; to Plinius Paternus, 164–5; to Trajan, 116–17, 174–83, 189
　patria potestas, 44
　patrons, 175–6, 179–83, 189
Pompeius Strabo, Cn. 22, 23
Pompey, 85, 86, 88, 89, 90, 93
Postumius Marinus, 182–3, 186
praetorian rights, 59
prostitution, 108
Protogenes, 138, 139
provincial Latin rights *see* municipal Latin rights
provincial Latinity, 38–9

Quintilian, *Minor Declamations*, 192–3

recensus, 87–8, 89, 90, 93–4
reproductive rights, 161–2
Riccardi fragment, 102–3, 216
Roman citizenship
　colonial Latinity and, 27–9
　corn dole and, 94
　desirability of, 8–11, 163
　formal manumission and, 1–3, 6
　Jewish community and, 96
　marriage and, 43, 44, 46, 64
　municipal Latin rights and, 21, 24–5, 32, 39–43: magistrates, 23, 31, 39–41, 43
　onomastic identification, 190
　onomastic studies, 51, 52–4
　Pliny's letters to Trajan, 176, 177, 178, 180, 182, 183
　Senatus Consultum Claudianum, 108
　signifiers of, 198–200; *see also* clothing; naming
　ways to acquire, 6–8, 109–12, 125, 127–9, 142, 195: *anniculi causae probatio*, 6–7, 67, 69, 81; church manumission, 138, 150; *manumissio iusta causa*, 118–19
　see also ius Quiritium
Romanisation, 54

Sallust, 87
Salvian of Marseille, 126, 140–1, 204–5
   Ad ecclesiam, 6, 158, 159, 203–4, 205–15: context, 205–11; slavery, inheritance and Junian Latins in, 212–14
   De gubernatione Dei, 205, 211
Seleukos of Rhosos, 42
Senatus Consultum, 113
Senatus Consultum Claudianum, 107–8, 124, 126–7, 137, 141, 148
Senatus Consultum Largianum, 116, 126
Senatus Consultum Neratianum, 131n
Senatus Consultum Orfitianum, 127
Senatus Consultum Tertullianum, 127
Severus Alexander, Emperor, 104, 105, 119, 120, 128
slave labour, 160–1
slave management, 10–11, 161–5
slaving, 164–5, 183–7, 191–2, 211, 212–14
Social War, 5, 71
Sozomen, *Historia Ecclesiastica*, 138
Spain, 103, 148–9
Suetonius, 193–4
   De Grammaticis et Rhetoribus, 191
   Life of Julius Caesar, 87–8
   Life of Augustus, 90, 97, 184, 216
   Life of Claudius, 105, 111, 128, 216
Summa Perusina, 146

tabula Heracleensis, 100
tabulae Herculanenses, 7, 103, 110, 110n
testamentary manumission, 3, 7–8, 98–9
testaments *see* wills
Thalelaeus, 144, 145
Theodosian Code, 124–5, 135, 136, 137, 138, 139, 218
Theophilus, 144
   Basilica, 144–5

Tiberius, Emperor, 60, 98, 99, 216
Tituli ex Corpore Ulpiani see Ulpian, *Rules*
toga, 191–4, 198–9; *see also* clothing
Trajan, Emperor, 128, 217
   correspondence with Pliny, 165, 174–83, 189
   iura cognationis, 45
   Roman citizenship, 110, 112, 115
tria nomina, 11, 53–5, 189–91, 198–9; *see also* naming; onomastics
Tribonian, 141–2, 192
tribunician laws, 91
Trimalchio, 194–5
Tullius Cicero, M., 22, 29, 39, 41, 42, 72, 86–8, 197

Ulpian, 32–3, 120–1
   Ad Sabinum (Ulpian), 134
   Rules (Regulae Ulpiani / Tituli ex corpore Ulpiani), 83–4, 112, 128, 133, 135, 148, 216, 217, 219
urban economy, 16–17

Valerius Paulinus, 126, 175, 177, 178
Verona cadaster, 24, 24n
Venidius Ennychus, L., 7, 103, 110, 110n
Vespasian, Emperor, 107, 108, 113, 126, 217
vigiles, 7, 95, 110, 122, 128n, 216, 217
Vincent, Bishop of Huesca, 149
vindicta see manumission (*vindicta*)
Visigothic kingdom, 148–9

wills, 68, 72, 100–1, 102, 192; *see also* inheritance; testamentary manumission
women, 2, 10, 18, 107–8, 127, 146, 161–5, 191; *see also* enslaved women